A History of the Western World

VOLUME II

A HISTORY OF THE
WESTERN
WORLD

VOLUME II
1600 to the Present

Bryce Lyon
BROWN UNIVERSITY

Herbert H. Rowen
RUTGERS UNIVERSITY

Theodore S. Hamerow
UNIVERSITY OF WISCONSIN

RAND McNALLY & COMPANY • Chicago, Illinois

RAND McNALLY HISTORY SERIES

Fred Harvey Harrington, *Advisory Editor*

All maps in color and the black and white maps entitled "Ancient Mesopotamia," "Ancient Egypt," "Ancient Athens," and "Industrial Revolution in England, 1750–1850" are from R. R. Palmer, *Atlas of World History* (Chicago: Rand McNally & Company, 1965). The maps entitled "Railways of Europe in 1850" and "Railways of Europe in 1940" are adapted from *Economic History of Europe,* Third edition, by S. B. Clough & C. B. Cole: D. C. Heath and Company: Boston, 1952. The map entitled "Economic Resources, 1914" is adapted from Harry Elmer Barnes, *The History of Western Civilization* (New York: Harcourt, Brace & World, Inc., 1935), II, 348, by permission of the author. The maps entitled "Density of Population in 1700" and "Density of Population in 1935" are adapted from Witt Bowden, Michael Karpovich, and Abbot Payson Usher, *An Economic History of Europe since 1750* (New York: 1937; New York: Howard Fertig, Inc., 1969); reprinted by permission. Cartography for all other maps in black and white is by Willis R. Heath.

Credits for illustrations are given with their listings in the Table of Contents.

Fourth Printing, 1972

Preface

THAT THIS WORK is a history of the western world rather than of the entire world is a considered decision of the authors. Each has devoted almost twenty years of research to various problems of western history and each has taught courses ranging from those at the introductory and advanced undergraduate levels to graduate seminars in European history. What each has written comes, therefore, from real familiarity with the problems and developments that have set the course of western history.

But the structure of the work is not based solely on the authors' interests. Learning from years of teaching history at numerous universities across the country that most introductory courses concentrate upon those aspects of western history considered essential for an understanding of the contemporary world, the authors decided to emphasize European history from the fall of the Roman Empire in the West down to the present. Aware also that in most introductory courses at least two-thirds of the time is allotted to modern European history, they have stressed the eighteenth, nineteenth, and twentieth centuries.

Two further observations are relevant. Since no student can comprehend the history of the western world without some knowledge of ancient history, the first three chapters discuss the ancient Middle East as well as Greek and Roman history. Also, since historical influences are reciprocal, the text constantly relates western history to that in other parts of the world. Western history, to be meaning-ful, must include sections on the ancient, medieval, and modern Middle East, on Byzantium, and on Africa and the Far East, especially in the modern period.

Maps, illustrations, tables, and plans have been appropriately placed through-out to supplement the text. To make it easier for the interested student to do further reading, at the end of each chapter there are critical bibliographies that emphasize only the most valuable books. An attempt has been made to indicate by an asterisk all titles that have appeared as paperbacks. Hopefully, the compre-hensive indexes of names, places, and topics at the end of each volume will lighten the student's task of finding his way about in this history.

The authors, who have critically read each other's contributions, have found that, in spite of occasional disagreement on certain interpretations and conclusions, in general they share similar views on the history of the West. Each is responsible for about one-third of the work. Bryce Lyon has written the first eight chapters on ancient and medieval history; Herbert H. Rowen the next six embracing the period from the Renaissance to 1815; and Theodore S. Hamerow the last six chapters that carry the account to the present. It is the hope of the authors that the student will learn as much from the reading of this work as they have from its writing.

Bryce Lyon
BROWN UNIVERSITY

Herbert H. Rowen
RUTGERS UNIVERSITY

Theodore S. Hamerow
UNIVERSITY OF WISCONSIN

Table
of Contents

Maps and Charts

MAPS IN COLOR

OTHER MAPS

CHARTS

Illustrations

ILLUSTRATIONS IN COLOR

OTHER ILLUSTRATIONS

A History of the Western World

VOLUME II

CHAPTER 11

The Age
of Absolutism
1600–1715

During the seventeenth century the transformation of the European world from medieval to modern continued in all its complexity and contradictoriness. By some historians it is seen as a century of crisis especially in England, France, and Germany, a century during which old forms and old ways of life collapsed in a paroxysm of failure and disaster to be replaced by essentially modern forms of thought and feeling and by the first truly modern governments. For others it was an age of reason when the rule of authority—tradition and habit sanctified and legitimized by their very age—gave way to the rule of reason— man's own judgment based on his own experience, aimed at his own purposes, and expressed most powerfully in the new sciences (see Chapter 12). For still others it was on the contrary the very age of authority, but authority based less and less upon tradition and habit and more and more upon reason, as practiced in the literature of French classicism. As we have observed, all attempts fail to pour the marvelous variety of human life into a single formula, no matter how supple; yet each of these characterizations gives an insight into some part of the experience of the seventeenth century.

1. *The Fabric of Society*

DUTCH ECONOMIC PREDOMINANCE

After the spectacular economic upsurge of the sixteenth century, the seventeenth was for most nations a time of doldrums and difficulties. After the Price Revolution of the previous century, prices leveled off and held fairly firm over the decades, although subject to the usual ups and downs in the short run, especially as a result of crop failures and wars. The population, too, ceased to grow rapidly and held steady in most countries that managed to escape the scourge of incessant warfare upon their own territories.

Only one nation found general prosperity in this time of trouble. For the Dutch the seventeenth century became their Golden Age. Already in the sixteenth century with the shift of trade routes to the Atlantic, the Dutch had begun to benefit by their central location at a point where the main east-west and north-south routes crossed. When the great port of Antwerp on the Scheldt River was recaptured by the Spaniards in 1584, it lost its century-old economic role as the principal port of Europe, because the Dutch who held the mouth of the river were able to cut off seagoing trade with the city. Then the merchants moved northward to Amsterdam which lay upon the great inlet which the Dutch called the South Sea (*Zuider Zee*). Amsterdam became the emporium of Europe. The countless ships of the Dutch seafarers, which outnumbered many times over those of all the rest of the European maritime peoples, brought in the commodities of every European country and all the European colonies and took them off again, by sea and by river, to the nations which wanted them. Amsterdam was the storehouse of Europe's grain (more precisely, of the surpluses which were not consumed locally and entered interregional trade), of the spices of the Indies, of sugar and cloth, leather and books, and all the great variety of products and manufactures which Europeans bought and sold.

Although Dutch prosperity ultimately rested upon this immense commerce, it extended to the whole of their economic life. The Dutch fisheries were the most extensive in Europe, supplying salted and pickled fish even to nations which lay upon the oceans. A wide variety of industries developed to supply the merchants of Amsterdam—ship building, sugar refining, book printing and publishing, armament manufactures, among the most important. Dutch agriculture could not hope to furnish enough grain to satisfy the needs of the dense population of the little country, so it imported its grain and developed instead an intensive market-oriented farming, producing industrial crops such as plant dyes, dairy products such as butter and cheese, and garden foods for the needs of the many towns, not to speak of the cultivation of fruits and flowers, which was marked by the mad speculation in tulip bulbs in 1636 and 1637.

MERCANTILISM

Other nations respected the diligence of the Dutch but they feared them even more. Indeed part of the reason for the Dutch success lay not in their undoubted abilities but in a combination of circumstances favorable to them and inimical to others. For the first half of the century the greatest powers of Europe were frequently engrossed in warfare, foreign and civil, and could give their attention only to the most immediate needs. The Dutch, on the other hand, achieved naval predominance early in the century, and no part of the heartland of their country knew the bloody taste of war after 1625 until the French invasion of 1672. The statesmen and merchants of other countries sought to counteract Dutch power as soon as their own political conditions permitted. Once the Dutch had defeated Spain (1648), the two greatest rivals they faced were the very powers which as allies had contributed most to the Dutch victory—England and France.

The means devised in England and France for economic competition with Holland were crystallized in the policy later called *mercantilism*. It was represented by the English Navigation Acts of 1651 and 1662 and by the protective tariff measures introduced in France under the leadership of Louis XIV's great minister, Jean Baptiste Colbert (1619–1683). Mercantilist policies were designed to impede or prevent Dutch imports by the imposition of high tariffs, by outright bans on the shipments of goods by ships of any country except one's own or the producer's, and by subsidies to one's own shippers and manufacturers. Colbert also sponsored the creation of government-owned and operated industries for the production of certain luxury goods. The most famous was the Gobelins tapestry works which are still in existence and the property of the French state. Colbert's mercantilist measures were more encompassing and systematic than those of Britain and became the pattern which other powers followed during his own time and through the eighteenth century.

The practice of mercantilism rested upon an economic theory which saw wealth as consisting primarily in money (reflecting Colbert's strong interest in expanding government revenues) and considered a country therefore to be richer when it had a favorable balance of trade, selling more than it bought. Mercantilism especially in England reflected as well a desire to favor the interests of domestic producers. French merchants, however, especially in such ports as Bordeaux and Marseilles, often opposed Colbert's measures to bar or limit imports, because they preferred to conduct their trade in combination with foreign importers, particularly the Dutch, rather than attempt to carry the entire operation from local producer to foreign wholesale purchaser, as the Dutch did.

In all three countries mercantilism was associated with the development of colonies. Even the Dutch, who favored the *free sea* in European waters, closed their colonies particularly in the East Indies to any but their own merchant companies.

THE DUTCH EAST INDIA COMPANY. To this vast warehouse, built in 1660 on the east bank of the Y River in Amsterdam, came the spices and other commodities of the Orient for the European market.

These merchant companies, notably the Dutch East India Company and the English East India Company, both established at the very beginning of the seventeenth century, and the French Company of the Indies, created later in an effort to repeat the successes of England and Holland, were different from the earlier companies of merchant adventurers in that they were broadly owned by means of shares; hence they were called *joint stock companies*. It was the company, not its members, which conducted the business, sent out its ships—the great *East Indiamen,* bought and sold beyond the seas, and exercised rights of sovereignty in its colonial possessions by delegation from its own government. Similar companies were created for trade with the West Indies but with lesser success; no nation was able to establish sole possession or even win predominance in the Caribbean, and the Dutch West India Company was unable to hold its colony in Brazil against the Portuguese after they threw off the rule of the Spanish king in their homeland in 1640.

The Dutch East India Company took over most of the Portuguese possessions in the East, especially in the huge Indonesian archipelago off the tip of southeast Asia and on the island of Ceylon. The English established a foothold on the subcontinent of India after 1662 when Charles II received Bombay from Portugal as part of the dowry of his queen, Catherine of Braganza. The French did not make important penetrations into this area until the next century. The Dutch took over and made more efficient the Portuguese practice of compelling local and interregional trade in the Indian Ocean to pay most of the costs of their colonial enterprise which was operated by the Dutch East India Company. Although the Dutch were able to establish a trading post on an island in the port of Nagasaki, they could not force their way onto the mainland of Japan, nor were they able to make progress in direct trade with China. The trade from the Indies constituted only a fairly small fraction of the total Dutch shipping and commerce, but it was a particularly profitable branch and one which excited great jealousy among the other European powers. The English sought to break into the Dutch East Indian monopoly in the Indonesian archipelago, and this rivalry was a principal source of the three Anglo-Dutch wars, but the British met with very little success against Dutch stubbornness.

In the West Indies, however, the English and the French were more successful. Together with the Dutch, they established themselves on various islands in the Caribbean. There they produced colonial crops for the European market, notably sugar, and engaged in smuggling trade with the Spanish American mainland which was unable to find adequate sources for imports within the framework of the legal trade monopoly maintained by Spain. The three countries also established colonies on the mainland of South and North America. The South American plantations in the Guianas were valuable mainly for the products of their forests, but the settlements on the North American mainland, beyond the limits of Spanish colonization, proved more important. The English held most of the territory from the Carolinas to Massachusetts, and during the second Anglo-Dutch War (1665–1667) they seized and kept the Dutch colony of New Netherland which became New York and New Jersey. The French settlements lay in the valley of the St. Lawrence River, farther north, but French traders ventured far westward past the Great Lakes. The English colonies were notable in that they were primarily settlements of immigrants who came to establish themselves as farmers and traders rather than as a new ruling class over a native population; in the English colonies the aboriginal Indians were either destroyed or driven out.

ABSOLUTISM, FOR AND AGAINST

Politically the seventeenth century was dominated by wars, foreign and civil. Wars put the states to the hardest test of survival. Because they were so immensely demanding in money, wars made the rulers seek every possible way to increase taxes and to enforce their decisions of policy more strictly. But the incessantly increasing demands upon subjects for money and the kings' efforts to impose their wills upon often recalcitrant subjects caused repeated outbreaks of riot and rebellion. Civil war plagued all but a very few states during the century. Even when conflict between rulers and ruled did not flare into outright armed combat, it sharpened the old tension between the sovereigns and the parliamentary assemblies which in most countries continued to have the right to approve taxation and legislation.

In defending the rights of subjects in general, these assemblies also specifically defended the established privileges of influential groups with status and wealth against encroachment by the sovereigns. Kings for their part continued the centuries-old process of political centralization, with the aim of ruling more effectively and by their sole authority, without the participation of subjects except as their agents. It was this kind of government—government in which the monarchs became the sole masters and ruled by means of professional bureaucracies and armies—that came to be called *absolutism*.

The alternatives of civil war and absolutism meant that the nations were confronted with a choice between liberty accompanied by disorder, turbulence, and havoc on the one hand, and order with compelled obedience and a high probability of misrule and tyranny on the other. The existence of these alternatives became the central theme of political thought during the seventeenth century. At first it was the proponents of order who were most eloquent and persuasive. The Englishman Thomas Hobbes (1588–1679), in the midst of civil war in his island homeland, argued that men created states and established sovereigns to escape anarchy; life without a supreme ruler was "nasty, brutish and short." In his *Leviathan* he proclaimed that this social contract was irrevocable; the ruler had no other duty towards his subjects than to govern them effectively, and subjects had no right whatsoever to impose their will upon him. The French theologian, historian, and political theorist, Bishop Jacques Bénigne Bossuet (1627–1704), argued for the advantages of absolute monarchy as exemplified in the rule of Louis XIV. He rested the rights of kings upon tradition and the gift of God (*divine right*) rather than upon a social contract; he was more sensitive than Hobbes to the needs of subjects but allowed them as little right of resistance to the will of the ruler.

The Dutch philosopher Baruch Spinoza (1632–1677) defended the absolute authority of the republican regime in Holland upon the basis of arguments drawn from Hobbes, but he conceived its total power as an instrument to be used for the welfare of subjects, in defense of their rights of free thought, and against the claims of the religiously intolerant. The English physician and philosopher John Locke (1632–1704), coming after Spinoza, saw the state as serving similar aims but argued instead against the very notion that a ruler could legitimately be absolute. Like Hobbes he envisioned the state as being actually or implicitly created by a social contract among the people to avert the inconveniences of an anarchical *state of nature* in which every man was a judge in his own cause; but he refused to grant, as Hobbes had done, that the sovereign thus established, in serving his own interests, automatically served those of the people. On the contrary, with Louis XIV and James II in mind, he saw the threat of tyranny as very real

HOBBES'S *LEVIATHAN*. The title page presents graphically Hobbes's theory of sovereign power. The figure of the ruler, absolute in power, encloses the innumerable tiny figures representing his subjects, whose lives he orders through the agencies of rule, political and ecclesiastical, illustrated in the boxes below him.

and depicted it as a kind of civil war fought by the ruler against his subjects. He advocated a mixed government by king and parliament, with the king responsible to the people who retained the ultimate right to use revolution as a weapon against tyrants.

With these thinkers—defenders and critics of monarchy alike—some of the most important dimensions of political debate in modern times were defined, and their arguments, constantly restated in new contexts, continue to be with us to this very day.

2. Wars and Diplomacy

MOST OF THE WARS of the seventeenth century were large, complex affairs involving many powers. Sometimes several distinct wars were fought simultaneously in different regions, more or less closely related to each other. One of the most striking traits of these wars was that, although peace negotiations began when the generals were demonstrably unable to produce final and total triumphs, the fighting continued meanwhile, each side hoping to improve its bargaining position. Long and protracted negotiations, in which the diplomats often seemed as helpless as the soldiers in bringing about peace, were the result. Yet, because the major wars of the century were long wars and even series of wars, the need for peace became constantly greater; the exhaustion of nations was immense, the strain upon the states' resources far larger than anticipated, and war began to feed upon itself and serve itself.

THE THIRTY YEARS' WAR

The first half of the century was dominated by the Thirty Years' War (1618–1648) in which Germany was the battleground and the victim. It was a war which began over mingled issues of religious and political liberty: the conflict between the Bohemian Protestants who wished to preserve both their faith and their estates form of government, and the Habsburgs who wished to make Catholicism predominant, establish their right of succession to the throne, and govern by prerogative. A Bohemian Protestant rebellion in Prague in 1618 led to the 1619 election of the Calvinist elector of the Palatinate, Frederick V, as king of Bohemia in place of the deposed Habsburg candidate, Ferdinand II, the newly elected Holy Roman emperor (1619–1637). The Bohemian rising was crushed by troops from Austria, but the fighting shifted to Germany where the Protestant princes were supported by neighboring kings, Christian IV (1588–1648) of Denmark and then Gustavus II Adolphus (1611–1632) of Sweden, both strong Lutherans.

For more than a decade Ferdinand kept the military advantage. His commanders, notably the Bohemian adventurer, Albert von Wallenstein (1583–1634), were more skillful on the battlefield. But Wallenstein developed a technique for making war without cost to the political ruler which was to be fateful for the further history of the conflict. Because the emperor's treasury could not sustain his army, Wallenstein forced the governments and residents of the territories where his troops were stationed to supply their pay and other needs. But Wallenstein, it turned out, could not be made to bend to the emperor's will, unlike generals who received their funds as well as their orders from the sovereign; eventually he was accused of plotting against the emperor, shorn of his command, and finally assassinated as an outlaw. By 1635 Ferdinand had forced Saxony, the principal German Lutheran power, to withdraw from the war, and he had held off the Swedish onslaught under Gustavus Adolphus. France now faced the specter of final and total Habsburg victory and was no longer able to stay out of the war; she had to do more than merely aid the foes of the Habsburgs with money subsidies. After Louis XIII declared war upon the emperor and his cousin, the king of Spain, the tide of war turned in Germany, but victory was still far away.

Negotiations for peace began in the Westphalian cities of Münster and Osnabrück in 1644 but did not conclude for another four years. The various treaties of 1648 which comprised the Peace of Westphalia brought an end to the wars of religion in Europe, for the three major creeds—Catholicism, Lutheranism, and Calvinism—were all made legal within the empire. Politically the victors were the imperial princes, for, though still legally the emperor's vassals, they received virtually all the prerogatives of fully sovereign potentates, including the right to wage war and make peace. But what the Habsburg emperor lost as feudal suzerain over Germany, he gained in the increased importance and power of his dynastic possessions in southeastern Europe which were taking shape as a distinct composite state under the name of *Austria*. France and Sweden gained too. The House of Bourbon defeated its great Habsburg rival in the Austrian branch which ceded its rights in Alsace to France. The Scandinavian kingdom maintained her possessions which formed a beachhead on the German Baltic coastline.

The people of Germany were immensely thankful for the peace, for it brought to an end a period of devastation, hardship, and depopulation such as the country had never experienced before. Many cities and villages had been sacked; trade, industry, and agriculture had all been disrupted; and Wallenstein's system of making the local population support the cost of the armies in their midst, especially when applied by all the belligerents, had piled new emergency taxes upon the old traditional levies. Restoration of prosperity did not come before one to two generations had done their work, and even then Germany did not catch up with the rapid advances of England and France upon the Atlantic.

France came out of the Westphalian Peace with advantage in Germany, but not in her other war with the Spanish Habsburgs. Indeed, one of the key reasons for the French victory in Germany had been that her Spanish Habsburg antagonist had been hamstrung by a two-front war in the Spanish Netherlands against French forces in the south and Dutch forces on the north. But Spain finally made a choice of enemies; she preferred to continue fighting France, the fellow-Catholic power, rather than the United Provinces—rebels to be sure, but without any desire to conquer the southern Netherlands themselves, or to see the French do so and become their neighbors. Early in 1648 Spain persuaded the Dutch to make a separate treaty at Münster, leaving France to continue the war against Spain alone.

THE WARS OF LOUIS XIV

The struggle between France and Spain continued for another eleven years. Not until the French bought the alliance of Cromwellian England, at the price of giving England a foothold on the continent at Dunkirk, could the back of Spanish resistance be finally broken. But in 1659 Madrid at last accepted defeat. By the Peace of the Pyrenees France gained territories to the north of the Pyrenees and on the edge of the Spanish Netherlands. A Spanish princess, Maria Teresa (called Marie Thérèse in France), was given as a bride to the French king, Louis XIV; she brought with her the opportunity for France to make a future claim upon the inheritance of the Spanish monarchy, even though she specifically renounced such rights.

The Dutch triumph over the Spaniards did not bring them the lasting peace they had long hoped for. Commercial rivalry, the English claim to sovereignty over the North Sea waters where the Dutch sailed and fished, and Cromwell's fears that the Dutch might assist the overthrown and exiled Stuarts, led in 1652 to a war fought all at sea. A well-equipped and well-commanded English navy defeated the unready Dutch, who accepted a humiliating peace in 1654. The rivalry between the two nations continued even after the Stuarts were restored in 1660, and a second round of the war began in 1665. This time it was the Dutch who were ready and the English who were not; the English not only saw their fleet outfought but also their shipyards at Chatham burned by Dutch raiders, and they had to accept the Peace of Breda in 1667. The Dutch kept Surinam, their conquest, and the English theirs, New Netherland; otherwise it was a standoff settlement.

That the Dutch were not as harsh upon their English opponents as they might have been was due to the outbreak of the first of the wars undertaken by Louis XIV after he took the helm of government in France in 1661. The War of Devolution (1667–1668) was designed to wrest the Spanish Netherlands from the Habsburgs. French military victories were thwarted by a quickly patched to-

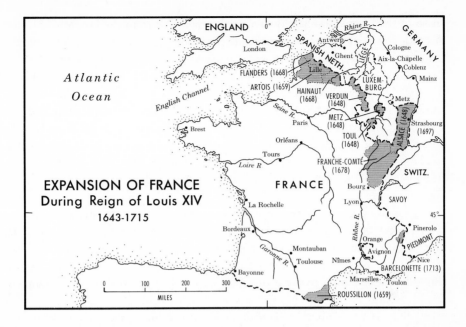

gether league of England, Holland, and Sweden (the Triple Alliance of 1668). Louis XIV accepted a settlement at Aix-la-Chapelle which gave him substantial territorial gains but not all that he had hoped for. He then bought over England's Charles II with whom he undertook a new war against the United Provinces in 1672. The Dutch barely managed to hold out against the French invasion by opening their dikes. But then they won allies in Spain and the empire and defeated the English at sea, compelling them to make peace two years later. When general peace came in 1678–1679, the price was paid not by the Dutch but by Spain who lost the ancient Habsburg territory of Franche-Comté to France.

During the next decade Louis XIV, his appetite for glory and aggrandizement sharpened to the verge of megalomania, nibbled away at the rights of his Spanish and German neighbors. His whole plan went awry when William III, prince of Orange, leader of the Dutch and organizer of the European resistance to Louis XIV, went to England in 1668 to take the lead in overthrowing James II and to become king of England himself. The War of the League of Augsburg, so called after a league of German princes hostile to France, was the result. It lasted from 1689 until 1697, when a compromise peace without gains for either side was made at Rijswijk (Ryswick) in Holland. By that time the paramount issue in European international relations had become who would succeed the ailing and childless King Charles II of Spain.

For several years both Louis XIV and William III attempted to avoid a renewal of their long and bitter wars over this issue. Twice they agreed to a partition of the Spanish monarchy among the claimants from the houses of France, Austria, and Bavaria. Their plans came to nothing and worse when the Spanish king finally willed his possessions as a whole to Philip of Anjou, grandson of Louis XIV. After some deliberation, Louis accepted the inheritance for Philip V (1700–1746); war between France and a Grand Alliance led by England ensued in 1702. The allies had the major advantage on the battlefields, as they also had had control of the sea since 1691, and finally obtained a favorable peace at Utrecht and Rastadt in 1713 and 1714. By it Philip V remained king of Spain, but the southern Netherlands and Spain's possessions in Italy went to Austria; the partition had come to pass, but only after more than a decade of fierce and costly war.

Thus the wars of the seventeenth century ended with decisive shifts in the arrangement of power. France replaced Spain as the greatest power upon the Continent, and England replaced Holland as the greatest power upon the seas. The alliance mechanism in the balance-of-power system had operated against the endeavor of France to dominate Europe, as it had thwarted the aspirations of the Habsburgs before it. The question now was whether it would operate with equal effectiveness against England if, as seemed so likely, she undertook in turn to enforce her mastery not merely upon France but upon the world.

3. The States of Europe

FRANCE: RICHELIEU AND MAZARIN

During the seventeenth century, when France replaced Spain as the leading power of Europe, her internal history became more than ever a crucial part of the general history of the Continent. She was, with Germany, one of the two most populous countries and was unquestionably the wealthiest and most powerful single state; yet her power in the end depended upon her unity.

When Henry of Navarre had followed Henry III upon the throne in 1589, civil peace had seemed as distant as ever. But civil peace had been restored by the mid-1590's and for the remainder of his reign Henry IV (1589–1610) worked to restore the prosperity of France. However, renewal of French rivalry with the Habsburgs brought both war and taxes, as well as the assassination of the king by a Catholic fanatic desperate over the threatening war against the Catholic Habsburgs. Henry's son, Louis XIII (1610–1643), once he had grown to manhood and thrown off the domination of his power-hungry but politically inept mother, Marie de' Medici, made Armand du Plessis, Cardinal Richelieu (1585–1642), his principal minister of state in 1624.

Richelieu became the most powerful prime minister in the whole history of

THE HOUSE OF BOURBON

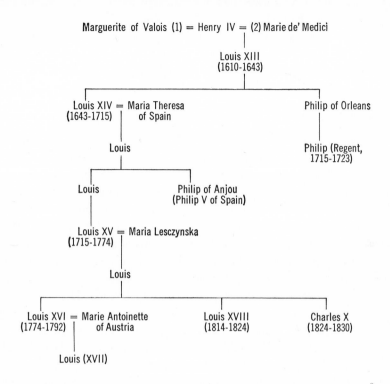

Marguerite of Valois (1) = Henry IV = (2) Marie de' Medici

Louis XIII
(1610-1643)

Louis XIV = Maria Theresa
(1643-1715)   of Spain

Philip of Orleans

Louis

Philip (Regent,
1715-1723)

Louis

Philip of Anjou
(Philip V of Spain)

Louis XV = Maria Lesczynska
(1715-1774)

Louis

Louis XVI = Marie Antoinette
(1774-1792)   of Austria

Louis XVIII
(1814-1824)

Charles X
(1824-1830)

Louis (XVII)

the French monarchy and, more than any other man except Louis XIV, the creator of absolute monarchy in France. To keep the royal power intact, safe, and strong was his constant purpose. To achieve it he tamed the nobility, seeking to make them effective and obedient servants of the king, and destroyed the quasi-independence of the Huguenots, although allowing them considerable religious toleration once they had ceased to be a "state within the state." Thus, by 1635 when French intervention in the Thirty Years' War became necessary to prevent a Habsburg victory, Richelieu had built an adequate basis of unity within France. But France's entry into the war also meant that Richelieu had to forgo the opportunity to make the internal government of France less burdensome upon its people; instead the Thirty Years' War meant a great increase in taxes and a sharpening of tensions with the people. With the support of the king and the assistance of a group of able and dedicated "creatures" in the administration, Richelieu was able to keep control of the situation until his death in 1642.

His successor, the Italian-born Cardinal Jules Mazarin (1602–1661), continued Richelieu's basic policies during the first eighteen years of the reign of the new king, Louis XIV (1643–1715). However, the sharpened fiscal demands of the government during the last years of the Thirty Years' War and the lessened prestige of the monarchy during the king's minority led to a civil war, the Fronde, in 1648. The Fronde hampered French prosecution of the war against Spain until it was finally put down in 1653. Even more important, it left in the mind of the young Louis XIV an implacable hatred not only of outright rebellion but of all claims of subjects to participate by right in the business of government.

FRANCE: LOUIS XIV

When he took over direct guidance of the work of the state after Mazarin's death in 1661, Louis XIV set about consolidating what he envisioned as the only rightful form of government for France, absolute monarchy. He forbade the courts, known as parliaments, to remonstrate against laws and edicts which they considered improper as they had been long accustomed to do. He appointed no prime minister in Mazarin's place and kept the ultimate power of decision firmly in his own hands, although he worked with servants of superb ability like Colbert and the war minister, François Michel le Tellier, marquis de Louvois (1641–1691). The use of *intendants,* royal officials sent to the provinces to supervise and direct the work of local authorities, was expanded and systematized. They made possible the effective exercise of royal authority but did not bring about any fundamental reform of governmental administration. The practice continued of selling offices outright to their holders, who could then bequeath them or sell them like almost any other kind of property.

Louis himself took the work of government very seriously; he was never bored by its detail or overwhelmed by its responsibility and did not permit himself to be distracted from it by the multifarious court ceremonials, his frequent love affairs, or his penchants for hunting, the theater, and music. The king's special interest was foreign affairs, the weaving of diplomatic policy, and the waging of wars, for he saw his paramount aim to be the achievement of glory such as only victorious wars could bring him. He had less interest in Colbert's work of economic innovation and fiscal consolidation; what mattered to him was that Colbert and his successors provide the funds needed for his vastly expensive wars and his grandiose building program which culminated in the construction of the immense palace at Versailles. Versailles was more than just a residence, but rather a little city where the entire court lived and the royal government worked most of the years from 1676.

Louis XIV's very success in expanding the central government and limiting or even excluding the work of provincial and local bodies, however, made it increasingly difficult for even a diligent monarch to keep track of everything of importance. As the size of the royal administration grew, the officials working under the king's authority and on his behalf gradually achieved a kind of autonomy different from that of feudal barons but no less real. Their professional training and experience made it increasingly difficult to replace them in their arduous tasks, while the growing complexity of their activities made it more and more difficult to direct them in practice. The monarch found himself almost unawares taking the details and even the main lines of his policies from his ministers and their subordinates, and his role of command was subtly transformed into one of deciding among alternative policies and competing ministers rather than in exercising his own initiative. Such advice might be wrong, but it was usually competent. More of a danger to the wisdom of his decisions, in the long run, was the never-ending flattery and the absence of effective criticism.

A rigid Catholic, although one whose shallow piety did not prevent a multiplicity of adulteries for the first several decades of his marriage, he was deeply convinced that all Frenchmen had a duty to share his religion with him. The *cujus regio, ejus religio* doctrine seemed self-evident to him. Thus, it was easy to persuade him that the immense majority of Huguenots were ready and eager to be converted to Catholicism. He accepted the harsh measures of military oppression organized by Louvois against the Huguenots as the price that had to be paid for religious unity. In 1685 Louis revoked the Edict of Nantes which, dating back almost a century to its grant by Henry IV, was the basis for religious toleration of the Huguenots. Proclaiming that there was now only one religion in his kingdom, Louix XIV made it a crime to remain a Huguenot and virtual treason for a Calvinist to preach. Although some Protestants changed faith under this threat and with the temptation of monetary rewards, most either fled abroad, bringing their valuable skills as businessmen, farmers, and artisans to such countries as England, Holland, and Prussia, or remained in their homes in peril of their liberty and their lives. But nothing deterred the king from the path he had chosen. He was ruling as he wished to rule, and although he came to admit at least in part that he had "loved war too much" and hurt his country gravely, he never questioned the ideal of absolute rule which he had followed and which he embodied.

It was an ideal which was not restricted to France. Louis XIV's success in this policy within France and the immensity of the power which he was able to bring to bear in France's foreign relations made his pattern of government a model which, even during his lifetime and for the following centuries, most kings and rulers attempted to follow.

ENGLAND: THE EARLY STUARTS

England continued to go her own way during the seventeenth century. She flirted with absolutism but never came wholly into its grip. James I (1603–1625), the Stuart king of Scotland who came south to succeed Elizabeth I in England, was a pedantic monarch who believed in the virtue and efficacy of unrestricted monarchy. In practice he was an ineffectual ruler, with greater pretensions than achievements. He vigorously supported the rights of the Anglican church but was unable to end the constant criticism leveled by the Puritans against its system of government by bishops and its retention of many rituals from Catholicism. Nor was James any more effective in ruling without Parliament; he needed the tax money which only it could grant and did not dare to disregard its hallowed rights as a partner in making laws. His foreign policy, too, was a sorry tale of high aspirations and deplorable failures. Although he inherited from Elizabeth the mantle of leadership of the Protestant states of Europe, he was reluctant either to exercise this role or to relinquish it.

What James I sowed, his son Charles I (1625–1649) reaped. He carried forward his father's absolutist ambitions with total conviction. When Parliament refused to grant him the taxes he wanted, he sent the lawmakers home and proceeded to govern without them. He extended the traditional *shipmoney,* paid by port towns for their naval protection, to the entire country and compelled the judges to enforce this measure, instituted on his own prerogative and without parliamentary legislation. He enforced a harsh anti-Puritanical policy in religion. Government by prerogative rather than with Parliament was successful for more than a decade, but at a price. Charles had to play a very passive role in foreign affairs while the Thirty Years' War was deciding the political fate of Europe since an active foreign policy

THE HOUSE OF STUART

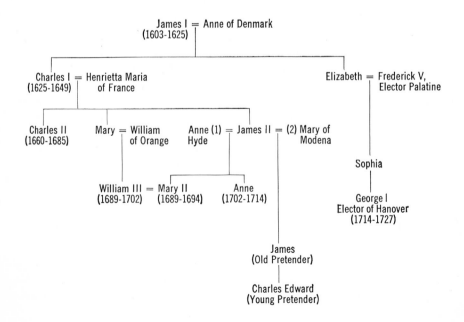

KING CHARLES I. Sir Anthony Van Dyck, who came from Flanders to be the portraitist of English society, here displays not only the easy elegance of the Stuart king but also his royal disdain.

would have created the probability of involvement in the war, and war in turn would have created the certainty of the expenditure of huge sums of money. Charles was able to do without Parliament without stirring up open rebellion only because he very largely lived within the traditional revenues of the crown, which did not require new legislative approval.

This policy of restraint collapsed when the king attempted to introduce episcopalian organization (government by bishops) into the church of Scotland which was staunchly Calvinist and presbyterian. A rebellion of the Scots revealed the paucity of the royal military forces in the northern kingdom, and the rebels carried the war to England itself. Charles was compelled to call Parliament back into session after an eleven-year interval (1629–1640), but this *Long Parliament* made the king's abandonment of his absolutist and anti-Puritanical policies a precondition for granting him the funds with which to expel or pay off the Scottish troops encamped in England. Charles, in desperation, sought to turn the Scots against their English compeers, but without success. Instead the Parliament joined the Scots in armed resistance, and civil war ensued for six years. A Parliamentary army, modeled on that of Gustavus Adolphus of Sweden, finally defeated the royalist Cavaliers. In 1648 Charles became the prisoner of the Parliamentarians who tried him for treason and executed him in January 1649.

ENGLAND UNDER CROMWELL

It was now Parliament's turn to establish an effective government upon a republican basis. But the English commonwealth proved to be based too narrowly upon the power of the army, without adequate support in the population. When a conflict arose between the lawmakers and the army commander, Oliver Cromwell (1599–1658), it was he who swept his opponents out of Westminster palace with a handful of troops. Cromwell became the monarch of England in all but name; even his title of Lord Protector, taken in 1653, was monarchial in spirit. Yet demands for a broader democratization of religion and society came from within the army. Outside were the Levellers and Diggers, revolutionary groups with ambitions to distribute power and property among the whole people. But their dreams were loftier than their strength, and they were easily put down. Under the dominance of the army, a stronghold of staunch Puritans, English life was strictly moralized, with dancing, games, and other traditional delights banned. Cromwell's power was such—displayed not only in the crushing of plots to restore Charles II, son of the late king, but also in successful wars against the Dutch and the Spaniards—that these policies were obeyed.

But, after Oliver's death in 1658, his successor, his son Richard, proved ineffectual and was ousted within a year. The army commanders into whose hands power fell were unable to agree among themselves on the future of government or society. At last restoration of Charles II, then in exile in the Spanish Netherlands, seemed

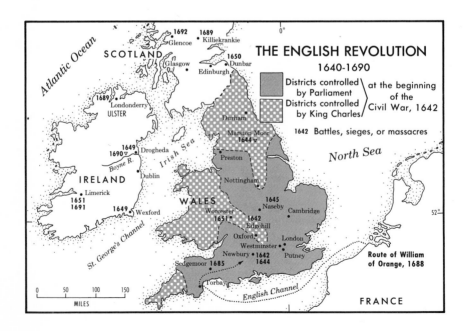

THE ENGLISH REVOLUTION
1640-1690

Districts controlled by Parliament
Districts controlled by King Charles
at the beginning of the Civil War, 1642

1642 Battles, sieges, or massacres

Route of William of Orange, 1688

the best solution. Charles, welcomed into the Dutch Netherlands en route home, promised in the Declaration of Breda that he would respect the religious freedom of the British peoples and govern with Parliament and under the law. In June 1660 he was restored to the throne amid great rejoicing.

ENGLAND: THE LATER STUARTS

As long as Charles II reigned (1660–1685), the Stuart monarchy survived all perils. But it took all the subtlety and stubbornness of this cynical monarch who was determined "not to go on his travels again" to achieve even a part of his purposes. These were essentially to govern by prerogative as much as possible, but at the same time to manipulate Parliament to achieve his aims, and to prepare the way for the restoration of Catholicism as the state religion if this could be safely done, or at the least to win official toleration for Catholics. Charles extracted grants of money not only from Parliament but also from Louis XIV, who wanted his alliance badly especially after the Triple Alliance of 1668 (see above, page 451). But the war against the Dutch in 1665–1667 was a debacle, and the renewed war against them in 1672–1674, if not a disaster, was bare of victories and ended in England's abandoning the French in 1674. The indications of Charles's fondness for Catholicism, his efforts to achieve toleration, and the conversion of his brother James, duke of York, to the Roman faith led to an upsurge of anti-Catholic feeling in the seventies and early eighties. But Charles, who had no legitimate children, fought off any attempt to exclude his brother from the succession to the throne, and James followed him peacefully in 1685.

James II, lacking the political astuteness of his brother, brought the smoldering conflict to open flame. He offended the most powerful and most numerous groups in the nation by suspending the anti-Catholic laws and by naming Catholics to leading positions in army, church, government, and the universities. He expanded the use of prerogative and thus moved strongly in the direction of absolutism, by means of which he sought to achieve his other goals. At first the Tories, the party of those who traditionally supported the king, remained willing to wait out the reign of James II, although his Catholicism deeply offended their strong Anglicanism, primarily because his two daughters, the heirs to the throne, were both good Protestants. However, when James, a widower, married an Italian noblewoman, Mary of Modena, and a son was born to them in 1687, the situation changed.

ENGLAND: THE GLORIOUS REVOLUTION

To prevent the establishment of a Catholic upon the throne, the Tories joined with the Whigs, their customary opponents who were committed advocates of parliamentary predominance and favored toleration of Protestant dissenters as well as strict laws against Catholics. James's nephew and son-in-law, William III, prince of Orange in the Netherlands (see below, page 462), was invited to head the resistance and came to England in 1688 with a fleet and a small army. James's supporters melted away, and he finally fled the country to take refuge in France. On the grounds that James had abdicated, the Parliament convened on orders of William III and gave the vacant throne to him and his wife, Mary II, in 1689 under conditions set down in the Bill of Rights, reaffirming the character of England as a constitutional monarchy.

In governing England, William kept in the front of his policy the war against France which followed immediately upon his English expedition. His reign saw the consolidation of the principles of constitutionalism, the permanent abandonment of the goal and the methods of absolutism in England, and close collaboration among the great aristocrats, the wealthy men of business, and the officials of state in the work of government. The central political issue of seventeenth-century England, whether sovereignty lay in king or Parliament, was thus decided once and for all in favor of the assembly that spoke for the nation, or at least for its dominant classes. William, who accepted that decision without question, was often unhappy with Parliament but recognized that his power depended upon persuading a body which he could not command.

When William died in 1702 (Mary II had died in 1694), he was succeeded by Mary's sister, Anne. Her reign, which extended until 1714, did not fundamentally change the settlement of 1689, although she was even more restless when her will was thwarted than William had been. She favored the Tories over the Whigs and endeavored to choose governments to her own liking. She did not overturn the Act of Settlement which conferred succession on the Hanoverian line in Germany, descended from Elizabeth, the daughter of James I who married Frederick of the Palatinate (see above, page 448), and excluded the direct line in the person of James II's son, "James III," who was living in France as a pensionary of Louis XIV. How the royal initiative in the formation of governments and the initiation and conduct of policy fitted in with parliamentary sovereignty—the right to make the ultimate decisions—remained uncertain, however, and continued to be an open question into the later eighteenth century.

The formation of the Bank of England and the acceptance of the principle that the national debt (for the obligations of the government were henceforth considered to be those of the nation and not just of the king personally) was sacrosanct, were signs of the new way of government. Its success was indicated in the ability of England, still much smaller in population than her opponent France, to rally her resources for two fierce, difficult, but finally victorious wars (1689–1697, 1702–1713). During these conflicts England took over the dominating position in European trade, shipping, and seapower generally which Holland had possessed during the entire preceding century.

WILLIAM II OF NASSAU AND ORANGE. Van Dyck endows his young subject with the qualities of self-assurance and purposeful strength which the prince displayed during his brief career as stadholder.

THE DUTCH REPUBLIC

The United Provinces of the Netherlands was an unparalleled political phenomenon in the seventeenth century—a federal constitutional republic that was also a great power. Provincial estates were the effective sovereigns within the country, the common government of the States General[1] being largely confined to the conduct of foreign affairs. The princes of Orange continued to serve the provinces as *stadholders* (governors) and the States General as chief commanders of the Dutch armed forces. The great political power wielded by the tiny republic was the direct consequence of the extraordinary development of Dutch economic life.

Tension between the House of Orange and the principal province, Holland, was the primary factor in Dutch political life. Holland's main concern was to win and maintain peace in order to keep and increase her prosperity; that of the princes of Orange was to enhance the influence and the power of their house. A crisis broke out in the summer of 1650 when William II attempted to crush a party hostile to him in Holland, seizing its leaders and besieging Amsterdam. He succeeded only in part and died later in the year, but the leaders of Holland had

---

[1] It is customary to call the Dutch assemblies *States* and those in France *Estates*, reflecting their national names. The terms are identical in meaning, however.

learned their lesson and decided to introduce government without stadholders. For twenty-two years the five principal provinces were ruled only by their town magistrates and provincial estates. French invasion in 1672 resulted in a wide wave of riots and near-rebellions on behalf of the young Prince of Orange, William III, and the stadholderate was restored. William, although offered the sovereignty over a rump republic by Charles II, his uncle, and Louis XIV, his cousin, refused to abandon the Dutch cause, and he led the European struggle against the Grand Monarch for the rest of his life.

But the structure of Dutch government was not yet finally fixed. On William's death in 1702 the political leaders, tired of his strong-willed rule, again refrained from naming a new stadholder. By this time, however, the superiority of the Dutch in trade and shipping had been lost to their English allies, the Golden Age was coming to an end, and the republic ceased to be a great power.

GERMANY

During the seventeenth century the Holy Roman Empire became an outright historical relic. The Thirty Years' War saw the last effort of an emperor, Ferdinand II, to beat down the aspirations of the German princes for sovereignty at the expense of the central authority. The Peace of Westphalia recorded his failure. The principalities became the true states of Germany, fully sovereign in rights and in almost everything but name.

From the holocaust of their imperial dreams the Habsburgs rescued the reality of their own dynastic power, both in the hereditary lands of Austria and in the various kingdoms assembled together under the Austrian archdukes, as Bohemia, Moravia, and Hungary. Austria—as we now begin to call the composite state ruled by the Habsburgs in central Europe—was defended against Ottoman assaults; the Hungarian lands lost to the Turks were fought for and rewon. Government within each of the Austrian lands continued along old patterns, but in each the Habsburg monarch ruled absolutely, except in Hungary where the resistance of the Magyar nobles compelled him to share power with the Diet.

No less significant in the long run than the emergence of Austria as a great power was the rise of Brandenburg to political strength. A conglomerate power with possessions from the Rhineland to the duchy of Prussia, the main center of Brandenburg lay in northeastern Germany around the capital city of Berlin. Frederick William became elector in 1644 when the fortunes of his land were at the lowest. The economic resources of Brandenburg were few, and Frederick William with cunning persistence, never losing sight of his basic goal, formed alliances with stronger powers and broke them as soon as it was to his advantage. He built up his army by taking foreign subsidies, threw off Polish suzerainty over the duchy of Prussia, and became a respected and even feared member of the com-

THE AUSTRIAN HABSBURGS

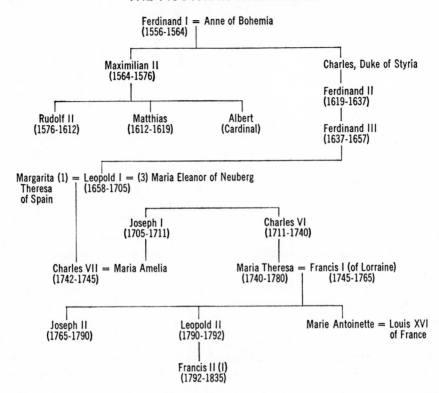

Ferdinand I = Anne of Bohemia
(1556-1564)

Maximilian II
(1564-1576)

Charles, Duke of Styria

Ferdinand II
(1619-1637)

Rudolf II
(1576-1612)

Matthias
(1612-1619)

Albert
(Cardinal)

Ferdinand III
(1637-1657)

Margarita (1) = Leopold I = (3) Maria Eleanor of Neuberg
Theresa　　　(1658-1705)
of Spain

Joseph I
(1705-1711)

Charles VI
(1711-1740)

Charles VII = Maria Amelia
(1742-1745)

Maria Theresa = Francis I (of Lorraine)
(1740-1780)　　　(1745-1765)

Joseph II
(1765-1790)

Leopold II
(1790-1792)

Marie Antoinette = Louis XVI
of France

Francis II (I)
(1792-1835)

munity of states. When Frederick William died in 1688, he had not yet made Brandenburg a great power, but his achievements won him the name of the Great Elector. In 1701 his son, Frederick III (1688–1713), used the position and the strength achieved by his father to take the royal title of king *in* Prussia with the permission of the emperor. The name *Prussia,* with its higher prestige, thereupon became the common name for all the territories of the elector of Brandenburg, and it was under the name Prussia that future greatness and tragedy was to come to this land.

EASTERN EUROPE

In eastern Europe the seventeenth century saw one power fall far away from its ancient greatness and another begin its rise to world stature. The first was Poland, the easternmost outpost of Latin Christendom among the Slavic peoples. Poland's government was an elective monarchy in which the nobility had picked away virtually all the prerogatives of the crown for their own advantage. The nobles were able to rule absolutely and ruthlessly over millions of peasants who fell deeper into the grip of serfdom. The once great Polish power which had extended from the Baltic to the Black seas flickered uncertainly and briefly, but final victory in wars with Sweden, Russia, and Brandenburg always went to the adversaries. Only once did the Polish forces win undisputed glory, when the army of King John III Sobieski (1674–1696) came to the rescue of Vienna against the Turks in 1683. But all the advantages went to the Austrians, and the Poles returned home with glory and nothing else.

Russia on the other hand began the century badly. The ancient Rurikian dynasty died out at the end of the sixteenth century with young Tsar Theodore, and a *Time of Troubles* ensued (1604–1613) during which the country was ravaged by civil wars, disputes for the throne, and invasions by Poles and Swedes who captured Moscow and enthroned their own candidates. But finally native Russian forces assembled around the new dynasty of Michael Romanov (1613–1645), the invaders were expelled, the rebellions were put down, and reconstruction began. Trade was maintained with western Europe principally through Dutch and English merchants, for Russia had not yet developed a native commercial class of any size. Despite the antipathy of the Orthodox Russians for the schismatic Christians of the West, some of the more thoughtful Muscovites recognized the superiority of the military and governmental techniques of the West and began to recruit westerners for aid in adapting these to Russian use. But Russia remained landlocked, both to the west and the south. Efforts to break through to the Baltic and the Black seas were unavailing until the reign of Tsar Peter I (1689–1725); but since most of his achievements come after the turn of the century, they will be treated in Chapter 13.

4. Intellectual and Religious Life

DURING THE SEVENTEENTH CENTURY there originated some of the most momentous transformations in the intellectual life of the western world, including the Scientific Revolution which will be the subject of Chapter 12. But the developments in the intellectual and religious worlds, though closely connected with the scientific changes, may be described here separately.

RATIONALISM

The specific change of greatest moment in the general intellectual life was the emergence of modern *rationalism,* a way of thought that placed the activity of reason ahead of all other ways of understanding and making use of the world. But reason can mean many things, and already did so in the seventeenth century. First of all it was the instrument of logic, created in antiquity by Aristotle, and then enormously amplified and refined during the later Middle Ages. From the beginning Christian thinkers had been aware of the potential conflict between logical reason and the method of faith which need not be bound by reason. However, modern rationalism, because it made the standard of reason paramount, carried with it from its emergence in the seventeenth century a latent hostility to the traditional systems of religious belief and argument. It was therefore a fundamental break with the medieval conciliation of reason and faith that had been achieved by St. Thomas Aquinas, in which the ultimate primacy was given to faith.

The more immediate problem faced by seventeenth-century rationalists was not the traditional theology but *skepticism* (called Pyrrhonism, after the ancient Greek thinker Pyrrho). The skeptics used the methods of reason to destroy confidence in reason; by calling into question the very process of knowledge, they made any certain or real knowledge of the world, either of things or of ideas, a logical impossibility. The most influential of recent skeptical thinkers had been the French essayist Michel Eyquem de Montaigne (1533–1592). Much of the meaning of Montaigne's thinking remains uncertain, particularly whether or not he intended his attack upon belief in certain knowledge to be a buttress for unreasoning faith. But there can be no question that Montaigne had forsworn either faith or reason as a basis for persecution of heretics or waging wars of religion. Montaigne's question, "What do I know?" deeply troubled most serious thinkers, who were usually unwilling, however, to settle for a world without certainties or a way of thought without certitudes.

The skeptics' question led directly into the work of the supreme philosophical thinker of the seventeenth century, René Descartes (1596–1650). A Frenchman by birth, education, and language, he spent most of his adult life in the tolerant Dutch Republic. Descartes, one of the greatest mathematicians of all time, desired to achieve in knowledge of the world—what was coming to be called *science* or *natural philosophy*—the same certainty that he found in algebra and geometry. He remained a believing Roman Catholic but relied on the doctrine of the two truths, which held that philosophy and religion were totally distinct and that what could be true in one could be false in the other, to permit himself to develop his philosophical ideas without perturbation by formal religion. Science was concerned only with the world of extension, the world in which things occupied space and moved; religion was concerned with the soul, which had no extension. Certitude in religion came from revelation and was therefore inviolable against the vitriol of rationalism; but certitude in science was not proof against the corrosive bite of skepticism, the apparent terminus of reason. Descartes took it as his task to use the very arguments of skepticism to defeat it and to build up a reliable science. This he did to his own satisfaction by showing that the very act of doubting implied a thinking doubter who had to say to himself, "I think, therefore I am." One's own existence therefore

THE PHILOSOPHER OF RATIONALISM. René Descartes, who sought to revolutionize science and philosophy, spent most of his productive years in tolerant Holland, where Frans Hals painted this portrait.

lay beyond the reach of doubt. From this rock of certainty Descartes, using elements of scholastic philosophy which he considered self-evident, developed such additional truths as the existence of God and of a real world. He then went on to elaborate a physical science not by investigation, but by proofs of logical and psychological necessity. This Cartesian[2] practice, lacking a base in experimentation, was ultimately displaced by the empirically-oriented rationalism of Galileo and Newton (see below, pages 485–488), but Descartes' methodological rules, with their emphasis upon precise distinction of ideas in analysis and their far-reaching combination in synthesis, became part and parcel of the new scientific method.

HISTORY

Where science was concerned with the understanding of nature, the understanding of men's activity to a large extent remained the work of history. History continued to be used as a form of rhetorical display and as a means of propaganda and agitation for one or another religion, nation, or group; but it also began to be practiced more and more as a disciplined form of knowledge in which sources are

---

[2] The adjective *Cartesian* comes from the Latin form of Descartes' name, *Cartesius*.

analyzed for authenticity, significance, and implications. But the two kinds of history already came into conflict. The efforts of various political controversialists to sustain their arguments by refutation of their opponents' sources and handling of sources was leading to that kind of study of the past and its significance for the present which a great modern historian has called "the discussion without end." Where, however, there were positions about the past which were accepted as sacrosanct, any treatment of them upon strictly historical terms, leaving the authority of tradition and revelation aside, became heretical.

This was most evident in the debate on the historical character of the Bible. It was a French Catholic priest, Father Robert Simon (1638–1712), philosophically a Cartesian, who initiated this controversy by attempting to prepare a critical edition of the Old Testament—critical not in the sense of incredulity and hostility, but in the sense of the working out of meaning on the basis of historical and philological evidence. When the Dutch philosopher Spinoza adapted Simon's technique in his *Theological-Political Treatise,* he called down on his head the wrath of the Calvinist theologians in Holland. For them the only permissible way of studying and using the text of the Bible was their own—as a huge congeries of citations studied without any historical awareness of the differences between the time of the writing and their own time, and applied to support positions already accepted.

RELIGION

In religious life the seventeenth century saw the passing of the great debates over religious problems at the highest level. It was a time not for the creation of new creeds but for the defense of those already established. The debates among Catholics and Protestants alike arose now over the specific meaning and content of orthodoxy, rather than over deliberate attempts to create new orthodoxies.

Catholicism was riven chiefly by the fierce and interminable conflict between a group of precisians called *Jansenists*—after the name of a bishop of Ypres, Cornelius Jansenius (1585–1638), who was active during the first part of the century. Jansenius had written a long treatise expounding the theological ideas of St. Augustine, with emphasis upon the notions of predestination and the bondage of the human will. Followers of Jansenius, with their center in the abbey of Port Royal near Paris, built upon these ideas a religious approach emphasizing strict morality. They denounced the laxist casuistry they attributed to the Jesuits, who were concerned to fit the ethical demands of Christianity to what could be achieved by a majority, not just a slim minority, of men. The most notable of the Jansenists, the great scientist and mathematician Blaise Pascal (1623–1662), in his *Provincial Letters* raised the issues from the personal and the occasional to the loftiest of human problems—the problems of man faced with his weakness and his aspirations, with a universe to which the new science seemed to give order but not meaning, and with a God whose purposes and ways seemed inscrutable. Pascal solved these soul-shaking anxieties by way of faith, rejecting the science to which he had contributed so much and expressing his qualms and his joys in prose of supreme lucidity and power.

A struggle similar to that which was waged between Jansenism and Jesuitism developed within Protestantism. In Holland it took the form of a struggle over the true character of Calvinism—whether God's predestination of men to election or damnation was as rigorous and absolute as the strict Calvinists, called Gomarians, held. In England the Puritans held beliefs very similar to those of the Gomarians, and they called their foes in the Anglican church by the name of Arminians, after the anti-Gomarians in Holland.

5. Arts and Letters

IN THE SEVENTEENTH CENTURY artistic and literary life evolved two sharply contrasted styles. One, the *Baroque,* gave expression primarily to feelings of tension—the relations among multiple and conflicting forces held momentarily under control by the artist's virtuosity, but not truly unified. The other style, *Classicism,* demanded even greater virtuosity of its practitioners, for it demanded that they take the complexities of human feeling and activity and bring them into authentic unity. Yet these movements of such utterly different quality voiced the moods and aspirations of the same society, often indeed of the same people. We must be wary therefore of identifying the Baroque with the turmoil and conflict of the early seventeenth century and Classicism with the reestablishment of authority after mid-century, unless we grant, as perhaps we must, that both characteristics remained strong within the societies and even within the individuals. In any case, one trait is shared by both Baroque and Classicism. Each was the further elaboration of Renaissance styles in art and literature; they arose at a time when the artist could no longer feel any personal triumph in creation in the Renaissance style but had to recognize that he was usually only doing well what others had already done superbly. Thus the energies of innovative creativity went into the evolution of new styles solidly based on the old practices.

THE FINE ARTS

Painting.   The linked duality of Baroque and Classicism may be traced in the various arts. Painting continued to be the form in which the highest quality of artistic force was achieved. The predominant style in the early part of the century was Baroque, and probably the most characteristic figure was the Flemish artist Peter

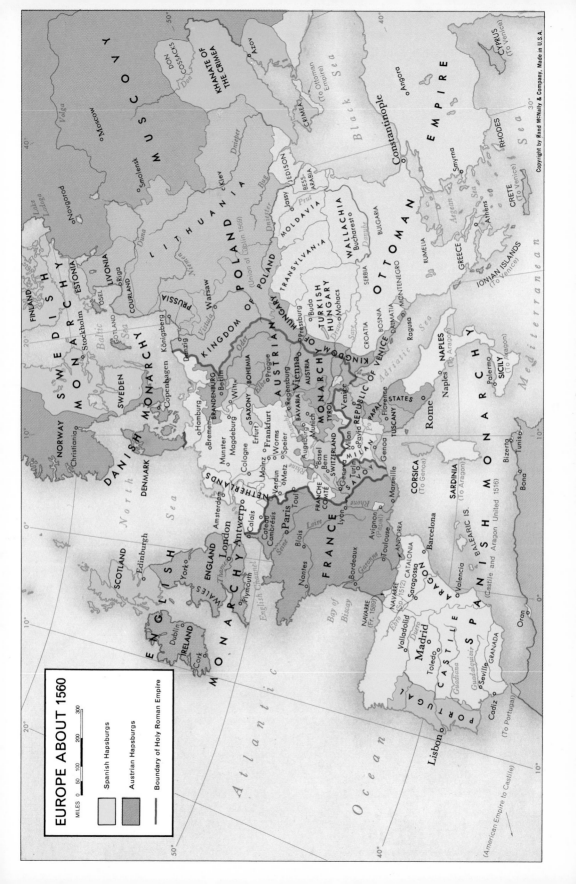

EUROPE ABOUT 1560

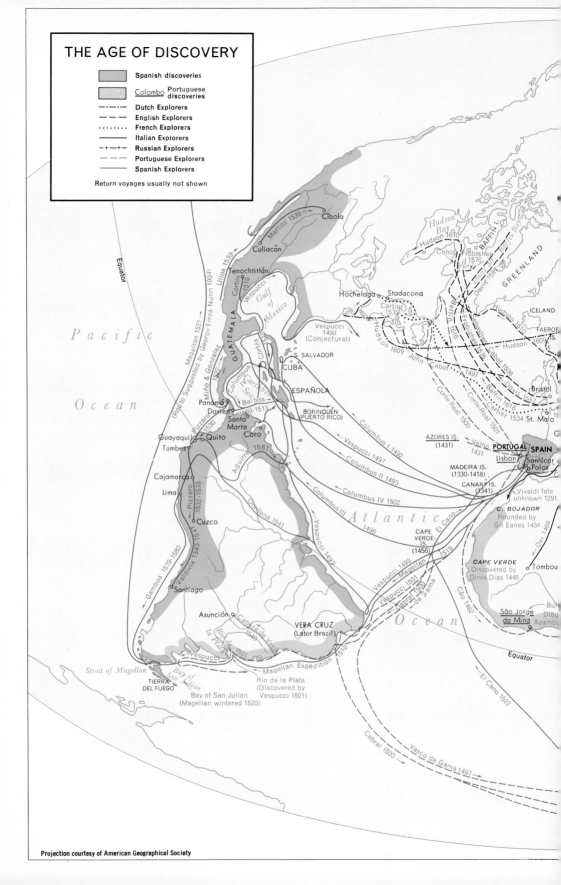

THE AGE OF DISCOVERY

Spanish discoveries

Colombo Portuguese discoveries

—·—·— Dutch Explorers

— — — English Explorers

········· French Explorers

———— Italian Explorers

—+—+— Russian Explorers

— — — Portuguese Explorers

— — — — Spanish Explorers

Return voyages usually not shown

Equator

Pacific

Ocean

Atlantic

Ocean

Equator

Císbola

Marcos 1539

Culiacán

Ulloa 1539

Tenochtitlán

Vespucci 1519

Cortés

Magellan 1521

(Route Suggested by George Emra Nunn 1934)

Miño & Gonzalez

GUATEMALA

Gulf of Mexico

Cortés

S. SALVADOR

CUBA

ESPAÑOLA

Vespucci 1498 (Conjectural)

Hochelaga   Stadacona

Cartier 1535

Cartier 1535 St. Malo

Hudson Bay

Hudson 1610

Cabot Frobisher 1576

BAFFIN I.

GREENLAND

Davis 1587

ICELAND

FAEROE IS. 1609

Hudson 1610

John Cabot 1497

Baffin 1616

Davis 1585

Bristol

Carribean Sea

Columbus

Panamá   Balboa

Darién 1509-1513

Santa Marta

Coro

BORINQUÉN (PUERTO RICO)

Columbus I 1492

Vespucci 1497

Columbus II 1493

AZORES IS. (1431)

Velho 1431

PORTUGAL   SPAIN

Lisbon   Sanlúcar   Palos

MADEIRA IS. (1330-1418)

CANARY IS. (1341)

Vivaldi fate unknown 1291

Guayaquil   Quito

Tumbes

Aguirre 1561

Columbus IV 1502

Columbus III 1498

C. BOJADOR Rounded by Gil Eanes 1434

El Cano

Cajamarca

Lima

Pizzaro 1530

Pizzaro 1532-1533

Orellana 1541

Vespucci 1499

CAPE VERDE IS. (1456)

El Cano 1519

CAPE VERDE Discovered by Dinis Dias 1445

Diaz 1489

Cuzco

Tombou

Gamboa 1579-1580

Valdivia 1540-1541

Santiago

Asunción   Cabeza de Vaca 1540

Río de la Plata

VERA CRUZ (Later Brazil)

Vespucci 1499

Magellan

Cabral 1500

da Gama

São Jorge da Mina

Bur Diog Azambu

Vespucci 1501

Magellan Expedition

Equator

El Cano 1522

Vespucci

Strait of Magellan   Bay of San Julián

TIERRA DEL FUEGO

Bay of San Julián (Magellan wintered 1520)

Rio de la Plata (Discovered by Vespucci 1501)

Magellan 1519

Cabral 1500   Vasco da Gama 1497

Projection courtesy of American Geographical Society

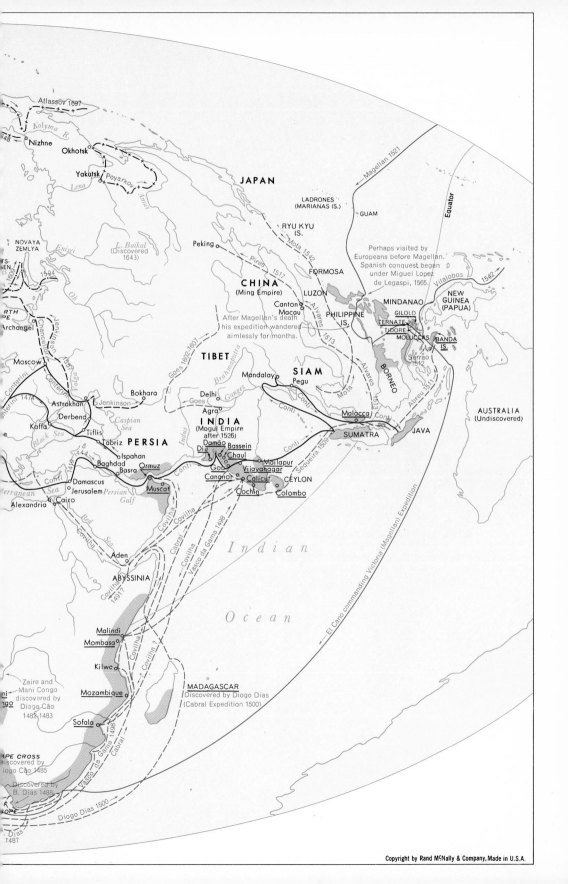

Atlassov 1697

Nizhne

Okhotsk

Yakutsk · Poyarkov

Kolyma R.

Lena

Amur

JAPAN

LADRONES
(MARIANAS IS.)

GUAM

Magellan 1521

Equator

NOVAYA
ZEMLYA

Enisei

L. Baikal
(Discovered
1643)

Peking

RYU KYU
IS.

Mota 1542

Perhaps visited by
Europeans before Magellan.
Spanish conquest began
under Miguel Lopez
de Legaspi, 1565.

Vilalobos

1542

Archangel

Chancellor

Ob

Pires 1517

CHINA
(Ming Empire)

FORMOSA

LUZON

MINDANAO

NEW
GUINEA
(PAPUA)

Moscow

Canton
Macau

After Magellan's death
his expedition wandered
aimlessly for months.

PHILIPPINE
IS.

Alvares 1513

GILOLO
TERNATE
TIDORE
MOLUCCAS

BANDA
IS.

Goes 1602-1607

TIBET

Brahmaputra

Mandalay

SIAM

Pegu

Conti

BORNEO

Serrao
1512

Abreu 1511

AUSTRALIA
(Undiscovered)

Contarini 1476

Bokhara

Jenkinson

Delhi

Ganges

Goes

Astrakhan

Derbend

*Caspian
Sea*

Agra

INDIA
(Mogul Empire
after 1526)

Conti

Malacca

Conti

SUMATRA

JAVA

Kaffa

Tiflis

Tabriz

PERSIA

Damão
Diu

Bassein
Chaul

Marlapur

Mota

1444

Ispahan

Goa

Vijayanagar

Sequeira 1509

Black Sea

Baghdad
Basra

Ormuz

Cananor

Calicut

CEYLON

Damascus
Jerusalem

*Persian
Gulf*

Muscat

Cochin

Colombo

Conti

Alexandria

Cairo

Mediterranean Sea

Red Sea

Covilha

Covilha

Cabral

Covilha

Vasco da Gama 1498

I n d i a n

Aden

ABYSSINIA

Covilha
1497

El Cano commanding Victoria (Magellan) Expedition

O c e a n

Malindi

Mombasa

Covilha ?

Kilwa

MADAGASCAR
Discovered by Diogo Dias
(Cabral Expedition 1500)

Zaire and
Mani Congo
discovered by
Diogo Cão
1482-1483

Mozambique

Sofala

Vasco da Gama 1498

Cabral

APE CROSS
iscovered by
iogo Cão 1485

Discovered by
B. Dias 1488

Diogo Dias 1500

Dias
1487

14. HUNTERS IN THE SNOW. Against a winter landscape drawn with minute and loving attention to detail, Pieter Brueghel the Elder has depicted with honesty and affection the Flemish peasants, highlighting the vigor and sturdy dignity of their everyday lives.

15. CARDINAL RICHELIEU. Philippe de Champaigne, who painted several portraits of Cardinal Richelieu, here portrays the intensity of purpose, the acuity of mind, and the sickly body of the man who governed France for Louis XIII for almost two decades.

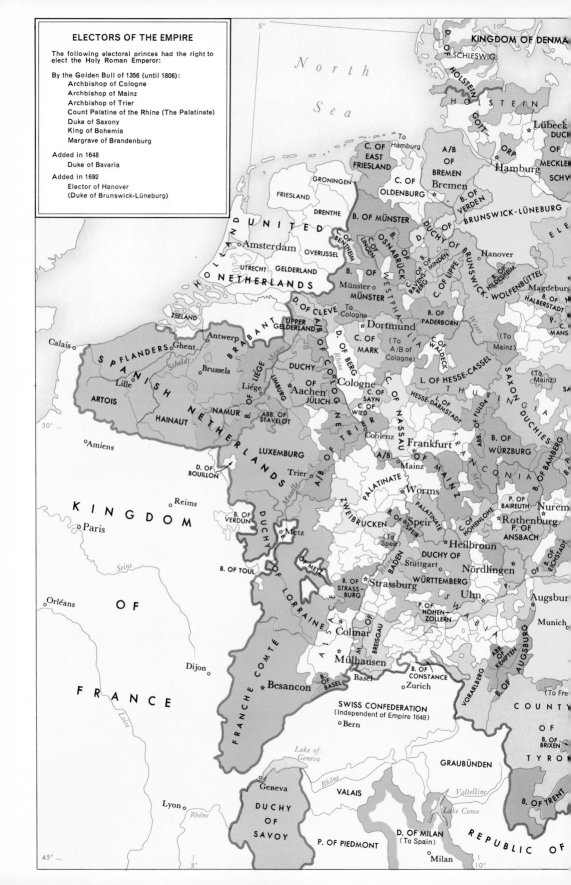

ELECTORS OF THE EMPIRE

The following electoral princes had the right to elect the Holy Roman Emperor:

By the Golden Bull of 1356 (until 1806):
  Archbishop of Cologne
  Archbishop of Mainz
  Archbishop of Trier
  Count Palatine of the Rhine (The Palatinate)
  Duke of Saxony
  King of Bohemia
  Margrave of Brandenburg

Added in 1648
  Duke of Bavaria

Added in 1692
  Elector of Hanover
  (Duke of Brunswick-Lüneburg)

KINGDOM OF DENMARK

D. OF SCHLESWIG

HOLSTEIN

HOLSTEIN

GOTT-

Lübeck
DUCH
OF
MECKLE
SCHW

ORP

Hamburg

North
Sea

To
Hamburg

C. OF
EAST
FRIESLAND

A/B
OF
BREMEN
Bremen

B. OF
VERDEN

GRONINGEN

C. OF
OLDENBURG

BRUNSWICK-LÜNEBURG

ELE

FRIESLAND

DRENTHE

B. OF MÜNSTER

DUCHY OF
BRUNSWICK

Hanover

B. OF N
HILDESHEIM

Magdeburg
HALBERSTADT

UNITED

B. OF
BENTHEIM

B. OF
LINGEN

OSNABRÜCK

C. OF
RAVENS-
BERG

C. OF LIPPE

B. OF MINDEN

WOLFENBÜTTEL

Amsterdam

OVERIJSSEL

B. OF

WESTPHALIA

P. C.
MANS

UTRECHT
GELDERLAND

NETHERLANDS

Münster o
MÜNSTER

B. OF
PADERBORN

(To
Mainz)

ZEELAND

D. OF CLEVE

UPPER
GELDERLAND

To
Cologne

Dortmund

C. OF
MARK

(To
A/B of
Cologne)

C. OF
WALDECK

L. OF HESSE-CASSEL

(To
Mainz)

SAXON DUCHIES

Calais o

Ghent

Antwerp

BRABANT

D. OF
BERG

C. OF

Cologne

L. OF
HESSE-DARMSTADT

THURINGIA

SPANISH FLANDERS

Brussels

LIÈGE

DUCHY
OF
COLOGNE

C. OF
SAYN

ABB. OF FULDA

B. OF
WÜRZBURG

Lille

Liège

Aachen

JÜLICH

C. OF
WIED

B. OF BAMBERG

ARTOIS

NAMUR

LIMBURG

ABB. OF
STAVELOT

A/B OF TRIER

C. OF NASSAU

FRANCONIA

HAINAUT

NETHERLANDS

Coblenz

Frankfurt

o Amiens

LUXEMBURG

Mainz

A/B

A/B OF MAINZ

P. OF
BAIREUTH

Nurem

50°

D. OF
BOUILLON

Trier

PALATINATE

Worms

C. OF
HOHENLOHE

Rothenburg

P. OF
ANSBACH

o Reims

B. OF
VERDUN

DUCHY
OF
LORRAINE

ZWEIBRÜCKEN

B. OF
WORMS

PALATINATE

Speir

B. OF
SPEIR

Heilbronn

KINGDOM

Paris

Metz

(To
Speir)

DUCHY OF

B. OF
EICHSTADT

o Metz

Stuttgart

Nördlingen

B. OF TOUL

BADEN

WÜRTTEMBERG

P.

Augsbur

OF

Orléans

ALSACE

B. OF
STRASS-
BURG

Strassburg

Ulm

SWABIA

Munich

Colmar

P. OF
HOHEN-
ZOLLERN

ABB. OF
KEMPTEN

B. OF
AUGSBURG

Dijon

FRANCHE COMTÉ

BREISGAU

Mülhausen

B. OF
CONSTANCE

VORARLBERG

B. OF
BRIXEN

FRANCE

Besançon

B. OF
BASEL

Basel

Zurich

(To Fre

COUNTY

OF

SWISS CONFEDERATION
(Independent of Empire 1648)

o Bern

GRAUBÜNDEN

TYROL

o Orléans

Lake of
Geneva

Rhône

Valtelline

B. OF TRENT

Geneva

VALAIS

Lake Como

Lyon o

Rhône

DUCHY

OF

SAVOY

D. OF MILAN
(To Spain)

REPUBLIC OF

P. OF PIEDMONT

Milan

45°

5°

10°

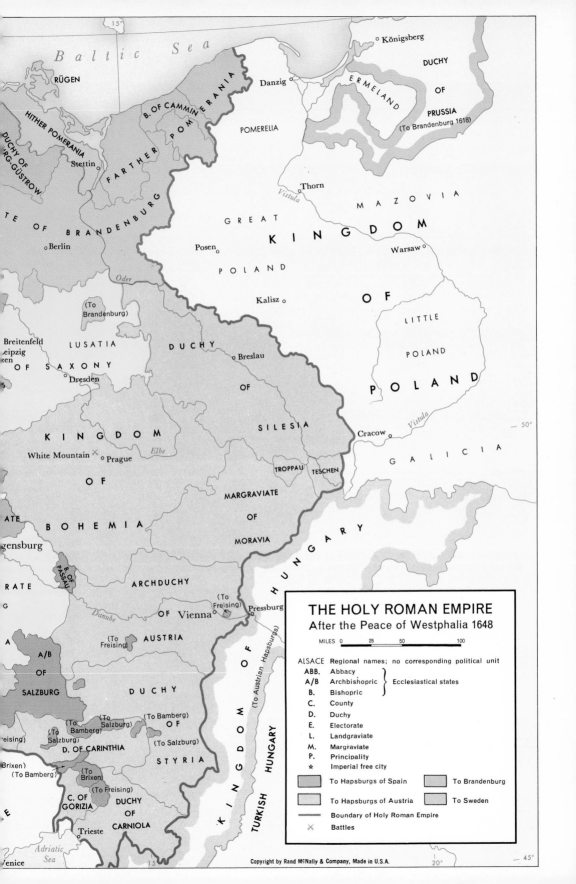

THE HOLY ROMAN EMPIRE
After the Peace of Westphalia 1648

MILES 0   25   50   100

ALSACE   Regional names; no corresponding political unit
ABB.   Abbacy   ⎫
A/B   Archbishopric   ⎬ Ecclesiastical states
B.   Bishopric   ⎭
C.   County
D.   Duchy
E.   Electorate
L.   Landgraviate
M.   Margraviate
P.   Principality
☆   Imperial free city

To Hapsburgs of Spain   To Brandenburg

To Hapsburgs of Austria   To Sweden

———— Boundary of Holy Roman Empire

×   Battles

Copyright by Rand McNally & Company, Made in U.S.A.

16. SURRENDER OF BREDA. Velasquez, in this remarkable representation of the surrender of Breda to Spain by the Dutch in 1625, uses a black screen of lances to symbolize the military might of the Spanish army in one of its last triumphs.

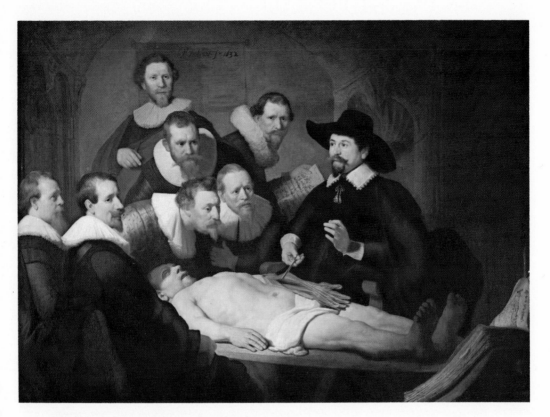

17. THE ANATOMY LESSON OF DR. NICHOLAS TULP. In this early masterpiece Rembrandt van Ryn shows the learned surgeon who was later to become the mayor of Amsterdam personally dissecting a corpse in order to teach the art of saving life from actual observation, not by reference to old books.

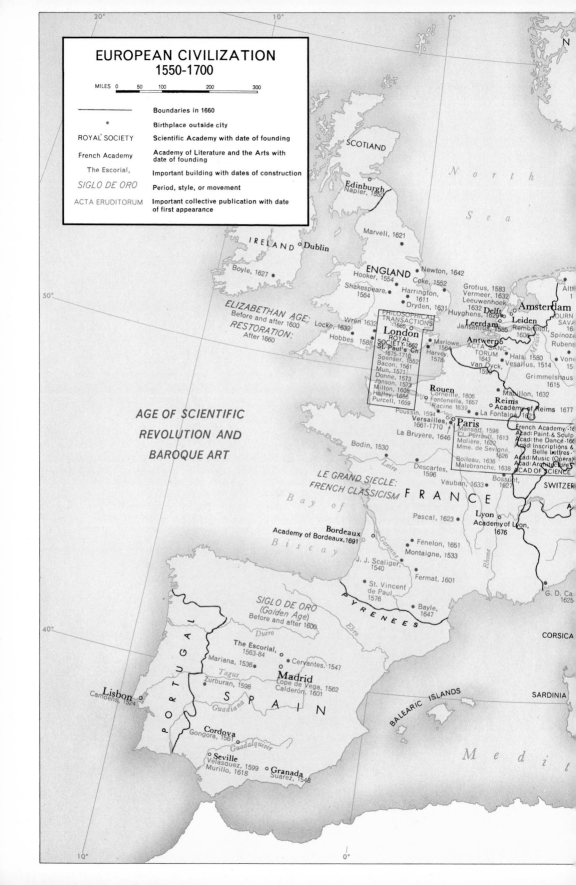

20°   10°   0°
                                                                    N

EUROPEAN CIVILIZATION
1550-1700

MILES 0   50   100   200   300

——————————— Boundaries in 1660

• Birthplace outside city

ROYAL SOCIETY Scientific Academy with date of founding

French Academy Academy of Literature and the Arts with
                date of founding

The Escorial, Important building with dates of construction

SIGLO DE ORO Period, style, or movement

ACTA ERUDITORUM Important collective publication with date
                of first appearance

SCOTLAND

North

Edinburgh
Napier, 1550

Sea

IRELAND ○Dublin

Marvell, 1621

ENGLAND • Newton, 1642
Boyle, 1627 •   Hooker, 1554   Coke, 1552
                                                Grotius, 1583   Alth
Shakespeare,   Harrington,   Vermeer, 1632   1
ELIZABETHAN AGE: 1564   1611   Leeuwenhoek,
Before and after 1600   Dryden, 1631   1632 Delft   Amsterdam
RESTORATION: Locke, 1632 • Huyghens, 1629○   OURN
After 1660   Wren 1632 •   Leiden   SAV
PHILOSOPHICAL   Leerdam Jansen, 1585 Rembrandt, 16
TRANSACTIONS   Hobbes, 1588 •   1606 Spinoz
-1665   Marlowe, Antwerp ○
London   1564   ACTA SANC- Rubens
ROYAL   St. Paul's Ch.   Harvey TORUM Hals, 1580 • Von
SOCIETY, 1662 1675-1710   1578   1643 Vesalius, 1514 15
Spenser, 1552   Van Dyck,
Bacon, 1561   159   Grimmelshaus
AGE OF SCIENTIFIC   Mun, 1571   1615
Donne, 1573   Rouen
Jonson, 1573   Corneille, 1606 Mabillon, 1632
REVOLUTION AND   Milton, 1608   Fontenelle, 1657 Reims
Halley, 1656   Racine 1639 Academy of Reims 1677
BAROQUE ART   Purcell, 1659   • La Fontaine, 16
Poussin, 1594
Versailles,   Paris   French Academy, 16
La Bruyère, 1646 1661-1710 ■ Mansart, 1598   Acad: Paint.& Sculp
CL. Perrault, 1613   Acad: the Dance-166
Bodin, 1530   Molière, 1622   Acad: Inscriptions &
Mme. de Sévigné,   Belle Lettres
Loire   1626   Acad: Music (Opera)
Descartes,   Boileau, 1636   Acad: Architecture
LE GRAND SIÈCLE: 1596   Malebranche, 1638 ACAD OF SCIENCE
FRENCH CLASSICISM F R A N C E   Bossuet,
Bay of   Vauban, 1633 •   1627   SWITZER
                                                        A
Pascal, 1623 •   Lyon ○
Academy of Lyon,
Bordeaux   1676
Academy of Bordeaux, 1691 Fénelon, 1651
Biscay   Montaigne, 1533
J. J. Scaliger,   G. D. Ca
1540   Fermat, 1601   1625
St. Vincent
de Paul   CORSICA
1576   • Bayle,
SIGLO DE ORO   1647
(Golden Age)
40° Before and after 1600

Duero

P O R T U G A L   The Escorial, ○
1563-84 ○ • Cervantes, 1547
Mariana, 1536 •
Madrid   SARDINIA
Tagus Zurburan, 1598 • ○ Lope de Vega, 1562
Calderón, 1601   BALEARIC ISLANDS
S P A I N
Lisbon ○
Camoens, 1524   *Guadiana*
Córdova
Gongora, 1561 •   *Guadalquivir*
○ Seville
Velasquez, 1599 ○ Granada
Murillo, 1618   Suarez, 1548 *Medit*

10°   0°

SWEDEN

20°

30°

istiania

o Stockholm

Baltic Sea

RUSSIA

Volga

o Riga

Dvina

openhagen

o Tycho Brahe,
1546

o Königsberg

Niemen

—50°

Elbe

Berlin

Oder

P   O   L   A   N   D

Vistula

Warsaw

Dnieper

O L Y

Leipzig o

A ERUDITORUM
1682-1776

eibniz, 1646
homasius, 1655

Böhme, 1575

Opitz, 1597

Pufendorf,
1632

o Lemberg

C A R P A T H I A N S

Dniester

O M A N

o Nuremberg

LEOPOLDINE ACADEMY
1687

Comenius,
1591

Danube

1571

Vienna

LEOPOLDINE
ACADEMY
1652

H U N G A R Y

o Buda

M   P   I   R   E

iladio, 1518

Cremona

everdi, 1567
divari, 1644

Venice

Malpighi, 1628

Torricelli, 1608

Florence

Academy della Crusca -1582

ACADEMY DEL CIMENTO -1657

alileo,
1564

Lully, 1633

Bellarmine, 1542

I   T   A   L   Y

Adriatic Sea

Danube

O   T   T   O   M   A   N

Black Sea

Constantinople

—40°

Rome

Palestrina, 1526

rench Academy at Rome -1666

cademy degli Arcadi -1690

ACADEMY DEI LINCEI -1603

t. Peters Church,
1506-1667

Tiber

Naples

ACADEMY ROSSANO
1695

Tasso, 1544
Bruno, 1548
Bernini, 1598
Scarlatti, 1659

Aegean Sea

E   M   P   I   R   E

Tyrrhenian Sea

Ionian Sea

Campanella, 1568

SICILY

RHODES

ranean Sea

El Greco, 1542

CRETE

20°

30°

18. TRIUMPHANT ENTRY OF LOUIS XIV INTO DUNKIRK, 1662. This tapestry from the Gobelins works portrays Louis XIV in a role he loved to play; he is shown as the conquering king, riding in to claim possession of his territory, although in actual fact he purchased Dunkirk from the English.

NEGRO HEADS. In these studies of the head of a black man—presumably a Negro visitor to Flanders—Peter Paul Rubens displays unaffected honesty and interest in and respect for his fellow man.

Paul Rubens (1577–1640). He combined the ability to draw simply but with the most extraordinary evocative power and a flair for the bold, dramatic, and emphatic. His paintings seethe with energy; his figures are robust and depicted in intense movement. The composition is full of swirling lines and turbulence that somehow never overmaster the artist. Among his works *The Descent from the Cross* and *The Elevation of the Cross* display his dramatic conception of religious experience, while *The Rape of the Sabines* and the *Venus and Adonis* express the classical interests of the late Renaissance, now an accepted element of intellectual and artistic life, all portrayed with Baroque virtuosity. His portraits, especially of his wife and children, however, are filled with the quiet strength of his affection without need for the Baroque touches of bravura.

Two other seventeenth-century painters, among the greatest ever known, defy easy classification by style and were the product of quite different societies. Diego Velásquez (1599–1660) was court painter to Spain's Philip IV, but he depicted his royal and aristocratic subjects with pitiless honesty although without hatred or scorn. He painted Philip IV forty times in all, as well as court figures like the duke of Olivares, but his interest also ran to startlingly human portraits of the royal jesters and dwarfs whom he showed with their masters and mistresses as well as to religious subjects. Rembrandt van Rijn (1606–1669), after an early, commercially

VERMEER AND THE VALIDITY OF THE PRIVATE WORLD. In this painting of an *Officer and Laughing Girl,* Vermeer fixes for all time a moment of Dutch domestic life, every detail lovingly delineated; the map in the background shows the province of Holland.

successful career as a painter of group scenes in which his patrons, the Dutch patricians, delighted, became an introspective delineator of the human soul. The huge *Night Watch* carries the portrayal of a civic group beyond mere depiction and flattery of the subjects to complex technical mastery of composition and color and subtle differentiation of personalities. The *Lesson in Anatomy* achieves similar results on a more modest scale with a depiction of the dissection of a cadaver under the direction of Dr. Nicholas Tulp, who was both a leading medical investigator and a mayor of Amsterdam. The *Pilgrims of Emmaus* is typical of Rembrandt's extraordinarily sensitive and moving biblical studies. The techniques of Velásquez and Rembrandt were very different but in both artists technique led past the externals—whether the magnificent court costumes of Velásquez's figures or the sober ornamentation of the Dutch burghers and the tatters of some of Rembrandt's later biblical characters—to the depiction of human feeling at its most intimate and least definable.

These were the qualities that were largely missing from the work of the popular portraitists of the century, like Anthony Van Dyck (1599–1641) in England and Hyacinthe Rigaud (1659–1743) at the court of Louis XIV. Their paintings are smooth, neat, and accurate, but they depict a historical personality as he wished to be remembered, rather than as a proud, passionate, and confused human being who

ST. JOHN ON PATMOS. Although Poussin's subject is religious, his setting and his manner are wholly neoclassical; he captures the essence of classicism with an ease sought but never quite achieved in the Renaissance proper.

happened to be a king, great nobleman, or minister of state. Strangely, the quality of inner authenticity was captured by Dutch artists who painted places and things as well as people. The scenes of Jan Steen (1626–1679) and Vermeer (1632–1675) were usually urban, as befitted Holland, the land of towns, while Jacob van Ruysdael (1625?–1682) caught the distinctive qualities of rural Holland's gentle land and cloud-filled sky.

The characteristics of Classicism fitted not only a Van Dyck and a Rigaud, but also a Nicolas Poussin (1594–1665), who was primarily a painter of pastoral scenes. His work is explicitly in the Renaissance tradition, being filled with ruins of Graeco-Roman architecture as well as shepherds and shepherdesses. In Poussin technique is so exquisitely controlled that it becomes invisible; there is no turbulence, no exaggeration, as in the Baroque, but balance, calm, ease. The appeal of the work is to the eye and to the mind, for the anecdotal and the symbolic elements are explicit and essential, as they are incidental although present in Velásquez.

Sculpture. In sculpture the dominance of the Baroque was almost complete. There was a shift away from the tomb decorations and mythological personalities emphasized during the high Renaissance and a new emphasis upon the portrayal of living or recently living persons. Baroque spirit came most easily to sculpture, because its very form—the depiction of life in lifeless stone—was the kind of challenge to which Baroque artists responded most enthusiastically. The supreme achievements came in the work of the Italian sculptor-architect Giovanni Bernini (1588–1680). The swirling vigor of Rubens' paintings is duplicated in Bernini's compositions. His bust of Louis XIV captures in marble not only the quality of the royal visage but even the pompous exaggeration of the king's lofty wig. Bernini's *Saint Teresa* is in content all striving muscle, in spirit all the utmost ecstasy of Teresa's mystical union with God, and in technique a successful defiance of the limitations of stone.

Architecture. In architecture Bernini represented the culmination of the Baroque impulse. To complete the visual impact of the basilica of St. Peter's in Rome, he added to the great building itself an immense entrance through a double portico of columns. The Baroque feeling in architecture expressed itself most vigorously in church buildings, where the classic simplicity of high Renaissance works was replaced by the emphasis on movement and tension in structures whose facades were marked by a whirlwind of complex ornamentation, often imposed upon buildings essentially simple in character in order to give them greater dramatic impact. The interiors of Baroque churches frequently used wall and ceiling paintings to give illusions of openness not upon the actual world but upon scenes of religious subjects painted as if they were occurring just beyond the building, whose walls and ceiling therefore visually vanished. In Austria and Germany late in the century

THE BAROQUE TENSION OF OPPOSITES. Bernini, supreme sculptor and architect of the Baroque, is able to make marble writhe and pant in *The Ecstasy of St. Theresa (above);* while in his interior of St. Peter's in Rome *(left),* the solidity of the architectural structure of the basilica vanishes beneath the swirling curves of the intricate and dramatic ornamentation.

similar techniques were used in a quite different spirit, with gaiety and jesting flourishes, to brighten and lighten the palaces and mansions of the princes and the nobles.

In France, however, the Baroque style in architecture failed to take hold. Instead the Neoclassical forms proved to be closer to the French artistic tradition which stressed balance and restraint. These qualities were retained even in the huge edifices erected for Louis XIV. They are notable in the colonnade for the Louvre designed by Claude Perrault (1613–1688), where the long line of columns avoids the sense of monstrous weight by its controlled proportions and adds to the essentially Renaissance design the majestic tone desired by the Sun King. The buildings of Sir Christopher Wren (1632–1723) in England were a unique blending of Baroque elements and French control, producing a sense not of mastered turmoil but of exquisite balance and grandeur.

LITERATURE

Stylistic forces similar to those in the fine arts were at work in literature. It may be noted that in both cases Italy lost leadership to other nations, notably to Spain, France, and the Low Countries. But in literature another name must be added, that of England. With the age of Elizabeth which extended into the very early seventeenth century, England took a lead among the literary nations which in the future she would share but never lose.

Poetry. These developments may be seen with particular clarity in poetry. Baroque elements were strong in the first part of the century. In Spain the exaggerated idiom and imagery of Gongorism gave an appearance of force with little inner resources of intellectual or spiritual strength, but in England the metaphysical poet John Donne (1573–1631) wrote equally elaborate verse that carried thought and feeling of the greatest moment. Later in the century the English John Milton (1608–1674) and the Dutchman Joost van den Vondel (1587–1679) merged the complex virtuosity of the Baroque with deliberate and strong Neoclassical language and forms. Each wrote a great epic on the same theme, but Vondel's *Lucifer* has remained a treasure only in his small country while Milton's *Paradise Lost* is a masterpiece known to the vast English-speaking world.

In France the emphasis early in the century already came to be placed upon clarity of thought and expression. French poetry developed a cult of lucidity, expressed in the didactic and critical work of Nicolas Boileau-Despréaux (1636–1711), *The Art of Poetry* (1674). The vivacity and wit of Jean de La Fontaine (1621–1695) in his *Fables* and *Tales and Stories,* the easy fluency of the dramatic verse of Jean Baptiste Poquelin, known by his stage and pen name of Molière (1622–1673), and the psychological richness of the dramatic poetry of Jean Racine

(1639–1699) were qualities of those of Boileau's contemporaries who had learned their craft before he wrote. Those who learned directly from Boileau lacked force and bite beneath the sparkle of their verse. In England, however, the Neoclassicism advocated by Boileau, when practiced by a John Dryden (1631–1700), achieved heights of pithy vigor.

Drama. The development of drama indicated the divergent tempos at which humanist impulses came to be felt in various art forms. Italian playwrights remained close to the classical forms, although the Italian popular plays, the *commedia dell'arte,* in which stock characters (the *pagliacci* later made famous by the opera of that name) improvised their plots and dialogue, remained vigorous and strongly influenced French playwrights of the seventeenth century (Molière's farces are masterly adaptations of the *commedia*). Spanish drama possessed extraordinary vigor during the century, achieving both fluency and force in the works of Pedro Calderón de la Barca (1600–1681) and Lope de Vega (1562–1635). French drama was most powerfully driven by the desire of the dramatists to make it a truly literary form; among the great French dramatists, only Molière was a practicing actor and director, not a man of letters as such.

The rules evolved from the Roman playwrights of antiquity, particularly Terence, Plautus and Seneca, were enforced or accepted as voluntary self-discipline; these required that the action occur in a single place and within the space of twenty-four hours, that the character of the play be unified, not garishly disparate. These rules were in conflict with the freer tradition of the Elizabethan theater in England, which was continued by some English playwrights in the seventeenth century and deliberately rejected by others, notably Dryden, in favor of the regulations of the French school. The French pattern achieved its supreme greatness in the work of two masters of tragedy, Pierre Corneille (1606–1684) and Racine, and one comic genius, Molière. In such plays as Corneille's *The Cid,* Racine's *Phaedra* and *Athalia,* and Molière's *The Misanthrope* and *The Miser,* these authors accepted the rules for their work but used them to intensify and focus their dramatic purpose—which was to portray men at their heroic best, fully aware of the consequences of their feelings and their deeds, or at their comic worst, the victims of their own obsessions. They imitated nature, but a nature purified of mere accidents of time and space and crystallized into characters at once supremely passionate and thoughtful in tragedy, or quintessentially human in their self-inflicted defeats. They willingly accepted the discipline of the classic unities and the Alexandrine couplets in which they wrote, and their plays do not have the sense of constraint and artificiality that was to overcome classical drama in the next century.

The Novel. The novel was a form that developed later and less rapidly, although it began with a work of unsurpassed genius, the *Don Quixote* of Miguel de Cervantes Saavedra. The Spanish writer made his parody of the Amadis de Gaul, a chivalric novel very popular in the late Middle Ages and the Renaissance, into more than a parody; it became an insight into and a comment upon the human situation, the never-ending, never-resolved tension between man's dream of the ideal and the implacable reality of life. Spain also initiated the other major form of prose taletelling, the picaresque novels of delightful rascals and charlatans who survive by their wits. The picaresque novels of Spain and France depicted the hard life of the poor in harsh colors lightened only by the brief triumphs of impecunious villainy over the self-satisfaction of the prosperous and the powerful.

MUSIC

In music the spirit of the century was easier to apply to externals, the literary form of the new *opera* invented in Italy by Claudio Monteverdi (1567–1643), for example, than to the tonal essentials. Although the older polyphony was no longer predominant, it still remained powerful in church music. The Lutheran church had never abandoned the tradition of using music for religious services, but the hymns of Luther's time were now amplified by chorales and organ works. The Dutchman Jan Pieterszoon Sweelinck (1562–1621) and the German Heinrich Schütz (1585–1672) were preeminent in this area, establishing a form and a tradition to be used in the eighteenth century by Johann Sebastian Bach. Catholicism continued to develop the traditional forms of church music, and secular music lived vigorously at the courts. Jean Baptiste Lully (1633?–1681), court composer to Louis XIV, set a style that combined majesty and dignity with grace. Henry Purcell (1659–1695), who served English kings from Charles II to William III in his short life, wrote music that combined ornamentation rich enough to please the most Baroque spirit with delicacy, taste, and utter mastery of melody and rhythm.

Further Reading

Unrivalled as an analytic survey of the period is *G. N. Clark, *The Seventeenth Century,* 2nd ed. (New York, 1961); for a narrative of events it may be supplemented by D. Ogg, *Europe in the Seventeenth Century,* 8th rev. ed. (London, 1961). *The New Cambridge Modern History,* Volume V, *The Ascendancy of France, 1648–1688* (Cambridge, 1961), is by scholars of many nations. *T. Aston, ed., *Crisis in Europe, 1560–1660* (London, 1965) presents the century as an age of transitional crisis. *C. J. Friedrich, *The Age of the Baroque, 1610–1660* (New York, 1952) and *F. L. Nussbaum, *The Triumph of Science and Reason, 1660–1685* (New York, 1953) boldly apply the concept of Baroque style to all history in their periods; *J. B. Wolf, *The Emergence of the Great Powers, 1685–1715* (New York, 1951) is a better informed and more effective interpretation. P. Laslett, *The World We Have Lost* (New York, 1965) is an innovating attempt to reconstruct the fabric of society. Mercantilism is thoughtfully analyzed in C. W. Cole, *Colbert and a Century of French Mercantilism,* 2 vols. (Hamden, Conn., 1939); *V. Barbour, *Capitalism in Amsterdam in the Seventeenth Century* (Baltimore, 1950) is briefer and highly factual; while C. R. Boxer, *The Dutch Seaborne Empire, 1600–1800* (New York, 1965) and C. Wilson, *Profits and Power* (New York, 1957) are both well informed and perceptive.

*C. V. Wedgwood, *The Thirty Years War* (London, 1938), although more vividly written, is less satisfactory as an overview of the great conflict than *S. H. Steinberg, *The Thirty Years War* (London, 1966). F. Watson, *Wallenstein, Soldier under Saturn* (New York, 1938) emphasizes the personality of the imperial general; while M. Roberts, *Gustavus Adolphus, 1611–1632,* 2 vols. (New York, 1953–1958) is both biography and history of a high order. *J. R. Jones, *Britain and Europe in the Seventeenth Century* (London, 1966) is useful; while H. H. Rowen, *The Ambassador Prepares for War: The Dutch Embassy of Arnauld de Pomponne, 1669–1671* (The Hague, 1957) is informative on both French diplomacy and Dutch domestic policies.

R. B. Merriman, *Six Contemporaneous Revolutions* (Oxford, 1938) compares the major mid-century uprisings. *G. Treasure, *Seventeenth Century France* (New York, 1966) is an up-to-date survey. *C. V. Wedgwood, *Richelieu and the French Monarchy* (New York, 1949) is brief and essentially traditional; *C. J. Burckhardt, *Richelieu: His Rise to Power* (New York, 1940) is the first part of a three-volume biography. *A. Huxley, the distinguished novelist, presents in *The Devils of Loudun* (New York, 1952) a suggestive study of the relation of religion and politics. P. Doolin, *The Fronde* (London, 1935) is concerned primarily with political theory rather than with events or personalities. *The Age of Louis XIV* by Voltaire, available in many editions, remains a literary masterpiece and useful history two centuries after it was written. J. B. Wolf, *Louis XIV* (New York, 1968) is a brilliant analytical biography. *W. H. Lewis, *The Splendid Century: Life in the France of Louis XIV* (Garden City, 1957) combines sparkle and scholarship. For England, the best surveys are *M. Ashley, *England in the Seventeenth Century,* 3rd ed. (Baltimore, 1961); and *C. Hill, *The Century of Revolution, 1603–1714* (Edinburgh, 1961). G. Davies, *The Early Stuarts, 1603–1660* (Oxford, 1937) and G. N. Clark, *The Later Stuarts, 1660–1714,* 2nd ed. (Oxford, 1955) are more detailed. *L. Stone, *The Crisis of the Aristocracy, 1558–1641* (New York, 1965) and *C. Hill, *Puritanism and Revolution* (London, 1958) are bold yet scholarly interpretations. *J. H. Hexter, *Reappraisals in History* (Evanston, 1961) presents a penetrating critique of simple explanations. See also *D. H. Willson, *King James VI and I* (London, 1956); C. V. Wedgwood, *The Great Rebellion,* 2 vols. (London, 1955–1958); *W. Haller, *Liberty and Reformation in the Puritan Revolution* (New York, 1955); and *M. Ashley, *The Greatness of Oliver Cromwell* (New York, 1957). For the later period valuable studies are A. Bryant, *King Charles II* (London, 1946); F. C. Turner, *James II* (London, 1948); S. B. Baxter, *William III and the Defence of European Liberty, 1650–1702* (New York, 1966); M. Ashley, *The Glorious Revolution of 1688* (London, 1966); and G. M. Trevelyan, *England under Queen Anne,* 3 vols. (New York, 1930–1934). K. Feiling, *The History of the Tory Party, 1640–1714* (Oxford, 1924) and *British Foreign Policy, 1660–1672* (London, 1930) are highly idiosyncratic but indispensable.

On the Dutch Republic P. Geyl's *The Netherlands in the Seventeenth Century,* 2 vols., rev. ed. (New York, 1961–1964) is a fundamental reevaluation by a great historian. For Germany see H. Holborn, *A History of Modern Germany,* Volume II, *1648–1840* (New York, 1963); and F. L. Carsten, *The Origins of Prussia* (Oxford, 1954). *S. B. Fay and K. Epstein, *The Rise of Brandenburg-Prussia to 1786* (New York, 1964) is a useful brief survey. F. Schevill, *The Great Elector* (Chicago, 1947) is sound.

For intellectual history see *P. Hazard, *The European Mind, 1680–1715* (London, 1953); and *B. Willey, *The Seventeenth Century Background* (London, 1934). J. E. King, *Science and Rationalism in the Government of Louis XIV, 1661–1783* (Baltimore, 1949) is an attempt to relate philosophy and the work of state. *J. N. Figgis, *The Divine Right of Kings,* 2nd ed. (Cambridge, 1922) and M. W. Cranston, *John Locke* (New York, 1957) are indispensable. *H. Haydn, *The Counter-Renaissance* (Gloucester, Mass., 1950) and N. Powell, *From Baroque to Rococo* (London, 1959) discuss literature and art respectively. On Descartes see A. Balz, *Descartes and the Modern Mind* (Hamden, Conn., 1952). M. Bishop, *Pascal: The Life of Genius* (New York, 1936) is an illuminating study of a complex figure.

CHAPTER 12

The Scientific Revolution

One of the most fundamental transformations in the history of the human race is the development of modern science as an effective means of understanding and controlling nature. The Scientific Revolution profoundly shook the character and structure of man's thought, making some ideas out of date and giving others unprecedented force. Yet the scientific method is not an ordinary or *natural* way of looking at nature; it requires the ability and readiness to turn from the rules of common experience and common sense and to accept instead the results of mathematical description and analysis of the events of nature. That even a relatively small number of men in the sixteenth, seventeenth, and eighteenth centuries were able to accept such a discipline of thought and method was itself the result of the developments of preceding centuries. Like all revolutions, the Scientific Revolution was the creation of the very institutions it overthrew.

1. The Science of Scholasticism

DURING THE MIDDLE AGES science, in the specific sense of the endeavor to know and understand nature, was not so much absent as different in character from the kind of knowledge that emerged from the Scientific Revolution. Medieval science was an adaptation of Greek science as set down by Aristotle, transmitted by Arab scholars, and fitted into the theologically oriented world view of medieval thought. Aristotle presented a teleological view of natural processes and events— his world view was based on the belief that everything that happens does so with a purpose. He built his science upon the basis of the systematic distillation of common experience and common sense. In it the events of the natural world were explained by analogy to the experiences of man. His science was largely descriptive and contemplative rather than experimental. It was designed not to give man greater power over the world of natural happenings but to lend to the outer world the same kind of meaning that man found within himself.

These characteristics of Aristotelian science were taken over in medieval science and linked more closely to contemporary theological philosophy, particularly after St. Thomas Aquinas had succeeded in combining Aristotelian philosophy and Christian theology in the system of scholasticism. The primary concerns of Scholasticism, of course, had been theology at the highest level and ethics at the specifically human. But a number of schoolmen undertook an examination and exploration of scientific problems in addition to their primary interest in theology. Much of their work was hardly to be distinguished from magic, but magic was not then the antithesis of science, as it is today, for it represented a deliberate effort to control the processes of the world. It was, at least in intention, a kind of technology of invisible events. Indeed, the fields of astrology and astronomy were scarcely distinguished, and most astronomers were practicing astrologers; furthermore, the very assumption of the astrologers that events in the sky act as causes in human affairs was a kind of anticipatory science in its assumptions, if not in its proofs.

A small number of scholastics went much further, attempting more precise analysis of natural processes although with limited use of mathematical description and analysis. Nonetheless, in general, since even they continued to accept as true and beyond question the science of Aristotle, their innovations consisted in assigning to his terms meanings quite different from those he intended. But the medieval scientists almost never resorted to the study of nature directly, except as it was met in ordinary experience; the *experiment,* a deliberately constructed query put to nature, had not yet been invented. Nevertheless the implications of Aristotelian science were carried very far, and some of the key problems were posed, or at least indicated, particularly in physics.

Fundamentally medieval science emphasized two principal points. First was the view that the world and its creatures other than man were, as the Book of Genesis said, made by God for the use of man, indeed that the entire universe was created for the use of man in some way, however indirectly. Second was the principle that everything in the world had meaning, in the sense of purpose, whether that of direct utility or as symbol: the universe was a fixed, definite, closed world where emptiness was impossible, emptiness physically and emptiness of meaning.

Medieval science, like medieval thought in general, took the Bible and Aristotle as its two fundamental authorities. Against them no appeal to nature or experience was possible or even suggested. Yet a very large number of questions remained open for debate, for the meaning of the Bible and the Philosopher was often far from clear. They constituted a truth beyond doubt, but one which required and permitted a variety of explanations. Indeed, medieval science was practiced in a world where disputation, or scholarly debate, lay at the heart of intellectual activity, and thus differences of interpretation were inevitably encouraged.

2. A New System of the World

THE SCIENTIFIC REVOLUTION began on one sector, not all along the front. Indeed, since one of the most fundamental aspects of the revolution was the effective application of mathematical models to the facts of the world, it was just in those areas of knowledge where this was most possible—kinematics, or the study of the motion of objects, and astronomy, the study of the skies—that the revolution first took place, and the first advances consisted precisely in the successful combination of kinematics and astronomy.

THE PROBLEM OF THE PLANETS

The first phase of the Scientific Revolution was the work of an astronomer who intended no revolution but sought only to improve the mathematical description of the movements of the sun, moon, and both kinds of stars, the fixed stars and the planets. But Nicholas Copernicus (1473–1543) of Poland was a revolutionary despite himself, for the consequences of his decision to shift the center of the universe from the earth to the sun, although it required more than a century for these consequences to be worked out by a series of scientists of genius, brought about a fundamental transformation of the accepted way of understanding both the universe and, ultimately, man's place in it.

The problem which Copernicus faced consisted essentially in explaining the movement of the planets across the sky. These "wandering stars," as the Greeks called them, do not remain in a fixed relationship to the other stars which rotate all together across the bowl of the heavens; instead they weave a complex path among the other stars, swinging from side to side as they proceed within a rela-

Non docet instabiles Copernicus ætheris orbes,
Sed terræ instabiles arguit ille vices.

NICHOLAS COPERNICUS. Described in this sixteenth-century print as teaching that the earth moves, not the "aetherial orbs," the Polish astronomer is here shown with a model of the earth orbiting the sun.

tively narrow band but occasionally even reversing the direction of their movement.

An explanation of the planetary motions had been given in the second century A.D. by the Greek philosopher-geographer Ptolemy, who had in turn incorporated ideas from predecessors, including Aristotle. Ptolemy placed all the fixed stars on a single great sphere or orb at a very great distance from the earth; this sphere, usually described as composed of some extremely light crystalline substance, revolved around the earth. Within this outermost sphere were other concentric spheres on which were located the sun, the moon, and the planets. To explain the erratic movements of the planets, Ptolemy located them not directly on their proper sphere but on a rotating circle which had its own center on another sphere, as the moon is located with respect to the sun in the heliocentric system. The system of epicycles, as such circles upon circles are called, enabled astronomers to describe the observed movements of the planets with fair accuracy, but the attempt to remove imperfections led to the creation of a vastly complex system of epicycles upon epicycles, and even worse of rotations having their centers at some distance from the centers of their proper spheres. Furthermore, there were motions of the planets which could not be even approximately explained by this system.

THE HELIOCENTRIC SYSTEM

Dissatisfied with this cumbersome system, Copernicus hunted through the writings of ancient astronomers for alternative explanations of the planetary motions. He decided to attempt to describe mathematically the implications of the heliocentric system suggested by Aristarchus of Samos (3rd century B.C.). His hypothesis had been rejected by all serious practising astronomers in antiquity and the Middle Ages because it involved the rotation of the earth and had no mathematical superiority over the geocentric system to which Ptolemy gave his name. However, by dint of enormous labors in calculation, Copernicus showed that it was possible to reduce the number of epicycles required for describing the planetary motions by more than half if the sun and not the earth were made the center of the universe. He did not propose that the concept of the sphere of the fixed stars be abandoned, and he held to the notion of circular orbits as firmly as any Ptolemaic astronomer. His system did not actually describe the planetary motions with significantly greater accuracy than the Ptolemaic, nor did it explain certain aberrations any more effectively, and practising astronomers were slow to adopt it.

Indeed, some of the adherents of the Copernican system considered it to be no more than an alternate mathematical device, and it was so explained by Andreas Osiander (1498–1552), who published Copernicus' master work, *On the Revolutions of the Celestial Orbs*, in 1543. But Copernicus himself fully believed that he was describing the world as it really was—in other words, that his system was not only mathematically consonant with the facts but also physically true.

KEPLER: THE TRIUMPH OF ELLIPSES

Although some practising astronomers adopted the Copernican system, it won little acceptance among the general public or even among learned men and was rejected by the greatest astronomical observer of the sixteenth century, the Dane Tyco Brahe (1546–1601). At an observatory built to his specifications at Uraniborg, Brahe brought naked-eye observations to never-repeated accuracy with instruments of his own devising and accumulated a vast amount of data on the movement of the heavenly bodies, the first fundamentally new data since antiquity. But he preferred to modify the Ptolemaic system rather than adopt the Copernican, in which he saw no practical advantage. Yet it was Brahe's data which enabled his disciple and successor, Johannes Kepler (1571–1630), to make the heliocentric system far more effective than the geocentric.

Kepler was deeply committed to the Copernican hypothesis, both for its astronomical advantages and because, a passionate Neoplatonist, he believed in the necessary mathematical harmonies of the universe as part of the mystical meaning of the world. He sought hard and long for some arrangement of the Copernican epicycles which would fit the data adequately, but with no success. He then turned to a quest for other mathematical figures to account for the planetary motions. When at last he tried the ellipse, placing the sun at one of its two foci, he discovered that the planetary paths were described simply and with greatly increased accuracy. The Copernican revolution was complete. The working out of its further implications required the integration of the new system of the skies with an adequate system of terrestrial mechanics.

GALILEO: THE MOTION OF TERRESTRIAL BODIES

In the multinational enterprise that the Scientific Revolution proved to be, the next phase of leadership fell to an Italian, Galileo Galilei (1564–1642). A professor of mathematics at the Venetian university of Padua, he returned to his native Florence under the patronage of the Medici grand duke. He was concerned not only with astronomy but also with terrestrial mechanics. He devised an effective telescope after he had heard no more than a report that such an instrument had been invented in the Netherlands. When he used it to examine the moon and the planets, he discovered that under magnification they did not correspond to the appearance required by the traditional doctrine that celestial bodies were pure,

GALILEO GALILEI. Scientist and visionary, what is he looking at with these thoughtful eyes? Galileo is portrayed here in the years of his greatest achievement by Joost Susterman, a Flemish painter active in Italy.

in contrast to the irregularity of the earth. The moon possessed craggy mountains and depressions, while Jupiter displayed a group of never-before-seen moons.

Galileo reported his discoveries in a little book, *The Message of the Stars*. Breaking with the tradition of writing on scientific matters in Latin, Galileo composed this work in a fluent, vivacious Italian; he was appealing directly to a broad audience of thoughtful laymen no less than to professional astronomers and mathematicians, and he was aware of the philosophical implications of his discoveries. He realized that he was contradicting the traditional medieval view that the earth and the celestial bodies had essentially different characteristics, terrestrial bodies being subject to change—which was equated with decline—while celestial bodies were unchanging and hence nearer to perfection. But in his astronomical observations, Galileo did not function as a mathematical astronomer who plotted the motions of the skies.

It was as a student of mechanics—the movement of bodies on *earth*—that Galileo applied not only his powers of insight but also his mathematical skills. Here his problem was to explain the movement of falling and thrown bodies. The Aristotelian conception distinguished between *natural* motions, like the fall of a body toward the earth, and *violent* motions, like that of a thrown ball. While falling bodies were thought to be in natural motion because they were returning to their *proper* place, circular motion was also considered to be natural because the circle was conceived to be a perfect geometric figure. Movements of other kinds, however, such as straight-line movement other than directly towards the earth or non-circular motions, were described as violent because they resulted from the application of force, on the analogy of the human need to apply effort to move objects.

Galileo, modifying the idea of *impetus* developed in late medieval times, sought to solve the difficulty of explaining the motion of projectiles which continue to move after losing contact with the propellant; impetus theory explained that the force was transferred to the object, not to the medium through which it moved. Galileo developed the notions that rectilinear motion was as natural as circular; that the application of force to an object resulted in increased velocity; and that continued application of force resulted in acceleration, or constantly increasing velocity.

It was in connection with these concepts that Galileo developed further the principle of deliberate experimentation as a means of obtaining fundamental data from nature and checking the theories developed to explain such data. But Galileo believed as strongly in what he called *thought experiments* (in which the relationships were handled abstractly and by imagination) as he did in empirical experiments. He was therefore important not only for his particular discoveries and theories but also for his emphasis on science as a study based on neither pure theory nor pure empirical observation but a combination of the two in which each contributes to the development of the other.

GALILEO AND THE INQUISITION

Galileo, because he elaborated the cosmological implications of the new astronomical ideas with great clarity even when these conflicted with the traditional cosmology which had come to be accepted in official Catholic teaching, finally met sharp resistance by the church. He was ordered by the Inquisition not to teach the new Copernican system, and, when he continued to do so, neither his quite orthodox Catholic beliefs in essentially religious matters nor his close friendship with leading figures in the church was able to save him from being condemned. The church was not yet able to reconcile the new cosmology, with its ultimate implications of an infinite universe and a multiplicity of worlds like our own, on the one hand, with the traditional earth- and man-centered doctrines of traditional belief, on the other. Galileo's condemnation did not by any means halt scientific work in the Catholic countries, but it made the results of such work increasingly redound to the disadvantage of the Roman faith.

Protestantism, although it had been much more hostile than Catholicism to the new emerging science during the sixteenth century—Luther had been absolutely opposed to the Copernican innovations, while Copernicus himself was a respected Catholic clergyman—during the seventeenth century adopted a stance of neutrality or sometimes even of favor to the new scientific developments.

NEWTON: THE UNITY OF EARTH AND SKY

What Galileo was still unable to do, to bring terrestrial mechanics and planetary astronomy into a single unified system, was the achievement of the Englishman Sir Isaac Newton (1642–1727). He brought to his work as a scientist mathematical abilities of the highest order: in a century of mathematical genius, he ranked at the very top, along with such giants as Descartes, Pascal, and Leibniz. But he was also a prodigious master of physics, with extraordinary powers of concentration and imagination. He appears to have done the fundamental thinking which resulted in his solution of the Galilean problem during a short period in the 1660's while he was still in his twenties. But it was two decades before he could be persuaded to set his ideas down in a major work, *The Mathematical Principles of Natural Philosophy*. Completed in 1686 and published the next year, it is unquestionably the greatest single piece of scientific writing of all time, one of the supreme accomplishments of the human mind.

What Newton did was to set forth a series of physical laws concerning the movement of bodies derived from Galileo's work, and then to show that these fitted the planetary orbits, including their shape and their distance from the sun, as they had been described by Kepler. The Newtonian laws completely reversed the concept of motion which had been held since Aristotle by the great majority

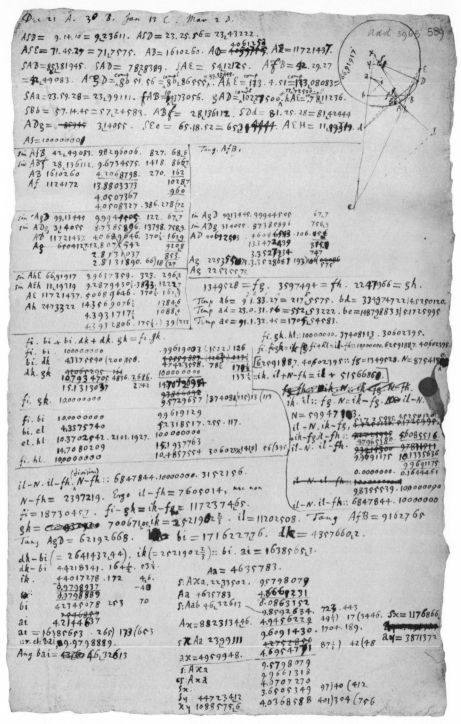

NEWTON'S CALCULATIONS CONCERNING THE ORBIT OF HALLEY'S COMET. This manuscript page in Newton's own hand is one of the immense number of pages of precise mathematical calculations which went into the preparation of his *Principia*.

of scientific thinkers. Newton linked the fall of bodies towards earth to their weight by means of the law of gravitational attraction, according to which bodies mutually attract each other in direct proportion to their relative masses and inversely in proportion to the square of the distance between them. He avoided explaining gravitational attraction by analogy with subjective human experience. Rejecting such "feigned hypotheses," he merely took observed data as it was and demonstrated in precise mathematical terms how bodies moved in response to gravity, not why they did so. Modifying Galileo in an essential point, Newton made motion of bodies in a straight line the only natural movement. The movement of a body in this way, in unchanging direction and at unchanged velocity, required no external thrust but only its own *momentum,* a term which replaced the *impetus* of medieval scientists. The force exerted by bodies in movement he described as a product of their mass (measured by their weight) and their momentum, and the forces thus exerted performed work against resistance forces of equal magnitude but opposite direction.

Newton thus abandoned the notions that *natural* motion is circular and that there is an *inherent* endeavor on the part of every body to return to its *proper* place. In so doing, he discarded the entire Aristotelian practice of explaining mechanics on the pattern of the conscious, deliberate behavior of living beings. Instead Newton explained physical actions and states by describing them mathematically and linking the descriptions logically in ways that permitted prediction and deliberate experimentation. *Natural laws* were distinguished from *laws of nature,* and thus there emerged the modern conception of scientific law. A *natural* or *scientific law* is a pattern of behavior in things which is followed uniformly. An *exception* is not possible; if there is an exception, it means that the law has not been correctly stated. A *law of nature,* on the other hand, is a moral prescription for right behavior which can be violated, with the violator subject to punishment.

In addition to showing the similarity of terrestrial and celestial motion, Newton made outstanding contributions in the other branches of physical investigation of his time, notably in the analysis of light. But his essential achievement lay in his solution of the problems of mechanics in a way that was not fundamentally revised, but only refined, until the emergence of relativity theory in the twentieth century.

LIGHT

During the Scientific Revolution the pattern of the new science—the mathematically organized study of nature—was fully achieved in mechanics and optics. Scientists studying light had long been able to describe with considerable accuracy some of the laws of optics, that is, the paths of light on reflection from mirrors and in refraction through lenses. The seventeenth-century accomplishment consisted primarily in Newton's use of the prism to demonstrate the structure of light. He showed that, contrary to the accepted notion, white light was not pure but a combination of all the visible colors. White light passing through a prism was separated into a spectrum which corresponded to the phenomenon of the rainbow, produced by the passage of sunlight through raindrops. It was not possible, however, to determine unequivocally the nature of light, which displayed characteristics of both waves and particles. Newton ultimately favored the corpuscular theory, while the great Dutch scientist Christian Huyghens (1629–1695) favored the wave theory. In any case, no connection could be shown between the theory of light and that of gravitation and mechanics, the central achievement of the Scientific Revolution.

MAGNETISM AND ELECTRICITY

The study of magnetism and electricity began in the sixteenth century. The phenomenon of the lodestone—a naturally magnetic rock—had been known since antiquity and had been used in the compass as a navigational aid. During the late sixteenth century the English scientist William Gilbert (1540–1603) demonstrated that the earth itself was a great magnet whose poles corresponded only approximately to the geographic poles (the ends of the earth's axis of spin). Gilbert suggested that the phenomenon of gravitation was magnetic in character, but in his own elaborate study of magnetism he was unable to evolve mathematical laws to describe its activity, an achievement that was to be delayed until the early nineteenth century.

During the seventeenth century, attention shifted from magnetism to the study of electrical phenomena, known only in the form of electrostatic charges caused by friction between such materials as amber and hair. Relatively large devices were invented to produce such charges and their accompanying sparks and shocks, but it was not until the invention of the Leiden jar (a metal-lined glass bottle) in the eighteenth century that a means of storing an electrical charge became available. This was followed by the discovery that the charges could be carried by wet thread and metal wire, which initiated the study of electrical currents. The phenomenon of electrical polarity—that some electrically charged bodies attract and others repel each other, and that these are associated with distinctive forms of electrical current—created a problem for the explanation, even the description, of this physical process.

Electricity had a special significance in the history of science because, unlike all previous discoveries in science, its primary data were not provided by ordinary experience through the primary sense organs but by deliberate manipulative experimentation. The electrical character of lightning was discovered by Benjamin Franklin (1706–1790), the American writer-statesman, in this way. Electricity was conceived of in various ways but Franklin most effectively described it by analogy with a flowing fluid. The work of experimenters in the laboratory of the Italian physicist, Count Alessandro Volta (1754–1827), showed that electricity acted upon the nervous system of frogs, and it was felt by some scientific thinkers that many life processes, notably the nervous system, were essentially electrical in character. But the connection between electricity and magnetism, the essential basis for fundamental progress in understanding and using both processes of nature, was not yet established.

VACUUMS AND GASES

Many other physical phenomena were explored and explained, at least in part, during the period of the Scientific Revolution. The Aristotelian assertion of the impossibility of vacuum was disproved when the German Otto von Guericke (1602–1686) and the Englishman Robert Boyle (1627–1691) invented effective air pumps. Further proof of the reality of empty space—space without matter—came with the development of the barometer. It not only registered the variation in atmospheric pressure at various times and altitudes but also produced a vacuum in the pocket above the column of mercury or other fluid. Boyle, although notable principally as a chemist, also developed a mathematical formula for the interrelationships of pressure, temperature, and volume in gases (known as *Boyle's Law*), which was the first important mathematically defined law of physics beyond the Newtonian mass-force laws and the laws of optics.

3. The Emergence of Chemistry

THE OTHER PHYSICAL SCIENCES were much slower than physics to make fundamental progress beyond the state which they had reached in the late Middle Ages. Chemistry, which concerns itself with the composition, interaction, and transformation of materials rather than with their motions, was still largely the purveying of pharmaceuticals to the medical profession and was taught mainly in medical schools until well into the eighteenth century. Thus most chemists were either medical practitioners or druggists.

OUT OF ALCHEMY

The emergence of chemistry as a rigorous and precise science was hampered by its long association with alchemy, the would-be art of inducing transformations, usually of *base* to *precious* metals, by means of processes partly magical and partly technical. But the early chemistry, like alchemy, was based upon the methods and principles of Aristotelian science. It sought to explain the characteristics and behavior of materials upon the basis of their sensory characteristics, such as color, moistness, smell, and touch. Within such a framework of ideas, the notion of transforming lead into gold was not a silly dream, for it meant changing only the sensory characteristics of the metal, not its underlying reality or substance. Some apparent transformations were achieved, notably in the industrial arts, and these were taken as signs of possible success; but even during the Middle Ages and the Renaissance less credulous obervers noted the absence of practical achievements by the alchemists as distinct from the work of assayers and others who worked with real rather than magical means.

A clear distinction between magic and science was only beginning to take shape, however, since both sought to give man control over nature. The manipulative successes of science were still meager, and their rationale at best hardly more accurate than that of the alchemists. The alchemists relied, too, upon the ingrained animism of the Aristotelian scientific view which imparted a kind of soul to all things, and it did not seem illogical to attempt to direct such *spirits* by verbal for-

THE ALCHEMIST'S SHOP. This etching, after a drawing by Pieter Brueghel the Elder, shows the interior of a medieval alchemist's shop, with the alchemist carrying out his experiments and the scholar engaged in his secret studies.

mulae when incantations against witches and demons were accepted practice and magical conceptions were widespread in virtually every branch of human activity. As we have seen with astrology, mathematics itself, the most abstract kind of human thought, was linked with hidden meanings and purposes by the Neoplatonic doctrines which had great influence upon religious and philosophical thinkers of the late Middle Ages and the Renaissance.

Such mystical considerations played little or no role in the work of successful miners, assayers, and forgemasters, even though they continued to believe that there was a kind of life in the very stones (as shown in the phrase *living rock* for unseparated bedrock), and that exhausted veins of ore were replenished by a process of growth over a fairly short time. But the development of printing encouraged the production of a whole series of manuals descriptive of the crafts of the men who transformed ores into metals. The best of these books was the *De Re Metallica* (*Of Things Metallic,* 1556) of George Agricola (1494–1555). These works were concerned with the accurate and realistic description of what was actually done by craftsmen but made no effort to explain the deeper reasons for the effectiveness of their operations. Lacking any adequate rational framework of theory, these books cannot be considered works of even a primitive science; but their hard-headed practicality spurred the empirical concern with the real world which was to be one of the two key elements in modern science.

ROBERT BOYLE

The first steps towards a true chemical science came in the seventeenth century when adherents of the ancient atomic theory of matter and of the new mechanical view of the universe undertook deliberate experimentation in order to test old scientific theories and create new ones. Groping in the dark, the new chemists had to base their findings on principles which led astray far more than they guided. The specific and limited relationships established by empiric practitioners remained more effective than those sought by theorists who began with common sense and the common senses but proved unable to get beyond these points of departure. Nonetheless certain key problems emerged from the plethora of vague verbalism. These problems centered on the linked phenomena of combustion (the combination of carbon and oxygen) and calcination (the combination of metals and oxygen). But this work in turn rested upon the studies of Robert Boyle, who sought to set chemistry firmly upon a physical basis.

Boyle was an ardent believer in the mechanical and corpuscular world system (see below, pp. 500–502). But to describe the world of chemical relations as the result of physical processes was in the later seventeenth century an act of poetry, not science; for there was as yet no chemical theory to explain chemical processes, nor for that matter a physical theory adequate to explain chemical theory. Yet it was Boyle more than any contemporary who set the stage for the development of chemical investigation and thought over the next century and more. This he did by directing attention to the importance of careful and strict quantitative analysis of chemical processes, in contrast to the characteristic qualitative methods of the traditional chemistry. Boyle also emphasized the importance of studying the gaseous state of matter, which was to provide a way of investigating the problems of combustion and calcination.

THEORIES OF COMBUSTION

In the period after Boyle, increased concentration upon the problems of combustion and calcination led to the formulation of a new theory to explain these processes. This was the doctrine that a gas called *phlogiston*, invisible and having negative weight, was released during burning or calcination, leaving behind ash or calx (the metallic oxide). This theory corresponded to what could be seen in a burning flame and it was assumed that the same process was at work in calcination. Not until chemists had worked out accurate methods for collecting and weighing the products of combustion and calcination, as well as for distinguishing the various components of the air, was it possible to see that the phlogiston theory was a reversal of the true process. Despite what the eye saw, combustion was shown to consist in the combination of an invisible gas, oxygen, with the carbon or metal. Oxygen had been discovered almost simultaneously by the Swede Karl Scheele (1742–1786) and the Englishman Joseph Priestley (1733–1804) in 1777.

The oxygen theory of combustion was set forth by the French financier-scientist Antoine Lavoisier (1743–1794) in 1783. It opened the way for a clearer definition of chemical elements, as suggested by Lavoisier, but atomic theory was only given adequate statement by John Dalton (1766–1844) in the early nineteenth century. It is noteworthy that Lavoisier's theory of combustion, like Newton's theory of gravitational mechanics of a century earlier, displayed a central characteristic of modern science. Not only did it link theory and practice, empirical experiment and logical (preferably mathematical) system, but it distinguished logic from ordinary common sense and accepted as real the results given by deliberate experimentation guided by theory rather than the immediate data of the senses. The role of theory, indeed, is illustrated by the historic usefulness of the phlogiston theory, which summed up the older notions in a more precise way, so that it was able to guide further research. Ultimately, when it could not produce answers to the questions it posed, it was replaced by the Lavoisier theory which formed part of a pattern of explanation that was larger and more inclusive, more complex and more fundamental.

4. Biology

THE SCIENTIFIC STUDY OF LIFE began at the same time as that of the physical world but made much slower progress. Crucial for the development of biology was the fact that it was dominated on the one hand by the practice of medicine and on the other by the demands of theology and philosophy.

GALENIC MEDICINE

Medical theory and practice rested upon doctrines derived mainly from Greek antiquity and brought to a new standard of philological authenticity by the Renaissance publication of accurate editions of Hippocrates (3rd century B.C.) and Galen (2nd century A.D.), the supreme Greek medical teachers. Galen in particular was taken as the basis for medical instruction in the universities. Even dissection, which was the key to the teaching of anatomy, was conducted not as a source of independent knowledge but as an illustration of Galen's text. If an organ as exposed on the dissecting table did not correspond to Galen, then a better-fitting example from animal anatomy was used; or the lecturer would simply repeat what Galen said despite what the dissecting operator revealed (medical professors did not usually perform these menial tasks themselves). The Galenic theory that the organism was governed by four *humors,* the sanguine, melancholic, choleric, and phlegmatic, remained the basis of most physiological thought.

Medical practice combined the use of a few pain-relieving drugs, such as laudanum, an opiate, and a few specifics, especially the quinine imported from Peru and used for malaria, with practices like blood-letting and violent purgations, which only weakened patients and lessened their chances of recovery. Many prescriptions were concoctions of fantastic or repulsive ingredients which presumably did no harm except to the esthetic sense and at best let the patient recover naturally. Yet surgery was already practiced, including the setting of broken bones, amputations, and relatively simple incisions as for gallstones; but no anesthetic was available to ease the pain of operations. Skeptical observers, like the great French playwright Molière in his farce, *The Doctor despite Himself,* saw that much medical doctrine was mumbo-jumbo, but they had no alternative to offer except Stoic courage or Christian resignation.

VESALIUS: SYSTEMATIC ANATOMY

Although only the beginnings of scientific biology were made during the period of the Scientific Revolution, these were of great importance in and for themselves as well as for their philosophical implications. The first true progress to-

VESALIUS. The muscles of the human body are precisely depicted against the background of a town scene in this characteristic woodcut from Vesalius' *Structure of the Human Body.*

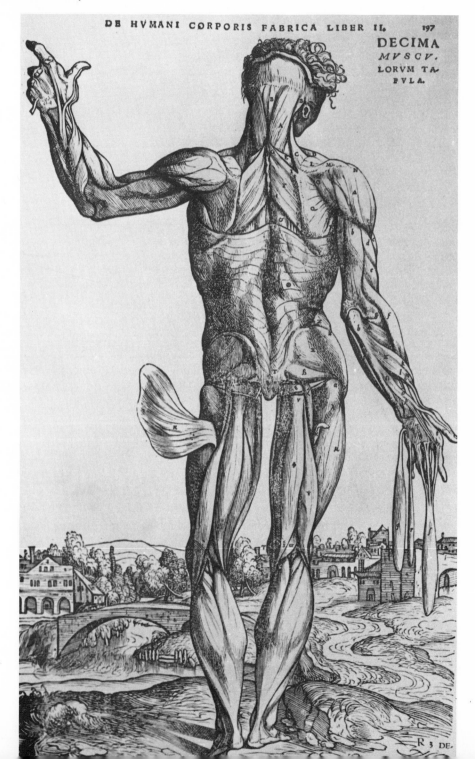

wards a biological science was made by the sixteenth-century teachers of anatomy, notably the Flemish-born and Italian-trained Andreas Vesalius (1514–1564), who capped his career by becoming physician to Emperor Charles V. As a brilliant young teacher of anatomy at Padua University, Vesalius systematically taught the anatomy of skeleton, muscles, and other organs from direct observation. Although a Renaissance humanist in his broad approach, he did not fear to dispute Galen, the classical authority, when observation did not confirm the Greek's teachings. Vesalius's findings were set down in a systematically organized work, *The Structure of the Human Body* (1543), in which the text was illustrated by a series of magnificent and informative woodcuts. Vesalius did not have a new or adequate physiology to explain the functions and operations of most of the organs he described, except for the obvious role of the skeleton. Yet his work clearly introduced that sense of the primacy of empirical observation over doctrinaire traditionalism which lay at the heart of the new scientific spirit.

DESCARTES: THE MACHINERY OF LIFE

Where Aristotelian scholasticism had emphasized the spiritual and rational elements which distinguished man from the animals, the advances of scientific biology tended to stress their basic identity. The most influential statement of this position was made by the early seventeenth-century philosopher Descartes. He taught that every living creature was a kind of machine whose functions were built into its structure and whose operations were the result of its natural movement, without the intervention of consciousness or a soul. The only exception to this universal materialism was man, whose rational soul, a purely spiritual entity, was able to react to material events and to direct the body, despite Descartes' radical distinction between spirit and matter as two utterly different substances. Although Descartes' attempts at biological explanation were not better than those he ventured in physics because of his penchant for accepting plausible hypotheses as "clear and self-evident" truth, he had laid down the philosophical principle for fruitful development of biological knowledge—to explain life processes as far as possible in physical and chemical terms, rather than in those of a spiritual vitalism which, however much it might maintain ultimate philosophical or religious truths, hampered scientific investigation in biology.

The spirit of Descartes' biology was indicated dramatically a century afterward by the attempt of a French doctor resident at the court of King Frederick the Great of Prussia to describe man in purely mechanical terms. However, *Man a Machine* (1748), by Julien de La Mettrie (1709–1751), was far more a rigorous statement of philosophical materialism than an effective analysis of the actual operation of the human organism.

HARVEY: THE HEART AS PUMP

More significant was the work of contemporaries of Descartes who studied specific organic structures in physical terms. The Italian anatomist Giovanni Borelli (1608–1679) viewed the structure of bones and muscles in strictly mechanical terms, as a system of levers, pulleys, and motors. He calculated relative forces and explained the role and size of a particular muscle by the work it was called upon to perform. More subtle by far was the explanation of the structure and operations of heart, lungs, and blood vessels as a unified system of circulation, given by the English physician William Harvey (1578–1657). In his system the heart was no more than a powerful pump, not the purifier of blood spirits, as Galen had taught. Harvey was thus able to describe correctly for the first time the path of flow of the blood out from the heart through the arteries and back again through the veins. Although Harvey did not discover the physical presence of the capillaries as the link between the arteries and the veins, he anticipated their eventual discovery in the lungs of a frog by the Italian Marcello Malpighi (1628–1694) in 1660. The Dutch microscopist Antoni van Leeuwenhoek (1632–1723) first observed the actual circulation of the blood in 1688.

The immediate medical consequences of Harvey's discovery of the circulation of the blood were virtually nil. Blood-letting continued to be practiced because the doctrine of humors had not been refuted. However, Harvey's work enabled the role of the lungs to be more adequately explained, particularly when the similarity between respiration and combustion began to be understood in the later seventeenth and eighteenth centuries.

MICROSCOPY

The collection of primary information about tiny organisms too small to be seen by the naked eye as well as about the equally small parts of the larger organisms, notably the individual cells, depended upon an adequate means of magnification. This proved to be the microscope, a system of lenses arranged in a tube so that one could see not the distant, as with the telescope, but the tiny. However, problems of distortion by glass lenses proved even greater in microscopes than in telescopes. The very best work in biological microscopy, perhaps even until the nineteenth century, was done by Van Leeuwenhoek with a single spherical lens. Van Leeuwenhoek, Jan Swammerdam (1637–1680), and other microscopists observed extremely small but independent life forms like mites, protozoa, and infusoria, as well as separate cells like spermatozoa and blood corpuscles.

The key problem of reproduction continued to be a biological puzzle of fundamental importance. It was not until well into the eighteenth century that the mammalian ova were discovered and the structure of the female reproductive system in mammals was explained; nor was the functional role of the sperm in fertilization understood. The continuation of species was attributed by many biologists, including some of the best, to the presence of a fully-formed miniature in the ovum, which needed only to grow in size to become an adult. But systematic studies demonstrated that the embryo and even the foetus were not structurally the adult of the species on a much smaller scale but went through genuine transformation.

SPECIES AND EVOLUTION

The question of species was centrally involved in the problems of identification, arrangement, and naming, which the scientist calls *taxonomy*. At first arrangement was done in such arbitrary ways as by the alphabetical order of Latin names, but gradually there were attempts to create systems based on similarities and differences in anatomy and physiology. These culminated in the grand-scale taxonomic achievements of the Swedish naturalist Carl Linnaeus (1707–1778), who devised the modern arrangement of orders, families (genera), and species, and the binomial system of nomenclature (the Latin name of the genus followed by that of the species).

Closely connected with the problem of distinguishing and arranging the species was that of explaining their origin. Most biologists during the Scientific Revolution continued to accept the principle of the permanence of species from their creation as described in the biblical Book of Genesis. Yet the possibility of evolution of the species was suggested both by the existence of fossils of extinct species in apparently impossible places (like maritime fossils on mountain tops), with the consequent implication that geological evolution had taken far longer than the biblical account indicated, and by familiarity with the practice of breeding livestock and plant varieties as well as such hybrids as mules.

A number of naturalists, including the Englishman Erasmus Darwin (1731–1802) and the Frenchman Jean Baptiste Monet de Lamarck (1744–1829), accepted the idea of evolution of species. Lamarck suggested a mechanism for such evolution in the process of adaptation of species to environment; he saw such changes as the adaptive transformation of the affected organs of a creature to the needs it faced. However, in the absence of the knowledge of any specific mechanism for the transmission of characteristics, any picture of the system of heredity and of the permanence or evolution of traits was at best an untested and as yet untestable hypothesis. Often it was only a kind of scientific myth accepted for its emotional plausibility or philosophical utility.

5. *The Organization of Science*

DURING THE AGE OF THE SCIENTIFIC REVOLUTION the interplay of individual and group activity in the evolution of knowledge became more complex and was adapted to the new needs. The primary characteristic of the new situation was that scientific work was not yet a profession, and it did not really develop such a status before the nineteenth century. Except for posts in mathematics and, more rarely, astronomy, there was no regular place in the universities for scientists as such until the eighteenth century, and then usually only for chemists and anatomists in schools of medicine, as we have noted. Otherwise, scientists for the most part were amateurs. Some were men of independent wealth and standing, like Otto von Guericke, mayor of Magdeburg, Robert Boyle, an Irish earl, or Antoine Lavoisier, a French financier; others were "little people," like the Dutch lens-grinder Van Leeuwenhoek; but most came from the broad class of educated men, like the American printer-statesman Benjamin Franklin.

At first contacts among scientists were purely informal, by personal meetings and correspondence; but early in the seventeenth century Francis Bacon, Baron Verulam (1561–1626), by profession a lawyer and by appointment Lord Chancellor of England, propounded in his *New Atlantis* a new view of science as an organized enterprise in which men of science would assemble in a research institute for joint investigation of agreed-upon problems. His ideal was beyond full accomplishment during the age of the Scientific Revolution, but a number of significant institutions were created more or less in line with his vision. The first were Italian academies sponsored by various rulers, of which the best known was the Academy of Lynxes (*Lincei*), established in 1601, to which Galileo was proud to belong. But its members met more to hear reports of individual projects and theories than to engage in collaborative enterprises.

The same was true of the first of the academies to achieve permanence, the Royal Society of England, founded in 1660 upon the basis of consolidating previous private groups. The patronage of Charles II and his successors on the English throne was permissive but nominal, for they gave no funds to the society; but the Royal Society was able nonetheless to encourage scientific investigation and to bring its results before the world in its *Transactions*. The French Academy of Sciences sponsored by Louis XIV, with the great minister Colbert as its organizing spirit, was more the kind of body Bacon had had in mind. Its members, including several distinguished foreigners like the Dutch physicist Christian Huyghens, were on the royal payroll, and the king footed the bill for their equipment. But especially when forceful ministers like Colbert and Louvois were its supervisors, the French academy was directed to tasks of immediate and obvious utility rather than toward the frontiers of knowledge. The Berlin and Moscow

Academies of Sciences created in the eighteenth century were modeled on the Parisian institute.

Nonetheless, in the formative period of the Scientific Revolution some of the most important organizational work in science was done on a completely informal basis by correspondents who reported in their letters the various new developments to those concerned. The most notable and effective of these scientific journalists was the French monk, Marin Mersenne (1588–1648). As a scientist he was well below the first rank but he was an indefatigable letter-writer and organizer of minuscule conventions in his monastic cell in Paris. Henry Oldenburg (1618?–1677), secretary of the Royal Society in its first decades, played much the same role during the second half of the seventeenth century. But by the eighteenth century the work of scientific communication began to be assumed by scholarly journals.

6. *The New World View*

MECHANISM

The Scientific Revolution rested upon an essentially new view of the nature of the physical world. Its roots lay in ideas which were already present but not yet combined in a single, coherent, general conception. Where the older view of the world had emphasized the doctrine that the world had been created for man and to serve his purposes, although man himself had been created to serve God, the new view based its conception of the physical world upon the model of a machine which works naturally because of the way it is organized and built, rather than upon the model of a servant who works upon command.

But the new view of the world also changed the character of man's description of the world as well as his attitude toward it. Where earlier the characteristics of things and processes in nature had been described primarily as they were directly experienced by man—distances were ordinarily given, for instance, in terms of the time it took to traverse them, rather than as line-of-flight measurements which disregarded difficulties of travel or anything but pure space—measurement now became king. Length, numbers, angles became the primary characteristics of physical objects; characteristics like color, texture, and temperature were conceived of as secondary and derivative, and qualities like utility or convenience more derivative still. But such a view of the universe was intensely impersonal and abstract; it treated all units of space or time as equal to each other, although it was obvious that they were experienced by men in different ways according to the varying circumstances.

The new view of the world drew upon the mathematical mysticism of the Neoplatonists who described the world in terms of mathematical arrangements but whose world was anything but abstract: for them numbers and harmonies had implicit and symbolic meanings, which led on the one hand to the affirmation of astrology that men's fates were governed by the movements of the planets, and on the other to the religious mysticism of the Jewish cabbala and its Christian imitators, which sought divine purpose and foreshadowing of future events in secret numbers. Yet it was from the habit of seeking to explain and describe the world in numbers that the new breed of mathematical physicists in part drew their inspiration.

But the numbers of nature gradually ceased to possess the magical significance that the Neoplatonists and Cabbalists ascribed to them, even though Kepler was still utterly gripped by such conceptions and Newton in his old age flirted with the possibility of such hidden meanings. As mathematics itself developed, evolving a powerfully effective symbolism covering operations (signs) as well as quantities, and as experimental practice served not only to provide data for formulating theory and checking its hypotheses but also to develop the habit of describing by counting and measuring, the direction of inquiry turned more and more toward seeking relationships through the most abstract mathematical procedures.

It was the extraordinary success attained by this apparently unlikely method —for physical nature turned out to be most precisely and concretely understood when the terms of description were most abstract—which spurred the effort to apply the same method to other spheres of nature and even to human behavior. In other areas of thought seventeenth-century rationalism claimed superiority over other philosophies; in natural science it triumphed.

CORPUSCULARISM

Mathematical abstraction was only one of the fundamental components of the new scientific world view. The other was the doctrine that the ultimate components of the physical world consisted in tiny little bodies which could not be further divided, hence called *atoms* (uncut) by the Greek philosophers who first propounded these notions. It was a doctrine still utterly untested in practice but a useful spur to experiment toward less distant goals. Yet such outstanding scientific minds as Newton and Boyle believed that the observed physical characteristics of the large bodies which man could observe directly were only the enlargement of the characteristics of the atoms below the threshold of sense perception. A sharp flavor, for instance, was attributed to prickly points on the atoms of which the food ultimately consisted. But these atoms were beyond any kind of observation, direct or indirect, then available to scientists; optical microscopes had been invented, but these were still crude instruments capable of only the coarsest magnifications. The atomic or corpuscular theory therefore served less as a working principle of science than as a metaphysical assumption that enabled scientists to reject more easily the animist doctrines of Aristotelian-Scholastic science and to grope toward and to accept more readily the mechanistic implications of the new science.

THE CLOCKWORK UNIVERSE

At the level of grand philosophical conceptions, the new science encouraged a view of the physical universe on the model of a great clock, the most elaborate kind of machinery then known. Judaeo-Christian ideas of the creation of nature by God as a form of existence distinct from Him, although designed and controlled by Him, fitted the clockwork doctrine no less easily than they did those of Aristotelian science. The various parts of the universe functioned as they did because their individual sizes, shapes, and masses determined their motions, but each acted as part of the larger mechanism, not singly and in isolation. The universe was therefore a system of nature, essentially different from a mere assemblage of pieces without interrelationship. None of the elements of the mechanism itself required anything other than its mechanical characteristics, but it seemed obvious that the design of the mechanism as a whole was distinct from that of its parts. Cogs and springs do not make a clock unless put together by a clockmaker, and on this analogy the universe required a Master Clockmaker.

Here a new view of the universe accepted and adapted a fundamental element of the older philosophy—the notion of God as creator and first cause. But God, conceived as a master mathematician and craftsman who created the world and set it into motion, was different from the older concept of a God who was the constant mover of the world. The new universe did not seem to require the intervention of God once He had set it into motion; and it was soon recognized that Newton's suggestion that God intervened now and then to make small corrections in the motions of celestial bodies implied both the imperfection of His own creation and inadequacy in the scientific study of it. The new science could not escape the implications of its own principle that the physical world was utterly determinist, that nothing happened in it except by an inherent orderliness called a natural law. Such a mechanism could be as easily described as existing by itself as by the fiat of a creator. This culmination of the new view was embodied in the reply given by the great astronomer Pierre de Laplace (1749–1827) to Napoleon I when the emperor propounded the notion of the Clockmaker God: "Sire, I have no need of that hypothesis." Belief in the deity was forced back into the sphere of faith, beyond proof or disproof by the methods of science.

Further Reading

The state of science at the end of the Middle Ages is sketched in *E. M. W. Tillyard, *The Elizabethan World Picture* (London, 1961). *G. Sarton, *Appreciation of Ancient and Medieval Science during the Renaissance* (New York, 1955) and *A History of Science and the New Humanism* (New York, 1931) are important for the complex question of the relation of science and humanism. *G. Sarton's *Six Wings: Men of Science in the Renaissance* (Bloomington, 1957) is informative. *H. Butterfield, *The Origins of Modern Science,* rev. ed. (New York, 1957) treats with clarity the philosophical basis of the new science; *T. S. Kuhn, *The Structure of Scientific Revolutions* (Chicago, 1962) and *C. C. Gillispie, *The Edge of Objectivity* (Princeton, 1960) carry the debate forward to important new questions.

The best general history of the rise of the new science is *A. R. Hall, *The Scientific Revolution, 1500–1800,* 2nd ed. (Boston, 1962). The *Brief History of Science* by A. R. and M. B. Hall (New York, 1961) is an excellent elementary introduction. *M. Boas (Hall), *The Scientific Renaissance, 1450–1630* (New York, 1962) and *A. R. Hall, *From Galileo to Newton, 1630–1730* (New York, 1963) are more detailed studies. Volume II of R. Taton, ed., *A General History of the Sciences* (New York, 1966) is a collection of more technical chapters by numerous specialists.

I. B. Cohen, *The Birth of the New Physics* (Garden City, 1960) is a useful overview. *T. S. Kuhn, *The Copernican Revolution* (Cambridge, Mass., 1956) clarifies the significance of the heliocentric astronomy. For Tyco Brahe see J. A. Gade, *The Life and Times of Tyco Brahe* (New York, 1947). *M. Caspar, *Kepler* (London and New York, 1959) is a brief biography. *L. Fermi, *Galileo and the Scientific Revolution* (New York, 1961) presents Galileo's achievement; while *G. de Santillana, *The Crime of Galileo* (Chicago, 1955) is a brilliant reinterpretation of his persecution. *E. N. Andrade, *Isaac Newton* (London, 1954) is a short biography; J. W. N. Sullivan's *Isaac Newton, 1642–1727* (New York, 1938) is somewhat fuller; while *L. T. More, *Isaac Newton* (New York, 1934) stresses the technical side of Newton's work.

M. Boas, *Robert Boyle and Seventeenth-Century Chemistry* (Cambridge, 1958) is fundamental. *B. Farrington, *Francis Bacon: Philosopher of the New Science* (New York, 1961) emphasizes the role of practical aims in the new science. G. N. Clark, *Science and Social Welfare in the Age of Newton* (Oxford, 1937) is more subtle. *R. F. Jones, *Ancients and Moderns: A Study of the Rise of the Scientific Movement in Seventeenth Century England,* 2nd ed. (St. Louis, 1961) is useful.

*A. Koyré, *From the Closed World to the Infinite Universe* (New York, 1957) analyzes the philosophical implications and consequences of the scientific revolution. R. S. Westfall, *Science and Religion in Seventeenth-Century England* (New Haven, 1958) shows the way devout scientists grappled with these questions.

CHAPTER 13

The Age
of Enlightenment
1715–1789

When the eighteenth century began France was the most powerful
state in Europe and seemed the model country of the Old Regime. Before the century reached its midpoint, however, the difficulties it faced were so grave and so
fundamental that a social and political crisis of the utmost significance could be
seen forming. In intellectual life the realization of what was happening gave rise
to the Enlightenment, a movement most explicit in its critique of the old order
and implicitly aiming at a new and better world, a New Regime.

1. The State of Society

THE CHANGES IN THE STRUCTURE of European society that characterize the modern
epoch began to emerge with clarity and force during this century. Although elements of modernity had been present for a long time, as we have seen, they had
remained scattered, without strong cohesion, and subordinate to the inherited
overall pattern.

[504]

THE INDUSTRIAL REVOLUTION BEGINS

One of the most fundamental changes was the Industrial Revolution. Actually this was a much more complex phenomenon than the name would indicate, and it will be discussed fully in Chapter 15. At this time, however, it is important to recognize that it was not so much a single revolutionary event as a long process affecting every form of economic activity—trade, agriculture, and the service fields, as well as industrial production. Indeed, the massive phase of industrialization did not take place before the nineteenth century. Until then, development of industrial production by power-driven machinery within factories employing great numbers of workers was confined almost exclusively to England.

Commercial capitalism, on the other hand, although it made greatest progress in England, was spread widely throughout western Europe. The volume of trade within England and overseas increased dramatically, much of it carried on by joint-stock companies. Merchant banking developed more broadly; in England it was already involved in the financing of the new industrial firms, a field which continental banks did not yet usually engage in. The establishment of the Bank of England late in the seventeenth century provided Britain with a financial institution which mediated between the general economy and the government treasury and provided the country with the foundations for a flexible yet strong credit system.

The importance of such an institution was illustrated by the consequences of the two great speculative booms which hit England and France during the 1720's, the *Mississippi System* in France and the *South Sea Bubble* in England. The former was a speculative frenzy to buy shares in the Mississippi Company, organized by the Scots-born financier John Law (1671–1729) to develop trade through New Orleans to the heartland of North America. Law, who linked the company to a new Royal Bank which took over the royal debt, was a wizard to some and a swindler to others. When the revenues from colonial trade could not sustain the profits promised by the Mississippi Company, it crashed. Speculators numbering in the thousands were ruined; those who sold out in time were enriched. Frenchmen in general reacted by developing a deep distrust of paper money, which had been issued by the Royal Bank. Thus the bank was abandoned at the very time when the need of the French state to organize its finances upon a sounder basis was becoming evident.

In England, on the other hand, the similar South Sea Bubble, consisting primarily in the creation of numerous joint-stock companies, most without prospects corresponding to their promises, did not interfere with Britain's economic development. When the Bubble burst, with a shift of wealth from greedy and credulous investors to greedy and unscrupulous promoters, the Bank of England remained intact, soundly-established joint-stock companies as well as family businesses continued to be active, and England's expansion in commerce as well as in industry continued with hardly any loss of momentum.

The Agricultural Revolution, which made it possible for an ever-smaller proportion of farmers to feed an ever-larger population, was essential to the eventual total transformation of European economy and society. It had been initiated in the Low Countries and northern Italy, as we have observed (see above, page 358), but the adoption and improvement of its procedures in England during the eighteenth century constituted the major shift in a general agrarian transformation. Englishmen learned how to replace the self-limiting open-field system with the more productive arrangements of artificial meadows planted in fodder crops, the use of root and leguminous crops, and more careful sowing, plowing, and harvesting. Other Europeans learned from the English rather than from the Netherlanders and north Italians who had originated these techniques. But not until the nineteenth century did western Europe find in North America, Argentina, and Australia, as well as in south Russia, sources of grain to sustain its industrial development and to free it from tight dependence upon its own capacity to grow bread crops.

In eastern Europe the impact of the European commercial capitalist development led during the eighteenth century to the completion of the paradoxical development by which the overwhelmingly agrarian economy of eastern Europe was oriented toward production for the western European market upon the basis not of expansion of capitalism or personal emancipation of the farming population, but rather upon serfdom so intensified as to resemble outright slavery.

DEMOGRAPHY

Toward the middle of the eighteenth century a new and rapid growth in population began. Where Europe had counted about 120 million people at the beginning of the century, it had grown to about 190 million by its end. No less significant was a shift in the distribution of population among the major countries. France, for centuries the most populous land in Europe, began to experience a falling-off in her growth rate which continued into the mid-twentieth century. At the same time Germany, now recovered economically from the devastation of the Thirty Years' War, and Russia, unified under the tsars and with population flowing into the lightly peopled areas of the south and southeast, began to expand their numbers rapidly and to outpace the French. England, too, whose population previously had numbered no more than a quarter of the French, began the swift expansion which was to lead her to equality with France in population by the middle of the next century.

The reasons for this demographic explosion are uncertain. The industrial revolution made possible the continuation and even acceleration of population growth but it does not explain its initiation, for the demographic upsurge preceded the economic and technological changes. Furthermore, similar demographic processes were occurring at about the same time in other parts of the world where the impact of the European industrial revolution was not to be felt for another century. More adequate food supplies due to the availability of more efficient crops, notably potatoes and maize (Indian corn), undoubtedly spurred the population growth, but it occurred even in countries which grew and consumed neither of these foods. Vaccination, invented in the eighteenth century, would bring the scourge of small-pox under control and eventually almost eliminate it, but it was not applied to the great mass of the population until the late nineteenth century. Hygienic improvements in towns were still not widespread and in any case were largely counteracted by the rapid growth of towns and town slums which were festering hell-holes of mortality.

The demographic revolution that began in the eighteenth century was unprecedented in a fundamental way. Under the previously prevailing balance between production and population, the size of the population could not grow beyond the limits of economic productivity without sooner or later creating disasters which cut population back, often well below the earlier balance level. Within decades, or at most a century or two, population growth would then fill the gap. However, when economic development constantly shifted the balance level upward and ultimately medical improvements limited epidemiological controls, the threat of famine and disaster began to come from the side of disturbances in the functioning of the economy and not from that of increases in the population—a situation that would begin to change later in the twentieth century when worldwide population expansion at an unprecedented rate raised the danger of inadequate resources.

SOCIETY

The character and relationships of social groups also began to undergo significant changes during the eighteenth century. In country after country the social preeminence and the political and economic prerogatives of the nobility as the elite order of society were strengthened and consolidated. Often, as in Prussia and Russia, this was a more or less explicit bargain between the absolute monarchs and the nobility. In exchange for unquestioned dominance over the peasant serfs, the nobles accepted the rulers' monopoly of sovereign political power.

However, where economic growth was directly the result of capitalist evolution, particularly in western Europe, the nobility began to face increasingly sharp and open competition from another elite class, the commoners of wealth and talent, the bourgeoisie. It was a class with fewer privileges in law and one for whom hereditary advantage played a much smaller role. Increasingly, too, it was the class which had been doing not only the business work of the society but also much of its detailed specific political administration. It was a class whose aspirations and self-confidence grew during the eighteenth century, but with mixed ideals. Especially in France during the earlier decades, the bourgeois aspired to rise and be admitted into the ranks of the nobility. After mid-century, however, as the nobles, resentful of the new "bourgeois gentlemen," obtained government measures closing off avenues of social mobility and became more of a caste, the bourgeois in turn began to stress their competitive rivalry with the aristocracy. Even though there were many titled nobility among the philosophes and their followers, the criticism directed by thinkers of the Enlightenment against traditional privileges appeared to more and more bourgeois to justify their own resentments. Usually the nobility responded to the bourgeois challenge by seeking—and in Prussia by obtaining from the "enlightened" king, Frederick II—the exclusion of commoners from the higher reaches of administrative and political careers. But sometimes the most thoughtful elements of the nobility, like the French reform minister Turgot, saw that the hope for more efficient society and government lay with the bourgeoisie, rather than with the nobility, who sought to protect advantages earned not by their own achievements but by those of their ancestors.

The possible talents of the third great group in society, the commoners without wealth, who were neither sought out nor trained, were undiscovered:

> Some village-Hampden, that with dauntless breast
>   The little tyrant of his fields withstood,
> Some mute inglorious Milton here may rest,
>   Some Cromwell, guiltless of his country's blood.

Thus the English poet Thomas Gray described them in his *Elegy Written in a Country Church-Yard* (1751). They therefore remained outside the competition between nobility and bourgeoisie. For the most part, the commoners were both envious and respectful of their *betters*. Yet riots flared now and again when economic privation or religious prejudice drove them to violence against tax collectors, foreigners, heretics, papists, or Jews. During the civil wars of the sixteenth and mid-seventeenth centuries, the leading combatants had been ready to make use of the almost mindless violence of the poor, but during the eighteenth century this risky maneuver was not usually attempted—at least until the outbreak of revolutionary movements in the last quarter of the century.

2. The Enlightenment

THE ENLIGHTENMENT IDEAL

The eighteenth century proudly called itself the Age of *Enlightenment*. Rightly so, for the Enlightenment was a significantly new way of looking at man and the world. Much of the moral content of the thought of the Enlightenment was traditional, inherited in the last analysis from the Judaeo-Christian and Greek ethical systems; there was still the same stress upon love of one's fellow man, the value of honesty, and the other traditional virtues. But two elements essential to historic Christianity were positively rejected. One was the role of sacramental religion as a means to man's salvation; the other was Christianity's central emphasis upon asceticism, the self-deprivation and self-punishment by which man sought to tame his selfishness and earn the greater happiness of salvation in an afterlife. Asceticism was replaced by a doctrine of ethical hedonism which upheld the goodness of ordinary human desires. Religious authoritarianism, resting upon a belief in the inborn evil nature of man and the necessity for the powers established by God to discipline him, was replaced by the doctrine of man's innate goodness, which was distorted only by harmful institutions. The ultimate dream of the Enlightenment thinkers, although they disagreed on many points and seldom set forth their aspirations for the future in a fully explicit picture, focused on a world without conflict, without harshness, with men of intelligence and goodwill working independently, each for his own welfare, yet all together for common interests as well.

THE ENLIGHTENMENT METHOD

The eighteenth-century thinkers of the Enlightenment called themselves philosophers but had a strong distaste for abstract philosophizing. It has become usual to use the French term *philosophes* for these men to distinguish them from academic professional philosophers. Such use of a French name for them is proper and natural, for France was the home of the most important of the enlightened thinkers.

The philosophes believed that both their goals and the means by which they hoped to achieve them were those of a new social science, essentially like that of the natural science which had triumphed so spectacularly with Newton. They therefore proclaimed the importance of fact and experience—but with the aim of finding the essential and inherent identity of social values. Since description produced a picture of chaotic discrepancies, the enlightened thinkers relied upon introspection to discover what all *right-thinking men* agree upon, and, strange to say, what they discovered was their own ideal of the good. But this discovery was presented in a new way and with a new purpose, as a means of criticizing the established values and institutions. In their place they defended a rational utilitarianism, the principle first clearly expressed by the Italian jurist Cesare Bonesana, marquis of Beccaria (1735?–1794?), and later made more famous by the English jurist Jeremy Bentham (1748–1832): the goal of society was "the greatest good for the greatest number," and this was the standard by which laws and policies should be judged.

ENLIGHTENED POLITICS

The philosophes sought to make essential changes in the character and content of many existing institutions, but they were not in favor of destroying existing states. On the contrary, they wished to make use of the states to achieve their purposes. They saw no other way to attain the new regime which they envisioned, in which there would be equality of all men before the law and the rule of law over all men including rulers; they did not wish to impose equality of property and, even less, common ownership of goods, but to give commoners and nobles the same rights. They seldom advocated abolition of noble titles and rank but only the withdrawal of the special powers and privileges attendant upon aristocratic status.

To create such a regime it was usually necessary to destroy the system of privileged estates. The philosophes saw only the kings as able to do this task and urged them to take it on. Ultimately, however, the philosophes had to face the problem that rulers without effective obstacles to their arbitrary power of command were as much opposed as the privileged orders to the kind of new world in which their enlightened, would-be advisers believed. Kings seldom wished to preside over social and political transformations which would sooner or later turn out to be at their expense too. Enlightened despots were usually more intent upon making themselves stronger and their governments more efficient than in building a New Regime.

THE PHILOSOPHES OF FRANCE

Movements that possess the breadth and duration of the Enlightenment are more varied than such a summary picture indicates. It displays certain common characteristics but not the individual traits especially of the major thinkers, nor the differences of the movement as it existed in various countries and during the many phases of its development.

The Enlightenment grew essentially out of two earlier movements, the rationalist and empiricist philosophies of the seventeenth century as they were merged in the new science, and the political opposition to absolute monarchy, directed in England against the Stuarts and in France against Louis XIV. The triumph of parliamentary sovereignty and political freedom in its early eighteenth-century form in England shifted the main impetus of the movement of critical thought to France where absolute monarchy continued as the form of government and where its application was erratic, sufficiently arbitrary and harsh to arouse resentment, but not tyrannical enough to crush opposition once and for all (see below, pages 517-521). The development of the Enlightenment in France may be observed in more detail in four thinkers who were its supreme exponents, Montesquieu, Voltaire, Diderot, and Rousseau, and one representative of the last generation before the revolution, Holbach.

Montesquieu. The role which the magistrates of the courts or parlements played in the resistance to absolutism is symbolized by the person of Charles de Secondat, Baron de la Brède et de Montesquieu (1689–1755). Montesquieu was by profession a judge, rising to the presidency of the parlement of Bordeaux before he retired to devote himself wholly to his writing. He was therefore a nobleman of the "robe," a baron by rank. In his master work, *The Spirit of the Laws* (1748), he painted the nobility as the class and the intermediate corporations like the parlements as the instruments which assured the rule of justice in the kingdom, equivalent in their function to the parliamentary legislature in Britain. Yet *The Spirit of the Laws* is far more than a defense of the narrow interests of the aristocracy; presenting a passionate argument on behalf of political and personal freedom and a profound analysis of the relations between social systems and forms of government, it is one of the early creative works of sociological thought. Its most direct impact came from its picture of the English constitution as a system of divided powers, with the executive, legislature, and judiciary each performing its own function while it checked the tendency of the others to govern badly. These twin ideas of the division of powers and a system of checks and balances became central to later doctrines of parliamentary regimes, as embodied in the constitution of the American republic adopted in 1789, in the French revolutionary constitution of 1792, and in innumerable constitutions of liberal states throughout the world in the nineteenth century. While *The Spirit of the Laws* was an assault upon the theory of absolutism, Montesquieu's earlier work, *The Persian Letters* (1721), was a witty and sardonic portrayal of the malpractices, injustices, and hypocrisies of the existing order as seen by an imaginary Persian visitor.

Voltaire. The qualities of *The Persian Letters*—indirection, satire, and grace—became the hallmarks of the writing of the playwright François Marie Arouet, who took the pen name of Voltaire (1694–1778) and made it world-famous through literary works of every kind: not only plays in the tradition of Corneille and Racine —which proved to be almost unreadable for later generations—but mock epics, philosophical tales, pamphlets in fantastic number, a philosophical dictionary which was in fact a tract for the times, philosophical studies, histories, and a great deal of verse. Voltaire possessed the gift of presenting complex and difficult ideas simply and easily, sometimes at the expense of their real meaning and full force. He achieved an early reputation as a writer of plays but was jailed in the Bastille for using his wit against a thin-skinned nobleman. On his release he went to England, where he came to accept the Newtonian system still largely rejected in France in favor of Cartesian physics and to admire the English political system. Returning to France, he lauded what he had seen in the *Letters on the English* (1734) and was launched upon his multifarious career. He became the central and characteristic figure of the Enlightenment. In religion he was a deist who believed that the Clockmaker God, without interfering in human life, bestowed rewards and punishments upon men for their deeds; but he rejected traditional Christianity (and Judaism as its parent), not only as a mass of superstitions he thought fit only for disciplining the stupid poor, but also as an infamous persecutor of heretics and disbelievers. In the notorious Calas affair, he fought unsuccessfully for a posthumous reversal of the death sentence against a Huguenot convicted of slaying his son, a convert to Catholicism.

In philosophy Voltaire was an advocate of common sense and a foe of what he saw as farfetched systems, like Leibniz's total rationalism, in which everything was really for the best in the best of all possible worlds. Voltaire satirized Leibniz's philosophy in *Candide* (1759), a tale which painted a world in which everything was for the worst until the protagonist decides that wisdom lies in "cultivating one's garden," an ambiguous symbol for Voltaire's ideal of life. Voltaire's skepticism and his hatred of the church set the pattern for anticlericalism in the French Revolution and the subsequent centuries.

Diderot.   Denis Diderot (1713–1784) represents the deeper complexities of thought in the Enlightenment, as Voltaire exemplifies its use of mockery. Diderot, scion

VOLTAIRE AND DIDEROT. *Left:* Sculptor Jean Antoine Houdon chiseled into marble the central quality of Voltaire's genius—a wit that combined a concern for the welfare of mankind with a mockery of its faults. *Right:* Jean Honoré Fragonard here uses the techniques he perfected in his idealized scenes of courtly life to convey the troubled wisdom of Diderot, one of the Enlightenment's most significant figures.

of a deeply religious family, turned aside from training for the priesthood to become the most subtle major thinker of the Enlightenment. On the one hand he was convinced of the truth of the empirical rationalism of the Enlightenment, which his tough-minded logic carried all the way to atheism; on the other he sought passionately to make the Enlightenment a new faith, full of the warmth, hope, and vigor he had known in the Catholicism in which he no longer believed. He preached the rejection of Christian asceticism and the acceptance of human desires as naturally good in his *Supplement to the Voyage of Bougainville* (not published until 1794), in which he portrayed a utopia of honest feelings openly expressed within rational institutions, with the scene laid in Tahiti. Diderot's outstanding accomplishment was the editorship of the *Encyclopédie,* a compendium of eighteenth-century learning which worked the teachings of the Enlightenment into its articles and became the major textbook for the followers of the philosophes for decades.

Rousseau. Jean Jacques Rousseau (1712–1778), who lived most of his adult life in France, was Genevan by birth, and the puritanical spirit and republican traditions of his native city gave a different quality to his handling of the central questions of Enlightenment thought. A man of profoundly troubled emotions, he lacked the gaiety of Voltaire or the self-control of Diderot; yet, perhaps more than any of his predecessors among the philosophes, he caught the imagination of men by the millions, not by the thousands. His immediate impact came in his philosophical novels, *Julie, or The New Héloïse* (1761) and *Émile* (1762). The former was an argument against artificial institutions which distort honest human feelings and relationships, the latter a tract in favor of natural education based on the inborn aptitudes and interests of the young instead of the enforcement of an external discipline of subject and method. Together these novels were among the strongest forces leading away from the prosy rationality characteristic of the Enlightenment to the affirmation of emotion that began in the late eighteenth century and developed into full-blown romanticism in the next century. Rousseau rejected the subtle artificialities of the *salon* culture where so many of the philosophes, for all the revolutionary implications of their work, found a hearing, sympathy, and support. In his *Discourse upon the Arts and Sciences* (1750), Rousseau painted the growth of civilization as a falling away from the honest morality of man in a "state of nature." In his *Social Contract* (1762), however, he accepted the argument of Hobbes and Locke that life without government was not feasible and sought instead to lay down the character of a political order in which obedience was freely given because sovereignty lay in the people and laws were the expression of their general will, which sought the welfare of all. Although Rousseau's concerns in the *Social Contract* were more ethical than political, his proclamation of popular sovereignty as the sole basis of just rule became, decades later, a central principle of the revolutionaries in France and elsewhere; but at the moment this book, with its mixture of dry argument and passionate assertion, made little appeal.

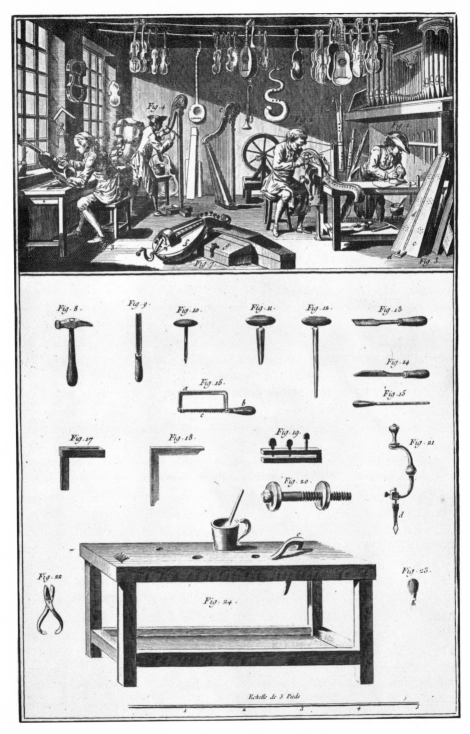

THE INSTRUMENT-MAKER. The plates illustrating Diderot's great *Encyclopédie* are a mine of technical and historical information; this engraving shows the workshop where lutes were made and the tools used.

By the 1770's, the decade when revolutionaries in British North America began to put many of the ideas of the philosophes into practice, the great age of the Enlightenment had come to an end. The last generation of the philosophes were at best writers of talent repeating what had been said before them, or grim sympathizers, like the German-born Baron Paul Dietrich d'Holbach. In a horde of anonymous works he denounced Christianity with a venom beside which even Voltaire's criticism paled; he preached total materialism and atheism as well as a rigorous utilitarianism. The man who wrote with the pen of an angry revolutionary was, however, in private life a kindhearted friend, a gracious host in his wife's famous salon, and an advocate of improvement by means of the authority of the royal government, with no taste whatever for the popular violence that was to play a central role in the revolution that broke out in France in 1789, the year of his death.

THE ENLIGHTENMENT IN EUROPE

The ideas of the Enlightenment spread throughout Europe and to the world of European colonists beyond the oceans. In each country they were adapted to fit native traditions and native conditions, losing much of their French flavor in the process. Elsewhere the new ideas did not take hold as fully as they had in France, and the resistance to them was also better organized and recruited better minds.

In England during the heyday of the Enlightenment intellectuals observed developments in France with close interest but were not spurred to direct imitation. The spirit of the philosophes was conveyed with accuracy and power, but without intellectual originality, in the long poem that Alexander Pope (1688–1744) called *An Essay on Man* (1733).

The Scottish philosopher David Hume (1711–1776), on the other hand, although he shared with the philosophes a distaste for political oppression and religious bigotry, did not accept their easy confidence in the power of reason. He picked up the thread of earlier skeptical thought to display the uncertainties of knowing and knowledge with unmatched rigor; his skepticism was directed not only against the tradition-bound defenders of the old intellectual and religious order but also at what he saw as the unwarranted self-assurance of the new thinkers. He even criticized the underlying assumptions of the new science by demonstrating the inability of philosophy to prove the notion of causality, on which all scientific thought rested. Hume's criticism, although it disturbed some of his friends among the philosophes, did not shake their convictions; he himself acknowledged that the need to believe was stronger than the will to accept the conclusions of philosophical analysis.

Later in the century, enlightened ideas combined with the native English tradition of democratic principles inherited from the seventeenth-century revolutions to produce the political and intellectual movement of the Radicals. Strongest among Protestant Dissenters, this movement favored democratic political reforms and full religious freedom instead of mere toleration.

In Germany the influence of the philosophes was found in the movement called the *Aufklärung,* the straightforward German word for *Enlightenment* (French has only roundabout terms like *les lumières* [illumination]). The *Aufklärung* emphasized the concepts of toleration and goodwill among men rather than hostility to religion. Its foremost exponent was the philosopher Immanuel Kant (1724–1804), who brought to its key ideas soberly powerful analysis. Kant's study of morality was built upon Rousseau rather than upon Voltaire, for he preached an ethics of self-imposed duty rather than the quest for satisfactions.

Elsewhere seeds of the Enlightenment fell on less fertile soil and put down shallower roots. In Italy the *Illuminismo,* as the movement was called, was strongest among legal reformers like Beccaria who enunciated a program for the reform of justice that would replace the traditional reliance upon death penalties, tortures, and haphazard sentences, by a systematic criminal jurisprudence based on the principle of making the punishment fit the crime. Italy's most original thinker of the century, the Neapolitan Gianbattisto Vico (1668–1744), whose *New Science* (1725) set forth the claims of history as opposed to science as a means for men to know and understand the world, found little response in his own time. In Spain the proposals of the philosophes which were aimed at making the state more efficient found an audience among some government officials, but notions of religious tolerance made no headway. Elsewhere in western Europe, especially where there were native traditions of personal freedom and participation by the people in government, as in Holland and Scandinavia, the new ideas were taken up more fully. But in countries without such traditions, like Russia, they were for the most part only part of the idle conversation of the more intellectual sections of the nobility. A nobleman like Alexander Radishchev (1749–1802), who dared to criticize the institutions of serfdom and absolutism and was exiled to Siberia for his pains, was the rarest of rarities.

The ideas of the philosophes played an important role in the revolutionary movements which broke out in the European world in the 1770's, but the creation of a sustained, coherent movement of intellectual opposition did not come about until the French Revolution of 1789–1799, discussed in Chapter 14, presented a political and military challenge to the old order far greater even than the one successful revolt of the 1770's, the American revolution against British sovereignty.

3. The States of Europe

THE FUNDAMENTAL PROBLEM facing almost all the states of Europe during the eighteenth century was to make monarchy work. During the first half of the century this seemed to involve only the rulers and the privileged orders in a contest between absolutism and the claims of the estates. But during the second half of the century, under the impetus of Enlightenment thought and the stormy growth of the business-capitalist sector of the economy, this question became complicated by the emergence of businessmen and other commoners as competitors for power and as potential enemies of both monarchs and estates.

FRANCE: THE HERITAGE OF LOUIS XIV

The eighteenth century was for France a period of crisis after the long wars of Louis XIV. He bequeathed to his successors an immense burden of debt which made government finance an apparently insuperable problem, even more of a problem than in less powerful states which had not undertaken such vast enterprises and did not have such tremendous ambitions. For the Sun King also gave to his successors and to the French nation a magnified sense of the grandeur of France. Military glory became more than ever the be-all and end-all of the most powerful groups in French society; for them peace was at best a time of preparation for war, at worst a humiliation and a degradation to be ended as quickly as possible. Finally, the Grand Monarch left behind him a tradition of total absolutism. Because he had been truly his own prime minister, subsequent kings of France, even when they lacked his dedication to onerous duty, held on stubbornly to their monopoly of power.

For most of the century the primary struggle was between the king and his officials on the one hand and the nobility on the other. The aristocracy now came more and more under the leadership of the judges of the parlements, who held their offices by inheritance or purchase and were therefore as a group virtually irremovable. The magistrates used their traditional right of remonstrance against legislation which they considered unconstitutional or unwise—a right which had been removed by Louis XIV and restored by the duke of Orleans, regent during the minority of Louis XV—to oppose the efforts of royal ministers to reform the tax system by eliminating or reducing the exemptions of the nobility and clergy or to take other measures which would limit or modify the privileges of the first two orders of the state. The magistrates proclaimed their purpose to be the defense of liberty by resistance to tyrannical measures, and hence they stepped to the fore as leaders in the defense of liberty in general. Such claims were weakened, however, when the judges of the parlements proved to be worse persecutors than royal officials, more ready to commit injustice in the name of the law, particularly in matters affecting the Huguenots. Not that the claim of the king's government to be the defender of law and justice was without flaw; the practice of arbitrary imprisonment, effected by sealed warrants (*lettres de cachet*) which deprived the prisoner of all access to the courts or other appeal, was a flagrant violation of the principle of justice for all.

The royal government's attempts at reform were made more difficult because fundamental fiscal reforms could not be introduced without deeply modifying the economic, social, and political structure of the country. A revolution from above designed to bring in a New Regime by the authority of the state was very far from the intention of the government leaders, with the single exception of Turgot in the early years of the reign of Louis XVI. Turgot's political failure, his inability to keep the support of the king against the resistance of both the royal family and the privileged orders, indicated how narrow were the chances for basic transformation under the guidance and authority of the state.

FRANCE: LOUIS XV

These problems came to the fore almost at once with the death of Louis XIV in 1715. His successor, Louis XV, was a boy of five years, whose uncle, Philip, duke of Orleans, governed as regent (1715–1723). Orleans, although dissolute in his personal life, was intelligent and aware of the need for change. He won the support of the parlements by returning to them their coveted right of remonstrance and instituted a government by councils dominated by the aristocracy. But leadership of state proved to need the hand of professionals, and the system evolved by Louis XIV was reinstituted after a few years.

When Louis XV came of age in 1723, he entrusted the reins of government to his beloved tutor Abbé Fleury (1653–1743) who was made a cardinal. Fleury, prime minister in everything but name, saw France's principal need to be a period of peace to encourage economic and fiscal recovery. In his pursuit of peace Fleury was willing to collaborate even with France's erstwhile enemy Great Britain; but a family compact between the French and Spanish Bourbons, which opened up the prospect of French trading privileges in Spanish America, led to French involvement in the conflict between Spain and Britain (the War of Jenkins' Ear), which broke out in 1739. It came just at the time when the wisdom of Fleury's policy of avoiding war and its gluttonous demands for money had been demonstrated; for the royal budget was balanced in 1739. For the first and the only time during the entire century, it became possible to reverse the apparently irresistible trend toward fiscal insolvency and bankruptcy, with its consequent peril to the political stability of the state.

This opportunity was lost before it could be used. Fleury was unable to thwart the war hawks who insisted that France join not only in the Spanish war against England but also in the Prussian war against Austria which broke out in 1740 (see below, page 524). Thus the two wars combined into one, which history calls the War of the Austrian Succession. Both conflicts went badly for France: the war against England because the British forces captured one French colonial stronghold after another; the war against Austria because the military successes won by

French arms in the Austrian Netherlands had to be given up when peace was made in 1748. Eight years later France was back at war, but only after the continued Austrian desire for revenge against Prussia prompted the Diplomatic Revolution of 1756, in which France became the ally of Austria against Prussia. Thus ended the centuries-old rivalry between the ruling dynasties of France and the House of Habsburg. England followed through by becoming Prussia's ally in the resulting Seven Years' War and reaped the fruits of victory by wresting away important segments of the French colonies, notably Canada and French India. The Peace of Paris in 1763 was the low point of French prestige at home and abroad. The haphazard and irresponsible conduct of foreign policy called attention to the often disastrous influence of royal mistresses upon the king's policy decisions as well as to the contest for influence and wealth among the courtiers. The immense costs of the war, when added to the already vast accumulation of royal indebtedness, pushed the state closer to bankruptcy.

In the final decade of his reign Louis XV was at last enough shaken by the situation to attempt a few essential reforms—primarily shifting some of the tax burden to the clergy and nobility—by the exercise of his authority. The parlement of Paris resisted the proposed reforms with adamantine hostility, denouncing them as virtual expropriation and the denial of inalienable rights. When the parlementarians undertook a strike by the courts of justice, Chancellor René Maupeou (1714–1792), with the support of the aging king, decided to remove them; the judges were exiled to a provincial town and new high courts were instituted in place of the parlement of Paris. In the new courts the magistrates held their posts by appointment, not as private property. Tremendous howls of protest and indignation were heard not only from the exiled magistrates, but also from most of the philosophes who saw in Maupeou's bold stroke simply the operation of royal tyranny. Only Voltaire among them threw his support to Maupeou, for he had seen the reality of the parlements' persecuting justice and their hostility to all true reform. By the time of Louis XV's death in 1774, the resistance to the Maupeou reforms, which were the key to all other reforms, was still loud but increasingly ineffectual as the new courts began to function.

FRANCE: LOUIS XVI

The new king, Louis XVI, grandson of the late monarch, was a man of goodwill, little intelligence, and even less strength of character. He wanted to rule well and did all the things that would win applause. Thus, he undid Maupeou's experiment which would have increased his own power to effect reforms and called the parlement back into session in Paris. However, he named as his principal minister Anne-Robert Jacques de Turgot (1727–1781), the most gifted practical reformer in France, who combined his theoretical work as an economist of the physiocratic

ANNE-ROBERT TURGOT. The practical and far-sighted minister of state who sought to put the power of the French monarchy at the service of economic reform is here depicted by the painter Charles Van Loo while he was still a royal intendant, although King Louis XVI, giving in to a storm of criticism, was later to remove him from office.

school with effective experience as an administrator in the provinces. Turgot attempted to reduce government expenditures while at the same time encouraging economic activity under the rule of *free trade* favored by the physiocrats. Both measures aroused the ire of influential groups, the courtiers and especially the royal family (including the queen, Marie Antoinette) who saw their incomes cut by economy moves, the magistrates who treated abolition of the guild system as a violation of the rights of property, and the general population who saw free trade in grain as a *pact of famine* designed to turn grain shortages into profits for a few insiders. He faced the angry condemnation of all entrenched interests.

Turgot's fall from office and power in 1776 was triggered by his attitude in the dispute over whether France should support the American rebels in their war of independence against England. The foreign minister, Charles Gravier, count of Vergennes (1717–1787), although an ideological conservative, favored doing so because it was an unmatchable opportunity to take revenge upon Britain for France's defeats in the wars of mid-century; but Turgot, whose ideological commitments might well have led him to support a revolution led by American philosophes like Jefferson and Franklin, opposed the alliance with the Americans because he felt it was beyond France's means. The king chose Vergennes's policy and dropped Turgot. French military and naval assistance enabled the fledgling American republic to win its independence in 1783 by the Peace of Paris. But France regained none of her territorial losses, and her assuaged vanity was bought at the price of heavy additional debt.

It was a bad time for the French treasury to assume the added burden. The French economy, after decades of commercial and industrial prosperity since the end of Louis XIV's wars, had slumped in the 1780's because of the impact of crop failures in grain fields and vineyards. There was deep anxiety among the common people who suffered from joblessness and the high cost of bread, their principal food. Louis XVI turned from one would-be financial magician to another, each promising somehow to solve the fiscal problems of the state without disturbing society, without stirring up the hornets' nests in the court and in the parlements, without reducing expenditures drastically. The magical device was credit. But to borrow in order to avoid belt-tightening, in order to avoid reforms, was only to pile up bigger problems for the future, and a future that was no longer far distant.

In 1787 and 1788 the crown faced not only sharply mounting deficits and an increased reluctance by lenders to provide money, but also in several provinces armed resistance to its authority, organized by the local parlements—an aristocratic *prerevolution,* as it turned out. The parlements made their central demand the convocation of the Estates General which had not met since 1614. In 1788 this demand was finally accepted. A decision to have the three orders meet separately, as the parlements proposed, brought a split between the privileged orders and the third estate even before the Estates General met in Versailles in May 1789. The fate of the monarchy and the nation was at stake.

ENGLAND

During the eighteenth century England consolidated the position of predominance among the European states that she had conquered during the later wars against Louis XIV. At the same time she consolidated her internal political organization upon the basis of the effective sovereignty of Parliament. Both achievements rested upon the success of the English in taking over the role of the Dutch as the merchants and carriers of Europe and their subsequent success in becoming also the manufacturers of Europe.

When Queen Anne died in 1714 the political settlement in Britain was in grave peril. The Tories were reluctant to stand by the Act of Settlement and Succession of 1701, which gave the crown not to James II's son, James Edward, "the Old Pretender," but to the elector of Hanover, George Louis. Nonetheless, when the Hanoverian was crowned as George I and the Old Pretender landed in Scotland in 1715 to lead a rebellion of Jacobites (from the Latin *Jacobus,* for James), the Tories could not bring themselves to follow James "III," a rigid Catholic. During the reigns of George I (1714–1727) and George II (1727–1760), the Tories exiled themselves from an effective role in politics by continued unwillingness to accept the dynastic consequences of the Revolution of 1688 which they had helped to carry out. The Whigs, lacking effective partisan opposition, therefore monopolized power, but political disputes and controversy did not end; they were played out within the framework of the dominant party, and party politics itself ceased to be of importance for half a century.

British politics became a matter partly of issues, partly of personalities, and partly of interest groups formed around leading families. The first two Georges were both Hanoverians in spirit as well as by birth, and they permitted English statesmen to govern their country with little interference. The leaders of the cabinet had to keep the confidence of both king and Parliament, so that their key task became to manage Parliament in order to obtain support for their policies. Thus Parliament became the foundation stone of English public life, and its legal (as contrasted to formal) sovereignty was beyond contest. In this situation leadership of state passed into the hands of the leaders of the cabinet—true *prime ministers,* although without the formal title. These were men like Sir Robert Walpole (1676–1745), the elder William Pitt (1708–1788), and his son, William Pitt the Younger (1759–1806), who were able to generate and execute policy in a way that made them difficult figures to replace. The other ministers, although not formally under the authority of the prime ministers, in practice became subordinates.

Party politics became significant again only with the accession of the English-born George III to the throne in 1760. He was determined to rule well and with the full prerogatives traditionally assigned to the king by the settlement of 1689 but neglected by his two predecessors. George's attempts to play a forceful role in political life finally broke the Whig monopoly, already weakened by the elder Pitt, a political independent who had imposed himself upon Parliament and crown during the Seven Years' War (1756–1763) because of his extraordinary ability and his support in the nation. George III was not suspicious of the Tories, who had gradually abandoned their Jacobite sympathies after the failure of the rebellion led by Charles Edward, the Young Pretender, in Scotland in 1745.

George III built his ministries primarily upon his own initiative, but they foundered one after the other upon the shoals of relations with the British North American colonies. The attempt to make the colonists share in the costs of the wars against France from which they benefited so greatly met colonial resistance which in turn generated attempts to impose the authority of the British crown and Parliament by military force. The failure of the king's ministries either to prevent the rebellion that broke out in America in 1775 or to defeat the rebels, and the resulting humiliation of the Peace of Paris of 1783 which acknowledged American independence, compelled the king to accept as his prime minister William Pitt the Younger, whose aim was to restore English power by political reforms and by a reconciliation with France. But Pitt faced a new situation when revolution broke

WILLIAM PITT THE YOUNGER. James Gillray, famous for his sardonic caricatures, here portrays the youthful and purposeful leader of England during the revolutionary era.

out in France in 1789, and he shifted his policies to brace England for the new trials that cóuld be foreseen.

PRUSSIA

The Holy Roman Empire became even more of a political nonentity during the eighteenth century. Except for the emperor, and he only as ruler of Austria, the German princes remained minor actors upon the stage of European politics. This situation changed only when Prussian power, slowly built up for a century, was put to use by a bold royal gambler.

Prussia was given the sinews of military power by Frederick William I (1713–1740). Known as the *Sergeant-King* because of his total commitment to the enterprise of creating a large and well-trained army, he concentrated political power more strongly than ever in his own hands. The merger of military and political institutions which had been begun by the Great Elector in the late seventeenth century was carried to the point where Prussia was virtually a population and a government existing to serve an army. Although Prussia was, in terms of resources, scarcely even a second-rate power, its army gave it the military strength of a first-rate power. But Frederick William was unwilling to risk this beloved instrument in

FREDERICK WILLIAM I OF PRUSSIA. This portrait by Antoine Pesne accords with the courtly style but does not reveal much of the hard and crude power which lay beneath the polished elegance of the "Sergeant King."

the gamble of war, particularly since the paucity of Prussian resources would make it extremely difficult to repair losses. As a consequence the Prussian army, instead of serving to achieve political objectives as in other states, became an object of idle display—except insofar as Prussia remained at peace, safe from aggression.

For Frederick William's son, Frederick II (1740–1786), the army was instead a means of asserting his personality and achieving glory. When Emperor Charles VI died some months after Frederick's accession, the new king of Prussia invaded the Austrian province of Silesia to which the Prussian house of Hohenzollern had some distant but not wholly invalid claim. There followed the long and bitter War of the Austrian Succession, with France as Frederick's ally and Russia and England on the side of Maria Theresa, Charles VI's daughter. In repeated battles, often against heavy odds, Frederick proved himself one of the outstanding military captains of all times and earned the sobriquet of *the Great*. When peace was made in 1748, he was able to retain Silesia, thanks to the support of his French allies.

Frederick then turned to the work of rebuilding his sorely tried kingdom, emphasizing efficiency and obedience but striving also for a strengthened rule of law. In order to assure the support of the nobility who constituted the bulk of his officer corps, Frederick permitted them to consolidate their grip upon the peasantry, especially in Brandenburg and Prussia. But the work of peace lasted less than a decade, because Silesia, which had brought half as many more people and a doubled wealth to Prussia, also earned Frederick the implacable hatred of Maria Theresa who would not yield in her efforts to regain her lost province. In order to pull France away from Prussia, she abandoned the old Habsburg enmity with the Bourbon power and brought about the Diplomatic Revolution of 1756. Frederick, fearing a monster coalition of Austria, France, Russia, and Saxony, decided to split the alliance by a sudden invasion of Saxony, the linchpin of the hostile war plan. The Seven Years' War followed, in which England, Frederick's ally, was helpful mainly by providing subsidies. But even a series of almost miraculous victories did not enable him to hold off permanently the tightening clamp of the allies. By 1761 the end seemed near, and Frederick contemplated suicide. He was saved by chance. Early in 1762 Empress Elizabeth of Russia died suddenly, and her successor, Peter III, who was an admirer of Frederick's, joined him. The Peace of Hubertusburg of 1763 brought no advantage to either side; but merely to keep Silesia meant a victory for Frederick.

For the rest of his reign Frederick resumed the rebuilding of his kingdom. He avoided all large-scale war but gladly participated with Catherine II of Russia

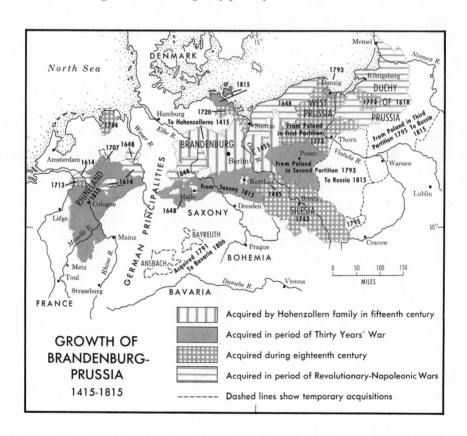

GROWTH OF
BRANDENBURG-
PRUSSIA
1415-1815

Acquired by Hohenzollern family in fifteenth century

Acquired in period of Thirty Years' War

Acquired during eighteenth century

Acquired in period of Revolutionary-Napoleonic Wars

- - - - - Dashed lines show temporary acquisitions

and Maria Theresa in the first partition of Poland (1772). Despite Frederick's own artistic interests and his genuine concern for the welfare of his subjects to whom he gave full religious toleration, he completed the work of militarizing the Prussian state which had been begun by his great-grandfather, the Great Elector. Prussia had risen to the rank of a great power but only at the cost of demanding the almost impossible of her people and making warfare the principal business of the country. Perhaps worse was that Frederick the Great's gamble had paid off, and future generations of Prussians, as well as many other Germans, were to accept the ideal of the military state that Frederick had made glamorous.

Frederick William II (1786–1797), a nephew who succeeded as king of Prussia in 1786, was anything but a new Frederick II. He took from his uncle only the ideal of absolutism, but he did not possess Frederick's qualities of intelligence and devotion to duty that had made absolutism work. The institutions of state and army remained fixed in form, while they slackened in fact. It was this Prussia which was to face the crisis of the revolutionary age about to break on the morrow of Frederick's death.

AUSTRIA: MARIA THERESA

If Prussia was the upstart among the German states, Austria was the established power that had to maintain herself against the aggressive competition of the new state on the other side of the empire. What was at stake at the time of Frederick's assault upon Silesia was not only the immediate loss of a cherished and valuable province but also the leadership of Germany itself. From the time of the Peace of Westphalia of 1648, but even more after the Peace of Utrecht and Rastadt (1713–1714), Austrian power had developed upon a double basis: the composite Austrian state, united under a single Habsburg ruling upon many thrones; and the predominance of Habsburg Austria within Germany where, until 1740, no effective rival had emerged.

During the reign of Emperor Charles VI (1711–1740) the wars against the Ottoman Turks were carried on but without substantial new successes. However, most of the Magyar provinces were now incorporated into royal (Habsburg) Hungary, and Austria was able to exert preponderant influence in Poland, her principal neighbor to the north. Charles was therefore able to devote his principal attention to a problem arising from the composite dynastic character of his state. When it became clear that his successor would be Archduchess Maria Theresa, the danger of division of the monarchy developed. Some of the Habsburg realms were governed by the Salic Law forbidding the descent of the crown to a woman, while Maria Theresa would be uncontested heiress in others. To avoid this splitting up of his realms and the consequent dispersion of the combined power which alone made Austria a great state, Charles obtained the assent of the parliamentary assemblies which did exist in his dominions and of the other powers of Europe to a *Pragmatic Sanction*. This edict overrode the Salic Law and instituted Maria Theresa as Charles's universal heiress.

During the two and a half decades of war and preparations for war which followed Frederick II's invasion of Silesia in 1740, Maria Theresa (her husband, Duke Francis Stephen of Lorraine, reigned as emperor from 1745 but was a political nullity) proved that her political abilities and her force of character were no less than Frederick's. She held together her disparate realms, even though in Hungary she was forced to return to the diet important governmental powers which her predecessors had wrested from it and to allow the Magyars to complete their domination over other nationalities within the Hungarian kingdom. Without attempting the revolutionary transformation of the internal system of the Austrian lands advocated by her son, Joseph, who had been deeply influenced by the philosophes of western Europe, she not only introduced reforms, particularly improvement of the conditions of the serfs where it was safe to do so, as in her own estates; she also more effectively centralized the general administration of finances and political decision-making. All in all, although unable to regain Silesia, she managed to keep her state of many parts together under the immense strains of the wars against Prussia.

AUSTRIA: JOSEPH II

On the death of Francis I in 1765 Joseph II became emperor; at the same time he continued as coruler of Austria with his mother. Not until 1780, when Maria Theresa died, was Joseph able to attempt to apply in practice the various reform ideas—principally increased efficiency and centralization of government, religious toleration and the subordination of church to state, and improvement of the status of the peasantry—which he had absorbed from the Enlightenment. He was able to have his way in religious matters because the domination of princes over the established religions had been common practice, even if not accepted doctrine, for at least two centuries.

But Joseph's political and economic aspirations rested upon too narrow a base, that fraction of the officialdom which was trained in and committed to the same fundamental ideas as the emperor. The mass of the nobility, the overwhelming majority of the ruling class, remained implacably hostile to ideas which could be introduced only at their expense. As for the peasantry, they were too ill educated, too lacking in political awareness, experience, or ability, to provide an alternative base for political action—even if Joseph II had been ready to make such a truly revolutionary break with state and society as to turn to the peasantry for his support.

In the final years of his reign rebellions broke out in many Habsburg dominions, notably Hungary and the Austrian Netherlands. These were movements on behalf of freedom—the traditional freedom, linked to the organization of society and government around the institution of estates—against the innovating, equalizing, centralizing monarchy. By the time of Joseph's death in 1790 he had already capitulated spiritually to the rebellions. His brother and successor, Leopold II (1790–1792), a more practiced innovator as a result of his experience as grand duke of Tuscany, could salvage a few reforms only at the expense of restoring the main elements of the old order. Enlightened despotism, resting upon the mind and will of the ruler and without a base in a broad group of the population accustomed to providing leadership, had failed in making a revolution from above in Austria. The lesson came at a most significant time, as revolution from below was at that very time taking France, Europe's leading country, into its grip.

RUSSIA: PETER THE GREAT

The Russian monarchy emerged upon the stage of Europe as an equal among the great powers only during the eighteenth century. Achieving this status for Russia was primarily the work of Peter I, called the Great. When he ascended the tsarist throne in 1689 (for a few years reigning jointly with his half-brother Ivan), a number of fundamental problems in Russia had been, or seemed to be, solved. One was the consolidation of a national dynasty, the Romanovs, after the extinction of the Rurikians at the end of the sixteenth century. By Peter's time it seemed beyond dispute that a Romanov would reign over Russia, but it was not yet clearly settled which Romanov. No fixed and explicit law of succession such as had been adopted in most hereditary monarchies in western Europe had come into force. Hence the danger of civil wars engendered by competition for the inheritance of the crown had not been eliminated. Second, the system of government inherited by the Romanovs from the Rurikians had not been fundamentally changed or even improved: there remained a huge assemblage of bureaus organized on no particular principle, with uncertain jurisdictions, with ill-trained and ill-paid personnel, but with an extremely elaborate system of ranks that made it difficult to reward ability and merit. Third, the Russian military apparatus had not kept up, or caught up, with the developments in the West.

Peter addressed himself to these problems with unmatched vigor, both mental and physical. A giant of a man, he was subject to fits of wrath which endangered those around him; yet he could adapt himself to the crudest conditions without complaint. He began his reign by an attempt to drive the Crimean Tartars from the mouth of the Don River, was defeated one year but in characteristic fashion learned the lessons of his defeat and won the next year. During his youth he had associated closely with westerners resident in Moscow's German (foreign) Quarter, and he sought to bring to Russia those aspects of the West that he admired and un-

THE HOUSE OF ROMANOV

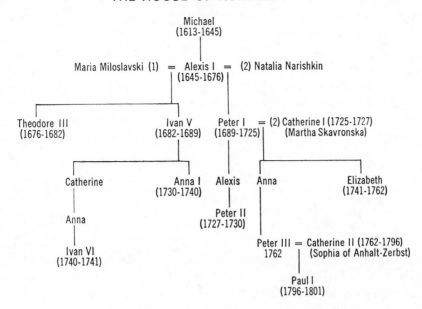

derstood: its technology, especially in warfare, and its efficient government. To learn these better he made a trip to the West. In Holland he worked incognito for a while in a shipyard. In England he visited Parliament as well as naval installations and his party shocked Englishmen by their barbarous naïveté. The trip was cut short by a revolt of the palace guards in Moscow, the stronghold of the old nobility who hated Peter's initial reforms; he returned to crush the rebels and became more determined than ever to modernize Russia.

• The nobles were compelled to educate their sons in the new, western fashion and to serve the monarch in army, navy, or government; and they had to share rank with upstarts whom Peter promoted, even to the very highest positions. He remodeled the government on the Swedish fashion, instituting as the highest body in the state an appointed Senate which operated through a series of ministries, again on the new western style. Most important, he reorganized the army and developed a navy on the best western models.

The first use of his new fighting force was not encouraging. Peter's primary aim was to achieve what his predecessors had not been able to do, to conquer and hold a Russian outlet to the Baltic Sea. But when he undertook to do so in 1700, he found as his opponent King Charles XII (1697–1718) of Sweden who swept Poles, Danes, and Germans before him with fantastic ease. Charles smashed Peter's proud new army at Narva, but the tsar resolved to come back. He rebuilt his army, and when he met Charles again in combat, at Poltava in 1709, he had lured the Swede far into the Ukraine, out of reach of Swedish bases on the Baltic. Charles, defeated at last, had to flee to Turkey with a remnant of his army.

Russia now had her *window upon Europe,* the northern Baltic provinces, and Peter proceeded to build a new capital at Saint Petersburg (present-day Leningrad) at the head of the Gulf of Finland. War continued until 1721 when Sweden acknowledged Russian sovereignty over the Baltic provinces. When Peter died in 1725, the question of whether the problems he had inherited had been solved still remained, and it was to take the entire eighteenth century, and more, to answer it.

RUSSIA: CATHERINE THE GREAT

The growth of Russia as a great power continued upon the base built by Peter the Great. Russian predominance in Poland was the achievement of German officials and generals from the Baltic provinces under Empress Anna (1730–1740), Peter's niece, during the War of the Polish Succession (1733–1735). Further gains were made toward the Black Sea, with the capture of the port of Azov from the Turks; but French mediation on behalf of the Turks deprived the Russians of conquests in Moldavia, the gateway to the Balkans. Anna's favoritism to Germans was reversed during the reign of Elizabeth, her cousin and Peter I's youngest daughter. Elizabeth modeled her court more closely upon the French model, and the Russian nobility took on the language and the manners of the French aristocracy. Higher learning upon the western European pattern was also introduced, with the establishment of the University of Moscow in 1755 and the Academy of Sciences under the gifted scientist Michael Lomonosov (1711–1756). Elizabeth threw her strength in the great mid-century wars against Prussia and its king, Frederick II, who indulged his taste for scurrilous sarcasm against her loose private morals. During the Seven Years' War, Russian armies played an important part in the alliance of Frederick's enemies and might have inflicted a final and total defeat upon him had not Elizabeth's death in 1762 brought to the tsarist throne her nephew Peter III, who idolized the Prussian king.

Peter ruled only half a year before he was overthrown and slain in a palace revolution led by a lover of his wife, the German-born Catherine. She reigned (1762–1796) as Catherine II and was called the Great because of her military conquests and her achievements as a political ruler who combined admiration for the principles of the Enlightenment with a keen sense of the realities of power. She was, or wanted to be, an enlightened despot; but her benevolence always stopped short before it could endanger her autocracy. She knew that the rebellion which brought her to the throne had been staged by regiments of guards made up of noblemen who wanted emancipation for their class from the obligation of services

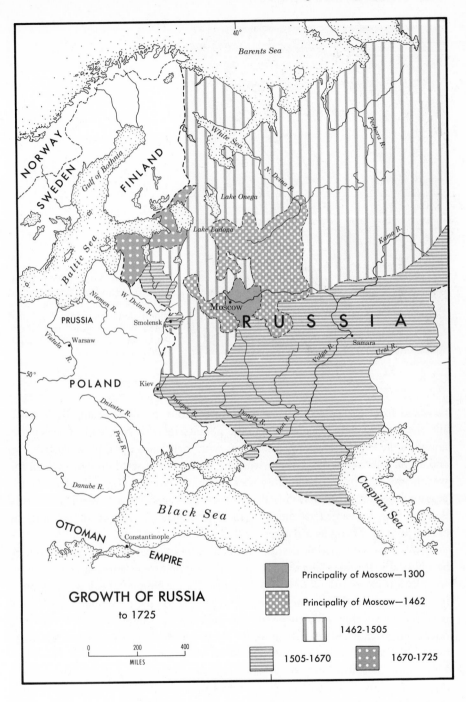

NORWAY

SWEDEN

FINLAND

Barents Sea

White Sea

Pechora R.

N. Dvina R.

Lake Onega

Kama R.

Gulf of Bothnia

Lake Ladoga

Baltic Sea

Niemen R.

W. Dvina R.

Moscow

R U S S I A

PRUSSIA

Smolensk

Volga R.

Samara

Ural R.

Vistula R.

Warsaw

POLAND

Kiev

Dnieper R.

Donets R.

Don R.

Dniester R.

Prut R.

Caspian Sea

Danube R.

Black Sea

OTTOMAN

Constantinople

EMPIRE

GROWTH OF RUSSIA
to 1725

| 0 | 200 | 400 |
MILES

Principality of Moscow—1300

Principality of Moscow—1462

1462-1505

1505-1670   1670-1725

CATHERINE THE GREAT. Catherine II of Russia, here portrayed by an anonymous artist, combined dedication to enlightened ideas with resolute absolutism, an affectionate nature with political ruthlessness.

inherited from earlier centuries and made rigorous and inescapable by Peter I, and she granted a charter of rights to the nobility in 1785. Although intellectually drawn to the teachings of the philosophes with their stress upon personal freedom and dignity, she refused to tamper with the institution of serfdom upon which the wealth and standing of the nobility rested. She put down with pitiless ferocity the peasant rebellion of 1773–1775, led by Emelyan Pugachev, a Cossack and army deserter. She responded to the nobleman Radishchev's critique of serfdom by exiling him to Siberia as a dangerous fool.

Nonetheless Catherine carried through such internal reforms as she felt to be politically feasible. These included more rational legislation suggested by a commission convened (1767–1768) to study codification of the laws and other improvements. In 1775, in the wake of Pugachev's rebellion, she reorganized local government systematically to provide more effective administration. Catherine's outstanding achievements lay, however, in the field of foreign affairs. She engineered election of a former lover, Stanislas Poniatowski, as king of Poland in 1764, enforced a Russian protectorate upon his country, and then dismantled it during the three notorious partitions (see below, page 534), expanding Russian territory hundreds of miles to the west. She also spread Russian sovereignty to the south, driving the Ottoman Turks from the northern shores of the Black Sea in 1774 and annexing the great peninsula of the Crimea in 1783. Later in her reign she resumed the Russian progress into the Balkans, conquering the region to the Jassy River from the Turks. In the northwest, although she was unable to extend the conquests of Peter the Great against Sweden, she held off the attacks of Gustavus III in 1788–1790, and strengthened Russia as a naval power in the Baltic. More than any other single Russian ruler during the eighteenth century, Catherine made permanent Russia's position as a great European power, a position which Peter had initiated.

POLAND

In Poland the institution of elective monarchy not only gave the nobility the means of enforcing a constantly tighter grip upon state and society; it also provided repeated opportunities for foreign powers to interfere in Polish affairs and contributed to the destruction of Polish independence before the end of the eighteenth century.

The contested elections of Augustus II, elector of Saxony, and Stanislas I Leszczynski, in 1697 and 1704 respectively, led eventually to a general European conflict called the War of the Polish Succession (1733–1735). Although this war was marked more by the bargaining of diplomats than the battling of soldiers, it

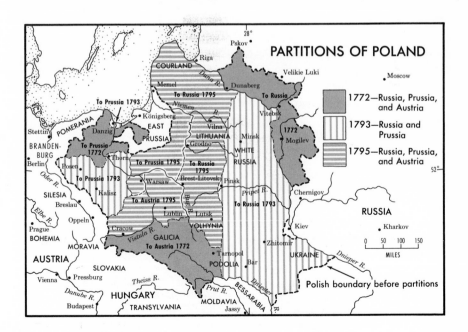

was in any case foreign power which made the decision that Augustus III would reign in Poland (1734–1763). The power of any member of the Polish diet to veto any proposal under discussion and in so doing to cause dissolution of the assembly was confirmed. This right of *liberum veto* and the elective monarchy became the key targets of advocates of political reform, as abolition or at least amelioration of serfdom was the goal of social reformers.

The opportunity for change came, paradoxically, when Catherine II manipulated the election of Stanislas Poniatowski as king in 1764. Stanislas II, like Catherine, was influenced by the doctrines of the Enlightenment, but he was readier than she to attempt to apply them, even though his regal powers were immensely smaller. Although himself a member of the great nobility, he could bring only a handful of his class to accept the need for reform. Nonetheless, after Poland lost large parts of her territory to Russia, Prussia, and Austria by the first partition of 1772, agitation for reform swelled. A new constitution, adopted in 1791, both established hereditary monarchy and abolished the *liberum veto*. Armed resistance to the reform constitution was sponsored by Russia, and a Russian army, joined by a Prussian force, backed the rebels. Another partition in 1793 led to a war of national independence under the leadership of Thaddeus Kosciuszko who had been a volunteer in America with Washington. Russian and Prussian forces again crushed the Poles, and King Stanislas resigned his throne. The third partition of 1795 distributed what remained of free Poland among her three great neighbors.

THE SPANISH HABSBURGS

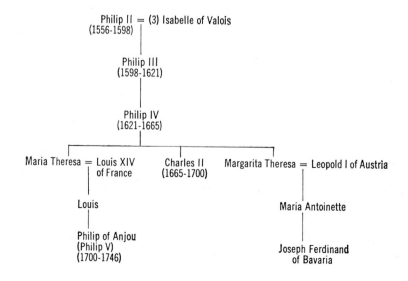

IBERIA

Under the new Bourbon dynasty Spain began to recover from the disasters that marked the end of Habsburg rule and even to venture upon the path of reform of her institutions. Philip V (1700–1746) did little but accustom the Spaniards to the new ruling family, but his son Charles III (1759–1788) cautiously but firmly introduced measures designed to improve Spanish commerce and agriculture and to increase the effectiveness of the work of government. But he had to cope with the sluggishness that had become endemic in Spanish public life. His measures were demonstrating more promise than fulfilled achievement when the crisis of the revolutionary age came upon Spain in the last decade of the century.

Portugal experienced an attempt at enlightened despotism under the ministry of the Marquis of Pombal (1750–1777). It was a more vigorous endeavor even than Spain's, with fundamentally the same aims, and in the end it had no more success, for it did not have the support of the people or any substantial group other than the officialdom.

4. *The Contest of States*

THE EIGHTEENTH CENTURY saw the culmination of the old states system of early modern Europe, that complex relationship among a multiplicity of states, each equal and wholly independent in principle but immensely unequal in actual power. As religion ceased to play any important political role at least in conflicts within the circle of European states, and as the ideological passions which arose in nineteenth- and twentieth-century Europe were not yet present, conflicts between states were stripped to the bare essentials of interests, power, and the ability of statesmen.

Even the primal emotions like hatred played a remarkably small role in relationships among states. During wartime noncombatants continued to travel unimpeded and were even welcomed in enemy states as long as their journeys were innocent, while officers in opposing armies dined with each other and played chess before battle.

Warfare itself became highly stylized. The battlefield saw the confrontation of two long lines of musketeers, aided by cavalry and artillery, whose movement was an elaborate if cruel ballet designed to bring men from the marching order to the line of battle. No longer did rulers and commanders rely upon the resources of local communities, swept up by foragers or even individual soldiers, to maintain their troops; an elaborate supply system freed the troops from dependence upon the resources of the countryside. Most soldiers continued to be volunteers in western

Europe, although conscription was more common in central Europe and furnished the huge manpower of the Russian army. Everywhere soldiers were separated by long terms of service from the civilian population and became a society unto themselves, difficult to control except by harsh discipline but having no particular independent purposes which might thwart those of the commander and the ruler.

Diplomacy too became an almost dispassionate art. The manipulation of policy was seen as a great chess game with more players, more—and less definite—rules, and bigger stakes. Soldiers fought to provide diplomats with additional pieces with which they bargained, especially in the great conferences which, since the Peace of Westphalia (1648), often were called into session while war continued. The stakes were primarily territorial aggrandizement and commercial advantage, and both were significant because they were the source of money, "the sinews of war." But especially in countries like England, France, and Holland where public opinion—that is, influential groups of the population able to reach the organs of power either through formal governmental bodies or by more indirect channels—was already visible, foreign policy was expected more and more to serve as well the needs of these groups.

RELATIVE PEACE

The settlement made at Utrecht and Rastadt in 1713 and 1714 did not at once restore complete peace to Europe. In the north, along the shores of the Baltic Sea, the Great Northern War continued to rage until 1725, when Sweden's defeat by Russia became definite and the Russian window upon Europe was opened wide. In southern Europe the struggle over the Spanish succession continued briefly, but with the former major antagonists—France, England, and Holland—all aligned against the effort of Charles VI of Austria to make good his claim upon Spain. Yet the major powers and their peoples were weary of war, and Sir Robert Walpole in England and Cardinal Fleury in France combined efforts to compromise over points of dispute between their countries and to maintain peace. They were largely successful until the end of the 1730's.

WARS FOR EUROPE AND THE WORLD

Little more than a generation passed before men forgot the price that war exacted and thought only of the advantages it could bring. The mid-century wars combined struggles for colonial empires and conflicts over territorial acquisitions in Europe. The link between them was France, Europe's great amphibian, pre-eminent among the land powers and now returning to the maritime challenge it had begun to offer Britain under Louis XIV.

The naval and overseas war did not come directly as a result of the rivalry between France and England, however, but rather through Spanish efforts to prevent English domination of Spanish America by interlopers. The War of Jenkins' Ear which broke out in 1739 (Robert Jenkins was an English sea captain who claimed a Spanish coast guard captain near Havana had sliced off his ear in 1731), soon involved France, upon whom fell the main burden of the fighting, and it merged with the continental War of the Austrian Succession (1740–1748). Some of the campaigning occurred in North America, where the British colonists fought to gain control over both the Ohio and ultimately the Mississippi valleys and the mouth of the Saint Lawrence River, the entryway to Canada. Other fighting occurred in India, where the English and French East India companies maintained trading stations and engaged in combat by means of small forces of Europeans joined with native allies. Naval warfare raged in the Atlantic and the Mediterranean.

The outbreak of the War of the Austrian Succession in May 1740, by involving France as a virtually automatic foe of Austria, linked the colonial and continental wars. The continental war stretched all the way to Russia, who joined Austria in an attempt to put down the ambitions of Prussia and thus keep open the way for the achievement of Russian aims in the West. The Peace of Aix-la-Chapelle (1748) was a standoff which satisfied none of the combatants except Prussia, who retained Silesia.

The statesmen spent the next years preparing feverishly for another war. England hoped to gain possession of the French colonial territories it continued to covet and to open up finally and for good the immense markets of Spanish America. Austria's fixed purpose was to regain the lost province of Silesia. France and Spain wished to keep what the others wanted. A new war, the Seven Years' War, broke out in 1756 as a result of the Diplomatic Revolution by which Austria and France became allies in the hope of improving their political and military positions. Prussia took the initiative by invading Saxony who was planning to join Prussia's enemies. Frederick II's frankly preventive attack renewed European attention to the Machiavellian doctrine of reason of state which made ordinary moral rules subordinate to the imperatives of political necessity. The Seven Years' War was an even more bitter struggle, fought in Europe, in America, and in India, but it brought clear victory to one side and definite defeat to the other. Prussia kept Silesia and England gained France's possessions in Canada and the Mississippi Valley to the east of the great river, as well as Florida from Spain. The balance of power in Europe had shifted massively in favor of the great English trading and manufacturing state which placed its primary and principal reliance upon its navy and kept control of the seas and hence of trade and profits.

THE ERA OF UNCERTAINTY

The British triumph after the two great wars was complete but it was not final. France remained a state with enormous resources although she was hampered

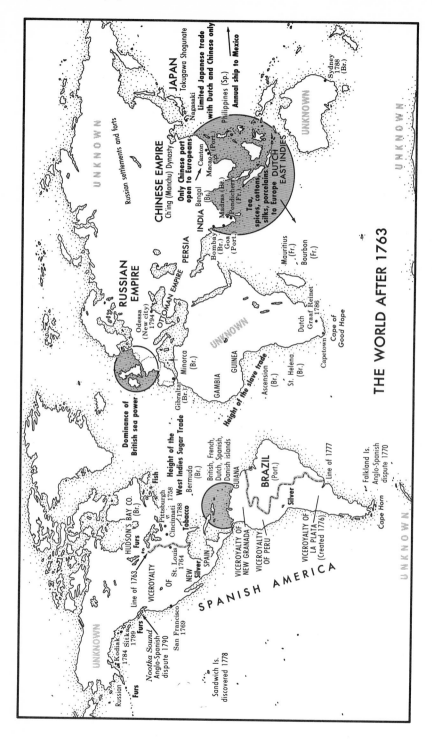

THE WORLD AFTER 1763

by increasing fiscal problems; and she had her own dream of political pre-dominance which she was not ready to abandon. The French opportunity came with the rebellion of England's American colonists. France became their principal ally and had the satisfaction of helping to pare down British power. But when peace was made in 1783, it turned out that France had served American interests without any direct or palpable advantage to herself.

At the end of the 1780's the hostility between Prussia and Austria, which had died down, flared again under the blast of Joseph II's ambitions in Bavaria. A brief, ill-prepared, and ill-conducted war (1778–1779), it did little damage except to the reputations of the aged Frederick II and the ambitious Joseph II.

5. *The Culture of the Enlightenment*

THE AGE OF THE ENLIGHTENMENT produced its own characteristic art styles and forms. Neoclassicism, with its stress upon reason and moderation, predominated but was becoming a mere rhetorical pattern, not a deeply felt esthetic necessity. The new style that took hold was the Rococo, a tasteful ornamentalism derived from Neoclassicism but more playful. Both Neoclassicism and Rococo failed to satisfy the stronger yet gentler emotions of men, so that by the final third of the century a reaction was beginning against rigid forms and the restraint of feeling. In Germany the new cult of sentiment took the form of the movement of *Storm and Stress* (*Sturm und Drang*), at the initiative of the poet-playwrights Johann Wolfgang von Goethe (1749–1832) and Friedrich Schiller (1759–1805). In England there was a similar movement, but it was less unified; it consisted in such things as a Gothic revival dedicated to misshapen gargoyles, admiration for ruined castles, and a delight in ghosts. In France Rousseau drove beyond the Enlightenment to an anticipation of the full-blooded romanticism of the nine-teenth century; he attacked the cult of reason and portrayed not only fictional characters but himself in the grasp of emotions more powerful than the rational faculties. A revolution in art and literature was in the making at the same time that Europe was on the threshold of an age of political and social revolution.

THE FINE ARTS

Painting reflected these general changes as closely as any field of art or litera-ture. Portraits of rulers and men of power and wealth continued to be important, but in a changed fashion. Dramatic intensity, with emphasis upon loftiness of status, tended to give way to greater emphasis upon personality, as indicated by qualities of lightness and charm. Landscape painting, Holland's achievement dur-ing the previous century, now became more common in other countries, but in ways characteristic of each national culture. The English stressed picturesqueness, while the Italians, notably the Venetian Antonio Canaletto (1697–1768), depicted a world of clearly defined outlines, basking in brilliant sun. French painters, like Jean Antoine Watteau (1684–1721) and Jean Honoré Fragonard (1732–1806), were less concerned with attempting to show reality than with creating an ideal world, fitting for the pastoral genres and the classical reminiscences which were still so strong in literature. A new kind of painting emerged in what was called genre style. To the Dutch still-lifes, with their amazing accuracy and verisimilitude, genre painters such as Jean Baptiste Greuze (1725–1805) added an anecdotal element, telling sentimental tales which appealed to the middle classes. Late in the century Neoclassicism was vigorously renewed when the Frenchman Jacques Louis David (1748–1825) began to paint heroic scenes from Roman antiquity, notably the *Oath of the Horatii* (1784). He used what he conceived to be Roman style, which meant the clear and bold lines of sculpture, and his figures were either nude or painted first nude and then clothed.

Classicism continued to control the art of sculpture. Portraiture in busts and full-length figures prevailed. At its best, in the work of the French sculptor Jean Antoine Houdon (1741–1828), the classicism of garb—Houdon puts Voltaire in a Roman toga—is relieved by a precise and effective individuality, a catching in stone of the essential intellectual and psychological quality of a specific and interesting human being. Other sculptors, like the Italian Antonio Canova (1757–1822), concentrated on works portraying the nude human body, combining the hardness of marble and the softness of flesh, but with little of human personality.

Architecture too made little fundamental advance during the century. The principles of classical imitation were worked out into accurate formulas but what originality there was consisted largely in the design of little palaces, as we might call them, like the Petit Trianon at Versailles—a shepherd's hut literally fit for a queen, fluffy with Rococo ornamentation—and Frederick the Great's charming *Sans Souci* at Potsdam, whose very name (Carefree) told its purpose. The first indication of a genuinely fresh approach in architectural design came in England where, during the latter part of the century, there arose an interest in constructing Gothic castles which were meant to convey gloom and mystery, already signs of an early romanticism.

LITERATURE

Writing also responded to the needs of an age of reason. Poetry did least well, for poets continued for decades to obey the rules of Boileau's *Art of Poetry*. Verse gained clarity and lost color. Reason stilled imagination. The best poetry tended to be epigrammatic, the distilled presentation of ideas, as in the work of the Englishman Alexander Pope. Not until after the middle of the century did

THE ROCOCO STYLE IN GERMANY. The dramatic exaggeration of the Baroque was made playful in German court architecture of the eighteenth century, as in this grand staircase, designed by Balthasar Neumann, in Augustusburg Castle at Brühl.

lucidity give way as an ideal to the ability to stir feeling. Curiously, it was the old English ballads and a deliberate fraud, *Ossian,* presented as a long-lost and newly discovered English saga, which first captured imaginations, in other countries as well as in Britain. Of more long-term importance was the work of the young *Sturm und Drang* poets in Germany, master craftsmen in verse who spoke to the soul rather than to the mind. Goethe and Schiller, greatest of them, also ventured into the drama; plays like Goethe's *Götz von Berlichingen* and Schiller's *The Robbers* imitated Shakespeare with not inconsiderable success. But eighteenth-century drama was at its best in comedy. The satires of the Italian Carlo Goldoni (1707–1793) and the Irish-born Richard Brinsley Sheridan (1751–1816) were among the most effective. In France the Rococo mood was brilliantly caught by Pierre de Marivaux (1688–1763), whose *The Game of Love and Chance* is all glitter but done to perfection. Social commentary came later, as in the two plays of Pierre Augustin Caron de Beaumarchais (1732–1799) featuring the character of Figaro. In *The Barber of Seville* and *The Marriage of Figaro* the criticism of the Enlightenment against privileges held by the titled orders at the expense of the common man's talents was expressed in the travails and ultimate triumphs of the barber-turned-valet, Figaro, over his lordly but inept employer, the Count of Almaviva.

The novel increased in popularity during this century. One of the new forms developed was the epistolary novel, in which two or more characters communicate the events of their lives as well as their thoughts and feelings in a series of letters. Subtle analysis of mood was achieved by Antoine François (Abbé) Prévost (1697–1763) in his *Manon Lescaut*, a tale of the thwarting of a simple girl's love for a young nobleman by his father, and her subsequent fall into a life of vice. Feeling became sentimentality in Samuel Richardson's (1689–1761) *Pamela* which won an enormous audience. It evoked in response the irony of unquenchable realism in Henry Fielding (1707–1754), especially in his *Tom Jones*. Realism was also the hallmark of the work of Daniel Defoe (1659?–1731). The narrative form also became the instrument for sardonic commentary upon the world in the philosophical tale. These included unforgettable masterpieces such as Voltaire's *Candide* and *Zadig*. Rousseau used the novel to present some of his most significant ideas, notably on education in *The New Héloïse*. In Germany it was again Goethe who used the novel form with consummate skill; when he was still young, he created works like *The Sorrows of Young Werther* which stirred the melancholy aspirations of a young generation that was beginning to tire of cold reason.

History gathered strength as a form of literature and a branch of learning. The sharp criticism of sources and their validity that Pierre Bayle (1647–1706) had displayed in his *Historical and Critical Dictionary* (1697) was a lesson to many historical writers; more attention was paid than before to the problems of evidence and plausibility. The Italian Vico had earlier made history the key to the understanding of mankind, but his work was not widely read in his own time because it generally lay outside the intellectual climate of the Enlightenment. For the philosophes, history continued to be primarily a form of moral edification, "philosophy teaching by example." Voltaire's *Age of Louis XIV*, Hume's *History of England*, *The Decline and Fall of the Roman Empire* of Edward Gibbon (1737–1794), Schiller's histories of the Revolt of the Netherlands and of the Thirty Years' War, were all in their various ways illustrations of philosophical themes. Voltaire's and Gibbon's histories have remained historical and literary masterpieces to this day because of their stylistic power and the force of their historical vision. Voltaire depicted an idealized reign of the Sun King, which he thought one of the supreme periods of history, when the monarchy was strong and culture prospered. Gibbon used his monumental history of the Roman Empire from its heights until the fall of Constantinople in 1453 to make Christianity the culprit in the degradation and loss of strength of a great civilization.

However, the belief that humanity remained essentially the same everywhere and at all times was dominant over the quest for the differences that mark off different peoples and different ages. A heightened taste for veracious history could be seen in the abandonment of rhetorical devices like spurious speeches. All historical writing, however, was hampered by its dependence on largely literary sources and memoirs, for the archives of states were seldom opened to the perilous curiosity of the historical searcher.

MUSIC

Least specific and yet most direct of the arts, music prospered and triumphed in the age of reason. The stringed instruments of the violin family were all re-designed and took on their modern form, achieving increased flexibility and force. Most wind instruments were also given approximately their modern designs. The harpsichord, in which the strings are plucked, was replaced by the clavichord, an early form of the modern piano, in which the strings are struck by hammers.

During the eighteenth century the central forms of modern instrumental music, the sonata and its large-scale form, the symphony, evolved out of the dance suite. Opera remained a static concert form for most of the century, with the principal emphasis upon florid singing. But Christoph Willibald Gluck (1714–1787) returned to Monteverdi's ideal of expressing feeling dramatically and musically at the same time in works like *Orpheus and Euridyce* which were full of passion for those who first heard them, however sedate they seem to a modern audience.

During the early part of the century music was composed predominantly in what is called the Baroque style by music historians, although that art style had long since passed in other arts. In music it meant emphasis upon ornamentation and delight in complication. But in the work of Johann Sebastian Bach (1685–1750), the Italian composers Arcangelo Corelli (1653–1713), Domenico Scarlatti (1683–1757), and Antonio Vivaldi (1680?–1743), and the Anglicized German George Frederick Handel (1685–1759), it also meant clarity of sound and unsurpassed expressiveness. Out of such work grew the Classical school of the later part of the century, with the figures of Joseph Haydn (1732–1804), Wolfgang Amadeus Mozart (1756–1791), and the young Ludwig van Beethoven (1770–1827) its supreme exponents. It enriched and developed the earlier musical forms, cast off merely florid ornament in favor of a more direct statement of ideas, and achieved a unique perfection in the balance of form and content. Haydn evolved the modern four-movement symphony for the full orchestra and the less emphatic but no less effective adaptation of the sonata form for the string quartet. His oratorios *The Creation* and *The Seasons* by their extraordinary vividness prepared the way for the romantic operas of the nineteenth century. Mozart followed Haydn in the use of the sonata form, moving during his short life to an ever-greater depth of expression. His operas, like *The Marriage of Figaro* and *Don Giovanni* in Italian and *The Magic Flute* in German, were not especially novel in form, but Mozart used the possibilities of the form with consummate craft. Beethoven's work falls mainly into the period of the revolutionary age and the early nineteenth century, but his early achievement brings the classic forms to their acme and displays a richness of feeling that was another harbinger of emerging romanticism.

Further Reading

*M. S. Anderson, *Europe in the Eighteenth Century, 1713–1789* (New York, 1961) is a good survey of the period. *The New Cambridge Modern History*, Volume VII, *The Old Regime, 1713–1763* (Cambridge, 1957) and Volume VIII, *The American and French Revolutions, 1763–1793* (Cambridge, 1965) have valuable chapters by noted specialists. Broadly conceived interpretations of the period are *P. Roberts, *The Quest for Security, 1715–1740* (New York, 1947); *W. L. Dorn, *Competition for Empire, 1740–1763* (New York, 1940); and *L. Gershoy, *From Despotism to Revolution, 1763–1789* (New York, 1944). R. R. Palmer, *The Age of the Democratic Revolution*, Volume I, *The Challenge* (Princeton, 1959) is a major interpretation of the decades before the revolution broke out in France.

*A. Goodwin, ed., *The European Nobility of the Eighteenth Century* (London, 1953) analyzes the governing class; while *G. Rudé, *The Crowd in History, 1730–1848* (New York, 1964) studies the people, especially as a violent intervener in politics.

Basic to a study of the Enlightenment thinkers is *E. Cassirer, *The Philosophy of the Enlightenment* (Boston, 1951); while M. Kraus, *The Atlantic Civilization: Eighteenth Century Origins* (Ithaca, 1949) includes both Europe and America in its view. *P. Hazard, *European Thought in the Eighteenth Century, from Montesquieu to Lessing* (New Haven, 1954) is systematic in scope and impressionistic in method. *C. Becker, *The Heavenly City of the Eighteenth Century Philosophers* (New Haven, 1932) emphasizes the element of faith in their thought; this theme is developed in C. W. Frankel, *The Faith of Reason: The Idea of Progress in the French Enlightenment* (New York, 1948). *K. Martin, *French Liberal Thought in the Eighteenth Century*, 2nd ed. (London, 1954) is by an admirer of the philosophes; while *J. L. Talmon, *The Origins of Totalitarian Democracy* (London, 1952) is highly critical. *R. R. Palmer, *Catholics and Unbelievers in Eighteenth-Century France* (Princeton, 1939) and *P. Gay, *Voltaire's Politics: The Poet as Realist* (Princeton, 1959) combine originality and soundness. P. Gay, *The Enlightenment: An Interpretation*, Volume I (New York, 1966) uses great learning to support challenging interpretations. On Rousseau see J. Guéhenno, *J. J. Rousseau*, 2 vols. (New York, 1966); and *E. Cassirer, *The Question of Jean-Jacques Rousseau* (New York, 1954). Other valuable biographies are *G. Lanson, *Voltaire* (New York, 1966); and A. M. Wilson, *Diderot: The Testing Years, 1713–1759* (New York, 1957). *F. E. Manuel, *The Prophets of Paris: Turgot, Condorcet, Saint-Simon, Fourier, Comte* (Cambridge, Mass., 1962) links the Enlightenment with nineteenth-century French social thought. L. Stephen, *History of English Thought in the Eighteenth Century*, 2 vols., 3rd ed. (New York, 1962) remains useful.

*A. Cobban, *A History of Modern France*, Volume I, *The Old Regime and the Revolution, 1715–1799*, 2nd ed. (Baltimore, 1962) is the best brief survey. H. Sée, *Economic and Social Conditions in France during the Eighteenth Century* (New York, 1927) requires some updating, but it is still a useful introduction. Important special studies are *F. L. Ford, *Robe and Sword: The Regrouping of the French Aristocracy after Louis XIV* (Cambridge, Mass., 1953); *E. Barber, *The Bourgeoisie in Eighteenth Century France* (Princeton, 1955); and D. Dakin, *Turgot and the Ancien Régime in France* (London, 1939).

*J. H. Plumb, *England in the Eighteenth Century* (Harmondsworth, 1950) is an outstanding survey; while B. Williams, *The Whig Supremacy, 1714–1760* (Oxford, 1939) is more detailed. R. Walcott, *English Politics in the Early Eighteenth Century* (Cambridge, Mass., 1956) furnishes the background for *L. B. Namier, *The Structure of English Politics at the Accession of George III,* 2 vols. (London, 1929) and *England in the Age of the American Revolution* (New York, 1930); while *R. Pares, *King George III and the Politicians,* rev. ed. (Oxford, 1963) also corrects traditional views. J. H. Plumb, *Chatham* (London, 1953) is a biography of England's greatest statesman of the century. S. Maccoby, *English Radicalism, 1762–1785* (London, 1955) and *G. Rudé, *Wilkes and Liberty* (Oxford, 1962) are essential for the new political forces.

*W. H. Bruford, *Germany in the Eighteenth Century* (Cambridge, 1935), as well as H. Holborn, *Modern German History,* Volume II, *1648–1840* (New York, 1963) are sound introductions. *H. Rosenberg, *Bureaucracy, Aristocracy, and Autocracy: The Prussian Experience, 1660–1815* (Cambridge, Mass., 1958) and R. A. Dorwart, *The Administrative Reforms of Frederick William I of Prussia* (Cambridge, Mass., 1953) analyze the creation of the Prussian state machinery and its political and social significance. The relevant chapters of *G. A. Craig, *The Politics of the Prussian Army, 1640–1945* (New York, 1955) are essential for this period. G. P. Gooch, *Frederick the Great: The Ruler, the Writer, the Man* (New York, 1947) is marked by cool respect. Austrian developments are studied in C. L. Morris, *Maria Theresa: The Last Conservative* (London, 1938); S. K. Padover, *The Revolutionary Emperor, Joseph the Second, 1741–1790* (New York, 1934); and E. Link, *The Emancipation of the Austrian Peasant, 1740–1792* (New York, 1949).

*B. H. Sumner, *Peter the Great and the Emergence of Russia* (London, 1950) is a brief but valuable sketch; I. Grey, *Peter the Great, Emperor of All Russia* (Philadelphia, 1960) is a full-scale biography; while *V. Klyuchevsky, *Peter the Great* (New York, 1959) is a subtle analysis of the tsar and the reign. *M. Raeff, *Origins of the Russian Intelligentsia: The Eighteenth-Century Nobility* (New York, 1966) and H. Rogger, *National Consciousness in Eighteenth-Century Russia* (Cambridge, Mass., 1960) are important special studies. I. Grey's *Catherine the Great* (Philadelphia, 1962) is by a specialist in Russian history; while *Z. Oldenbourg, *Catherine the Great* (New York, 1965) is brilliantly written by a distinguished novelist. G. P. Gooch, *Catherine the Great and Other Studies* (New York, 1954) is useful. For Poland see H. H. Kaplan, *The First Partition of Poland* (New York, 1962) and R. H. Lord, *The Second Partition of Poland* (Cambridge, Mass., 1915). R. Herr, *The Eighteenth Century Revolution in Spain* (Princeton, 1958) is an important reevaluation.

*A. Sorel, *Europe under the Old Regime* (Los Angeles, 1947) is a classic introduction to the European system of states; while A. T. Mahan, *The Influence of Sea Power upon History, 1660–1783* (Boston, 1890) is fundamental for the relation between naval and political power. R. Pares, *War and Trade in the West Indies, 1739–1760* (Oxford, 1936) is an important case study.

CHAPTER 14

The Age
of Revolution
1789–1815

The events in France in 1789 changed the very meaning of the word revolution. From an image of the eternal swing of man's fate up and down, as if he were bound to a point on a turning wheel, it became a metaphor for total and violent transformation. Some such shift had already been foreshadowed in England by the seventeenth-century revolution that failed, the Puritan revolt, and by the one that succeeded, the Glorious Revolution of 1688–1689. But only with the quarter-century of immense and multitudinous changes in the western world that began with the convening of the Estates General in France in 1789 did the idea of revolution come to encompass not only the system and the personnel of politics, but the whole range of economic, social, and intellectual life as well.

1. From an Old to a New Regime

HISTORICAL CHANGE seldom occurs with catastrophic instantaneity and did not in the age of the French Revolution: but fundamental changes did occur with a rapidity seldom recorded before in history. Western society was transformed from an Old Regime, based on a hierarchy of inequality and privilege sustained by law and custom, to a New Regime dedicated to equality and liberty, in law if not always in fact. Yet the Revolution of the West was not only a destroyer and innovator; it was also a continuator and preserver which brought to completion and accomplishment strivings of many decades and even centuries. But it did so in several new ways, adopted by the new government in France and by old governments elsewhere which found themselves compelled to adapt many of the revolutionary innovations in France in order to save themselves from defeat and overthrow.

Furthermore, the French Revolution brought to the very forefront of political debate the roles of violence and ideology in public affairs: ideology as the deliberate construction of a system of beliefs and values which defines the purpose and content of public life; and violence as the ultimate recourse of political action, long taught by Machiavelli to a Europe only half-willing to believe such diabolic doctrine. Although the pen was mightier than ever in an era of almost ceaseless revolts, it was strong only as it guided the sword of force: the force of mobs and the force of armies. Convictions again armed passions as they had done during the wars of religion of the sixteenth century, and Europe was again torn apart even more deeply. The problem of creating and maintaining law, peace, and order, since ancient times the goal of men of good will, seemed more insoluble than ever, but the goal itself became more desirable to the millions.

2. The Revolution in France, 1789–1799

As WITH ANY GREAT AND COMPLEX EVENT, but especially one whose consequences still affect the lives of men everywhere, the origins and causes of the French Revolution are much disputed. Nonetheless there are certain broad facts which are generally considered beyond dispute, as well as many specific details and general interpretations which are not.

THE CAUSES OF THE REVOLUTION

In one way or another historians distinguish the *immediate* from the *long-term* causes of the revolution, although the distinction has little logical validity. By long-term or fundamental causes historians mean the structure of society and government which not only gave rise to tension among the major elements of the French population but also made the effective solution of these conflicts increasingly difficult to achieve, even a solution based on the definitive victory of one group over another.

These *fundamental* causes have been implicit in our account of French history during the medieval and especially the early modern period, but they came more into the open during the eighteenth century. They include the closing off of entry into the ranks of the nobility—the acknowledged badge of elite status—for men of wealth and talent who had frequently been able to move upward in the immediately preceding centuries; the increase in numbers and economic power of businessmen and men in the professions caused by the rapid increase in commercial and industrial activity in the half-century since the end of the wars of Louis XIV, at the very time when the ability of these members of the bourgeoisie to influence political decisions was declining; the wide acceptance of the criticisms of merely traditional and customary practices put forward by the thinkers of the Enlightenment; the institution of venal office which ensured that efforts by the crown to bring about important reforms on its own initiative would meet adamant resistance from the very people called upon to carry them out; the attack upon the notion of royal omnipotence as equivalent to tyranny; the financial difficulties of the king's government which not only made it less and less possible for it to operate effectively, but also deprived it of freedom to maneuver; and finally the unwillingness of the government to accept a pacific and hence passive role in foreign affairs as the price for limiting expenditures and hence averting the otherwise virtually inescapable bankruptcy toward which the French monarchy was rushing.

The *immediate* causes which triggered the breakdown of absolute monarchy in 1789 were the crisis which hit the French royal treasury when French and European bankers refused to make any more loans to it after the failures of Necker, Brienne, and Calonne, Louis XVI's last three principal ministers, to find a way out of the crown's dilemma; and the economic depression which struck France during the decade of the 1780's after decades of dramatic economic advance. The decline resulted in part from years of bad harvests in the vineyards and the grain fields and in part from the market difficulties faced by French industry when English merchants were able to ship in goods almost without tariff hindrance after the trade treaty made with England in 1786, the so-called Eden Treaty. Economic difficulties, by reducing the effective tax base of the French treasury, compounded the difficulties France faced.

THE PREREVOLUTION

Nonetheless the revolution in France, in the specific sense of the loss of power by the absolute king, began with a rebellion not of the commoners but of the nobility, not of the third but of the second estate. As we have seen, the finance ministers from Turgot on had all seen clearly that the revenues of the state could be expanded only by bringing under taxation the immense properties of the clergy and nobility, although these ministers differed on the urgency of the need to reduce the expendi-

NE POUR LA PEINE

Reueille matin de Campagne

But des gens de Campagne Tailles payee

Collecteur

L'ABEILLE ny mouche à miel Chacun a part à ses trauaux

qu'iles animaux

LA VACHE

par son moyen lon boit et mange

LE COCHON

Il est meprisé et necessaire

du paysan

LA POULE

sa journée est d'un petit prix

attributs

L'acquisition

qui ne nourrit rien na rien

N. Guerard inv et fecit

L'homme de Village

Tous les jours au milieu d'un champ.　　Trauailler tant que lannée dure.
Par la chaleur par la froidure.　　Pour amasser par son labeur
Lon voit le pauure paysan.　　Dequoy payer le collecteur.

Se Vend à paris chez N. Guerard Graueur rüe St Jacques à la Reyne du Clergé proche St yues　C.P.R.

BORN FOR TOIL. The burden of the poor countryman, "born for toil," according to this contemporary cartoon, is to work every day, all year long, so that he can pay the tax collector, especially the *taille*.

tures of the crown and the court. But the first two orders were not ready to abandon their valuable privileges. Furthermore, the nobility, led by the parlements, had been struggling for decades and centuries to create in France a kind of constitutional monarchy in which the sovereignty would be shared by the crown and the estates, with the parlements standing in for the estates when they were not in session. Indeed, the fiscal crisis of the state itself intensified the demands of the nobility for an end to royal tyranny; if they had to give way on taxation to some extent, it would only be in exchange for the political means to protect their property rights and their special status against renewed threats of reform from above. Even as late as 1787 the principal danger to established privilege arose from the royal government and from ministers who themselves were usually noblemen but who had taken on, indeed had sought, the responsibility of directing the work of government.

This was the paradox of France on the eve of revolution: that the government seeking reform could do so only by means of an exercise of authority which was admittedly absolute and which its opponents called tyrannical; while the leading foes of such tyranny sought not freedom for all and participation in government by all, but freedom for themselves against both the reforming interventions of the crown and the egalitarian aspirations of commoners directed against the privileges of the first and second estates. Yet, when the aristocratic revolution began in 1787, aristocrats and consumers were still in their immense majority leagued against the tyranny of absolute government under the intellectual aegis of the Enlightenment. But this alliance against absolutism fell apart during the prerevolution of 1787–1789 when the government was compelled finally to call the Estates General into session. The demand of the parlement of Paris that the representative assembly continue to vote by order or chamber and not by head effectively blocked any possibility that the commoners could impose their solution to the crisis at the expense of both crown and privileged orders. However, the government acknowledged in part the legitimacy of the commoners' claims by conceding to them double membership to the chamber of the third estate.

THE TRANSFER OF POWER

The hesitancies and inconsistencies of royal policy under Louis XVI became only the more evident when the Estates General convened at Versailles in May in an atmosphere of great hopes for fundamental reform and improvement. These were soon dashed. Jacques Necker (1732–1804), the Genevan-born Protestant banker who was the king's principal minister and basked in the not-quite-deserved admiration of the multitude as a reformer, presented the government's policy. In a long and tedious speech, he proposed no program but only a reaffirmation of the government's needs. The initiative thus carelessly abandoned passed at once into the hands of the deputies of the third estate, who had been elected not only by urban businessmen and professionals but by virtually all commoners possessing property and paying direct taxes, including a majority of the peasantry. The deputies themselves were in the large majority lawyers and other professional men to whom the peasantry had habitually looked for leadership. The third estate at once demanded that the Estates General be reorganized as a single chamber in which their double number, reinforced by support from reform-minded deputies of the nobility and clergy, would carry the day. When this demand was not granted by the king, the third estate refused to carry on until unification of the three estates was ordered. The king, characteristically wilting before firmness, then instructed the three chambers to merge. The united body took the name of *National Assembly* and the task of writing a constitution for the country. When its constitution-writing function was emphasized, this assembly was also called the *Constituent Assembly*.

But the National Constituent Assembly, before it could begin effective work, had to face a challenge to its very existence and the personal liberty of its members. Louis XVI, still faithful to the image of government inherited from Louis XIV, began to respond to the appeals of his youngest brother, the count of Artois, and other diehard defenders of the Old Regime that he dismiss the National Assembly

JUSTICE TIPS THE SCALES. The Third Estate is shown in this cartoon as winning over the Clergy and the Nobility with the help of Justice, who "is on the side of the strong this time."

AP.

and arrest the troublemakers in its ranks. Troops were brought in from the frontier garrisons to posts near Versailles, and Necker, still the symbol of reform, was dismissed on July 11. An unanticipated response came from the populace of Paris who rose in rebellion on July 14, stormed the prison-fortress of the Bastille, seized the other strongholds of royal power, and demanded the restoration of Necker to office. Fearing to undertake a siege of Paris in arms, the king gave way: the National Assembly was saved, and the revolution moved on. The lesson had been well learned that force could be met by force, the force of regular troops by that of an armed populace. The news of the fall of the Bastille and the success of the Parisians in saving the revolutionary cause released a flood of enthusiasm not only in France but throughout the European world among all those whose minds were moved by the ideals of the enlightened philosophes and dreamed of freedom and a better world. At the same time the irreconcilable foes of the revolution in France, led by the counts of Artois and Provence, began to emigrate abroad.

THE NATIONAL CONSTITUENT ASSEMBLY

The lesson of July 14 on the uses of force had also been learned in the countryside. During July the peasantry in many parts of France rose in arms in a movement called *The Great Fear*. Nominally directed against marauding brigands, the movement was in fact a peasant rebellion against the landlords, their exactions and their power. Faced by this immense demand for the abolition of seignorialism (*feudalism* in the then-current terminology) and fearful of asking the king to use troops, yet troubled by any assault upon property (much manorial land and many seignorial rights were actually owned by bourgeois), the assembly during the night of August 4 decreed the abolition of feudalism, with compensation for such seignorial rights as were considered to be property rather than powers of local government. The peasantry largely disregarded such limitations. Seignorialism was effectively extinguished, although it was not until the National Convention ruled France in 1793 that its last vestiges were legally abolished. The destruction of feudalism, together with the transfers of landed property that ensued during the next years, made the majority of the peasantry staunch defenders of the new economic order; they became an essentially satisfied class neither desiring further revolutionary changes nor counter-revolution. On occasion, as in the Vendée in western France, they even joined counter-revolutionary forces in support of the church and in resistance to conscription.

The urban populace, especially in Paris, was anything but pacific. Fully aware now of their ability to use mob action, or the threat of it, to influence political developments, they intervened forcefully in events. In October 1789 a group of Paris women marched to Versailles to bring the king and his family to Paris, again the capital of France, where the monarch and his Austrian queen could be watched.

It was a far from pointless precaution, because the king's brothers and many noblemen had already gone into self-imposed exile and begun a campaign to persuade Louis XVI's fellow-rulers to invade France to restore his powers. Indeed, the king and queen were secretly corresponding with her brother, Emperor Leopold II, seeking such aid.

Meanwhile the National Assembly settled down to its work of writing a constitution while it legislated for current affairs. But it first set forth a Declaration of the Rights of Man and the Citizen, adopted August 27, 1789, which became the world-wide program of the New Regime. The declaration dismantled the Old Regime and its system of hierarchy and privilege; in its stead it established a world of equality, of free men under one law, and of a government that was not the master but the servant of a sovereign people. But it was an equality which consisted in the abolition of the old, privileged orders, not in the extinction of classes as such. The authors of the declaration took for granted the continued existence of rich and poor, of property owners and propertyless men, and they were wholly committed to the principle that only men of property should have political, as distinct from civil, rights.

This was the principle that was embodied in the constitution that was adopted by the Constituent Assembly in October 1790 but not ratified by the king until the next July. It declared all men to be citizens but gave the vote only to those who paid a moderate direct tax. Voters chose electoral assemblies that in turn named members of the new Legislative Assembly. The constitution formally confirmed the transformation of France into a limited, constitutional monarchy; the king became a hereditary chief executive, strictly bound by his dependence on the legislature which alone could grant tax revenues and enact laws, and over which he had only a suspensive veto.

The constitution included provisions for the reorganization of the Catholic church in France. The state was to take over church-owned lands as *national wealth,* and in exchange churchmen were assigned salaries to be paid out of the national treasury. But bishops and priests were to be elected by their districts, and not merely by lay Catholics but by all voters, Catholic or not; the Papacy would be notified of their election but have no right of rejection nor even of investiture: the battle lost by medieval German emperors against the Papacy was now being won by French revolutionaries. The so-called "national wealth" was of key importance in the effort to solve the fiscal crisis of the treasury; these former church lands were to be sold at auction and could be paid for by *assignats,* a kind of combination bond–and–paper money issued by the government to meet its obligations.

The constitution accomplished the dream of most philosophes—a political system based on the principles of liberty and equality—but whether revolution could generate fraternity among all Frenchmen, or between Frenchmen and other Europeans, still depended upon the ability of the king and the people of France to make the new constitution work.

DECLARATION OF THE RIGHTS OF MAN. This contemporary print gives the text of the Declaration of the Rights of Man and the Citizen, adopted by the National Assembly in France on August 27, 1789.

The prospects for such collaboration were poor. The king, who had been browbeaten into accepting the constitution despite the inclusion of the civil constitution of the clergy, finally attempted to flee the country in June 1791. Caught with his family at Varennes, not far from the frontier, he was brought back to Paris a virtual prisoner but reinstated because the dominant political party of constitutional monarchists needed a king, even despite Louis's obvious reluctance to play his assigned part.

THE LEGISLATIVE ASSEMBLY

As was to be expected, the experiment did not work. The issue of the king's position and his safety became paramount. The monarch continued his secretive efforts to obtain support from his fellow-rulers abroad, even suggesting that a war would provide a pretext for invasion and rescue. A group of moderate republicans, called *Girondins* (because some of their leaders came from the department of the Gironde, around Bordeaux), faced savage criticism from the more extreme republicans (called the *Mountain* because they occupied the higher rows of seats in the Legislative Assembly). The Girondins came to look on war as a means of rallying the country behind them and discomfiting their rivals, monarchists on the right and Mountain on the left.

War finally came only after the rulers to whom Louis and Marie Antoinette had appealed for help were nudged into a position they did not want to take. Frederick William II of Prussia and Leopold II of Austria made a sly effort to evade pressure for a combined invasion of France by issuing a declaration at Pillnitz on August 27, 1791 that they would undertake intervention when and if all powers, including England, agreed to join in the alliance—which London then had no intention of doing. The subtlety of this evasion escaped the French revolutionaries, however, who took the Pillnitz warning at face value as a threat of invasion. The Girondins, the party of bellicose republicans, had to be given control of the government by the king, and they responded to the establishment of a formal alliance between Austria and Prussia in February 1792 by a declaration of war upon them on April 20.

Thus far the revolution had been driven forward at key moments by the violence of the populace; now the far greater difficulties of foreign war became an even more important force in the development of the revolutionary situation. The cocky assurance of the Girondins was soon destroyed when the French armies, led in large part by generals and officers who saw the revolutionary regime as their true enemy, suffered a series of military defeats. By mid-June the Girondin ministry had fallen from power, and the mob attacked the royal palace of the Tuileries. The Prussian commander-in-chief then threatened to destroy Paris if the royal family were harmed, but he miscalculated as badly as the Girondins before him; the king was seized on August 10, and a provisional government was formed which ordered election of a Convention.

Like the National Constituent Assembly three years earlier, the Convention had the task of writing a new constitution—but on a republican basis—and governing the country in the interim. In September monarchist suspects held in prison in Paris and other cities were massacred by mobs enforcing the verdicts of improvised tribunals. A pattern of terror was initiated that was to mark the revolution for the next two years. But the victory of a French army composed of regulars and volunteers over Prussian invaders at Valmy on September 20 demonstrated that the revolution could at last defend itself effectively on the battlefield.

THE CONVENTION

The Convention met on September 21 and declared the monarchy abolished and the republic established. Enormous tasks faced the new assembly. Invading armies were still encamped on France's northern and eastern frontiers, and the economic crisis which had helped bring on the revolution three years before had only been made worse by continuing political disorder. The armed populace of Paris, which had now twice broken the resistance of counter-revolution, was a powerful force. Suffering increasing hardships, the Parisians demanded governmental measures to assure their bread and vigorous action against all suspected of collusion or sympathy with the invaders; they were ready to use the weapon of mob violence again to gain their will. In the meanwhile the municipal government of Paris was in their hands.

The support of the radical Parisians enabled the Mountain, led by Maximilian Robespierre (1758–1794), to overthrow the Girondins who had become the conservative party within the Convention. Robespierre brought personal integrity of character—he was called *The Incorruptible*—and fervent revolutionary ideas to the leadership of France. His ideal, and that of the Jacobin party, was a calm, peaceful, and sedate society of men of modest property, living the life of reason, adoring the deists' God, and practicing justice upon earth. Those who did not share this image of the heavenly city, and even more those who disagreed with him about the way to achieve it—by the violent destruction of all enemies of the revolution—had themselves to be destroyed. He believed wholeheartedly in the sovereignty of the people taught by Rousseau in the *Social Contract,* but he saw democratic government as a thing to be put into effect only when the revolution had been triumphant over all enemies, domestic and foreign. In the interim, while the war against invaders and counter-revolutionary rebels continued, the Convention, more specifically the Committee of Public Safety, and ultimately Robespierre himself, leading the Jacobin party, had to wield power in dictatorial fashion.

French armies at first continued to win victories after the Jacobins took power. The revolutionary troops drove out the invaders and brought the German Rhineland and the Austrian Netherlands (Belgium) under their power. The break with France's monarchial past was made total and irreparable by the trial and execution of Louis XVI, found guilty of treason to the nation by a bare majority of the Convention in January 1793.

The execution of the king was followed almost at once by a declaration of war against Great Britain, the United Netherlands, and Spain (who, together with Prussia and Austria, formed the First Coalition against France). At the same time Belgium was formally annexed. Not only was revolutionary France deliberately increasing the number of its foes, but it was embarked upon a program of territorial aggrandizement which would make immensely more difficult the eventual task of reestablishing peace. To make matters worse, revolutionary bravado was again quickly punished by a series of military reverses. On the Belgian front, the French commander, General Charles Dumouriez (1739–1823), actually went over to the Austrians. A royalist revolt erupted in the western region of the Vendée, where the peasants remained faithful to the nobility and the church and were bitterly hostile to the calling up of troops.

THE REIGN OF TERROR

The Jacobins reacted to the new perils by organizing a revolutionary government for this emergency; it was composed of two executive committees, the Committee of Public Safety and the Committee of General Security. The Committee of Public Safety, led by Robespierre, became the effective ruler of France for a year. It mobilized the energies of the French nation for the task of waging war against the external and internal enemies of the revolution.

The Committee of Public Safety did not rely merely upon the fervor of its supporters but instituted a Reign of Terror—dictatorial government enforced by frequent use of imprisonment and the guillotine (the new scientific method of beheading by machine instead of by sword). Terror was employed not only against competitors and dissenters within the government; Girondins and Parisian extremists alike went to the guillotine. A *law of the maximum* established a ceiling on prices of essential commodities, and supplies were acquired by ruthless requisitioning and were paid for by constantly inflated paper money (assignats). Members of the Convention were sent on special missions to the armies and rebellious provinces to supervise the work of regular authorities and to assure victory by making death the price of defeat. A mass levy of the male population provided the armies with recruits by the hundred thousand.

A new, strongly democratic constitution was adopted in June 1793, but Robespierre proclaimed the principle of democratic dictatorship—that democracy had to be defended in the crisis by means of dictatorship, for "there is no liberty for the enemies of liberty." Hence the constitution of 1793 was enshrined but never applied. Meanwhile measures to complete the revolution and transform the old world into the new were introduced: a revolutionary calendar based on weeks of ten days and renamed months was established and remained in use until the early years of the Napoleonic empire; quasi-religions, the Cult of the Supreme Being and the Cult of Reason replaced outlawed Christianity; the institutional reforms begun by the National Assembly, like the abolition of the last vestiges of feudalism and seignorialism, were completed.

The divisions among the population over religion, already exacerbated by the disputes over the civil constitution of the clergy and the measures of reprisal against churchmen who refused to swear allegiance to it as well as to the political constitution, were further envenomed by the new hostility to Christianity. The various rationalist and deist cults fostered by Robespierre and his successors until the end of the decade were particularly blasphemous in the eyes of devout Catholics because of the otherwise ludicrous imitation of Catholic rites in the new ceremonies. The anti-Christian cults won the revolution few if any new friends but turned against it many, especially among the peasantry who wanted to remain loyal to the old church even while they enjoyed the benefit of the revolution's political and economic changes. The long-term consequences were equally significant; for the dispute between Christians and anti-clericals deepened the cleavage between those to whom the revolution was history's greatest achievement and those to whom it was its worst abomination. Often during the next century and a half the division was to become an abyss which could not be bridged.

The combination of impassioned endeavor and unrestrained terrorism brought the desired results. The allies were first slowed and then forced to withdraw from France; by the summer of 1794 the French revolutionary armies again occupied Belgium and the Rhineland. Yet it was a triumph which undid Robespierre, for only the threats of invasion by counter-revolutionary armies had persuaded a majority in the Convention to accept his boundless rule of terror, his desire to create a "republic of virtue," and his willingness to compromise with the demands of the poor. Victory ended Robespierre's spell, and on July 27 he and his companions were denounced and condemned by the Convention and executed the next day.

The revolution was not yet at an end, but a fundamental impetus of the revolutionary movement had been taken away—the aspiration to build a heavenly city upon earth, a utopia of perfect government and perfect men. The Thermidoreans (so called because July 27 was the 9th Thermidor in the revolutionary calendar) had no such ideal, but only the coldly realistic purpose of consolidating the gains of the revolution and their own. They wanted France to be ruled by the men of property and education who constituted the bourgeoisie. They wanted no more of popular uprisings and interference with the normal course of business. Hence they repealed the law of the maximum and used troops to put down attacks upon the Thermidorean Convention by discontented mobs. But neither did they want the restoration of the Old Regime—neither the return of confiscated church lands and noble estates to the old owners, nor the reestablishment of absolute monarchy and privileged orders.

At the same time the Thermidoreans were unwilling to pay the price their foreign opponents demanded for the peace which could have made such consolidation of the revolution possible. The Thermidoreans were enthusiastic patriots, proud that revolutionary France had extended the nation's territories far beyond what even Louis XIV had achieved, and they were determined to accept no peace which involved the abandonment especially of Belgium—that corner of Europe for which the Grand Monarch had fought so long and with such limited success. But as long as the French held Belgium, the enmity of England was certain, and the wealth and strength of Great Britain was the heart of all the coalitions that were formed against France from 1792 until 1815. Thus, although Prussia and Spain made peace with France in 1795 and Holland became a satellite republic, general peace seemed no nearer at hand.

THE DIRECTORY

The Thermidoreans consolidated their authority by adopting a new constitution. The new government was called the Directory, after its executive board of five *directors*. A council of 250 *ancients* and a *Council of Five Hundred* shared legislative power in such a way that a renewal of the kind of legislative omnipotence held by the Convention would be impossible. The directors effectively solved the problem of consolidating the institutional achievements of the revolution and of restoring monetary and economic order so far as this was possible under conditions of continuing war. The assignats, having suffered astronomic inflation, were withdrawn in favor of a more stable paper money directly convertible into land. The willingness of the new government to employ armed force against the populace enabled it to begin effective collection of taxes, far beyond the capacity of any revolutionary government since 1789.

There were two fundamental problems which the Directory could not solve. The first was to find an adequate political base for itself. Convinced and dedicated republicans were reluctant to support the Directory because they thought it had betrayed the revolution by abandoning its utopian ideals; the flagrant corruption and flaunted self-indulgence of the dominant party offended moralists who remembered Robespierre's incorruptibility. On the other hand, monarchists, of whom there remained large numbers despite all the efforts of Jacobin propaganda and terror, looked upon the directors as a band of irredeemable republicans who might be made use of but would be discarded as soon as the monarchists could obtain a majority in the two councils. The directors meanwhile were engaged in destructive rivalry among themselves. Political victory came to rest neither in elections, which were quickly undone when, as always, they turned out wrongly for those in power, nor even in votes of the legislature, but in the intervention of the force of the army. Its support enabled one or another group of directors to win out in a series of coups d'état that marked the five-year history of the regime of the Directory. More and more, therefore, the inability of republicans to create stable government upon the basis of their own principles put the effective decisions about politics into the hands of generals.

The role of the generals was becoming steadily more important in other respects. The armies drew their resources not so much from the French national treasury as from the territories which they occupied and exploited ruthlessly. Few political leaders thought back to the perils run by the Habsburg emperor during the Thirty Years' War because his army was not only commanded but also created and paid by Wallenstein whose financial independence made possible his political disobedience. Furthermore, the military commanders were in the politically advantageous position of winning campaigns, while peace, which would reduce their powers and prerogatives, remained distant as long as England could not be defeated.

The most successful of the Directory's generals was the Corsican Napoleon Bonaparte (1769–1821). In the Italian campaign of 1796–1797, he swept the Austrians out of the peninsula and imposed upon the emperor the treaty of Campo-Formio, which ceded Belgium and the left bank of the Rhine to France. Yet Bonaparte's expedition to Egypt in 1798–1799, designed to cut England's trade route to India, despite initial successes ended in debacle after the English admiral Horatio Nelson (1758–1805) destroyed the French fleet at Abukir Bay (August 1, 1798).

The immediate result of this triumph was the reconstitution of the alliance against France. The Second Coalition included England as always, together with Russia, Austria, and some lesser states, but neither Spain nor Prussia. The tide of battle remained uncertain until the Russians, who had penetrated to Italy and Switzerland, quarreled with the Austrians and left the alliance. Meanwhile political crisis had broken out again in France and the directors Emanuel Joseph Sieyès (1748–1836) and Roger Ducos (1748–1816) turned to General Bonaparte, who had returned alone from Egypt, to provide military assistance in putting down hostility from their fellow directors and the legislative councils. The coup d'état of 18th Brumaire (November 9, 1799) went off successfully and Bonaparte became First Consul of a new government devised by Sieyès. A general had become the head of the republic.

3. *The Revolution in Europe, 1789–1799*

EMIGRATION AND COUNTER-REVOLUTION

For Europe the revolution in France began with the storming of the Bastille on July 14, 1789, rather than with the assembly of the Estates General on May 5. Just as the Enlightenment had to some extent won the minds of almost all educated men, so the revolution was greeted as the birth of a new freedom and the beginning of a new era in which the ideals of the Enlightenment would be made real in France. Just what the common man with few worldly possessions and little education thought is hard to say: most, probably, heard very little or nothing about the events in that far-off land.

But the rulers and ministers of state were not dismayed or fearful at this time that their own peoples would follow French example, except of course in the Austrian Netherlands where revolt had broken out against the enlightened despotism of Joseph II even before revolution started in France. The nearer their states lay to France, the more relieved were the rulers; for what they saw happening was not so much a new class coming to power in Paris as the laming of the power of the French kingdom, the most powerful state on the continent of Europe. They saw in the French troubles an opportunity to achieve ambitions which France otherwise might have been able to thwart. This was especially true of Prussia and Austria, which were in the midst of suspicion-filled negotiations with Russia directed toward another partition of Poland. England, too, saw the crisis in France, which left her greatest rival without effective government, as an opportunity to complete British dominion of the seas and overseas lands. Bourbons ruled in Spain but there was little affection left between the two branches of the dynasty, and the Iberian kingdom itself was gripped by the ugly comedy of a simpleton king and a wayward queen whose lover was her royal husband's chief minister.

Those who preached a crusade against revolutionary France were far away, at the ends of Europe. One was Gustavus III (1771–1792) of Sweden, a one-time philosophe faced with conspiracies among his own nobility (he was to be slain by a plotter at a masked ball). The other was Catherine II of Russia, cured for some time now of her flirtation with the Enlightenment. She hated revolutionary ideas and hoped to entrap her rivals in Poland, the Prussian king and the emperor, in trouble with France, thereby leaving her with free hands in Poland. But neither Prussia nor Austria was ready to fall into Catherine's trap, nor were they ready to give more than a clucking sympathy to the appeals of the French royal princes and aristocrats who fled their homeland to take refuge abroad, particularly in the Rhineland, and proclaimed the restoration of their rights and the king's to be the cause of all Europe. But neither could they bring themselves to scorn openly the pathetic

TWO FACES OF COUNTER-REVOLUTION. This cartoon, as seen on the *left,* depicts a disgruntled figure entitled "An Aristocrat Cursing the Revolution"; when turned upside down, *right,* he becomes the leering figure entitled "An Aristocrat Believing in the Counter-Revolution."

appeals from the royal couple in Paris or the incessant demands for action from the émigrés, most of whom were dependent for their livelihood upon gifts from those to whom they were teaching their duty. But the decision to satisfy these demands by hard words instead of action misfired, for, as we have seen (see above, page 555), the threats, however insincerely meant, were taken seriously and led to terror and war.

The fighting against revolutionary France turned the other states into a counter-revolutionary block, especially after sympathizers with the French began to be active. The ideological threat from France was felt more sharply, and measures for the repression of Jacobins were adopted in Austria, England, Spain, Italy, and Germany. The episode of enlightened despotism came to a swift and total halt; the lines were now clearly drawn for and against Voltaire and Rousseau, for and against revolutionary France, for and against the New Regime. The old competition between nobility and crown, which had been the primary political contest of the Old Regime in most of Europe for untold centuries, was ended by the discovery of a common interest in defeating the revolutionaries, with their slogans of liberty, equality, and fraternity.

The Englishman Edmund Burke (1729–1797), who had defended the American colonists in their rebellion against England because he saw their cause as the preservation of the historic rights of free-born Englishmen, led the intellectual assault against the doctrines of the French Revolution. In part Burke's *Reflections on the Revolution in France,* written only months after the fall of the Bastille, was an expression of the offended vanity of a social climber; but the book was more important by far than a mere outburst of snobbish venom against the insolence of the poor and the unwashed who dared to insult a queen. It was directed against the argument of the English radical Dr. Joseph Priestley, better known as the great chemist who first discovered oxygen, that all legitimate power, like that of the king of England, depended upon a grant from the sovereign people. To this Burke replied with a denial that the king of England held his rule upon such a basis; history and the practice of ages were its true source. Tradition was the proper teacher of social wisdom, pure reason no more than a false guide.

Although not immediately influential, Burke's philosophical exposition of the principles of political and social conservatism became the starting point of a whole series of similar works in the revolutionary era, notably by the German Friedrich von Gentz (1764–1832), the Savoyard Joseph de Maistre (1753–1821), and the Frenchman Louis de Bonald (1754–1840). But it was a conservatism different from that which had characterized almost all political theories before the Enlightenment; adherents of sixteenth- and seventeenth-century revolutionary movements had argued that they were restoring the past which their innovating opponents had destroyed. The conservative thinkers of the revolutionary epoch, on the contrary, made the doctrine of progress their central target, denying both the possibility and the desirability of deliberate, planned improvement of the human condition.

EXPORT OF REVOLUTION

The debate was not limited to the arena of theoretical treatises, however. French revolutionary armies carried with them the institutions of the New Regime, while the armies of the coalitions restored those of the old society. The new French order was introduced all down the line in the territories annexed by France. Elsewhere French conquest brought not outright incorporation into the French Republic but the destruction of the old governments and the establishment of new regimes under the leadership of the adherents of enlightened reform. Such regimes were the Batavian Republic which replaced the government of stadholder and estates in the United Netherlands in 1795, the Helvetic Republic created in Switzerland in 1798, and a series of frequently reorganized republics in Italy.

These governments lived under the shelter of French military might and had to accept the plundering of their countries by their protectors. But the attitude of most of their leaders was mixed; they were seldom mere imitators of the French but usually represented indigenous movements of some importance. They accepted French rule because in practice they had no choice, but they sought to limit the

French exploitation, although without much success. In most cases, French defeat meant jail or death for them. They were often compelled by French generals and commissioners to readjust their constitutions to follow the systems evolved in France during changes there; but they were encouraged, and sometimes required, to carry through fundamental social and economic changes: the abolition of serfdom and feudalism, of titles of nobility and privileged orders, and the creation of more or less representative governments. Yet, because they seldom had the support of more than a minority of their own peoples, they dared not accept the verdict of elections or even permit honest balloting. Harbingers of the transformations that would reshape their countries during the nineteenth century, defenders though they were of the rights of the sovereign people, at least in principle, they have seldom been honored by later generations of nationalist historians who felt more sharply the indignity of collaboration with an invader than the desirability of the creation of the New Regime. Thus the situation created for Europe by the wide-ranging conquests of Napoleon was prefigured by the status of the satellite republics during the regimes of the Convention and the Directory.

4. Napoleon: The Revolutionary Emperor, 1799–1815

THE CONSULATE

The overthrow of the Directory in France, brought about at the instigation of Sieyès by General Bonaparte, initiated a new stage in the revolutionary development of France. Bonaparte seized the opportunity provided by the overthrow of the Directory to build a personal grandeur and glory that compelled the admiration of millions throughout Europe and the world, even among those who feared and hated him. He was a man of keen intelligence and driving will who exercised a magical charm upon those who came into contact with him, especially after he wielded the full power of the state. He saw the French nation as the instrument for achieving his own greatness and played with skill upon the patriotic fervor of Frenchmen. He despised the revolutionary ideology of the past decade and brutally used his police to shackle all forms of free expression in the press, the theater, and meetings. His spies penetrated every part of society, for he trusted no group and no man, especially those who displayed signs of nostalgia for political and intellectual liberties. Napoleon I (as Bonaparte was called after he took the title of emperor in 1804) dominated France with the force of his personality and power as not even Louis XIV, the Grand Monarch, had been able to do.

The transformation in economic and social institutions during the previous decade was consolidated in the fifteen years of Napoleon's rule in the form in which

19. ITALIAN COMEDIANS. Antoine Watteau, supreme master of pictorial worlds in which Rococo elegance is tinged with sadness for fleeting happiness, catches in this picture of a group of Italian actors—players in the *commedia dell' arte*—the charm and, more subtly, the tragedy of their life.

EUROPE IN 1721
After the treaty of Utrecht, 1713,
and Associated Treaties

Miles 0   50   100   200   300

——— Boundary of Holy Roman Empire
×   ×   Dutch Barrier Forts

Atlantic

Ocean

SHETLAND ISLANDS

Bergen

ORKNEY ISLANDS

Stavanger

North

Sea

HEBRIDES

SCOTLAND Aberdeen

KINGDOM

Edinburgh
Glasgow

OF

Belfast

GREAT   BRITAIN

IRELAND Dublin

York

(To Hanover

NETHERLANDS

Liverpool

Nottingham

WALES   ENGLAND

Norwich

THE UNITED

Amsterdam

Cork

Cambridge
Oxford

The Hague
Utrecht

Bristol

London

Ryswick

AUSTRIAN

Plymouth

Portsmouth Dunkirk

Antwerp
Neerwinden

Aache

BEACHY HEAD

Thames

Oudenarde
Lille

Ramillies

English Channel

LA
HOGUE

Rouen

Fontenoy

NETHERLANDS

Malplaquet

(1714)

Brest

St. Malo

Paris

Reims

Seine

Nancy

Lorient

LORRAINE

Strassbu

Orléans

Nantes

Tours

Loire

Besançon

Basel

FRANCE

Rochefort

Limoges

Lyon

Geneva

Bay

Angoulême

SAVOY

of

Tur

Biscay

Bordeaux

Garonne

CAPE FINISTERRE

Bayonne

Toulouse

Montpellier

Avignon

(To the
Pope)

PIE

Marseille

Toulon

Oporto

PYRENEES

Burgos

Ebro

CATALONIA

Valladolid

Duero

Saragossa

Barcelona

CO
(To

Madrid

Alcantara

Tagus

SPAIN

Toledo

Valencia

SARDIN
(To Hapsburgs
(To Savoy 17

Lisbon

Guadiana

(To Bourbons, 1713)

BALEARIC ISLANDS

MINORCA
(To Great Britain 1713)

Guadalquivir

MAJORCA

CAPE ST. VINCENT

Seville

Granada

Cartagéna

Medit

Cadiz

CAPE TRAFALGAR

Gibraltar
(To Great Britain
1713)

Algiers

KINGDOM OF SWEDEN

FINLAND

20°

30°

40°

L. Ladoga

Nystad
Åbo
Helsingfors
Viborg
KARELIA
St. Petersburg
INGRIA
Novgorod

Uppsala

Gulf of Finland
Narva
ESTONIA
LIVONIA
(To Russia 1721)
Riga

RUSSIAN EMPIRE

nia

Stockholm

GOTLAND

Baltic Sea

COURLAND

Dvina

Vitebsk
Smolensk

Moscow

Calmar

Copenhagen
Lund

Memel

LITHUANIA

Niemen

Vilna

Minsk

K

(To Prussia 1720)
Königsberg
Danzig

PRUSSIA

Grodno

Dnieper

50°

mburg

Stettin

BRANDENBURG
Berlin
Zorndorf

(King of Prussia)
Oder

Thorn

Posen

Warsaw

POLAND

Kiev

Kharkov

Poltava

SAXONY
Glogau
Leipzig
Dresden

Elbe

SILESIA
Breslau

Lublin

Bar

Targovitza

Bug

HOLY
ROMAN
EMPIRE

Prague

BOHEMIA
MORAVIA

Cracow

Lemberg

Dniester

Czernowitz

Cherson

erg

AUSTRIA

BAVARIA
Munich

Vienna

Salzburg

Danube

Buda
Pest

Thiss

KINGDOM OF HUNGARY

MOLDAVIA

BESSARABIA

CRIMEA

ruck

TYROL

Laibach
Trieste

Drave

Agram

Zenta

Temesvar
BANAT
(To Hapsburgs 1718)

TRANSYLVANIA

Prut

ona

Po

Venice

REPUBLIC OF VENICE

CROATIA

SLAVONIA

Karlowitz

Belgrade
Passarowitz
(To Hapsburgs 1718-1739)

WALLACHIA

Bucharest

Silistria

Danube

Black Sea

Bologna

PAPAL STATES

Adriatic Sea

BOSNIA

Sarajevo

SERBIA
Nish
Sofia

BULGARIA

Florence
TUSCANY

Tolentino

Ragusa

MONTENEGRO

OTTOMAN EMPIRE

Adrianople

Constantinople

40°

Rome

KINGDOM OF NAPLES
(To Hapsburgs 1714-1735)

Bari

Salonika

Naples

Otranto

CORFU
(CORCYRA)

Aegean Sea

Smyrna

Tyrrhenian Sea

Palermo
Reggio

Athens

MOREA
(To Ottoman Empire 1718)

Syracuse
SICILY
(To Savoy 1714)
(To Hapsburgs 1720-35)

ean

Sea

CRETE

20°

Copyright by Rand McNally & Company, Made in U.S.A.

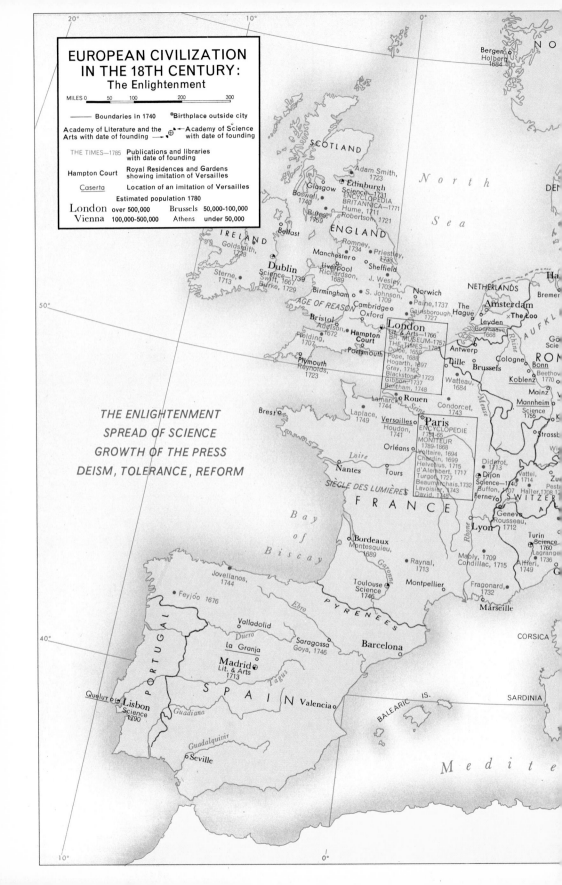

EUROPEAN CIVILIZATION IN THE 18TH CENTURY:
The Enlightenment

MILES 0   50   100   200   300

——— Boundaries in 1740   • Birthplace outside city

Academy of Literature and the   ⊕ ← Academy of Science
Arts with date of founding   →   with date of founding

THE TIMES—1785   Publications and libraries
                  with date of founding

Hampton Court   Royal Residences and Gardens
                 showing imitation of Versailles

Caserta   Location of an imitation of Versailles

                 Estimated population 1780
London over 500,000   Brussels 50,000-100,000
Vienna 100,000-500,000   Athens   under 50,000

THE ENLIGHTENMENT

SPREAD OF SCIENCE

GROWTH OF THE PRESS

DEISM, TOLERANCE, REFORM

Bergen
Holberg
1684

N O

North Sea

DE

SCOTLAND

Adam Smith,
1723
Glasgow   Edinburgh
           Science—1731
Boswell,   ENCYCLOPEDIA
1740   BRITANNICA—1771
           Hume, 1711
Burns,   Robertson, 1721
1759

Belfast   ENGLAND

IRELAND

Goldsmith,
1728

Sterne,   Dublin   Romney,
1713   Science—1739   1734   • Priestley,
           Swift, 1667   Manchester   1733
           Burke, 1729   Liverpool • Sheffield
                           Richardson,
Birmingham   1689
           • S. Johnson,
AGE OF REASON 1709   Norwich   NETHERLANDS   Bremen
           Cambridge o   Amsterdam
           Oxford   • Paine,1737 The
           Gainsborough The Hague Leyden × The Loo
Bristol   1727   Boerhaave
Addison,   Hampton   1668   Go
1672   Fielding,   Court   London   Scie
           1707   Lit. & Arts—1766 Antwerp Cologne ROM
Plymouth   Portsmouth BR. MUSEUM—1753   Bonn Beethov
Reynolds,   THE TIMES—1784 Lille Brussels 1770
1723   Defoe, 1659   Koblenz
                                   Pope, 1688
                                   Hogarth, 1697   Mainz
Brest o   Gray, 1716   Mannheim
                   Lamarck,   Blackstone, 1723   Science
                   1744 Rouen   Gibbon, 1737   1755
           Laplace,   Bentham, 1748
           1749   Versailles Condorcet,
           Houdon,   1743   Strass
           1741   Paris
           Orléans ENCYCLOPEDIE   Diderot,   Wi
                   1751-65   1713
           Loire   MONITEUR   Vattel,
Nantes   Tours   1789-1868 Dijon   1714   Zu
                   Voltaire, 1694 Science—1740 Pest
SIÈCLE DES LUMIÈRES Chardin, 1699 Buffon, 1707 Halter,1708 1
                   Helvetius, 1715   Ferney o SWITZER
           F R A N C E d'Alembert, 1717
                   Turgot, 1727   Geneva   A
           Bay   Beaumarchais,1732 Rousseau,
           of   Lavoisier, 1743   1712
           Biscay David, 1748
                                   Lyon   Turin
                                           Science
Bordeaux   1760
Montesquieu,   Lagrange
1689   • Raynal,   Mably, 1709   Alfieri,
           1713   Condillac, 1715 1736
Jovellanos,   1749
1744   Toulouse   Montpellier   Fragonard, G
           Science   Fragonard, 1732
• Feyjóo 1676 1746   1732   Marseille

Valladolid   CORSICA

La Granja Saragossa
           Goya, 1746
Madrid   Barcelona
Lit. & Arts
1713   SARDINIA
S P A I N Valencia o
                   BALEARIC IS.
Quelux o Lisbon
          Science
          1790 Guadiana

Seville   M e d i t e r

20°   10°   0°

50°

40°

10°   0°

SWEDEN

20°   30°

St. Petersburg
Science—1725
Peterhof ◦Tsarskoe Selo
        Slutsk

↑ Lomonosov, 1711
(Near the White Sea)

Upsala ⊕
Science
1728

◦Stockholm
Science—1741
Drottningholm
Swedenborg, 1688

Volga

◦Moscow
Radischev,
1749

Linnaeus,
1707

⊙Copenhagen
Science 1743

Dvina

RUSSIA

Baltic Sea

Niemen

◦Königsberg
Kant, 1724

• Herder, 1744

POLAND

—50°

Winckelmann
• 1717 Berlin
Y—   Science
Potsdam   1700
ck   Lit.& Arts
            1703
• Handel 1685   Charlottenburg
◦Weimar   • Lessing,
Erfurt   1729
science   Dresden
1754
MANACH DE   ◦Prague
GOTHA—1778
• Gluck, 1714

Vistula

Warsaw•

◦Breslau
Wolff,
1679

Cracow◦ CARPATHIANS

Oder

Dnieper

uremberg

IRE   AUSTRIA

Dniester

ymphenburg   *Danube*
◦Munich   Vienna⊙
Science   Lit. & Arts
1759   1704   Haydn,
Salzburg   Schönbrunn 1732 Budao Pest
Mozart,
1756

HUNGARY

*Black
Sea*

Canova,
• 1757
ona

◦Venice
Tiepolo, 1696
Goldoni, 1707

ologna
science
1712
orence

Adriatic Sea

Constantinople

—40°

LUMINISMO   • Galiani,
                1728
ome

ITALY

OTTOMAN

EMPIRE

Naples ◦ • Pompeii
Vico, 1668 Ruins discovered
Filangieri,   1748
1752

Caserta

*Aegean
Sea*

*yrrhenian
Sea*

*Ionian
Sea*

•Athens

◦Palermo

SICILY

ean   *Sea*

CRETE

20°

30°

Copyright by Rand McNally & Company. Made in U.S.A.

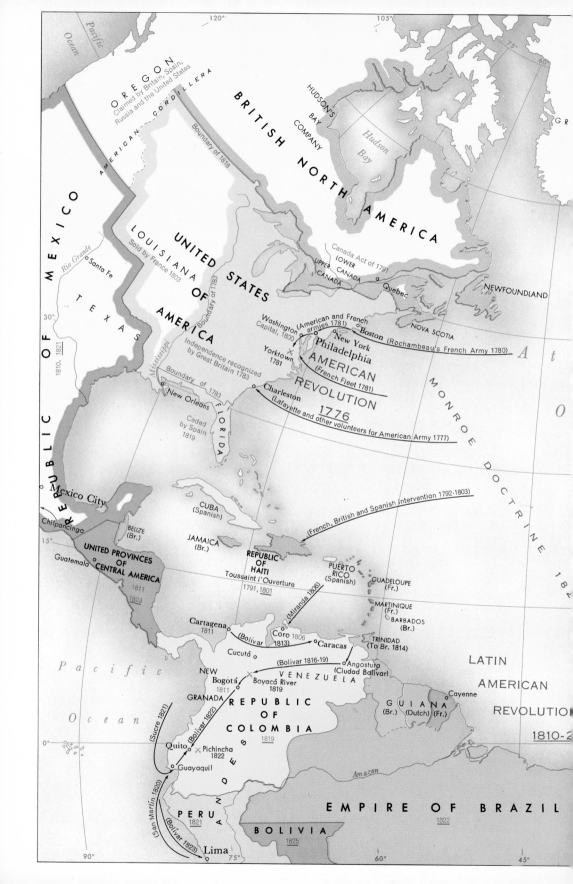

Pacific Ocean

OREGON
Claimed by Britain Spain,
Russia and the United States

AMERICAN CORDILLERA

Boundary of 1818

BRITISH NORTH AMERICA

HUDSON'S BAY COMPANY

Hudson Bay

G R

REPUBLIC OF MEXICO
1810, 1821

Rio Grande

Santa Fe

T E X A S

UNITED STATES OF AMERICA

LOUISIANA
Sold by France 1803

Boundary of 1783

Mississippi

Independence recognized
by Great Britain 1783

Boundary of 1783

New Orleans

FLORIDA

Ceded by Spain 1819

Canada Act of 1791

UPPER CANADA

LOWER CANADA

Quebec

NEWFOUNDLAND

NOVA SCOTIA

Washington (American and French
Capital, 1800   armies 1781)   Boston

New York   (Rochambeau's French Army 1780)

Yorktown   Philadelphia
1781   AMERICAN

REVOLUTION   (French Fleet 1781)

Charleston   1776
(Lafayette and other volunteers for American Army 1777)

MONROE   DOCTRINE   182

A t
o

Mexico City

Chilpancingo

UNITED PROVINCES
of CENTRAL AMERICA
1811
1823

Guatemala

BELIZE
(Br.)

CUBA
(Spanish)

JAMAICA
(Br.)

REPUBLIC OF HAITI
Toussaint l'Ouverture
1791, 1801

(French, British and Spanish intervention 1792-1803)

PUERTO RICO
(Spanish)

GUADELOUPE
(Fr.)

MARTINIQUE
(Fr.)

BARBADOS
(Br.)

(Miranda 1806)

Cartagena
1811

(Bolivar)

Coro 1806
1813

Caracas

Cucutá

(Bolivar 1816-19)

NEW
Bogotá
1811

GRANADA

Boyacá River
1819

VENEZUELA

Angostura
(Ciudad Bolivar)

TRINIDAD
(To Br. 1814)

LATIN

AMERICAN

REVOLUTIO

1810-2

(Sucre 1821)

(Bolivar 1822)

A   N   D   E   S

REPUBLIC
OF
COLOMBIA
1819

GUIANA
(Br.) (Dutch) (Fr.)

Cayenne

Quito

Pichincha
1822

Guayaquil

Amazon

EMPIRE   OF   BRAZIL
1822

(San Martín 1820)

PERU
1821

(Bolivar 1823)

Lima

BOLIVIA
1825

Pacific

Ocean

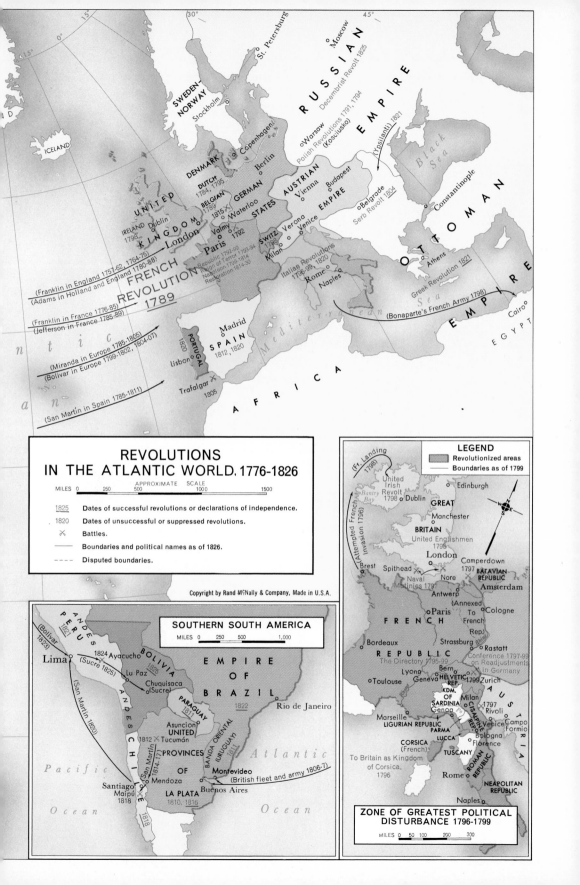

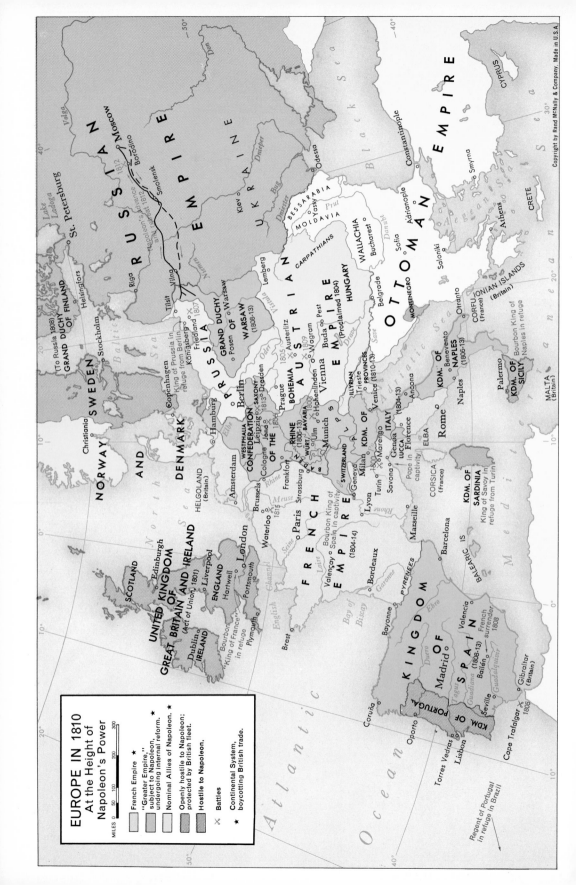

EUROPE IN 1810
At the Height of
Napoleon's Power

French Empire ★

"Greater Empire,"
subject to Napoleon,
undergoing internal reform. ★

Nominal Allies of Napoleon. ★

Openly hostile to Napoleon;
protected by British fleet.

Hostile to Napoleon.

× Battles

★ Continental System,
boycotting British trade.

MILES 0 50 100   200   300

Copyright by Rand McNally & Company. Made in U.S.A.

NORWAY AND SWEDEN

DENMARK

GRAND DUCHY OF FINLAND
(To Russia 1808)

R U S S I A N   E M P I R E

Moscow
Borodino
1812
Napoleon's advance and retreat 1812
Smolensk
Vilna
Tilsit
1807
Friedland 1807
Königsberg ×
King of Prussia in
refuge from Berlin

St. Petersburg
Helsingfors
Riga
Lake Ladoga
Volga
Don
Dnieper

Stockholm
Christiania
Copenhagen
Hamburg

GRAND DUCHY OF WARSAW
(1808-13)
Posen o Warsaw

U K R A I N E
Kiev
Dniester
Bug

P R U S S I A
Berlin
Königsberg

WESTPHALIA
COLOGNE
Cologne
Brussels
Amsterdam
HELGOLAND
(Britain)

CONFEDERATION OF THE RHINE
(1806-13)
Leipzig ×
1813 Dresden
SAXONY
Jena ×
1806
Prague
BOHEMIA
Frankfurt
Strassburg
WÜRT.
BAVARIA
Ulm ×
Munich
Hohenlinden 1800
1805 Austerlitz

AUSTRIAN EMPIRE
Vienna
Wagram 1809
Buda Pest
HUNGARY
(Proclaimed 1804)
Belgrade
Lemberg
Vistula

Danube
Drave
Save

BESSARABIA
MOLDAVIA
Iassy
Prut
Odessa

CARPATHIANS
WALLACHIA
Bucharest
Sofia

O T T O M A N   E M P I R E
Constantinople
Adrianople
Salonki
Smyrna

Black Sea

Aegean Sea
Athens
CRETE
CYPRUS

ILLYRIAN PROVINCES (1810-13)
Trieste
Venice
KDM. OF ITALY
(1804-13)
Milan
Marengo 1800
Genoa
Turin
Florence
Pope in captivity
LUCCA
(1805-14)
Savona
Lyon
Geneva
SWITZERLAND

Adriatic Sea
MONTENEGRO
CORFU / IONIAN ISLANDS
(Britain)
CORFU
(France)
Bourbon King of
Naples in refuge
Otranto

KDM. OF NAPLES
(1806-13)
Benevento
Ancona
Rome
ELBA
Naples
Palermo
KDM. OF SICILY
Bourbon King of
Naples in refuge
MALTA
(Britain)

F R E N C H   E M P I R E
(1804-14)
Paris
Waterloo 1815
Bordeaux
Bayonne
Marseille
Brest
Loire
Seine
Meuse
Rhine
Rhône
Garonne
Bourbon King of
Spain in captivity
Valençay

CORSICA
(France)
KDM. OF SARDINIA
King of Savoy in
refuge from Turin
BALEARIC IS.

UNITED KINGDOM OF
GREAT BRITAIN AND IRELAND
(Act of Union 1801)
SCOTLAND
Edinburgh
ENGLAND
London
Liverpool
Hartwell
Portsmouth
Plymouth
"Bourbon
King of France"
in refuge
Dublin
IRELAND

K I N G D O M   O F   S P A I N
(1808-13)
Madrid
Valencia
French surrender 1808
Bailén
Seville
Barcelona
PYRENEES
Duero
Ebro
Tagus
Guadiana
Guadalquivir

KDM. OF PORTUGAL
Oporto
Lisbon
Torres Vedras
Coruña
Cape Trafalgar ×
1805
Gibraltar
(Britain)
Regent of Portugal
in refuge in Brazil

North Sea
Baltic Sea
English Channel
Bay of Biscay
Atlantic Ocean
Mediterranean Sea

they have fundamentally remained even to the present day. From the point of view of the adherents of the Old Regime, the revolution continued under Napoleon without essential change: there was no longer any division of society into estates; the law was the same for all, rich and poor; seignorialism and feudalism became mere historic memories; and the modern system of freehold property was universally in force. But the years of Napoleon's rule saw no important additions to the innovations introduced during the revolutionary decade.

From the point of view of the bourgeoisie which had so quickly taken the leadership of the revolution and still was the most influential social force in the country, revolutionary economic and social change had come to an end at the precise point which corresponded most closely to its interests. Even the establishment of an imperial nobility by Napoleon did not shake the satisfaction of the bourgeoisie with its class triumph. Napoleon's nobility was not a closed caste, as the aristocracy of the Old Regime had become during the eighteenth century; entry into the ranks of this new nobility was an honor paid to talent and wealth rather than to birth as such, and hence became again what the bourgeoisie had earlier conceived its proper role to be—the culmination of personal or family success in the careers of business, the professions, or government service. Indeed, the reestablishment of firm order within the country and the end of insurrections and riots were for the property owners of France boons for which they were deeply grateful.

The revolutionary transformation was also consolidated and completed under Napoleon in the field of government administration. The revolution had swept away the fantastic hodgepodge which the machinery of government under the Old Regime had been even after centuries of centralization and systematization. It had laid down in its place the framework of a modern, rational government: the division of the country into fairly equal departments, all except Paris identically administered; the full development of ministries with functionally assigned duties; the effective centralization of power so that no neofeudalism of territorial magnates could arise. Napoleon made the whole system more effective by setting prefects over each department as the local representatives of the central power; they were a revival of the intendants of the Old Regime, but with more clearly defined tasks and powers as the agents of the political arm of the state. Indeed, the institution of prefects proved so useful that this office has not been abandoned by any of the vastly different regimes which succeeded Napoleon's during the subsequent history of France to this day. The system of authority might change at the top but the instrument of authority was to change little in more than sixteen decades.

But Napoleon's establishment in power, which constituted a consolidation of the revolution in the fields of social relations, economic institutions, and governmental administration, was its very opposite when it came to the source and purpose of political power. From the beginning the political ideal of the revolution had been in some form the rule of a sovereign people, no matter how much debate there had been over identifying who *the people* were and defining those institutions by which they were to exercise their sovereignty. Revolutions may arise from social and economic strains—certainly in very large part they do—and they may give rise to important and even fundamental transformations, but they are in the first instance shifts in political power and usually, in consequence, changes in the structure of politics; they are ultimately transfers in sovereignty and the instruments of sovereignty. Politically, however, Napoleon brought the revolution in France to a clear and decisive end. He reestablished a regime of authority effective even beyond the dreams of Louis XIV and based it upon a dynastic monarchy directly imitating the power of the Sun King.

During the first stage of Bonaparte's transformation of France into an imperial monarchy, the state remained externally republican in character. But already, as First Consul (together with two other consuls) under the new constitution adopted in December 1799, Napoleon gave himself an effective monopoly of the executive and legislative power in France, even though a legislative chamber of three hundred members preserved the form of popular sovereignty.

THE PEACE THAT FAILED

The first important political act of the First Consul was to renew war against Austria in 1800, after his offers of peace upon his own terms had been rejected. On the battlefield Bonaparte won the battle of Marengo in Italy by a slim margin, but the victory of a separate French army in Germany at Hohenlinden opened Austria to a double French invasion from north and south. The Habsburg emperor thereupon accepted the bitter peace of Lunéville (February 9, 1801), which marked the beginning of the end for old Europe.

Bonaparte confirmed his position within France by removing the last ferment of counter-revolutionary passion within the country, the hostility of the Roman Catholic church to the revolutionary regime. In 1801 a Concordat concluded with the Papacy gave the French government a grip upon the church such as Francis I and Louis XIV had not fully obtained. Archbishops and bishops were to be named by the state and invested with their authority by the Pope. All clergy were to be paid by the state. Catholicism was recognized as the religion of a majority of Frenchmen, something short of the full status of state religion which it had had under the Old Regime. That the Concordat was granted on Napoleon's terms and did not constitute a return to the conditions of the Old Regime was further emphasized by the separate recognition given to Protestantism and Judaism, which were also accorded state support. Education, especially at the higher level, was made totally subordinate to the government authority.

The next year, in March 1802, Great Britain acknowledged the impossibility of continuing the war against France without continental allies and concluded the Peace of Amiens with France. But Napoleon in turn had to accept the conquest of French, Spanish, and Dutch overseas possessions by the British during the past decade. The Peace of Amiens was fundamentally a peace on the basis of the military and political status quo; it did not remove the suspicion between the two great powers, even though it was the necessary first step if they were to turn back to the work of reconstruction after a decade of immense military effort. But the conduct of both states did not ease the tension between them. Napoleon extended his power in Italy by becoming president of an Italian Republic which he had created and by annexing Piedmont and Elba to France. His predominance in central Europe was made more complete when the provisions of the treaty of Lunéville for the reorganization of the Holy Roman Empire were carried out. It was French, not Austrian, deputies who guided the territorial rearrangement of Germany; France received the west bank of the Rhine and the former possessors were indemnified at the expense of the minor imperial princes. A large reshuffling of possessions took place, and the reorganization of Germany was under way.

EMPEROR OF THE FRENCH

In 1804 Bonaparte completed the political transformation of France from the more or less democratic republic which he had overthrown in 1799 to an imperial monarchy. Proclaimed as hereditary *Emperor of the French* in May, Napoleon I was consecrated by Pope Pius VII (1800–1823) on December 2; but unlike Charlemagne, who had been crowned by the pontiff in the famous ceremony at Rome in 800, Napoleon placed the crown upon his own head. It was a gesture full of symbolic meaning. Napoleon was the ultimate self-made man, who in a favorable situation used his abilities and his willfulness to impose himself upon the world. He was not the creature of institutions, as the monarchs of the Old Regime had been, but their creator. His crowning of himself was also an act of total arrogance. Without it the history of the next decade, during which Napoleon came within a hairsbreadth of conquering Europe and then was conquered by it, cannot be understood.

Napoleon governed France with a fist of iron which he scorned to conceal in a velvet glove. The police operated without restraint from laws or courts. A Napoleonic cult was enforced in which the emperor's vanity and his recognition of the popular love of panoply were both present. France had become a mixture of the new and old regimes not only in her institutions but also in her spirit.

The British reply to this and other demonstrations that Napoleon was not settling down to govern France peaceably but was continuing with his assertive foreign policy was to refuse to return the strategic Mediterranean island of Malta to the Knights of Malta, as had been provided for in the treaty of Lunéville. War began in May 1803, and in 1805 England won the support of Russia, Austria, and Sweden in the Third Coalition. The fundamental relationship of forces—that France was the master of the land and Britain of the seas—was demonstrated again. In October 1805 the British admiral Horatio Nelson destroyed the combined French-Spanish fleet (Spain, under its Bourbon king, having become a French ally) off Cape Trafalgar. Thereafter for the duration of the war with Napoleon and until the First World War, British warships held the seaways of the world under their effective command.

Napoleonic France had to continue its combat with the island power with the resources of a land power; French corsairs, however successful at times, could do no more than inflict painful pinpricks upon the English. But on land France proved herself mightier than ever. In December 1805 Napoleon defeated the combined armies of Austria and Russia at Austerlitz and compelled Austria to make peace at Pressburg (Bratislava). France received territory in northwestern Italy, and the kingdom of Italy (as the republic had been renamed), with Napoleon its monarch, got the former Venetian territory. Austria ceded other territories in Germany to French allies.

THE GRAND EMPIRE

Napoleon followed up this triumph by setting up his brother Joseph as king of Naples, after the Bourbon monarchy was declared abolished by decree of the French emperor. This was the first of a series of measures by which Napoleon created a ring of satellite kingdoms and principalities around France. Their monarchs were members of Napoleon's newly-created dynasty, their dukes and princes lesser members of the imperial entourage. But in all these states the will of the emperor of the French was law, and any efforts of the vassal kings to rule independently on behalf of their own people were thwarted by the adamant insistence of Napoleon on being sole and total master in the Grand Empire, as the whole territory in which he ruled, directly and indirectly, was called.

In 1806, shouldering aside the shadowy Holy Roman Empire of which Francis II (1792–1806) of Habsburg still legally wore the crown, Napoleon established the Confederation of the Rhine which he dominated as protector. Francis II, who had already proclaimed himself Francis I, emperor of Austria, two years before, now acknowledged the extinction of the Holy Roman Empire. He also stayed out of the war which ensued between France and her most persistent foes, England and Russia, who were joined by a Prussia made desperate by the French preponderance in Germany. The simultaneous battles of Jena and Auerstädt on October 14, 1806 destroyed the Prussian army, still boastful of the heritage of Frederick the Great, and left Napoleon in occupation of Berlin, the Prussian capital.

From the Prussian capital the French emperor issued a decree instituting a *Continental System,* which declared a blockade of England by closing to it all the ports on the Continent. The system, reinforced a year later by the Milan decree of December 17, 1807, was designed to strike at the vital arteries of Britain's credit, and hence at her ability to wage war, by cutting off access to the Continent. But the blockade proved a barrier of paper; officials in dependent countries doggedly refused to enforce it strictly, and smuggling operated with the connivance of populations and officials. British trade with European countries was seriously hampered, to be sure, but there was too great a need for her products and too many holes in the blockade for the Continental System to achieve its purpose. This was all the more true because Napoleon underestimated the resilience of the British financial system after a century of economic growth and sound fiscal policy on the part of its government.

Meanwhile the campaigning continued. After the French triumph at Friedland (June 14, 1807), the defeated tsar Alexander I (1801–1825), joined by the Prussian king, Frederick William III (1797–1840), made peace with Napoleon aboard a raft in the Niemen River at Tilsit (July 7–9). Russia and Prussia recognized both the satellite kingdoms and the French-sponsored reorganization of Germany, including the Confederation of the Rhine, and agreed to join in the Continental System. Prussia was reduced to a fragment of her former size; most of the lands she had taken from Poland during the three partitions were ceded to a French-dominated Grand Duchy of Warsaw; and she became another satellite state in the Grand Empire. Yet the inner hostility of the Prussian king and his people to the conqueror was unabated and they awaited an opportunity to shake off the yoke.

THE EMPEROR FAILS: SPAIN AND RUSSIA

Within less than a year after Tilsit, Napoleon's myth of unconquerability began to lose its luster. In Spain, where he transferred his brother Joseph as king after ousting the Bourbons, a national guerrilla war broke out against the French. Many of Napoleon's best generals lost their reputations in the Peninsular War, especially after the English general Sir Arthur Wellesley, later the duke of Wellington (1769–1852), came with English regulars to stiffen the wild *guerrilleros*. In Spain the force of nationalism turned against Napoleon and his conquering empire with unexpected force; the Spanish rebellion could not drive out the French, but it took a constant toll of the forces supporting Joseph.

Hopeful that Napoleon was mired beyond rescue in Spain, Austria again took up the challenge to Napoleon in 1809, calling upon all Germany to rise in a war of national liberation. Only the old Habsburg province of Tyrol, which had been ceded to Bavaria in 1805, responded by a revolt, and it was crushed. The Austrians were defeated in battle after battle; even their capital, Vienna, fell into French hands. Finally Francis I accepted his fate and made peace. Not only did he make further cessions of territory to French satellites in Germany and in Illyria (in modern Yugoslavia); he also accepted the counsel of his chief minister, Clemens von Metternich (1773–1859), to swallow his pride and give his daughter Archduchess Marie Louise in marriage to the French usurper, to take the place of Napoleon's divorced first

THE DAY OF DEATH. Goya, who also painted the royal court, depicts in *The Third of May, 1808* the execution of Spanish nationalist rebels by Napoleon's troops in Madrid.

wife, Josephine, who had borne him no children. Metternich's subtle aim was to make Austria seem a loyal French ally while she recovered her strength in anticipation of the time when another coalition against France would permit the Habsburg empire to take revenge for its defeat and humiliation.

That opportunity came only after Napoleon undertook a campaign in 1812 to compel Russia to become an obedient junior partner in the alliance of the two emperors, to accept continued expansion of French territory and that of French dependencies, and to enforce to the letter the blockade measures of the Continental System. Perhaps the most profound reason for the failure of Franco-Russian collaboration, however, was the insatiable jealousy felt by tsar Alexander towards his over-proud and over-mighty friend, a feeling of which Napoleon was only too aware. Russia won the alliance not only of England but also of Sweden, where the crown prince, Jean Baptiste Bernadotte, was a former marshal of France who now broke with his one-time commander-in-chief and sovereign. France, however, included among her allies both Prussia and Austria.

The Grand Army which Napoleon sent into Russia finally numbered more than six hundred thousand men, including troops from every state in the Grand Empire and the French allies. The invasion began in June but Napoleon met a new kind of strategy upon the part of the Russians. Reluctant to allow him to destroy their forces in a single great battle, they retreated, destroying the countryside as they withdrew. At Borodino, on the Moscow River, they attempted to hold but lost heavily; but the French, although able to cross the river and reach Moscow on September 14, had also suffered great losses. In the Russian capital no one remained to make peace, and the city went up in flames. Yet the stubborn French emperor-commander kept his troops camped there amid the ashes for five weeks before he began a westward retreat in frigid climate under harassing attacks, suffering a military catastrophe worse than any Napoleon had inflicted upon any enemy. Less than a sixth of his force finally escaped into Poland.

THE EMPEROR FALLS

This was the chance awaited by Prussia and Austria. In February Frederick William III broke openly with Napoleon, and he was followed by Austria after a brief peace congress at Prague proved vain. The new coalition was again supported, like its predecessors, by English subsidies, which enabled Prussia and Austria to put three armies in the field. Napoleon won a victory at Dresden in late August but suffered a crushing defeat at Leipzig in a three-day battle in mid-October. The French empire collapsed as the Napoleonic satellite states were swept away by the allies and the French armies in Spain were overwhelmed by Spanish and English troops. The allies, still fearful of Napoleon's often-demonstrated ability to pull victory out of apparent defeat, offered him terms of peace: he could continue to rule in France, which would be allowed to retain Belgium and the Rhineland. But Napoleon, ever the defiant gambler, rejected these terms, and the allies invaded France. When Napoleon defeated them in a series of battles in February, they again offered peace terms including the boundaries of 1792, but Napoleon again demanded more than they would give. Now the fighting finally went against him, and the allies entered Paris on March 31, 1814. Twelve days later Napoleon abdicated and withdrew to the island of Elba as its ruling prince and with an imperial title.

In France he was succeeded by the Bourbon claimant to the throne, Louis XVIII, whom the allies had finally turned to after the failure of their negotiations with Napoleon. Despite the biting accusation that the returning Bourbons had learned nothing and forgotten nothing during their quarter-century of exile, Louis XVIII had indeed grasped much of what happened. He agreed to govern France as a limited, constitutional monarch. He attempted to bring about a reconciliation among Frenchmen of almost all groups, republicans and Bonapartists as well as royalists and returned émigrés, on the basis of retention of the New Regime in its fundamentals as well as measures of restitution for returned émigrés, but the tension between these disparate elements remained sharp. Since the restored French king was considered by the allies not to bear the responsibilities of the defeated Napoleon, he was permitted to participate in the peace congress that convened in Vienna in September 1814. There his envoy, Charles Maurice de Talleyrand (1754–1838), took full advantage of disputes among the victors to strengthen the French position.

THE HUNDRED DAYS

Before the Congress of Vienna could complete its work (which, because it is the basis for European restoration and political structure until the mid-nineteenth century, is described below in Chapter 16), Napoleon made a last effort to recover his immense power. He returned to France on March 1, 1815. The French armies sent to capture him joined his banners, the Bourbon monarch fled to Belgium, and Napoleon entered Paris on March 20. A new reign began, called the *Hundred Days* because it lasted only until June 29. Napoleon's return ended the bickering among the allies who sent a million men under the high command of the English duke of Wellington to destroy him. Bold as ever, Napoleon carried the fight to the enemy and met Wellington south of Brussels at Waterloo on June 18. A battle as fierce as any Napoleon had ever fought finally turned against him at the end of the day and he fled with a shattered army. Abdicating again, he took refuge on a British war-

NAPOLEON'S NEMESIS—WELLINGTON. The Duke of Wellington is shown in this portrait by Sir Thomas Lawrence astride "Copenhagen," the horse he rode for sixteen hours at the battle of Waterloo.

ship, trusting London's honor more than the vengefulness of his continental foes. He was sent into exile in the distant, lonely island of St. Helena in the south Atlantic. He remained there, closely guarded, until his death in 1821, but not before he had created, through his writing and discussions with his aides, the Napoleonic legend of the fallen eagle. He described himself now as the French patriot who had fought only for his country's greatness. This myth became a powerful political force during the remainder of the nineteenth century, obscuring the reality of a ruler who was not only a great captain and a skilled administrator, but also a vain and vainglorious dynast.

Meanwhile the allies returned to their deliberations at Vienna which led shortly to peace and restoration.

The Old Regime, with its mixture of medievalism and modernity, was finally ended. A new order had come into being, changing even those who sought to resist it and who now met at Vienna. The effort to clamp a system of watertight castes upon Europe had failed; a social order based on classes in which wealth became more important than birth was the pattern of the future. Hierarchy and traditional privilege as such became difficult to defend, instead of being the unquestioned shape of social arrangements. The bourgeoisie were consolidated and invigorated; they knew they had the capacity to rule no less than to make wealth in trade and industry. The common people, too, had had a taste of power, briefly and mainly in France, and they brought to the new century a thirst for improving their conditions and a hope of establishing a world in which they would have something to say. For the moment, however, the decisions lay with the representatives of the victorious dynasties, to whom the old order was something to be regained if possible.

Further Reading

Modern historical study of the French Revolution begins with the classic work by *A. de Tocqueville, *The Old Regime and the French Revolution* (orig. French ed., 1856), which retains scholarly value as well as philosophical power. *A. Mathiez, *The French Revolution* (New York, 1929) is somewhat outdated by G. Lefebvre, *The French Revolution,* 2 vols. (New York, 1962–1964), the outstanding contemporary survey. R. R. Palmer, *The Age of the Democratic Revolution,* Volume II, *The Struggle* (Princeton, 1964), and the briefer J. Godechot, *France and the Atlantic Revolution of the Eighteenth Century, 1770–1799* (New York, 1965) view the events in France as part of a general revolutionary movement in western civilization. L. Gottschalk, *The Era of the French Revolution (1715–1815)* (Boston, 1929) and L. Gershoy, *The French Revolution and Napoleon* (New York, 1933) are useful textbooks. *G. Rudé, *Revolutionary Europe, 1783–1815* (Cleveland, 1964) reflects recent scholarship; and an anthology of key studies can be found in *J. Kaplow, ed., *New Perspectives on the*

French Revolution (New York, 1965). *C. Brinton, *A Decade of Revolution, 1789–1799* (New York, 1934) combines an ironic spirit and incisive judgment. *C. Brinton's *The Anatomy of Revolution,* rev. ed. (New York, 1965) compares the French and later revolutions.

The origins and onset of the French revolution are brilliantly analyzed in *G. Lefebvre, *The Coming of the French Revolution, 1789* (Princeton, 1947). *G. Rudé, *The Crowd in the French Revolution* (Oxford, 1959) is a systematic study of participants in revolutionary mobs. *J. M. Thompson, *Robespierre and the French Revolution* (New York, 1953) is a useful sketch, briefer than his full-length biography, *Robespierre,* 2 vols. (Oxford, 1935). *R. R. Palmer, *Twelve Who Ruled: The Committee of Public Safety during the Terror* (Princeton, 1941) is a series of illuminating short biographies. G. Bruun, *Saint-Just, Apostle of the Terror* (Boston, 1932) is a perceptive biography of Robespierre's leading supporter. C. Brinton, *The Jacobins: An Essay in the New History* (New York, 1930) analyzes the composition of the Jacobin clubs; while *C. Tilly, *The Vendée* (Cambridge, Mass., 1964) does the same for the counter-revolutionary insurgents in western France. D. Greer, *The Incidence of the Terror during the French Revolution* (Cambridge, Mass., 1935) and *The Incidence of the Emigration during the French Revolution* (Cambridge, Mass., 1951) are important essays in quantitative history. *G. Lefebvre, *The Thermidoreans and the Directory* (New York, 1964) and *A. Mathiez, *After Robespierre: The Thermidorean Reaction* (New York, 1931) survey the period after Robespierre's downfall. D. Thomson, *The Babeuf Plot: The Making of a Republican Legend* (London, 1947) studies an important episode.

A. T. Mahan, *The Influence of Sea Power upon the French Revolution and Empire, 1793–1812,* 2 vols. (Boston, 1892) is a classic work in naval history. J. H. Rose, *William Pitt and the Great War* (London, 1912) traces the development of British resistance to the revolution in France; while G. P. Gooch, *Germany and the French Revolution* (New York, 1920) describes both favorable and hostile movements.

Sound biographies are F. M. Kircheisen, *Napoleon* (New York, 1932); H. A. L. Fisher, *Napoleon* (New York, 1945); and J. M. Thompson, *Napoleon Bonaparte, His Rise and Fall* (New York, 1913). *H. Butterfield, *Napoleon* (New York, 1956) is both brief and penetrating; while *P. Geyl, *Napoleon: For and Against* (New Haven, 1949), in tracing the attitudes of French historians toward the emperor, adds incisive analysis of its own. O. Connelly, *The Gentle Bonaparte: The Story of Napoleon's Elder Brother* (New York, 1968) is a brilliantly told biography of Joseph Bonaparte. *C. Brinton, *The Lives of Talleyrand* (New York, 1936) blends paradoxical wit and good scholarship. *R. B. Holtman, *Napoleonic Propaganda* (Baton Rouge, 1950) is an important special study.

O. Connelly, *Napoleon's Satellite Kingdoms* (New York, 1965) is an invaluable pioneering work on the Grand Empire. C. Oman, *Studies in the Napoleonic Wars* (London, 1929) and R. Grenfell, *Nelson the Sailor* (New York, 1949) are useful studies of land and sea fighting. Important studies of the political resistance to Napoleon are E. N. Anderson, *Nationalism and the Cultural Crisis in Prussia, 1806–1815* (New York, 1939); A. Cecil, *Metternich, 1773–1859,* 3rd ed. (London, 1947); W. C. Langsam, *The Napoleonic Wars and German Nationalism in Austria* (New York, 1930); and L. I. Strakhovsky, *Alexander I of Russia: The Man Who Defeated Napoleon* (New York, 1947). *C. L. Hibbert, *Waterloo: Napoleon's Last Campaign* (New York, 1967) is a modern study of Napoleon's most famous battle.

CHAPTER 15

The Rise of
an Industrial
Society

The transition from enlightened absolutism to middle-class liberal-
ism could not be halted, however much the victors who assembled in Vienna in
1814 favored the Old Regime; for the new political orientation was facilitated by a
transformation in the economy of Europe resulting from the application of mechanical energy to production. Revolutionary changes in politics, in other words, were
to a large extent a response to revolutionary changes in economics. Benevolent despotism had been a form of government adapted to the needs of a static agrarian
society, just as parliamentary institutions came to reflect the needs of a dynamic
industrial society. Innovations in the methods of manufacture, furthermore, led to
an alteration in the interrelationship of social classes. The men who lived through
the early period of industrialization did not always realize that they were witness-
ing the beginning of a new way of life. But now, after the passage of more than
two centuries, it is clear that the factory system introduced a revolution in the history of the West more sweeping than that which overthrew the Bourbons in France
or ended the colonial empires in the New World. The development of Europe
since the fall of the Old Regime is incomprehensible without an understanding of
the changes in the economy which have taken place, for the contemporary world

has been as profoundly affected by the new technology as by the ideals of liberty, equality, and fraternity.

1. The Factory System

THE TERM *Industrial Revolution* is popularly used to describe this process of economic change. The beginning of industrialization cannot be determined with the same degree of precision with which political events are dated. But that the Industrial Revolution has transformed the structure of European society fundamentally and irrevocably is undeniable. At the end of the nineteenth century the economic historian Henry de Beltgens Gibbins could still assert that "the change . . . was sudden and violent. The great inventions were all made in a comparatively short space of time. . . . In a little more than twenty years all the great inventions of Watt, Arkwright, and Boulton had been completed and the modern factory system had begun." Today such an interpretation seems oversimplified. Yet in the sense that men's lives were drastically altered by basic innovations in the methods of production there has been and continues to be an Industrial Revolution.

MECHANIZATION OF MANUFACTURE

A basic characteristic of this revolution was the application of mechanical energy to the processes of manufacture. Some machines, to be sure, had been known in the days of Galileo and even Columbus. Yet the techniques of production at the beginning of the eighteenth century were basically no different from those employed by the Romans or, for that matter, the Egyptians at the dawn of history. They were built on human energy and skill, supplemented at times with the strength of draft animals. Mills and ships had also harnessed the power of air or water currents, but no fundamental change in the methods of making goods had been introduced since the invention of the wheel. The first step in the industrialization of the economy of Europe was therefore the use of machinery exploiting new sources of productive energy.

The mechanization of manufacture first developed on a significant scale in England in the eighteenth century. British commerce and British colonialism had helped build a vigorous middle class with a sizable volume of risk capital. The abundance of coal provided the pioneers of industrialism with their basic raw material. And the royal navy maintained military and political security which stimulated business enterprise. The first branches of the economy to feel the effects of mechanical invention were textiles and mining. The fly shuttle invented by John Kay in 1733 speeded up the weaving of cotton and woolen cloth. James

Hargreaves' spinning jenny, introduced in the 1760's, was the first successful device for spinning more than one thread at a time. In 1712 Thomas Newcomen constructed an engine which was used to pump water out of mines. And in 1769 James Watt patented "a new method of Lessening the Consumption of Steam and Fuel in Fire Engines," by which a rotary motion turning shafts and wheels could be harnessed to drive machines.

On the Continent there were also inventors who experimented with various devices for adapting mechanical force to production. Most of these early engine builders were self-made men, small shop owners, skilled artisans, or ingenious mechanics, who on their own initiative began to transform the economy of Europe. Great Britain was the mother of industrialism, but even before the outbreak of the French Revolution the first effects of mechanization had been felt in France and the Austrian Netherlands. In the course of the nineteenth century all of the West entered an era of industrialism. Not everyone welcomed the changes in the established way of life which accompanied material progress. There were those who were repelled by the bustle and unabashed commercialism of industrial society. During the 1820's the literary giant of Germany, Johann Wolfgang von Goethe, wrote that "machinery, which is gaining the upper hand, worries and alarms me. It rolls on like a thunderstorm, slowly, slowly. But it has taken aim,

REPLICA OF HARGREAVES' SPINNING JENNY. Despite their primitive appearance and clumsy construction, machines such as this formed the basis of the Industrial Revolution.

it will come and strike." Yet there could be no turning back to the placid life of a preindustrial era. A new age had begun whose problems had to be met and solved.

The process of industrialization became more complex as its potentialities became more apparent. Eventually the ingenious inventor without education began to give way to the trained scientist. The machines became so complicated and costly that only an engineer with special skills and financial resources could undertake to construct them. In the nineteenth century there was still room for the self-taught genius whose talents might carry him from rags to riches, but in the twentieth century such achievements became possible only on the screens of motion-picture theaters. The raw materials of early industrialization, coal and iron, were largely superseded by oil and steel. In place of the skilled artisan who had once controlled the production of goods came intricate mechanical devices manufacturing countless articles swiftly and cheaply. Yet the miracles of industrialism were achieved at the cost of social dislocation. Those whose way of life depended on a preindustrial mode of manufacture reacted to the factory system in a variety of ways. Some bowed to the inevitable, becoming workers in the mills. Others petitioned governments and parliaments for laws restricting the use of machinery. Still others tried to destroy the factories in riots which usually ended in defeat and imprisonment for the rioters. And many simply hungered in silence.

During the revolution of 1848 the guildsmen of Germany protested against an economic system "which enables the man of wealth, who already has more than he needs, to rob . . . the oppressed handicraftsman of his last bit of bread and to force masses of these children of the state into the misery of the proletariat. . . . Yet history has shown beyond a doubt that . . . out of the overthrow of the old order arose an industrial struggle exceeding rule by violence in its evil consequences, a struggle in which dishonest labor triumphed over the honest, in which usury, gambling, and fraud triumphed over diligence and skill." But nothing could stop the advance of industrialism. The advantages of mechanized methods of production were so great that no government could afford to prohibit them. The increase in the output of goods was in the long run bound to raise the standard of living of the population at large. This progress, however, was made possible by the suffering of the artisan masses who had once occupied an important position in the towns of Europe. The problem of automation, as it has come to be called today, is as old as the Industrial Revolution itself.

CONCENTRATION OF LABOR

The factory system involved changes not only in the methods of production but also in the organization of labor. In preindustrial society the typical manufacturing establishment was headed by a master artisan who might be assisted by a few journeymen and apprentices, perhaps as many as a dozen or even more. But

INDUSTRIAL REVOLUTION IN ENGLAND 1750-1850

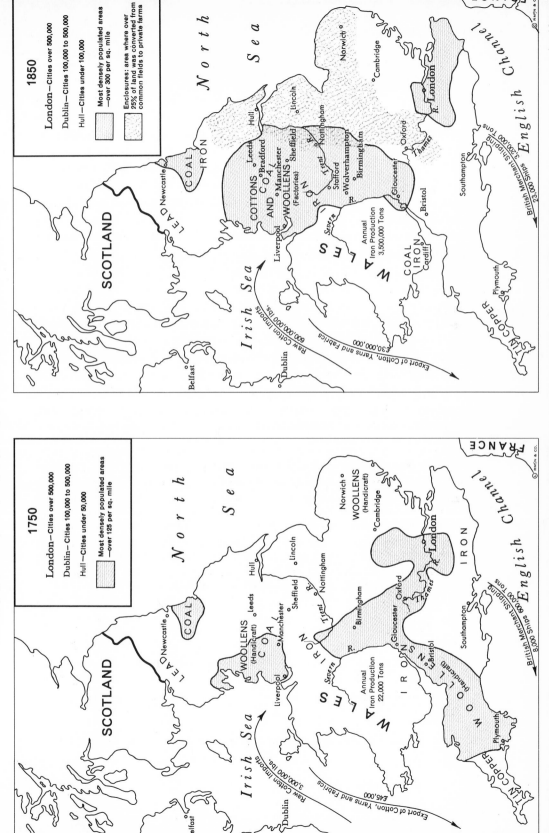

1850

London—Cities over 500,000
Dublin—Cities 100,000 to 500,000
Hull—Cities under 100,000

Most densely populated areas —over 300 per sq. mile

Enclosures: area where over 25% of land was converted from common fields to private farms

1750

London—Cities over 500,000
Dublin—Cities 100,000 to 500,000
Hull—Cities under 50,000

Most densely populated areas —over 125 per sq. mile

employer and employee knew each other personally and could even enjoy a common participation in their occupation. Indeed, the worker often lived in the house of his master, slept under his roof, ate at his table, and married into his family. Since the tools of trade were few and simple, no great resources of capital were required to start in business. Through their guilds the handicraftsmen controlled methods of production, conditions of labor, hours, wages, even prices and profits. The effect was to reduce competition and provide a secure financial return and social position for those engaged in manufacture. The attractions of such a system of corporative industrial organization should not be exaggerated. It was open to serious abuses, and even at best it tended to discourage initiative. The intangible psychological satisfactions which it provided, however, helped to make up for its inefficiency.

The Industrial Revolution changed all that. It made the tools of production so expensive that only a relatively small group of employers could afford to buy them. The introduction of machinery in a manufacturing establishment, moreover, often meant the employment not of a handful of workers, but of dozens, hundreds, or even thousands. The result of mechanization was therefore a high concentration of labor. Instead of a large number of producing units, each with a few workers, there emerged a few producing units, each with a large number of workers. This change in the distribution of the labor force impressed even the early writers on the Industrial Revolution. Andrew Ure, a Scottish chemist-turned-economist, stated in his *Philosophy of Manufactures:*

> The term *Factory,* in technology, designates the combined operation of many orders of work-people, adult and young, in tending with assiduous skill a series of productive machines continuously impelled by a central power. This definition includes such organizations as cotton-mills, flax-mills, silk-mills, woolen-mills, and certain engineering works. . . . The principle of the factory system then is to substitute mechanical science for hand skill, and the partition of a process into its essential constituents, for the division or graduation of labour among artisans. On the handicraft plan, labour more or less skilled was usually the most expensive element of production . . . ; but on the automatic plan, skilled labour gets progressively superseded, and will, eventually, be replaced by mere overlookers of machines.[1]

Ure recognized that the factory system was changing the function of labor. In many branches of manufacture it was destroying the demand for the skilled operative who had mastered the entire process of production from the preparation of the raw material to the polishing of the finished product. Mechanical devices could do such work more efficiently. The task of the mill hand as opposed to the trained

---

[1] Andrew Ure, *The Philosophy of Manufactures: or, an Exposition of the Scientific, Moral, and Commercial Economy of the Factory System of Great Britain* (London: Charles Knight, 1835), pp. 13, 20.

artisan became to tend the machines or perform the same simple operation over and over again. The joy in a creative occupation which the trained handicraftsman often felt was usually denied the unskilled laborer in the big plant. The close association between the master and his journeyman, moreover, was increasingly replaced by the impersonal relationship between the factory employer and the factory employee. Not only was the former separated from the latter by an insurmountable social barrier, but the two led different lives, lived in different parts of the city, had different economic prospects. In most cases they did not even know each other. They were held together only by what the British writer and social critic Thomas Carlyle called the "cash nexus."

The factory labor force was recruited in part from declassed artisans whose livelihood had been destroyed by the mechanization of production, but more commonly from peasants driven from their villages by hunger or overpopulation. In the course of the eighteenth and nineteenth centuries millions of rustics migrated to the big cities in search of greater economic opportunity. The extent to which their hopes were realized is still the subject of controversy. That life in the urban slums and working conditions in the mills of the early Industrial Revolution were harsh cannot be questioned. The hours were long, the wages low, the living conditions brutalizing. A commission investigating child labor in England during the 1840's found that "the most common age for boys to be taken to labour in the coalmines of this district [Oldham in Lancashire] is at seven, eight, or nine. But in the 'mountain mines,' or smaller collieries towards the hills, . . . they will go down as early as six, five, or even four years of age; some are so young they go in their bedgowns. One little fellow whom I endeavored to question could not even articulate, although his father, between whose legs he hid his little black face as he stood before me, answered for him that he was seven years old."

Yet the daily existence of the lower classes in the countryside during the preindustrial era had also been cruel. The peasant had toiled long and hard to eke out a meager livelihood; his life was shortened by the squalor in which he dwelt; his children were put to work when they were very young. Would not therefore almost any change have been an improvement? Andrew Ure was convinced that the introduction of machinery had actually raised the standard of living of the industrial worker: "Since the comfortable wages of factory labor have begun to be enjoyed, the mortality has diminished in the proportion of thirty-two and a half to forty-one and a half; that is, only three persons die now, where four died in the golden age of precarious rural or domestic employment." And Edward Baines, Jr., another economic commentator of the first half of the nineteenth century, wrote enthusiastically about "that energetic and persevering industry which, combined with the highest mechanical skill, large capital, and mercantile intelligence and enterprise, . . . has added more to the wealth, population, and power of England than . . . the boldest could have thought possible."

BREAKER BOYS. Of all the social hardships accompanying the growth of industrialism, none was more tragic than the employment and exploitation of child labor.

There is thus no clear-cut answer to the question of whether the factory system in its early development raised or depressed the level of well-being of the masses of Europe. Conditions varied from region to region and from industry to industry. By and large there was no significant decline in the standard of living of the lower classes, and there may well have been an improvement. But the social and psychological consequences of industrialization were often unfavorable. Within a short span of time countless peasants were uprooted from their villages, removed from a way of life which had endured for centuries, and dumped into cities growing helter-skelter in response to new economic stimuli. The result was bound to be a decline in moral values.

Atomized and alienated, the worker in the factory lost the sense of belonging which had made the hardships of rural life more bearable. The physical privation he had to endure was probably no greater than before, but the problem of adjustment to a new way of life seemed at times insurmountable. Here was the source of that demoralization of the laboring classes which so many contemporary observers noted. In *The Condition of the Working Class in England in 1844* Friedrich Engels, the militant socialist who was at the same time a successful industrialist, claimed that "next to intemperance in the enjoyment of intoxicating liquors, one of the principal faults of English workingmen is sexual license. But this, too, follows with relentless logic, with inevitable necessity out of the position of a class left to itself, with no means of making fitting use of its freedom. . . . The consequence is that the workingmen, in order to get something from life, concentrate their whole energy upon these two enjoyments, carry them to excess, surrender to them in the most unbridled manner." The changed position of labor arising out of the factory system had created a spiritual vacuum. Only gradually did the urban working class begin to fashion new values and loyalties out of the experience of the Industrial Revolution.

INCREASE IN OUTPUT

Whatever its cost in physical hardship and emotional insecurity, the factory system brought about an increase in production which eventually led to a great improvement in the material well-being of society. From the beginning of time man had lived amid privation. It had become an axiom that human toil could not produce enough commodities to meet human demand. Poverty was therefore accepted as a hard but inescapable fact of life. The biblical declaration that "ye have the poor always with you" described a timeless reality. For had there ever been an age when most people could satisfy their need for the basic necessities? It was taken for granted that the nature of production made it inevitable that only a small minority would enjoy sufficient affluence to devote itself to higher pursuits; the great mass of mankind was condemned to live from hand to mouth. The class system on which the community had been built, its political institutions, social relations, and economic practices, its philosophy, theology, and literature, even its art and architecture had developed on the assumption that mass impoverishment was immutable and eternal.

The factory system changed all that. It created for the first time the possibility of meeting the demand for consumer goods. Mechanized manufacture and concentrated labor altered the structure of the economy on which every previous society had been based. The Industrial Revolution made it possible for the community to enter an era of continuous mass consumption. Moreover, not only could the domestic need be fully supplied, but the prosperity of the economic system came to depend in large part on the purchasing power of customers abroad. Government authorities therefore offered encouragement to the export trade, they sent commercial missions to foreign countries, they even conquered colonies to assure a captive market for the national economy. The standard of living of the mass of mankind has risen more in the last two hundred years than in the preceding two thousand. Not since men first ceased to be nomadic hunters and learned to produce their food through animal husbandry and farming has there been such a momentous change in their way of life. In its long-range implications the Industrial Revolution dwarfs any of the major political changes of modern history.

The adjustment of society to this drastic change in its way of life has lagged behind the advance of the factory system. The ideas and institutions by which men live have continued to reflect to a considerable extent the traditions of a preindustrial age. Wherever sharp class distinctions exist, wherever mass poverty prevails, wherever culture reflects aristocratic bias, wherever oligarchies of wealth or birth rule, the full potentialities of the Industrial Revolution are not being realized. For it is clear that the general improvement in the standard of living made possible by the mechanization of production has provided the material basis for a democratic organization of the community. As time goes on, the fundamental distinction between patrician and plebeian which has characterized every previous social order will continue to decrease. It is no coincidence that the era of industrialization has also been the era of democratization. All the possibilities inherent in a condition of popular affluence have not been recognized. The world is still going through a difficult transition from an economy of scarcity to an economy of abundance, and there are serious problems of physical and psychological adaptation to be solved. But there is also inherent in the factory system the promise of a richer life.

2. Transportation and Communication

The Industrial Revolution denotes a series of interrelated revolutions in the production and distribution of goods. The factory system is an essential part of it, to be sure, but its effects could be felt only when there was a significant improvement in the methods of transmitting goods from producer to consumer. In other words there was no point in increasing output unless there was a way of shipping manufactured articles swiftly and cheaply to distant markets. Industrialization necessarily presupposed new techniques of locomotion, and mass production became possible only with the introduction of mass transportation.

NEW METHODS OF DISTRIBUTION

The earliest response to the need for better methods of shipping was the improvement of roads and canals. There was nothing novel about this process; it simply extended techniques which were already familiar. In 1761, for example, the Duke of Bridgewater completed a canal seven miles long to transport coal from Worsley to Manchester where the price of coal then fell to half of what it had been. When the new canal was then extended to the Mersey River, the cost of shipping goods by water from Manchester to Liverpool declined to less than 20 per cent of what was charged on the overland route. At the same time the construction of highways proceeded so rapidly that one British writer asserted: "There never was a more astonishing revolution accomplished in the internal system of any country." After the middle of the eighteenth century ingenious road builders like the Scotsmen Thomas Telford and John L. McAdam evolved techniques for producing hard surfaces which could carry traffic at any time of the year. Not only the volume of freight but also the speed at which it was transported was greatly increased. When in 1826 the coach between Liverpool and Manchester reached the unheard-of velocity of fourteen miles an hour, there were loud outcries against such reckless disregard of health and safety. Yet the advantage of completing the trip from Edinburgh to London in two days instead of fourteen was too great to be abandoned. As the expense of shipping declined, regional price differentials began to diminish. Ideas and attitudes, moreover, became more uniform. The economist John Ramsay McCulloch observed in 1835 that "manners as well as prices are reduced nearly to the same standard. . . . Everything is, as it were, brought to a level."

The first great innovation in the techniques of distribution came with the application of mechanical energy to water transportation. The idea of a steamboat had long attracted inventive minds on both sides of the Atlantic. But its first successful demonstration came in 1807, when the American Robert Fulton launched the *Clermont,* which traveled 150 miles up the Hudson River in 32 hours. Amazed observers on the shore saw "the Devil on the way to Albany in a saw-mill." Yet steam vessels were at first restricted to inland waters, for their crude construction could not withstand the rigors of ocean travel. Even when the *Savannah* finally crossed the Atlantic in 1819, she used sail for twenty-six days out of thirty. The early steam engines were so inefficient that it was impossible to carry coal for more than a small part of the voyage. One of the experts went so far as to say that a crossing from New York to Liverpool using mechanical energy was "perfectly chimerical, and they might as well talk of making a voyage from New York to the moon." Yet in the course of the 1830's the various technical difficulties were overcome, and at the end of the decade Samuel Cunard founded the first great steamship enterprise by contracting to carry mail fortnightly between Liverpool, Halifax, and Boston. In 1850 the entire European steamship registration was only 186,000 tons, but by 1870 the figure came close to 1,500,000, by 1890 it had passed 7,500,000, and in 1910 it reached 19,000,000. Navigation was now completely transformed.

The most revolutionary innovation in transportation, however, was the railroad. Its background was the familiar story of mechanics, tinkerers, and visionaries who in the late eighteenth and early nineteenth century experimented with steam engines. The first convincing demonstration of the feasibility of such a form

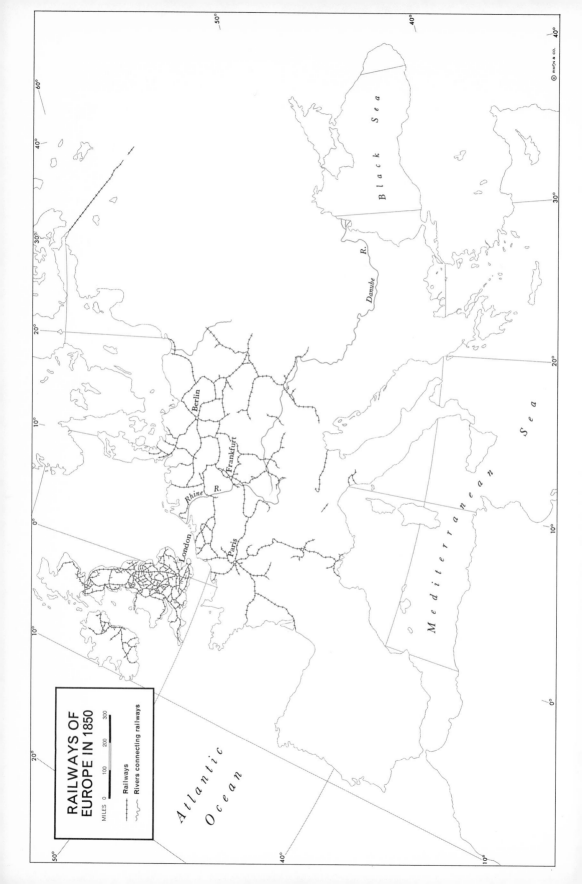

RAILWAYS OF
EUROPE IN 1850

MILES 0   100   200   300

━━━━━ Railways
〜〜〜 Rivers connecting railways

Berlin

Frankfurt

Rhine   R.

London

Paris

Danube   R.

Black   Sea

Mediterranean   Sea

Atlantic
Ocean

© RAND & CO.

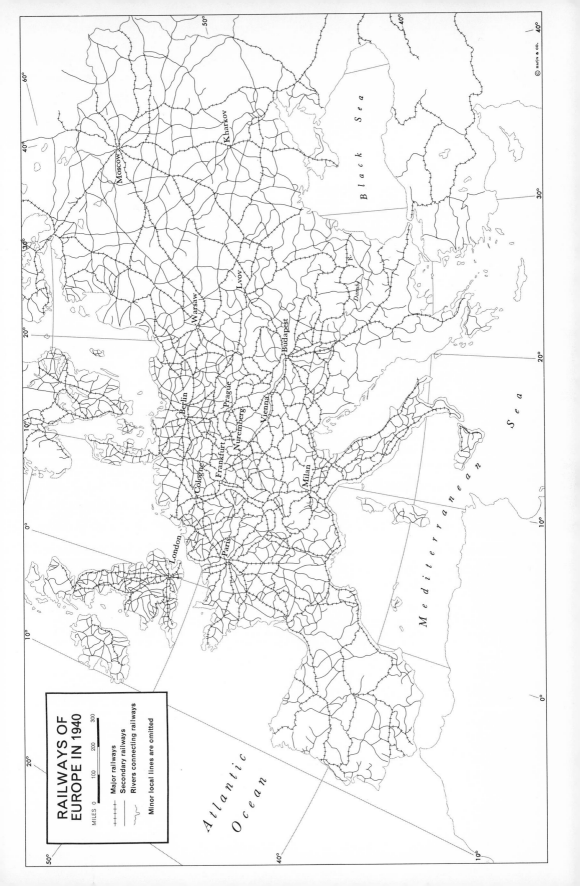

RAILWAYS OF
EUROPE IN 1940

MILES 0   100   200   300

—⊢—⊢— Major railways
———— Secondary railways
~~~~~ Rivers connecting railways

Minor local lines are omitted

Moscow

Kharkov

Lvov

Warsaw

Budapest

Berlin

Prague

Nürnberg

Vienna

Frankfurt

Cologne

Milan

London

Paris

Danube

Black Sea

Mediterranean Sea

Atlantic Ocean

© RMCN & CO.

60°
50°
40°
30°
20°
10°
0°
10°
20°

50°
40°
30°
20°
10°
0°
10°
20°
30°
40°

THE OPENING OF THE STOCKTON AND DARLINGTON RAILWAY, 1825. The quaintly amusing little railroads of the early nineteenth century introduced a revolution in European transportation.

of overland locomotion came in 1829, when the British engineer George Stephenson introduced the *Rocket,* an engine which had an improved boiler design and could move at speeds ranging between thirteen and sixteen miles an hour. In the succeeding half century a railroad mania swept over Europe. In one country after another investors rushed to pour their money into rail enterprises which promised to make them rich. Scandals, bankruptcies, and shattered hopes were often the result of speculative recklessness, but the network of railways continued to grow steadily. In the United Kingdom the number of miles of track rose from 500 in 1838 to 6,600 in 1850, 15,500 in 1870, and 20,000 in 1890. Some people, to be sure, were less than enthusiastic about the new mode of transportation. King Frederick William III of Prussia failed to see what difference it made whether one arrived in Potsdam a few hours sooner or later. His postmaster general, moreover, complained that while empty stagecoaches traveled across the country daily, there were now demands for trains, of all things. But when a traveler could go from Berlin to Cologne by rail in less than half the time required by stagecoach, when the cost of shipping a ton of coal declined from forty pfennigs per kilometer to thirteen, there was no sense in yearning for the good old days. The young German poet Karl Beck sang in his verse of the progress which the locomotive was making possible:

For these rails are bridal bracelets,
Wedding rings of purest gold;
States like lovers will exchange them,
And the marriage-tie will hold.

The railroad, which in the course of the nineteenth century destroyed the economic importance of the horse-drawn vehicle, was in turn threatened during the twentieth century by further advances in transportation. The automobile and the airplane began to attract a growing volume of passenger and freight traffic. Their effect was felt most strongly in the United States where the internal-combustion engine transformed the way of life of the country. But in Europe the motorization of travel also increased steadily, especially after the Second World War. Even many working-class families began to find that a motorcycle or a small car was not beyond their means. Air transportation is making impressive gains as well. The railroad still dominates the shipping of heavy goods, but technological progress is now making this supremacy insecure.

At the time of the Napoleonic wars men and their possessions moved no more rapidly than in the days of the Caesars, but since then a revolution has taken place. Fruit picked in the orchards of Spain can be eaten two days later in the restaurants of Sweden; a businessman can breakfast in London and then attend a luncheon meeting in New York. Under such conditions distances lose their meaning. The problems of transportation created by an industrial economy have been solved as effectively as the problems of production.

TRANSMISSION OF INFORMATION

The emergence of the factory system gave rise to the need for improved methods of communication. Not only did the volume of information which had to be exchanged between distant points grow tremendously, but it became important to increase the speed with which it could be exchanged. At first an effort was made to solve the problem by improving established techniques. A semaphore system of signaling introduced by Claude Chappe during the French Revolution made it possible to send a message from Strasbourg to Paris, a distance of some 250 miles, in seven minutes. But it required transmitting stations every few miles and was useless in fog, rain, or darkness. The *penny post,* introduced in Great Britain in 1840 as a result of the investigations of Rowland Hill, was another important advance in communication. Previously the cost of sending a letter had depended on the number of sheets of paper, the weight, and the distance to be covered. Now a uniform rate of a penny was applied to all letters up to half an ounce traveling within England. There was no longer any need to count the sheets, check for enclosures, and spend a great deal of time weighing and computing. The advantages of the new arrangement were so obvious that it was soon adopted by countries on the Continent as well.

Yet the need for the rapid transmission of information remained. The penny post increased the volume rather than the speed of communication. The problem of sending news rapidly was not solved until the introduction of the electric telegraph. While the Englishman Charles Wheatstone and the German Wilhelm Eduard Weber contributed to its invention, major credit is usually given to the American Samuel F. B. Morse because of his method of relay and his system of dots and dashes. In 1844 he succeeded in sending a message from Baltimore to Washington, and two years later the first British telegraph company was formed. By 1851 a submarine cable had linked Dover with Calais, and the British network was then connected with lines running to Moscow and the Mediterranean. Calcutta near the Bay of Bengal was reached in 1865, the Atlantic coast of North America in 1866, and Australia in 1871. As early as 1860 there were seventy-five thousand miles of telegraph wire in the world carrying almost nine million messages annually. The demand for a device which could send information over great distances swiftly, reliably, and inexpensively had now been met. While it could be used as an adjunct to the postal system for the transmission of personal communications, its chief beneficiaries were government and business.

Another important advance in the distribution of information came with the invention of the telephone by an American who had been born in Scotland, Alexander Graham Bell. A teacher of deaf-mutes, he became interested in the study of acoustics, and this in turn led him to the problem of communicating sound across space. He was not the first to consider the feasibility of transmitting human speech by means of electricity, nor even the first to find a solution to the problem. But he was the first to invent a practicable telephonic instrument. He exhibited his device at the Centennial Exposition of 1876 in Philadelphia, where it attracted immediate attention. The telephone, which was at first slow and defective, found it difficult in the early years to compete with the telegraph and the postal system. Indeed it has never become as popular in Europe as in the United States. But its value for the conduct of business gradually became apparent. There is no important economic enterprise in the world today which does not rely on telephonic communication. The ability to talk directly with people in distant places has become indispensable for modern industry, commerce, and finance. Plans can be discussed, agreements reached, and contracts concluded by men thousands of miles apart. The cost of long-distance telephoning is such that for many transactions ordinary mail or the telegraph is preferable. But when speed and the direct give-and-take of ideas are important, the telephone becomes an indispensable tool of the modern economic system.

Wireless telegraphy and telephony represent the final triumph of technology over the obstacles to instantaneous communication. The wired telegraph and telephone, important though they are, depend on the maintenance of a direct physical connection between the stations exchanging information. They are therefore useless for the establishment of contact with desert, jungle, and polar regions, or with ships, trains, and airplanes. Their reliance on wire restricts their effectiveness to settled communities. The great breakthrough in the removal of this last barrier to communication came in 1896, when the brilliant Italian inventor Guglielmo Marconi patented the radio. His work was essentially an application of the discoveries made a few years earlier by the German physicist Heinrich Hertz regarding the transmission of electromagnetic waves through space. Before the decade was out Marconi succeeded in sending a message across the English Channel, and in 1901 he established contact over a distance of more than three thousand miles with the other side of the Atlantic. The use of the radio then spread swiftly, first to military posts and government offices, then to business, and finally to entertainment. As with most inventions, several improvements had to be made in order to exploit the full possibilities of the new method of communication. Among the most important of these was the vacuum tube, a major electrical achievement by the American Lee De Forest. The introduction of television in the middle of the twentieth century was a further development of Marconi's work with great importance for the dissemination of information.

GROWTH OF THE MARKET

The increase in production and the improvement of distribution transformed the economy of Europe. Until the Industrial Revolution the exchange of raw materials and manufactured articles was carried on under conditions which inhibited commercial activity. Since transportation was slow and expensive, international trade was largely limited to wares which were neither bulky nor perishable. Spices from the Far East, precious metals from the New World, and textiles from the Low Countries were typical items of wholesale commerce in the preindustrial age. Foodstuffs, metalware, ore, coal, and iron, on the other hand, were considered unsuited to exportation. Trading was thus narrowly limited. A merchant might offer his goods for sale at the local village fair, at the marketplace of the nearest city, perhaps even in the neighboring province or region. But to ship them from one end of the kingdom to another was a risky undertaking, and to send them abroad required considerable courage. The businessman who succeeded in making a sizable sale to customers in a distant part of Europe could earn a fortune, yet if he was careless or unlucky, he faced bankruptcy. Profits in wholesale commerce were great, because risks were great. Most men preferred to buy and sell in a market which was local in scope; it might not offer much variety, but it was at least safe.

Improvements in transportation and communication led to an expansion of trade. Perishable foodstuffs which once had to be consumed locally could now be shipped abroad in a day or two to earn handsome profits. Butter from Denmark, cheese from Switzerland, oranges from Spain, and pork from Serbia became staples of wholesale commerce. Sweden sold iron ore to Germany, England sold coal to Italy, Germany sold steel to Russia, Russia sold wheat to England. The economic factors restricting the export of goods ceased to operate. The tonnage of vessels clearing British ports rose from 2,444,000 annually during the 1820's to 15,398,000 during the 1860's. The importation of wheat in these forty years grew sixteen times, of cotton five times, and of wool almost nine times. Exports increased at an equally impressive rate, of coal twenty-nine times, of iron and steel sixteen times, of machinery and millwork twenty-two times, of woolen goods and yarn four times, and of silk goods seven times.

While the United Kingdom was the biggest trader in the world, there was a substantial growth of commerce in all countries. The total value of French imports and exports climbed from $185 million in 1830 to $375 million in 1850, $1135 million in 1870, and $1854 million in 1880. For Germany the figures for these years were $165 million, $525 million, $1060 million, and $1494 million. Even countries which were less advanced economically made impressive gains. The Russian statistics on the volume of foreign trade were $100 million in 1830, $160 million in 1850, $500 million in 1870, and $605 million in 1880, while the Italian statistics for these years were $55 million, $130 million, $370 million, and $331 million. This data provides a graphic description of the economic consequences of the progress in production and distribution and a measure of the great increase in the consumption of goods made possible by the Industrial Revolution. But those who benefited most from this new opulence were those who were already opulent. It was the upper and middle classes of society who most enjoyed the advantages of the factory system and of world trade. For the poverty-stricken peasants of Sicily or Poland, Swiss chocolate and French silk remained unattainable luxuries. But with the passage of time the masses also began to achieve a higher measure of material well-being.

The age of the railroad and the steamship made possible a degree of economic specialization unthinkable in the age of the stagecoach and the sailing vessel. Since it was now easy to import from abroad goods which could not be produced efficiently at home, each country began to emphasize those branches of industry and agriculture for which local conditions were best suited. Why should Holland try to develop heavy industry when steel and machinery could be bought cheaply in Germany? Why should England worry about the decline of her dairy farming when Danish butter and eggs were so readily available? In other words the development of the economy since the Industrial Revolution has led to an increasing interdependence among nations and the emergence of a world market. During the Middle Ages and in the early modern period Europe had been largely independent of trade with overseas regions. Even individual states were to a considerable extent self-sufficient, so that the interruption of their commerce with foreign countries did not necessarily have a serious effect on their domestic production. But the rise of industrialism meant that the era of autarchy had come to an end.

Great Britain, the mother of the factory system, felt this change most directly. Thanks to her lead in the mechanization of manufacture, she enjoyed an economic supremacy in Europe which lasted more than a hundred years—until the end of the nineteenth century. Her concentration on industrial production, however, forced her to rely more and more on imported foodstuffs. Her existence came to hinge on the ability to sell manufactured goods abroad with which to pay for the purchase of food and raw materials. Germany is another case in point. Around 1850 she was still an agrarian land of small towns and villages, exporting grain and trying to protect her undeveloped industrial production against English competition. Fifty years later she had become the largest manufacturing country on the Continent, challenging Great Britain on all the markets of the world. Yet she too paid a price for economic progress by becoming dependent on imports of cereals and raw materials, a factor which during the First World War proved to be her Achilles' heel. The other European states also became to a greater or lesser degree reliant on a worldwide exchange of goods. By the 1930's national self-sufficiency was only a dream of the fascist dictators whose pursuit of the impossible contributed to their downfall. The Industrial Revolution has created a global economy in which "no man is an island, entire of itself."

3. The Finances of Industrialism

THE INCREASE IN THE OUTPUT OF GOODS resulting from the Industrial Revolution created the need for a new system of management and investment. The typical businessman of the sixteenth or seventeenth century had been an industrialist, merchant, and financier in one. He had supervised the process of manufacture, frequently taking a direct part in it; he had made arrangements for the purchase of raw materials and the sale of finished products; and he had found the money required for his enterprise by drawing on his private resources, borrowing from friends, or taking in partners. The scope of his economic activity had usually been so limited that he could perform all of the functions involved in production and distribution. There were men who became well-to-do or even rich under this uncomplicated system of doing business. But they never succeeded in creating the kind of economic empire exemplified in the twentieth century by General Motors, I. G. Farbenindustrie, or the Royal Dutch Shell Company. The financial needs of even the biggest enterprises could still be met by forming partnerships or private companies. The problems of management were simple enough to be mastered in their entirety through practical experience and hard work. The Industrial Revolution, by complicating manufacture and commerce, introduced a new era of economic organization.

MANAGEMENT AND CREDIT

One of the immediate results of the rationalization of industry was the separation between the producing and distributing functions of business. The supervision of workers in the performance of their labor was assigned more and more to foremen who understood the technical processes of manufacture but who were incapable of dealing with the problems of planning and marketing. There arose a new professional class of managers whose task was merchandising rather than output. Their concern was not to oversee the making of the product but to adjust the volume of production to supply and demand. They were unfamiliar with the mechanics of their industry, since their major purpose was the adaptation of production to market conditions, and they could work with equal effectiveness for a railroad company, a steel mill, or a colliery without knowing the first thing about engineering or mining. Their talent lay in the determination of the optimum conditions for buying and selling; they became the bureaucrats of the new economic age. Trained in the counting room or the school of business rather than the factory, they constituted the patriciate of the business world. Those directly engaged in production were subordinated to those responsible for marketing. The executive suite became a term suggesting an arcane world of all-powerful managers controlling the modern economy.

The methods of financing industrial output grew as complex as the methods of its operation. The factory system created the possibility of vastly increasing the volume of production but only through a vastly increased volume of investment. The difference in cost between a charcoal furnace and a Bessemer converter is a measure of the extent to which the demand for capital rose after the introduction of mechanized manufacture. The credit structure was forced to adjust to new pressures. As a rule no one man nor group of men, however wealthy, possessed the enormous amounts of money required for large-scale industrialization. The result was the emergence of new forms of corporate financing, particularly the joint-stock company. The basic principle behind the latter was old and simple: invite the public to contribute funds to a new venture, the profits to be distributed in proportion to the amounts invested. As early as the 1550's a group of English capitalists raised six thousand pounds by selling shares of twenty-five pounds each for "the discovery of the northern parts of the world." Some fifty years later 218 venturesome businessmen formed the East India Company to carry on trade between Great Britain and the Orient "by a joint and united stock."

Throughout the sixteenth and seventeenth centuries joint-stock financing continued to prove its value in commercial capitalism. But its full potentialities were not realized until the coming of the Industrial Revolution.

In the years after 1815 the corporate form of business structure made possible the rapid expansion of production and transportation. Railroads, mines, steel mills, and textile factories were irresistibly attracted to the joint-stock method of financing. These new enterprises, however, were a far cry from the small pioneering companies which had once engaged in trade with the Far East or the New World. The investors in a modern corporation numbered thousands and tens of thousands, while the capital which they provided totaled millions or even billions. The organization of the modern industrial establishment, moreover, was infinitely more complex. Management was usually in the hands of a small group of financiers and administrators who sat on the board of directors. But ownership was legally vested in a large number of stockholders, whose rights of possession were represented by the shares they had purchased on the stock exchange. As a rule the investors knew little about the technical operation of the business firm which was in theory their property. Their interest was limited to its earning capacity. The intricacy of the corporate economic structure thus created a gulf between production and finance which grew wider with the rising complexity of manufacture and trade.

Yet the great advantages of the joint-stock form of business organization were undeniable. As early as the 1850's the German financier Gustav Mevissen presented a remarkably penetrating analysis of the fundamental changes in the structure of ownership which were beginning to take place in Europe:

> The alliance within the field of industry of capital and intellectual forces in the form of the joint-stock company has increasingly become a striking feature of the present time. . . . On the basis of what has already occurred it seems clear today after the passage of a few decades that the joint-stock company has developed in modern society with the energy and speed of a force of nature. As a result of conditions in Europe and America it has arisen simultaneously in all states which have assumed the great task of material progress; it has in a sense re-established the corporate association on the ruins of a bygone era. The energies united within its form have in the course of a few decades created works of material civilization before which even the great works of antiquity and the Middle Ages must bow. Like all natural manifestations of the spirit of a given period it has found no pre-existent forms. Its legal position and the legislation which governs it are divergent. The extent of the authority granted to this new corporate association varies enormously, depending on the differences among the states, from fearful mistrust and the most minute supervision of its every move to the most complete and unconditional acceptance of its creative power. Besides, the resistance which develops against all new creations bearing the seeds of a great future has not been and is not absent. But so far the young giant has overcome all his opponents, and every day enlarges his power. . . . The newest achievements of modern times,

the railway and steamship companies, allied with the banks and insurance companies belonging to an earlier period, were the first to be molded in the form of the joint-stock company. Based on these fields the form has gradually gained control of a number of branches of industry in which capital plays the leading role, and individual activity and talent a secondary one. It seeks to penetrate deeper and deeper into the domain of industry.[2]

The passage of a hundred years has only confirmed the accuracy of this analysis.

DEVELOPMENT OF BANKING

The joint-stock company and related forms of corporate economic organization, despite their vast resources, failed to meet all the financial needs of the modern industrial system. They were too inflexible to satisfy the constantly shifting demand for funds. A manufacturing firm could not issue more shares every time it needed a short-term loan, nor could it always find a public willing to invest the capital necessary for its successful operation. A more convenient method of financing was therefore required to serve the credit market. The result was the rise of a new type of lending institution. Some banking functions had been performed by the money-changers of antiquity and the Middle Ages. The great importance of the financier, however, began with the economic expansion of Europe in the early modern period. The Medici in Italy and the Fuggers in Germany are the best-known examples of bankers who became powerful in the fifteenth and sixteenth centuries by advancing money to governments and by financing commercial ventures. Their wealth supported popes and emperors; it paid for the wars of Spain and Austria; it controlled trade and mining all over Europe. This tradition of private family banking was carried on in the eighteenth and nineteenth centuries by several great firms like Rothschild and Baring Brothers, whose members used the power of credit to achieve a position of eminence in the economy of their time.

These older banking institutions, however, were frequently reluctant to adapt their business practices to the needs of large-scale industry. For one thing, they continued to favor investment in government securities which offered a relatively safe and predictable return. Second, their resources based on private wealth were too limited to satisfy the voracious appetite for credit generated by the factory system. In the course of the nineteenth century, therefore, there emerged new financial firms characterized by their readiness to provide risk capital for industrial enterprises and by their reliance on funds supplied by the public through a joint-stock structure. One of the first of these investment banks was the French Crédit Mobilier, founded in 1852 by the Péreire brothers. It puts its money into railroads,

---

[2] Joseph Hansen, *Gustav von Mevissen: Ein rheinisches Lebensbild, 1815–1899*, 2 vols. (Berlin: Georg Reimer, 1906), II, 532–533. Trans. by Theodore S. Hamerow.

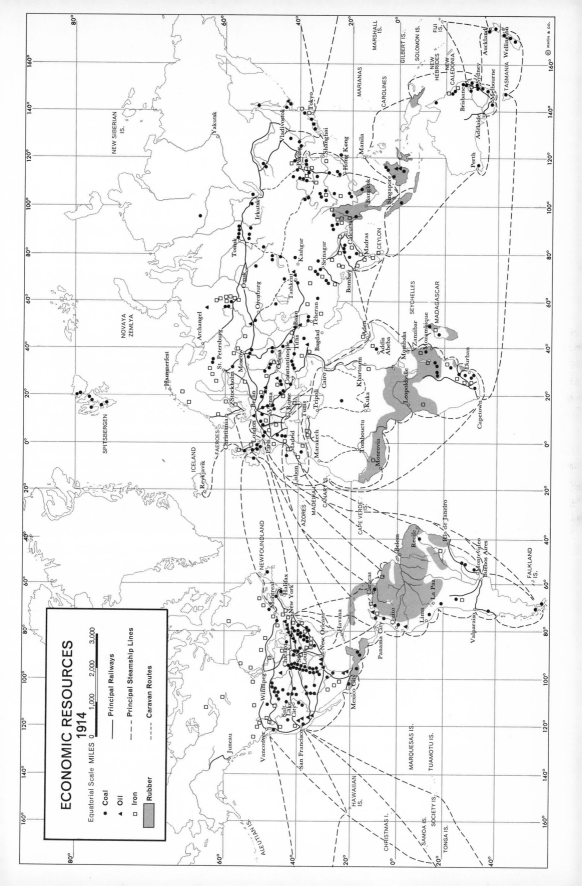

ECONOMIC RESOURCES
1914

Equatorial Scale MILES 0 1,000 2,000 3,000

- ● Coal
- ▲ Oil
- ▢ Iron
- ▨ Rubber

——— Principal Railways
– – – Principal Steamship Lines
– · – · – Caravan Routes

© RAND McNALLY & CO.

shipping, and real estate, paying dividends of more than 40 per cent at one point. Its success made it reckless, however, and after 1866 it entered a decline which ended in collapse. But the experience had been an eye opener. Before long other lending establishments appeared which imitated the example of the Péreires with greater caution and greater success. There were the *big five* in England: the Midland, Westminster, Lloyds, Barclays, and the National Provincial. Germany had the four *D banks*: the Darmstädter Bank, the Deutsche Bank, the Dresdner Bank, and the Diskontogesellschaft. The giants of French finance became the Comptoir National d'Escompte, the Crédit Industriel, the Crédit Lyonnais, and the Société Générale. By the beginning of the twentieth century the new joint-stock system of banking had gained the upper hand over the old private firms.

In finance as in industry the initial stage of pell-mell growth was followed by a period of consolidation. At first everybody was eager to found banks which would hopefully emulate the profits earned by the Crédit Mobilier. "Each city, each state, however small, wants to have its bank and its lending establishment," observed the French consul in Leipzig in a dispatch to his government in 1856. "It seems as if there is as much determination to cover Germany with a network of credit institutions as there was to cover her with a network of railroads." But after the first boom in banking passed, the weak and the unlucky collapsed or were absorbed by their stronger and more fortunate competitors. In each country a small group of lending financial firms arose which dominated the credit system as effectively as the big corporations dominated steel, coal, oil, or electricity. On the eve of the Second World War, for example, the big five in England controlled close to five-sixths of the lending business, owning 9,891 banking offices in the kingdom out of a total of 12,200. Finance capitalism, in other words, was displaying the same tendency toward expansion accompanied by concentration as industrial capitalism.

POWER OF THE PURSE

Since the volume of investment required by production and transportation increased enormously, the connection between finance and industry became inextricable. In the eighteenth and even the nineteenth centuries it had still been possible to establish a new business and develop it into a major enterprise with the modest resources provided by private savings, a family inheritance, a partnership, or a small joint-stock company. The shipper Samuel Cunard in England, the munitions manufacturer Alfred Krupp in Germany, and the oil king John D. Rockefeller in America are proof of that. But with the increasing cost and complexity of economic growth, the age of unlimited opportunity came to an end. The successful conduct of business came to depend on an alliance between big industry and big finance. Leading bankers would join with leading manufacturers to dominate entire segments of a country's economy through exclusive agreements and interlocking directorates. While the United States sought to oppose this tendency toward concentration by means of antitrust legislation, in Europe government authorities placed no serious obstacle in the way of giant combinations such as cartels, which could wield vast power over national or even international production. In both the New World and the Old the moneyed interests were able to extend their sway over manufacture and commerce through the mechanism of credit which they controlled.

The financial community could even exert influence over affairs of state, so that the protection of its investments became the concern of diplomats and generals. In the 1870's, when the Egyptian government proved unable to meet payments on the loans it had received from European bankers, Great Britain intervened to enforce the claims of the lenders. Some fifteen years earlier, in response to the complaint of French creditors that the Mexican authorities were defaulting on their debt, Napoleon III had organized an international expeditionary force to obtain a resumption of payment. At the beginning of the twentieth century Germany participated in a blockade of Venezuelan ports to help collect the amounts owed her investors. Yet the relationship between financiers and statesmen was not one-sided. Bankers usually responded favorably to government requests that they support the diplomatic policy of their nation. The French stock exchange floated Russian bonds to cement the alliance concluded between the two countries in 1894. The German money market made important loans to the Ottoman Empire after 1890 at the urging of the foreign office in Berlin. The Viennese bankers backed the diplomats by refusing to extend credit to Serbia after 1903, when the latter embarked on a course hostile to the Dual Monarchy. In short, economic power became closely allied with political power, the two working together in defense of their respective interests.

The growing influence of the world of finance brought with it serious problems for the entire economy. It made industry and commerce largely dependent on the ups and downs of the money market. It led to recurring cycles of prosperity and optimism followed by depression and gloom. In good times hopes for a quick profit would start a boom in which reckless buying on the stock exchange raised prices of shares to exorbitant heights. Then, after it became obvious that production could not keep pace with the inflated growth of paper values, a collapse would occur, causing numerous bankruptcies, wiping out unlucky investors, slowing down business activity, and creating unemployment and privation. This pattern of boom and bust was by and large unrelated to output, representing rather the fluctuation of expectations on the money market. While economic crashes had been known before the nineteenth century, their scope and severity became much greater with the rise of large-scale financial organizations. Between the end of the Napoleonic era and the outbreak of the Second World War depressions of varying intensity occurred in Europe at approximately twenty-year intervals. There seemed to be no way of avoiding them. They were regarded as acts of fate which had to be accepted in the same spirit of resignation as sickness or bad weather. The German economist Albert Schäffle, writing shortly after the depression of 1857 which began in America and spread to the Old World, compared its course with that of an elemental force of nature:

> The avalanche from the banks of the Ohio, where it was set in motion by the insidious activities of a few speculating rascals, advanced with devastating violence irresistibly eastward. It crushed the Atlantic states of the great republic, and after a mighty leap across the ocean fell upon England and the mainland of the European continent, reaching as far as the plains around the Baltic Sea (North Germany, Poland, Scandinavia). Everywhere it has brought all branches of business more or less to a standstill. Like a thief in the night it has surprised the world of speculation and production which had climbed to dizzying heights. In a time of the most profound political peace, after a generally rich harvest, that same edifice collapses which in years of scarcity and . . . war had towered on high like a fairy castle springing out of the wilderness. Its rise as well as its fall border on the incredible.[3]

In the course of the twentieth century, however, governments as well as popular opinion began to adopt a less fatalistic attitude toward the cycles of good and bad times which had previously been considered inevitable. The great depression following the crash of 1929 was especially important in creating a resolve to prevent the recurrence of such an economic disaster. Its political and social consequences made it clear that the community could not afford to remain idle in the face of demoralization, hopelessness, and privation. Attempts to deal with the causes of financial crises concentrated partly on the regulation of the money market, and partly on government intervention in the operation of the economy. First of all promoters of new business ventures were required to provide more accurate information concerning their resources and prospects, so as to reduce the danger of wild speculation. More important, it came to be accepted as a legitimate practice that the state should use its vast financial power to counteract unhealthy tendencies within the business community. If in a time of depression the private investor is spending less, then the public treasury should spend more. If employers are firing, the state should be hiring. If the big corporations are retrenching, government agencies should be expanding. Such unorthodox policies were not adopted without dire warnings from the economic traditionalists. Nor is it by any means established that they can in fact prevent a financial collapse in the future. But the twentieth century has refused to maintain a hands-off policy toward the ups and downs of the economy. The social dangers arising out of material hardship appear too serious to be tolerated.

------

[3] [A. E. F. Schäffle], "Die Handelskrisis, mit besonderer Rücksicht auf das Bankwesen," *Deutsche Vierteljahrs-Schrift*, XXI: 1 (1858), 256. Trans. by Theodore S. Hamerow.

4. *The Agricultural Revolution*

THE CHANGES which the Industrial Revolution effected in production, distribution, and finance would have been impossible without comparable changes in agriculture. For how could more and more people be employed in manufacture, trade, and banking, if the farmer did not produce more and more food to support the growing urban population? There had to be an increase in agricultural output equivalent to the increase in industrial output. During the preindustrial period of economic development most men had been employed in husbandry not only because there were few other pursuits, but because their labor was needed to provide society with sustenance. The efficiency of agriculture was so low that a heavy investment of labor was required to yield the surplus food required by the nonagricultural classes of society. The wasteful three-field system of farming, which left much of the land fallow in order to increase its fertility, was common throughout Europe. The villager's holdings were often widely scattered, so that he lost a great deal of time moving from one to the other. The methods of fertilization were uneconomical, and the tools of farming primitive. In 1770 the agricultural reformer Arthur Young published a description of the backwardness of agriculture in northern England which could have been applied to many parts of the Continent:

> 1. Large tracts of land, both grass and arable, yielded but a trifling profit, for want of draining. In wet clays, the rushes and other aquatic rubbish usurped the place of corn and grass; the seasons of tilling were retarded, and even destroyed; and those pastures which ought to have fed an ox, scarcely maintained a sheep.
> 2. The pastures and meadows of this country were universally laid down in ridge and furrow, a practice highly destructive of profit, and detestable to the eye; and the manner of laying down such lands was as miserable as their product denoted poverty; for after many years ploughing of numerous crops but insufficient fallows, when the soil was so exhausted as to disappoint the expectation of corn, a parcel of rubbish called hay-seeds was scattered over the surface, and the field left to time for improvement. A villainous custom, and too much practiced in all parts of the kingdom.
> 3. The culture of turnips was become common, but in such a method that their introduction was undoubtedly a real mischief; *viz.* without hoeing, so that the year of fallow, in the general management, was the most capital year of slovenliness and bad husbandry.
> 4. The implements used in agriculture through this tract were insufficient for a vigorous culture, and consequently the husbandman sustained a constant loss.
> These circumstances, among others, shew how much the husbandry of this country wanted improvement.[4]

---

[4] Arthur Young, *A Six Months Tour through the North of England. Containing, an Account of the Present State of Agriculture, Manufacturing and Population, in Several Counties of this Kingdom,* 4 vols. (London: W. Strahan, 1770), I, 308–309.

The Agricultural Revolution was the process by which this backward form of farming was improved.

RATIONALIZATION OF HUSBANDRY

The first step was the consolidation of small and scattered parcels of land, held individually or communally, into sizable farms and estates offering the advantages of large-scale production. This more efficient organization of the soil often meant the elimination of marginal farmers, whose holdings became part of larger agricultural units. The latter could achieve increased output through specialized farming. In Great Britain, where this process of consolidation was known as the *enclosure movement* because it involved the fencing of fields, a report on the condition of Scottish agriculture during the early nineteenth century, noted that "even the appearance of inclosures indicates comfort and security; and landlords never fail to draw very advanced rents from well-inclosed lands, which generally let from 20–50, and in some cases, even 70 *per cent* higher than open lands of the same description in the neighbourhood; the value or rate of rent continuing to advance, as the inclosed soil goes on to improve. . . . The landlord often has an opportunity to appropriate many waste spots, and otherwise useless corners, for plantations; to the great embellishment of his property, and the solid emolument of himself or his successors." In other words, the concentration of landholding increased output in agriculture for the same reason that the concentration of manufacturing increased output in industry. It made possible a more productive form of ownership.

A second factor in the Agricultural Revolution was the application of scientific knowledge to husbandry. Before the nineteenth century little was known about the chemistry of plant growth. Experience had shown that the fertility of the soil would be rapidly exhausted if it were not replenished by rest or fertilization. Farmers therefore tried to improve the yield of their fields by enriching them with a variety of waste materials: rags, refuse, garbage, ashes, soot, leaves, and sweepings, as well as manure. The publication in 1840 of *Organic Chemistry in Its Relations to Agriculture and Physiology* by the German chemist Justus von Liebig was a landmark in the development of scientific agriculture. Although not free from error, it identified the elements in the air and soil which are essential for the life of a plant. By supplying his land with these elements the farmer could increase and prolong its output. The hit-and-miss methods of fertilization, which had remained basically unchanged since the beginning of agriculture, were now replaced with precisely measured additions of nitrate and phosphate prescribed by soil chemistry. Chance in husbandry, while not eliminated, was greatly diminished. By maintaining a sufficiently high level of fertility on his land the agriculturist could raise production and reduce the danger of crop failure. For the first time the volume and quality of farm output became to a large degree controllable.

The third major factor in the Agricultural Revolution was the invention of mechanical devices to meet the needs of husbandry. An increase in productive energy was as important for the growth of farming as for the growth of manufacturing. While there had been several Europeans in the early years of the nineteenth century who tried to improve the tools of agriculture, the lead in this field soon passed to the United States. During the 1830's Jerome I. Case laid the foundation for what became the greatest thresher works in the world, while Obed Hussey and Cyrus H. McCormick patented reaping machines which they had invented independently. At the international exhibitions in London in 1851 and in Paris in 1855 American agricultural machines beat all comers in competitive trials. The vast plains of the New World were ideally suited to large-scale mechanized cultivation, but the landowners of Europe were also impressed with the advantages of farm machinery. Between 1862 and 1892 the number of threshing machines in France grew from 101,000 to 234,000, of planters from 11,000 to 52,000, of mowing machines from 9,000 to 39,000, and of reapers from 9,000 to 23,000. Equally rapid was the mechanization of agriculture in Germany, where mowing machines on large farms of over one hundred hectares increased from 1,493 in 1882 to 6,746 in 1895 and 137,624 in 1907, while the figures for threshing machines during the same years were 173,000, 428,000, and 743,000. The Agricultural Revolution like the Industrial Revolution depended on machinery.

THRESHING IN THE DAKOTAS WITH STEAM-POWERED ENGINES, 1879. While the United States was a pioneer in the use of machinery in agriculture, European farming soon followed its example.

EXPANSION OF FARM PRODUCTION

The result of the rationalization of husbandry was an increase in output which promised to end once and for all the threat of famine. The last great hunger in Europe came in the 1840's, when widespread crop failures across Europe, in the area between the Shannon River in Ireland and the Oder River in Germany, drove hundreds of thousands of emigrants across the ocean to the western hemisphere. But thereafter the Agricultural Revolution began to insure an adequate food supply. There were still occasional local famines to be sure: Russia, for example, experienced severe privation in the early 1890's. But under normal conditions the farm production of the Old World and the New was enough to feed their combined populations. Only when war or revolution disrupted the international market was there a serious danger of food shortage. Germany during the First World War suffered hunger because of the blockade imposed by the Entente Powers. After the Bolsheviks seized power in Russia in 1917 there was widespread starvation due to civil war and the sudden transformation of the country's economic system. During the Second World War people in Poland and Greece died of malnutrition because of the ruthless policies of the Axis occupation. But the sense of horror which such tragedies inspired merely underlined the extent to which society had forgotten what had once been a common experience. The hardships which men formerly accepted as inevitable now filled them with pity. This change in attitude was a measure of how swiftly the food supply of Europe had grown during the previous one hundred and fifty years.

What made the increase in agricultural yield all the more remarkable was that it had been achieved by a diminishing proportion of the labor force. While output had been growing at a very high rate, the number of people employed in farming had been declining. The harsh economic necessities which had kept the bulk of society tied to the soil had vanished. The production of food had ceased to be the occupation of the great majority of Europeans. A basic change in the forms of human employment had occurred, made possible by expanding surpluses in agriculture. Without these surpluses there could have been no shift of population from country to city, from husbandry to manufacturing. The rise of modern industry, commerce, and finance depended on the ability of fewer and fewer people to produce more and more wheat, rye, milk, beef, and pork. In Germany during barely three decades between 1878–1879 and 1901–1910 the yield of wheat per hectare rose from 1,350 kilograms to 1,960, of rye from 1,060 to 1,630, of barley from 1,360 to 1,900, and of potatoes from 7,110 to 13,510. The French wheat crop was 19 per cent higher in 1906–1909 than in 1876–1885, while Russian wheat production grew from 274,000,000 bushels in 1890–1895 to 757,000,000 bushels in 1909–1914. The average weight of German livestock rose between 1883 and 1912 from 321 kilograms to 360 for cattle, from 116 to 126 for pigs, and from 34 to 42 for sheep.

Such figures suggest the dimensions of the increase in output arising out of the rationalization of agriculture.

More than that, the adjustment of production to an international rather than local market led to a high degree of specialization in farming. Denmark is a case in point. A hundred years ago the country was an exporter of grain and meat. But when after 1860 the price of butter rose while rye and wheat began to fall, the farmers turned to *arable dairying,* that is, growing fodder roots and grains for animal husbandry. By the First World War Danish agriculture had become a major supplier of the butter, eggs, and bacon eaten at the British breakfast table. Holland went through a similar experience but concentrated on cheese and condensed milk rather than butter and eggs. The fruit growers of southern Italy and Spain found customers north of the Alps and the Pyrenees. The great improvements in ocean transportation introduced during the nineteeth century made it possible for farmers overseas to feed and clothe the European consumer. Wheat grown in the United States and Canada began to cross the Atlantic. Argentine beef and Australian wool invaded the Continent. In short, subsistence farming was everywhere forced to retreat before commercial farming. In this respect the parallel between agriculture and industry was striking. The quest for efficiency had led to the expansion of the market and the specialization of production, until self-sufficiency had become a mirage. The price of economic progress had been an economic interdependence which political boundaries and military rivalries were powerless to halt. The material welfare of mankind was increasingly based on a vast world market in which the interests of all nations converged and interacted.

DECLINE OF THE COUNTRYSIDE

The way of life associated with agriculture changed drastically as a result of the growing productivity of the soil. While the availability of food increased more rapidly than population, the proportion of people living in the countryside diminished. This was a result of the greater efficiency of farming and of the greater attractiveness of city life. The decline of the village characterized in varying degrees every nation of Europe. In Great Britain, where the effects of the Industrial Revolution were felt first, about 50 per cent of the inhabitants lived in rural communities as of 1851. By 1891 the ratio had fallen to 28 per cent, and in 1911 it amounted to only 22 per cent. In Germany in 1871 the percentage of the population living in villages of less than two thousand inhabitants was 64, but by 1900 the figure had diminished to 46, and by 1910 to 40. In France industrialization was slower. Yet, while in 1851 75 per cent of the French population lived in the countryside, by 1910 the proportion had become 53 per cent. In other words, after the coming of the Industrial and the Agricultural Revolutions there was a large-scale movement of people from the country to the city. In the course of about a century and a half a demographic pattern which had remained unchanged for thousands of years underwent a transformation. Men began to abandon the land to find new homes in big urban communities.

This shift in the distribution of population was bound to have an effect on the class structure of Europe. Its most obvious consequence was a weakening of the position of the landed aristocracy. Since the days of the earliest civilized societies ownership of the soil had been an instrument of power and a mark of distinction. It had signified participation in the most important of human activities, the production of food. The nobility, to be sure, performed vital functions in the community and the government in addition to farming. Not only were they traditionally responsible for the military defense of the state, but they occupied leading positions in the bureaucracy and the church. Yet the economic foundation of their eminence was agriculture. Whether the aristocrat engaged in husbandry directly or preferred to let others manage his estates, he remained a proprietor of the most valuable of commodities, land. But once the importance of farming diminished, his right to predominate in society was open to challenge. After 1815 industry rather than agriculture became the crucial sector of the economy; industry rather than agriculture promised the greatest profit; industry rather than agriculture attracted people who wanted to get ahead. The result was a decline in the economic supremacy of the aristocracy which gradually undermined its political and social supremacy as well. For a nobleman in the nineteenth century life was not all cakes and ale. In the mid-century the conservative German politician Baron Philipp von Künssberg-Mandel was one of many aristocrats who, frightened by the spreading disintegration of established authority, lamented that they were doomed to live in a time out of joint: "No class is any longer satisfied with the lot assigned to it; each man wants to climb higher. Everybody seeks only one goal, namely, wealth and pleasure. Everything is sacrificed to this idol, and today appearances count for more than realities."

The diminishing economic significance of agriculture also meant the decline of another social class which derived its livelihood from the soil, the peasantry. The consolidation of landholding and the growth of the large estate were essential for efficient husbandry, but they meant the uprooting of countless small subsistence farmers. The latter became a landless proletariat seeking relief from poverty in flight, either abroad or to the city. As early as 1770 the English writer Oliver Goldsmith portrayed in his *Deserted Village* a rural community which had fallen victim to the enclosure movement:

> Sunk are thy bowers, in shapeless ruin all,
> And the long grass o'ertops the mouldering wall;
> And, trembling, shrinking from the spoiler's hand,
> Far, far away, thy children leave the land.
>   Ill fares the land, to hastening ills a prey,

Where wealth accumulates, and men decay:
Princes and lords may flourish, or may fade;
A breath can make them, as a breath has made;
But a bold peasantry, their country's pride,
When once destroyed, can never be supplied.

Even those rustics who were not forced off the land often drifted to the big city in search of greater economic opportunity or a more exciting life. The labor force of the factory system was made up largely of villagers who had abandoned the ancestral fields to try their luck in mills and collieries. The peasantry became part of what Karl Marx called the "industrial reserve army," shifting the balance of economic power in favor of the manufacturer as opposed to the landlord.

The decline of the countryside could also be seen in a less tangible form in the altered popular attitude toward rural life. In the preindustrial age farming had been considered the mother of those virtues on which civilization rested. After defeating the enemies of Rome, Cincinnatus returned to the plow. George Washington, when he was not leading armies or presiding over the republic, managed his plantation. Even George III of England was pleased to be known as "Farmer George" because of his interest in agriculture. But with the coming of industrialism, husbandry lost its honored place among human pursuits. The city began to attract the new leaders of society. They might still maintain a country home or own an estate as a decorative symbol of high status. But few men of ambition devoted themselves primarily to agriculture, because it had ceased to be a major avenue of economic or social advancement. The rustic became more and more an object of ridicule and a butt of countless jokes about the slow-witted farmer. The best minds in the village began to drift to the town where lights and prospects were brighter. After a long reign agriculture bowed down before industry.

5. The Course of Urbanization

THE BIG CITY was a child of the factory system. Urban communities were nothing new to be sure. They were already in existence thousands of years before the birth of Christ. But their size and number were limited by an economic system in which manufacturing and farming were by modern standards inefficient. Since the food surplus which the peasant produced was small, most men had to live on the land. The techniques of industry were too primitive for mass production and mass employment. Until the nineteenth century, therefore, the countryside supported the great bulk of the population. Around 1800 there was only one city in all of England with over one hundred thousand inhabitants; in France there were two;

in the Holy Roman Empire three. Communities which would soon become major centers of manufacture and trade were still sleepy provincial towns. Liverpool had a population of 82,000, Manchester 77,000, Birmingham 71,000, Antwerp, 62,000, Lille 60,000, Cologne 50,000, Leipzig 30,000, and Essen 5,000. The Industrial Revolution transformed the face of Europe by creating an economic need for rapid urbanization.

EMERGENCE OF THE BIG CITY

The basic reason for the swift growth of population in urban centers during the nineteenth and twentieth centuries was the demand for manpower generated by the factory system. Since the concentration of labor was one of the basic requirements of large-scale production, industrialization led to the employment of vast numbers of workers in manufacturing establishments. Both mill owners and mill hands began to gravitate to the towns, where they could best satisfy their economic needs. The important urban communities were sometimes big cities like London and Paris, which became even bigger through the influx of factory employees, or they might be provincial towns like Belfast or Lyon, which suddenly expanded under the stimulus of an industrial boom. In either case manufacture and commerce altered the community drastically, filling it with new people, infusing it with new energy, defacing it with new slums. Urban life offered a startling juxtaposition of wealth and poverty. Sometimes only a few streets separated the imposing residences of the new-rich from the noisome hovels of the eternally poor. But they might as well have been on different planets. People with a tender social conscience deplored the destruction of an older, more stable way of life. They contrasted the serenity of the village with the ceaseless striving for gain in the big city. Yet urbanization was an essential part of an economic process which was irreversible. By the time of the First World War eight out of ten Englishmen, six out of ten Germans, and nearly five out of ten Frenchmen lived in urban communities. An ancient way of life had been suddenly and radically transformed.

Urbanization did not affect all cities equally. It varied from place to place, depending on the volume of industrial investment and the opportunity for industrial employment. Its effects were felt most directly by large communities. Between 1871 and 1931 the proportion of the population of England and Wales living in villages with fewer than two thousand inhabitants fell from 38.3 to 20.1 per cent, while the proportion in towns with between two thousand and twenty thousand inhabitants declined more slowly from 19.7 to 14.8 per cent. For cities of twenty thousand inhabitants or more, on the other hand, the population increased substantially, from 42.0 to 65.1 per cent. The movement of population to the big urban centers is illustrated even more clearly by statistics from Germany. Between 1871 and 1900 the proportion of the citizens of the empire who lived in communities of more than two thousand inhabitants rose from 36.8 to 54.3 per cent, while the proportion living in large cities of more than one hundred thousand inhabitants rose from 4.8 to 18.9 per cent. Virtually every city in Europe grew as a result of the Industrial Revolution, but in some cases the rate of increase was extraordinarily high. Between 1800 and 1950 the population of London rose from 959,000 to 8,325,000, of Paris from 600,000 to 4,950,000, of Berlin from 172,000 to 3,345,000, of Vienna from 247,000 to 1,615,000, and of Rome from 153,000 to 1,625,000. Yet not only national capitals expanded so enormously. Birmingham went from 71,000 to 1,110,000, Glasgow from 77,000 to 1,088,000, Barcelona from 115,000 to 1,277,000, Milan from 134,000 to 1,270,000, Hamburg from 130,000 to 1,621,000, and Essen from 5,000 to 610,000. In response to compelling economic stimuli a town which was little more than an overgrown village could turn into a booming metropolis within the space of three or four generations.

The emergence of the big city was not a planned process. Like the factory system it developed as a result of powerful but uncoordinated forces. Here and there some entrepreneur would establish a mill or a foundry, soon a new industry would come into existence, shrewd real estate dealers in search of a quick profit would lay out streets and jerry-build houses, merchants would move in to serve an expanding market for consumer goods, landless peasants looking for work

THE RAG PICKERS, 1868. The poverty of the lower classes in the cities was a common effect of urbanization a century ago as well as today.

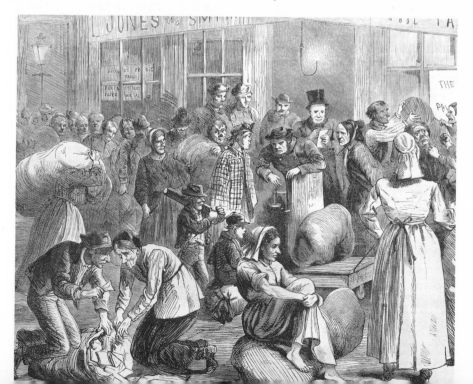

would begin to appear in growing numbers—and a small town was on its way to becoming a big urban center. Under such circumstances city life was bound to be harsh and ugly. There was no one to worry about sanitation, transportation, recreation, or public health. Since men had never before had to cope with rapid urbanization, they did not know how to control it. There were few sights in the nineteenth century as depressing as the industrial slums of London, the working-class quarters of Paris, or the rented barracks of the factory proletariat of Berlin. Yet little by little order began to emerge out of chaos. Public opinion recognized the need for urban planning and even urban beautification. Municipal authorities soon learned to deal with many of the problems created by large masses of people living and working close together. The difficulties of city government seemed at times to multiply more rapidly than the solutions devised for them. But at least society was no longer blind to the needs arising out of urbanization. Men became aware of the magnitude of the task confronting them, and the leaders of the community began to grapple with it in earnest. The process of urban growth was gradually regulated without destroying the spirit of innovation and independence bred by the big city.

NEW WAYS OF LIFE

The rise of the modern metropolis had political, social, and intellectual consequences of the greatest importance. For the urban environment became the matrix of new ideas and ideals in European society. During the Middle Ages the saying that "city air makes free" had a literal meaning: the peasant who settled in the city escaped the manorial obligations which had weighed on him in his native village. But in another sense city air continued to make men free. It weakened the grip of custom, convention, tradition, and authority. Every revolutionary movement of the last two hundred years found its most devoted following in urban centers. Not only new civic ideologies, not only bold hypotheses in scholarship and science, but exciting experiments in literature, music, painting, and architecture have flourished in the environment of the city. The way of life of the preindustrial age was more serene, but its horizons were narrow and its demands limited. It provided a sense of security based on fatalism and ignorance. The industrial city, on the other hand, made men restless. It questioned accepted beliefs and challenged established institutions. It expressed those vital forces in modern society which had led to the overthrow of the static political and economic order of the Old Regime.

Yet at first people could not see much good in the city. It was physically ugly and socially disruptive. It was a threat to all the values inherited from an earlier age of agrarian tranquillity. Thomas Jefferson, the American apostle of liberal republicanism, argued that "those who labor in the earth are the chosen people of God, if ever He had a chosen people, whose breasts He has made His peculiar deposit for

THE PROBLEMS OF RAPID URBAN GROWTH. These views of the coal-mining town of Hanley, England, before the Second World War (*above*) and of a present-day slum area in Chicago, Illinois (*below*), show clearly that the physical environment in which men have had to live since the beginning of large-scale urbanization has often been depressing and demoralizing.

substantial and genuine virtue. . . . The mobs of great cities add just so much to the support of pure government, as sores do to the strength of the human body." At the other end of the political spectrum the German statesman Otto von Bismarck, a pillar of monarchical conservatism, psychologized at the dinner table about the fundamental difference between the rustic and the townsman. Big cities were less practical than the countryside, which came into closer contact with life and nature and hence fostered sounder judgment. "Where so many people are close together," he expatiated, "individual qualities can easily cease to exist. They intermix. All sorts of opinions arise out of the air, out of hearsay and repetition, opinions which have little or no foundation in fact. But they are spread through newspapers, public meetings, conversations over a glass of beer, and then they become fixed, indestructible. . . . That is the case in all big cities."

In the course of time, however, urban life won a grudging acceptance by society. For one thing, a concentration of economic power on such a vast scale could not simply be ignored. The big city which manufactured the goods, imported the raw materials, and advanced the loans needed by the countryside was obviously essential for material progress. Even the inveterate countryman had to acknowledge its importance. The tastes and attitudes of the village, moreover, were increasingly shaped by the example of the metropolis. The farmer might rail against the sinfulness of London, Paris, or Berlin, but he was eager to wear the clothes, imitate the manners, affect the airs, and share the pleasures of the city dweller. The urbanization of popular mores proved an irresistible process. The city also became the undisputed center of cultural life. Even before the coming of industrialism, to be sure, the urban environment had attracted men of scholarly or artistic talent. Yet the provinces had also had their geniuses. The English scientist Isaac Newton, the French philosopher René Descartes, the German writer Johann Wolfgang von Goethe, the Austrian composer Franz Joseph Haydn, all had flourished in a small-town milieu. But after the rise of the factory system the big city began to dominate European civilization completely. It offered stimulation, recognition, companionship, and financial reward. Intellectuals might talk longingly about the days when the artist had lived close to the elemental things in life, but they continued to flock to the cafés and salons of the metropolis. Finally, while the politicians ritualistically extolled the simple virtues of the village, they courted the voters of the city. The combination of economic, cultural, and political influence made of the great urban center a vital force in modern society.

CHALLENGE OF THE METROPOLIS

The rise of the big city created problems of social organization which mankind had never faced before. There was the enormous task of satisfying the basic needs for housing, sanitation, transportation, and recreation of masses of people crowded into a limited area. Entire regions like Lancashire in England or the Ruhr district

of Germany became chains of industrial commu
provided a livelihood for millions. How was this h
shelter? How were all these people to get to their pla
they to protect their health? How were they to sp
the questions with which municipal authorities had
of the automobile as a private means of transportation
the metropolis. It made possible a migration from the c
the evening and on weekends countless commuters e
hurly-burly of the office or the factory. But it also impose
urban centers which were not designed to support the
by a daily mass migration to and from work. The dangers
politan community increased in direct ratio to its rapid gro

The solutions offered for the problems of urban life vari
one was reconstruction. Every city in Europe as well as Americ
streets, building roads, digging tunnels, and constructing byp
pressure of traffic. Whether this alleviated the crowding or inter
ing still more automobiles was an open question. Some city p   ..ated
the decentralization of the metropolis, that is, its subdivision into smaller communities separated by belts of greenery. Urban centers might thus recapture the simplicity and wholesomeness of the village. Others urged the acceptance of the
concentration of population in cities, proposing the erection of huge complexes of
buildings containing facilities for housing, shopping, recreation, and even for office
and industrial employment. Such self-contained units would decrease traffic by
reducing the need for movement within the community. There was general
agreement, however, that the growth of the city had to be regulated to provide not
only for material well-being but for esthetic satisfaction as well. Public parks, public
gardens, public playgrounds, public concerts, and public art galleries were as
much a part of municipal planning as public housing and public transportation.
Never before had the development of the community been so carefully studied.

But adjustment to an urban way of life meant more than the proper ratio of
floor space and sanitary plumbing to population. The experience of industrial
society showed that the force of custom which helped maintain an acceptable
standard of behavior in the country declined in the city. The degree of lawlessness
in the modern metropolis was perhaps exaggerated by a sensationalist press and by
small-town moralists, but it was an undeniable fact that the incidence of crime was
greater in large communities than in medium or small ones. The impersonality
of urban existence contributed to antisocial behavior, but it was only one of the
factors. The sharper contrast between affluence and poverty, the lack of a time-
honored social tradition, the constant fluctuation of population, the greater opportunity for escaping detection, all were related to the higher rate of criminal activity
in the big city.

It takes time for men to adjust to a new physical and social environment. The metropolis is still a recent phenomenon. For the great bulk of the population of the world it is less than a century old. While it has undermined established customs and beliefs, it has not yet developed a system of values expressing its unique character. But the metropolis is too important a factor in the material and cultural development of society to be destroyed. The community is gradually learning to modify its traditions in accordance with the demands of life in the big city and to meet the challenge of the metropolis.

6. *Industrialization and Society*

DURING THE LAST TWO HUNDRED YEARS the West has undergone a transformation unparalleled in its history. The methods of manufacturing and distributing goods have been mechanized and rationalized. The forms of ownership and finance have become infinitely more complex. The techniques of food production have been improved to the point where a diminishing minority of the population can feed the community better than it has ever been fed before. Finally, there has been a disruptive but irreversible flow of population from the countryside to the city. Yet the Industrial Revolution, which initiated this entire complex of economic change, has also had far-reaching demographic and social consequences. It has altered traditional relationships among individuals and classes. And this alteration in the structure of the community is among the highly significant results of modern technological progress.

GROWTH OF POPULATION

The most striking demographic development in Europe since the coming of industrialism is the enormous increase in the number of inhabitants. It has been estimated that in 1650 the population was about 100,000,000, in 1750 140,000,000, and in 1800 187,000,000. Since then, however, the curve has moved upward with remarkable rapidity. The figure for 1850 was 266,000,000, for 1900 401,000,000, and for 1950 579,000,000. That is to say, during the largely preindustrial period between 1650 and 1800 the population rose 87 per cent, while in the next 150 years of rapid industrialization it rose 210 per cent. The rate of growth has been uneven, but every country has experienced a substantial expansion. England and Wales grew from 8,900,000 inhabitants in 1800 to 20,000,000 in 1860, 32,500,000 in 1900, and 44,300,000 in 1954. During the same years the figures for Germany were 25,000,000, 38,100,000, 56,400,-000, and 69,900,000; for Russia 30,000,000, 63,700,000, 103,600,000, and 216,000,000; for France 27,000,000, 35,800,000, 39,000,000, and 42,800,000; and for Italy 18,100,000, 25,000,000, 32,500,000, and 48,700,000. There is evidence that the increase is leveling off, for there has been a recent decline in the rate of growth. But the population of Europe continues to rise, although at a slower pace.

This demographic increase has not been the result of an expansion in the birth rate. On the contrary, it is clear that the birth rate tends to be higher in preindustrial than in industrial societies. It was not unusual for a European married couple prior to the nineteenth century to have ten, twelve, fourteen, or even sixteen children. The peasant masses, without hope for a better future, expected their offspring to lead the same hard life they themselves had known, but each new child was an asset to his family because after only a few years he would be put to work in the pasture or the field. Methods of contraception were primitive or altogether unknown, so that to most people it seemed simplest to let nature take her course. The Industrial Revolution changed the popular attitude toward childbearing. The birth rate remained high for a few generations after the introduction of the factory system, but then it began to decline steadily. The improvement in the standard of living awakened new expectations and aspirations. Parents wanted to provide their children with training, with education, perhaps even with a little property. The fulfillment of these hopes meant limiting the size of the family. The result was a decrease of human reproduction. The birth rate in England and Wales fell from 32.6 per 1,000 in 1841–1850 to 29.9 in 1891–1900 and 16.3 in 1930. For Germany the comparable figures were 36.1, 36.1, and 17.5; for France 27.4, 22.2, and 18.1; and for Belgium 30.9, 29.0, and 18.6. Even in the economically less advanced countries the ratio of births to population dropped, in the case of European Russia from 49.2 per 1,000 in 1891–1900 to 43.8 in 1930, and in the case of Italy during the same period from 34.9 to 26.2.

What accounts for the growth of the European population during the last century and a half is not an increase in the birth rate, but a decrease in the death rate. A rising standard of living combined with remarkable advances in medical science to prolong life, thereby augmenting the total number of people. The vital statistics for Germany illustrate this point. The death rate in the period 1851–1860 was 27.8 per 1,000. During the 1860's, 1870's, and 1880's it remained high: 28.4, 28.8, and 26.5. Then it declined to 23.5 in the 1890's, and in the first decade of the twentieth century it fell to 19.7. The most important factor in the increase of the average life-span has been a reduction in infant mortality. Before the Industrial Revolution there were periods when more than half of all children born in any given year did not reach their first birthday. Neglect, mishandling, malnutrition, and childhood diseases decimated the offspring of even the well-to-do classes. But after 1800 economic and medical progress led to a steady decrease in the death rate of children. In England and Wales as late as 1910 the number of deaths per 1,000 infants less than a year old was still 128. By 1930 the proportion had dropped to 68, and by 1950 to 30. In other countries the decline in infant mortality was equally impressive. The figures for Germany during the same years were 186, 94, and 55; for France 132, 89,

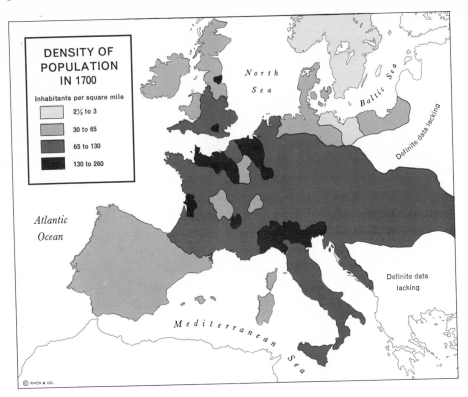

DENSITY OF
POPULATION
IN 1700

Inhabitants per square mile

2½ to 3

30 to 65

65 to 130

130 to 260

*North
Sea*

Baltic Sea

Definite data lacking

*Atlantic
Ocean*

Definite data
lacking

*Mediterranean
Sea*

© RM_N & CO.

and 47; and for Sweden 84, 59, and 21. The result of a reduction in the overall death rate was an extension of longevity. The life expectancy at birth of females in England and Wales rose from 42 years in 1845 to 52 in 1905 and 72 in 1950. In France the comparable ages were 41, 49, and 69, and in Sweden 47, 57, and 72.

One effect of the Industrial Revolution, then, has been an increase in population, occurring at first at a very rapid pace, then more slowly. During most of the nineteenth century the birth rate remained high, while the death rate declined. But after the opening of the twentieth century the birth rate also began to go down, so that the relative demographic growth diminished. The vital statistics for England and Wales provide a good example of this trend. Between 1760 and 1780, before the factory system had become firmly established, the population of the kingdom rose 11 per cent. Between 1780 and 1800 the percentage climbed to 23, and it remained high for the next 100 years: 34 per cent for 1800–1820, 33 for 1820–1840, 26 for 1840–1860, 30 for 1860–1880, and 25 for 1880–1900. Then came a drop to 17 for 1900–1920, 11 for 1920–1940, and 10 for 1940–1960. The pattern of demographic expansion in the other countries of Europe has been by and large the same. After an initial swift growth in population during the early stages of industrialization, there has been a decline in the birth rate and a relative reduction of population growth. Europe's

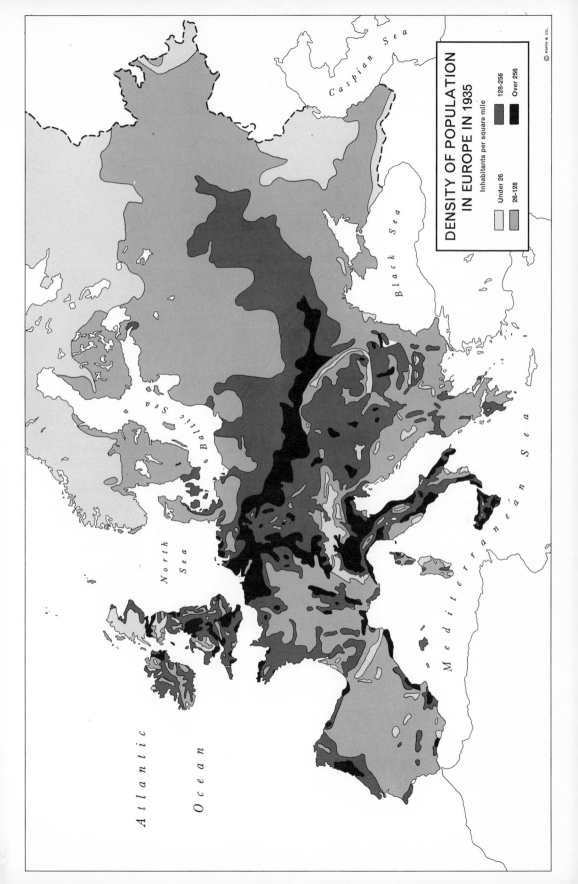

DENSITY OF POPULATION
IN EUROPE IN 1935

Inhabitants per square mile

Under 26

26-128

128-256

Over 256

© RAND & CO.

Caspian Sea

Black Sea

Baltic Sea

North Sea

Atlantic Ocean

Mediterranean Sea

population continues to increase, but the rise in productivity is greater than the rise in population. There are parts of the world which face the problem of a *population explosion,* that is, an expansion in the number of people substantially larger than the expansion of the manufacturing and agricultural output. Such an imbalance in the rates of economic and demographic growth is bound to lead to a decline in the standard of living. But European society does not face this danger. Industrialized and urbanized, prosperous and educated, it has achieved a sound equilibrium between material resources and human needs.

CHANGES IN CLASS STRUCTURE

The Industrial Revolution has also altered the social system of Europe. By reducing the importance of agriculture it reduced the importance of those classes which derived their livelihood from agriculture. The most obvious consequence has been the disappearance of the landed nobility as a vital force in public life. Their decline coincided with and was caused by the industrialization of the economy. Some great landowners managed to retain a measure of political, military, bureaucratic, and even economic influence in central and eastern Europe until the Second World War. But the new order which emerged out of that terrible conflict destroyed their power once and for all. Today there is hardly a country in the world in which a title of nobility is more than a social ornament. Those aristocrats who have managed to survive the disintegration of their class have done so only by allying themselves with bourgeois forces in industry, commerce, or finance.

The peasantry, although more prosperous since the coming of the Industrial Revolution, has also declined. The last two hundred years have destroyed the legal and economic shackles which had kept the villager subservient to the landed aristocracy. A new system of capitalistic agriculture based on free ownership swept away the last remnants of serfdom and manorialism. The growing demand for industrial labor, moreover, absorbed the surplus population of the countryside, strengthening the position of those who remained on the soil. Finally the great social upheavals of the twentieth century which crushed the agrarian nobility improved the status of the rustic. They made him an independent proprietor or a participant in a collective farm. The material well-being of the European peasant is greater than it was a hundred years ago, although many pockets of rural poverty remain in such regions as southern Italy and Spain. Yet while the standard of living in the village has risen, its influence has diminished. The peasantry has become a declining class, living in the shadow of the big urban centers which dominate the economy of the West. The farmer cannot disappear because the function he performs for society is indispensable, but his interests, attitudes, customs, and beliefs are steadily losing their importance in the community.

The first and greatest beneficiary of the Industrial Revolution was the bourgeoisie. The men who established factories and collieries, who built railroad and steamship lines, who organized banks and insurance companies, who imported raw materials and exported manufactured goods, who founded newspapers and periodicals, who became managers and directors, who practiced law, engineering, medicine, and journalism, such men played an increasingly important role in the life of Europe. They gradually gained a dominant position in the political, economic, and social system. They began to acquire a decisive voice in the determination of state policy; they began to control a major share of the national wealth; they began to exercise a powerful influence over public attitudes and values. The nineteenth century became the golden age of the European middle class. The growth of free trade, the emergence of liberal parties, the spread of parliamentary institutions, the popularization of the virtues of sobriety and hard work, all reflected the triumph of the self-made man in the community. Even after these classic manifestations of his power came under attack in the twentieth century, he retained considerable authority. The passing of the era of rugged individualism in economics reduced the preponderance of the bourgeoisie without destroying it. The world is still dominated in large part by the needs and interests of the middle class.

The Industrial Revolution was also responsible for the rise of another important group in society, the factory proletariat. This group was made up of those people, most of them uprooted peasants and artisans, who derived their livelihood from employment in mills and mines. A common way of life gradually produced among them a sense of solidarity which found expression in proletarian economic and political associations. As the laboring masses of the factory system recovered from the bewilderment produced by their transplantation from a rural to an urban environment, they began to organize for the purpose of improving their position. The first significant expression of their growing class consciousness was the formation of labor unions, which proposed to raise the workers' standard of living through collective action. The strike became their most effective weapon in the struggle to win a larger share of the profits of industrialism. At first the governments of Europe, controlled by the well-to-do classes, tried to suppress the young labor movement. But these efforts failed, and by the end of the nineteenth century the unionization of the European factory proletariat was far advanced.

In most countries, moreover, the working class was won over to the cause of socialism which taught that the basic problems confronting the propertyless groups in society could be solved only through public ownership of the means of production and transportation. The established order sought initially to destroy the socialist parties with even greater determination than it sought to destroy the labor unions. Yet here too it was gradually forced to accept what it could not overcome. The workingman was more and more attracted to radical doctrines which rejected the entire system of values of bourgeois society. Still, the combined effect of unionism, socialism, industrial growth, and agricultural progress was to improve the lot of the lower classes. By the middle of the twentieth century the factory proletariat, organized, prosperous, and assertive, was challenging the dominance of the bourgeoisie in Europe. Its rise was the most momentous social consequence of the Industrial Revolution.

THE STANDARD OF LIVING

The far-reaching changes in the structure of the community resulting from industrialization have produced relatively little class violence. Never before did established economic relationships undergo such complete alteration in such a short time. Yet this historic process was by and large peaceful. There were a few middle-class uprisings in Europe during the nineteenth century, notably in 1848, but they were brief and relatively bloodless. The proletarian revolutions of the twentieth century, especially the establishment of a communist regime in Russia in 1917, were accompanied by considerably more turbulence. But the transition from an agrarian to an industrial society was on the whole calm, considering its magnitude. The basic reason for the widespread acquiescence in the transformation of the community was the rising standard of living of the population at large. Economic conflicts became amenable to compromise, when all men could expect to share the bounty of expanding production. The rationalization of industry and agriculture meant that the well-being of one social class no longer needed to be won at the expense of another social class. Man did not have to exploit man in order to advance his welfare. It became possible to create more goods for more people in less time with less effort. The golden age of security and leisure about which human society had dreamed throughout its history could now be placed not in the irrevocable past but in the attainable future.

The Industrial Revolution brought about a remarkable improvement in the European way of life. The population quadrupled and longevity doubled, while the standard of living continued to rise. The volume of commodities available for consumption grew more rapidly than the number of inhabitants. For the broad masses the rationalization of the economy has meant an increase in material well-being. The amount of physical labor required to produce manufactured and agricultural goods has declined, so that leisure, once the prerogative of wealth, has become a common experience even for the lower classes. The work week of 60, 65, and 70 hours has been reduced to less than 45 in many countries, and a figure of 35 or even 30 is a probability in the not very distant future. An unchecked increase in population could slow the rise in the standard of living, but statistical evidence suggests that a prosperous industrialized society tends to limit its rate of reproduction. An equilibrium has been established in Europe between demographic and economic growth which makes possible a continuing expansion of popular affluence.

The mitigation of economic conflict, moreover, should lead to a mitigation of political conflict. Wars among nations have had a variety of causes: dynastic aspirations, territorial ambitions, military rivalries, ideological differences, even religious prejudices. But no cause of international discord has been more constant than the desire for greater material well-being. The conviction that the standard of living of one people can be enhanced only through the subjugation of another people underlay the calculations of every aggressor from Tiglath-pileser and Cyrus to Napoleon and Hitler. But this conviction ceases to make sense in the light of the experience of the Industrial Revolution. The development since the Second World War of countries like Germany, Italy, and Japan demonstrates this point. During the 1930's they had been ruled by expansionist regimes which insisted that their growing populations could be supported only through the acquisition of additional territory, in other words, through war and conquest. Yet today those same populations, larger even than a generation ago and compressed within narrower boundaries, are living better than ever before. The industrialization of the economy thus makes possible the advancement of material well-being without recourse to arms. One of the most important factors leading to war is losing its efficacy, and the result is likely to be a gradual decline in international tension.

The Industrial Revolution has opened before mankind exciting new possibilities. These possibilities involve difficulties and dangers, but there is no reason to

POWER BY THOMAS HART BENTON. A well-known contemporary American artist has here sought to capture the spirit of modern mechanization.

believe that the rationalization of life must lead to its dehumanization. While the problems of social adaptation to industrialism are serious, they are not insuperable. They are no more serious than those which man overcame when he first ceased to be a hunter and became a farmer, or when he first abandoned the primitive villages of prehistory to found the cities of the ancient Near East. Each of these earlier adjustments meant an important step forward to a more civilized form of human existence. The transition to an industrialized economy holds the same promise of progress.

Further Reading

There are several good general accounts of the Industrial Revolution, among them *T. S. Ashton, *The Industrial Revolution, 1760–1830* (London, 1948); and N. S. B. Gras, *Industrial Evolution* (Cambridge, Mass., 1930). *P. Mantoux, *The Industrial Revolution in the Eighteenth Century* (London, 1928) is an outstanding study of the origins of the factory system. For the economic development of the leading countries there are J. H. Clapham, *An Economic History of Modern Britain*, 3 vols. (Cambridge, 1926–1938) and *The Economic Development of France and Germany, 1815–1914* (Cambridge, 1936); R. E. Cameron, *France and the Economic Development of Europe, 1800–1914* (Princeton, 1961); and P. I. Liashchenko, *History of the National Economy of Russia to the 1917 Revolution* (New York, 1949). The standard of living of the lower classes before and after the advent of industrialism is discussed by M. C. Buer, *Health, Wealth and Population in the Early Days of the Industrial Revolution* (London, 1926); and J. L. and B. Hammond, *The Village Labourer, 1760–1832* (New York, 1920). *A. P. Usher, *History of Mechanical Inventions* (Boston, 1959) depicts the technological advances which formed the basis of the Industrial Revolution. *W. W. Rostow, *The Stages of Economic Growth* (Cambridge, 1961) presents an original interpretation of the process of industrialization.

L. C. A. Knowles, *Economic Development in the Nineteenth Century* (London, 1932) contains a sound treatment of modern progress in transportation and communication. For the interconnection between finance and industry see A. Plummer, *International Combinations in Modern Industry* (London, 1938); and J. Riesser, *The German Great Banks and Their Concentration* (Washington, 1911). The complex question of economic depressions is examined in W. C. Mitchell, *Business Cycles: The Problem and Its Setting* (New York, 1928); and J. A. Schumpeter, *Business Cycles: A Theoretical and Statistical Analysis of the Capitalist Process* (New York, 1964). C. K. Hobson, *The Export of Capital* (London, 1914) and *H. Feis, *Europe, the World's Banker, 1870–1914* (New Haven, 1930) are important studies of the role of European banking in the world economy. E. Corti, *The Rise of the House of Rothschild* (New York, 1928) and C. Wright and C. E. Fayle, *A History of Lloyd's* (London, 1928) depict two giants of international finance.

A good introduction to the development of agriculture in the West may be found in N. S. B. Gras, *A History of Agriculture in Europe and America* (New York, 1940).

J. A. Venn, *The Foundations of Agricultural Economics* (Cambridge, 1933), analyzes the rise of modern farming. There are several other works dealing with various aspects of English farm life. See, for example, N. S. B. and E. C. Gras, *The Economic and Social History of an English Village* (Cambridge, Mass., 1930); and R. E. P. Ernle, *English Farming* (Chicago, 1962). Conditions on the Continent are described by J. Blum, *Noble Landowners and Agriculture in Austria (1815–1848)* (Baltimore, 1948); and J. B. Holt, *German Agricultural Policy, 1918–1934* (Chapel Hill, 1936).

No one has written about the problems of urbanization more imaginatively than L. Mumford. Among his works dealing with this subject are *Technics and Civilization* (New York, 1934) and *The Culture of Cities* (New York, 1938). N. Anderson, *The Urban Community* (New York, 1959) and N. Carpenter, *The Sociology of City Life* (New York, 1931) deal with the way of life created by the rise of the metropolis. An analysis of the growth of the big city is presented by R. E. Dickinson, *The West European City* (London, 1951). For the civilization which metropolitan existence is shaping see N. A. Berdiaev, *The Bourgeois Mind* (London, 1934); and A. N. Pack, *The Challenge of Leisure* (New York, 1934).

The best survey of demographic expansion is still A. M. Carr-Saunders, *World Population: Past Growth and Present Trends* (Oxford, 1936). But it should be supplemented with such studies as E. M. East, ed., *Biology in Human Affairs* (New York, 1931); and H. P. Fairchild, *People: The Quantity and Quality of Population* (New York, 1939). J. A. Field, *Essays on Population* (Chicago, 1931) and E. Bowen, *An Hypothesis of Population Growth* (New York, 1931) examine the increase of population in the West. For an analysis of the social implications of industrialization see S. Chase, *Men and Machines* (New York, 1935); H. O. Rugg, *The Great Technology* (New York, 1933); and *E. Mayo, *The Human Problems of an Industrial Civilization* (New York, 1933).

CHAPTER 16

The Liberal Era
1815–1871

A different Europe emerged from the fires of the French Revolution
and the Napoleonic era. More than twenty years of war had destroyed the political
structure of enlightened despotism, intensified the economic effects of industrialism,
and altered the traditional class structure of continental life. The conservative statesmen who gathered in Vienna in 1814 might dream of a return to the stable civic
order which European society had known under the Old Regime, but there could
be no turning back the clock. The eighteenth century was over, and the legitimists
of Metternich's school soon discovered that a new age had opened which pursued its
own goals by its own methods.

1. The Conflict of Ideologies

THE CHANGED SOCIAL ENVIRONMENT in which men found themselves after the restoration of peace was bound to alter their civic faith. In the benign atmosphere of the
Enlightenment it was easy to believe that some day a philosopher-king would

[624]

exercise his absolute authority to inaugurate a humanitarian millennium on earth. But after the terrible ordeal of revolution and warfare which ended at Waterloo such a hope began to seem naïve. The great doctrinal need of the new age was a statement of belief voicing its distinctive political ideals and aspirations.

LIBERALISM

The ideology which best expressed the dominant mood of this new age was liberalism. Liberalism brought to the middle class of Europe a view of man and society which harmonized with its own experiences and interests. It condemned the aristocratic bias of the benevolent absolutism of the preceding century without embracing the egalitarian principle of Jacobinism. While it sought to deprive the landed nobility of its monopoly of political influence, it did not flirt with the great unwashed who respected neither life nor property. It followed the path of what the French called the *juste-milieu,* the straight and narrow path between despotism on the right and radicalism on the left. Wherever the factory system went, the industrial bourgeoisie followed, and behind the industrial bourgeoisie came liberalism.

Theoretically liberalism relied on the political teachings of the Age of Enlightenment which justified opposition to royal tyranny—the teachings of Locke, Voltaire, and Montesquieu. Practically it drew on the experiences of the revolutions of the seventeenth century in England and the eighteenth century in America and France. It maintained that government was based on a social contract between governor and governed by which the latter agreed to obey the former in return for protection of the inalienable rights of the individual. Among these rights—guaranteed by God and nature alike—were life, liberty, property, and the freedom of speech, press, petition, assembly, and religion. The state was limited in its power over the citizen, for it could not deprive him of fundamental privileges which were his birthright. One of the most famous liberal documents, the American Declaration of Independence, argued that "all men are created equal," equal in the sense that they all possess as their natural heritage lifelong personal rights. It therefore followed that instruments of political repression and censorship, laws conferring special privileges on hereditary aristocracies, and legal discriminations because of race or religion were unjustifiable in theory and evil in effect. Individual freedom was the hallmark of liberalism.

Yet if all men were equal in the protection which they enjoyed against oppression, that did not mean that they were equal in the right to direct state policy. It was self-evident that the ignorant, the stupid, the reckless, and the subversive could not be entrusted with the determination of the fate of a nation. Only those who had proved their ability and intelligence ought to have a voice in government, and the best way to prove ability and intelligence was to accumulate property. In a speech before the French legislature the eminent liberal statesman François Guizot described his formula for social progress with disarming simplicity: *"Enrichissez-vous* [get rich]!" For Guizot, as for most liberals, the best of all governments was a constitutional monarchy in which the king reigned without ruling and in which the masses obeyed without questioning. The state should retain the trappings of royalty because they gave the nation a sense of tradition and stability, but the real power behind the throne ought to be a parliament elected by a highly propertied suffrage. The ruler might perform the executive functions of government: he might appoint civil and military officials; he might conduct foreign affairs; he might even declare war and conclude peace. All legislative enactments, however, especially the adoption of budgets, must have the approval of a parliamentary assembly representing the well-to-do elements of society. Ideally, moreover, the functions of the crown should be exercised by a ministry appointed by the monarch but responsible to the legislature. Since the crown was to enjoy the shadow but not the substance of authority, and since the masses were to be carefully excluded from a voice in government, the dominant role in the state would fall to the main beneficiary of industrialism, the educated and propertied bourgeoisie.

In economics as well as in politics, liberalism preached an individualistic freedom and reflected middle-class interests. Rejecting the mercantilistic theories of the preceding age, it advanced the principles of *laissez faire* propounded by the classical school of English economists. From Adam Smith's *The Wealth of Nations,* published in 1776, it borrowed the view that the free competition of nations and individuals, unrestrained by protective duties and monopolistic practices, must in the long run result in the greatest possible economic well-being of society. For the enlightened self-interest of millions of individuals engaged in the pursuit of profit would lead each to seek gain in that branch of industry or agriculture for which he was best fitted, and the consumer would be the beneficiary of this natural economic specialization. From Thomas Malthus' *Essay on the Principles of Population* (1798) liberalism learned that the unemployment, hunger, and suffering which followed in the wake of the Industrial Revolution were not the result of economic dislocation caused by the factory system, but the natural and inevitable outcome of the laws of population growth. Since men tended to multiply at a faster rate than their food supply, providence itself arranged for the reestablishment of a balance between population and nourishment by such means as wars, epidemics, and famines. Finally the dismal science of laissez-faire economics accepted the doctrine advanced by David Ricardo in his *Principles of Political Economy* (1817) that the wages of labor are governed by a natural "iron law" with which man cannot tamper. They will not fall below the subsistence level, for then the worker will be unable or unwilling to perform his job; but neither can they rise above that point of remuneration at which the laboring population increases so rapidly that a shortage of work develops and wages fall once again:

There is no means of improving the lot of the worker except by limiting the number of his children. His destiny is in his own hands. Every suggestion which does not tend to the reduction in number of the working people is useless, to say the least of it. All legislative interference must be pernicious.

DEMOCRACY

Armed with a consistent philosophy of state and society, liberalism marched forth into the nineteenth century to remake the world in its own image. But its outlook was too narrow and its interest too exclusive to win the support of all opponents of royal absolutism. Among the lower middle class, among small businessmen, petty shop owners, independent tradesmen, lawyers, journalists, and intellectuals, there arose an ideology known variously as radicalism in England, republicanism in France, and democracy in Germany. It too condemned the teachings of divine-right monarchism, but it sought to replace them with the tenets of the Jacobin Republic of Virtue. Its heroes were not Locke and Washington but Rousseau and Robespierre. It spoke of the sovereignty of the general will, it approved manhood suffrage, it favored a republican form of government, and it advocated governmental measures to improve the lot of the masses through the supervision and regulation of economic life. It believed in the freedom of the individual and in the sanctity of private property no less firmly than liberalism, but it also argued that a stable government must be based on the consent of that "rabble" whom middle-of-the-road bourgeois statesmen regarded with contempt. In the final analysis it was prepared to subordinate property rights and even personal rights to the ideal of the greatest good of the greatest number.

Throughout the early nineteenth century the democrats remained a persecuted political faction opposed by both conservatives and liberals. In Great Britain William Cobbett spent two years in jail and Jeremy Bentham found himself under attack as a dangerous subverter of society. In France Godefroy Cavaignac and A. A. Ledru-Rollin were subjected to police surveillance and bureaucratic harassment. In Italy the views of the exiled radical Giuseppe Mazzini were propagated by a small band of his devoted followers who often paid for their convictions with imprisonment. In Germany Gustav von Struve and Friedrich Hecker were forced to disguise their republican leanings behind a facade of subtle innuendoes. Only after 1870 did democracy become a respectable political faith in Europe capable of exerting a significant influence over national parliaments and over the voting public.

SOCIALISM

At first the industrial worker was in sympathy with the teachings of democracy. The conservatives preached to him only the virtues of obedience and piety, while the liberals made little effort to disguise their distaste for the lower classes. The urban proletariat, therefore, was favorably disposed toward a radicalism which advocated manhood suffrage and social equality. Before long, however, its attention was attracted to another political doctrine. If liberalism was essentially the ideology of the mill owner, socialism became the ideology of the mill hand. By the end of the nineteenth century it had emerged as the secular faith of the European worker, who often sacrificed for its sake his religious belief and his dynastic loyalty. In return it provided him with a purpose and an ideal; it explained his sorrows and resentments; it assured him of a final judgment which would avenge his years of oppression. In the meantime he could attend socialist party meetings, relax at socialist party dances, find a wife in the socialist party women's auxiliary, take his family to the socialist party picnics, pay his medical bills through the socialist party sickness insurance, and be sure that eventually the expenses of his burial would be paid through the socialist party funeral fund. Socialism was more than an ideology, more than a movement; it was a way of life.

The basic notion of socialism—the notion that the government ought to destroy the profit motive as the driving force of economic life by assuming ownership of the means of production and transportation—had its roots in antiquity. But only since the advent of industrialism had it been able to acquire a consistent theoretical foundation. The factory system had given birth to a new class in western society, the industrial proletariat. Torn from its roots in the village and unassimilated by the older urban population, it was in need of a social philosophy to define its position in the community. Socialism satisfied that need. It brought a measure of hope and a sense of security to those millions who had abandoned the rural way of life followed by their ancestors for centuries to find a new existence in the slums of London or Paris or Berlin or Vienna. Socialism's successes must be explained in terms not of its economic teachings, which were as a matter of fact open to serious criticism, but of the emotional satisfactions which it provided for the uprooted and the dispossessed who were the spiritual victims of the Industrial Revolution.

The earliest exponents of modern socialism were usually men of upper- or middle-class origin who for humanitarian reasons sought to eliminate the economic hardships which accompanied the factory system. They shunned mob violence and class conflict; they were even ready under certain circumstances to tolerate a degree of capitalism. What they wanted was the creation of a system of voluntary cooperative ownership of industrial enterprises in which the advantages of communal proprietorship would soon become self-evident. Count Henri de Saint-Simon and Étienne Cabet described imaginary societies in which men lived and worked not for selfish profit but for the common good. Charles Fourier and Louis Blanc presented detailed blueprints of socialistic communities and undertakings which could offer the individual economic security and personal satisfaction. Robert Owen tried to translate these plans into reality by founding an experimental colony in New Harmony, Indiana (1825–1828). But the pioneer socialists relied almost invariably

20. NAPOLEON CROSSING THE ALPS. Jacques Louis David, here abandoning the classicism of his earlier works, depicts Napoleon as the First Consul, preparing to cross the Alps at the head of his troops before the great victory at Marengo in 1800.

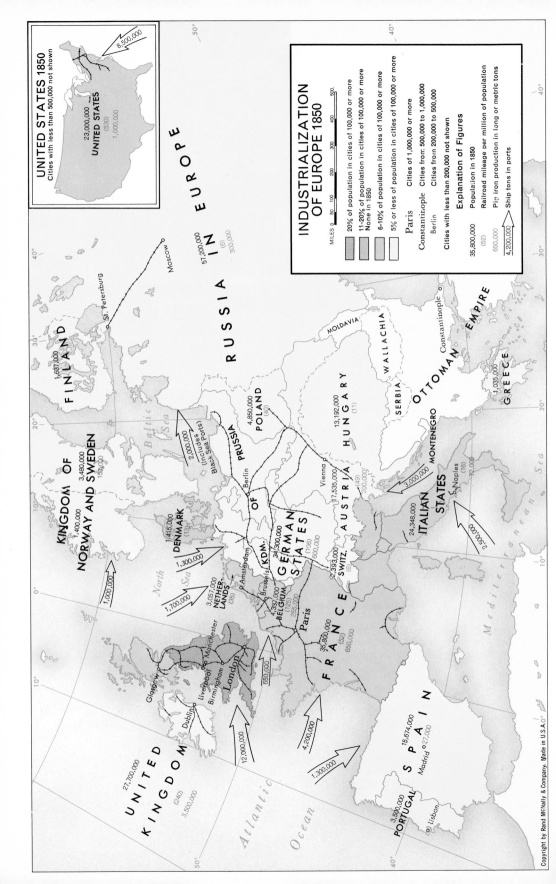

UNITED STATES 1850
Cities with less than 500,000 not shown

8,500,000

23,000,000
(530)
UNITED STATES
(1,000,000)

INDUSTRIALIZATION OF EUROPE 1850

MILES 50 100 200 300 400 500

20% of population in cities of 100,000 or more

11-20% of population in cities of 100,000 or more
None in 1850

6-10% of population in cities of 100,000 or more

5% or less of population in cities of 100,000 or more

Paris   Cities of 1,000,000 or more

Constantinople Cities from: 500,000 to 1,000,000

Berlin   Cities from 200,000 to 500,000

Cities with less than 200,000 not shown

Explanation of Figures

35,800,000   Population in 1850

(52)   Railroad mileage per million of population

650,000   Pig iron production in long or metric tons

4,200,000   Ship tons in ports

EUROPE

IN

RUSSIA

Moscow

51,200,000 (6)
300,000

FINLAND
1,687,000

St. Petersburg

**KINGDOM OF
NORWAY AND SWEDEN**
1,400,000   3,480,000

Baltic Sea

2,000,000
(includes
Black Sea Ports)
150,000

PRUSSIA

Berlin

POLAND
4,850,000
(40)

DENMARK
1,415,000
(13)

1,300,000

1,700,000

Amsterdam

**NETHER-
LANDS**
3,057,000
(35)

Brussels

BELGIUM
4,337,000
(125)
255,000

KDM.

**GERMAN
STATES**
34,300,000
(106)
600,000

Vienna

AUSTRIA
17,535,000
(49)
200,000

HUNGARY
13,192,000
(11)

MOLDAVIA

WALLACHIA

SERBIA

OTTOMAN EMPIRE

Constantinople

GREECE
1,035,000

North Sea

1,000,000

Glasgow

Liverpool   Manchester

Birmingham

London

650,000

**UNITED
KINGDOM**
27,700,000
(240)
3,500,000

Dublin

12,000,000

4,200,000

Paris

FRANCE
35,800,000
(52)
660,000

SWITZ.
2,393,000
(6)

1,300,000

**ITALIAN
STATES**
24,348,000

Naples
(16)

3,000,000

MONTENEGRO

2,500,000

SPAIN
15,674,000

Madrid
27,000

PORTUGAL
3,500,000

Lisbon

Atlantic

Ocean

Mediterranean Sea

Copyright by Rand McNally & Company. Made in U.S.A.

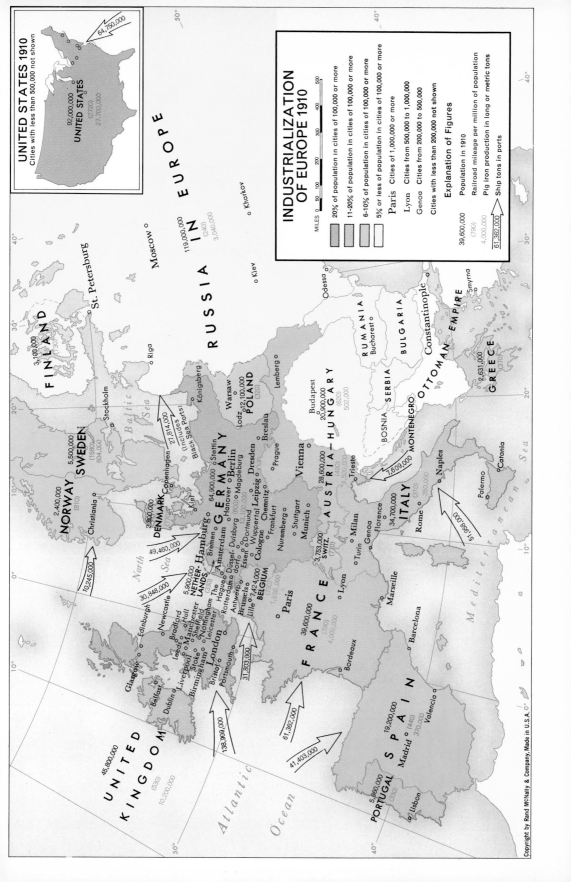

UNITED STATES 1910
Cities with less than 500,000 not shown

64,750,000

92,000,000
UNITED STATES
(27,700)

27,700,000

INDUSTRIALIZATION OF EUROPE 1910

MILES 0 50 100 200 300 400 500

20% of population in cities of 100,000 or more
11–20% of population in cities of 100,000 or more
6–10% of population in cities of 100,000 or more
5% or less of population in cities of 100,000 or more

Paris   Cities of 1,000,000 or more
Lyon   Cities from 500,000 to 1,000,000
Genoa   Cities from 200,000 to 500,000
Cities with less than 200,000 not shown

Explanation of Figures

39,600,000   Population in 1910
(790)   Railroad mileage per million of population
4,000,000   Pig iron production in long and metric tons
61,362,000   Ship tons in ports

EUROPE

RUSSIA

119,000,000   (240)
3,040,000

Moscow
St. Petersburg
Kharkov
Kiev
Odessa
Riga

FINLAND
3,100,000
(30)

NORWAY
2,400,000
(810)
Christiania

SWEDEN
5,500,000
(1580)
604,000
Stockholm

DENMARK
2,800,000
Copenhagen   27,814,000
(includes Black Sea Ports)
Kiel

Baltic Sea
North Sea

GERMANY
64,900,000
(600)
13,100,000
Hamburg   49,460,000
Bremen
Hanover   Berlin
Magdeburg
Leipzig   Dresden
Chemnitz
Prague

Stettin
Königsberg

POLAND
12,100,000
(320)
Warsaw
Lodz
Lemberg
Breslau

NETHER-LANDS
5,900,000
(330)
Amsterdam
The Hague
Rotterdam
30,848,000

BELGIUM
7,424,000
(290)
1,890,000
Antwerp
Brussels
Lille
Düsseldorf
Duisburg
Essen
Cologne
Dortmund
Wuppertal
Frankfurt
Nuremberg
Stuttgart

AUSTRIA–HUNGARY
28,600,000
(440)
502,000
Vienna
Budapest   20,900,000
(620)
502,000
Trieste

RUMANIA
Bucharest

SERBIA
BOSNIA
MONTENEGRO
BULGARIA

OTTOMAN EMPIRE
7,603,000
Constantinople
Smyrna

GREECE
2,631,000
(370)

UNITED KINGDOM
46,800,000
(590)
10,200,000

Glasgow
Edinburgh
Belfast
Dublin
Newcastle
Bradford
Leeds
Hull
Liverpool
Manchester
Sheffield
Stoke
Nottingham
Birmingham
Leicester
London   138,909,000
Bristol
Portsmouth
31,803,000
10,245,000

FRANCE
39,600,000
(700)
4,000,000
Paris
Munich
Lyon
Bordeaux
Marseille
61,362,000
3,753,000
SWITZ.
(770)
Turin
Milan
Genoa

ITALY
34,700,000
(370)
350,000
Florence
Rome
Naples
Palermo
Catania
619,866,000

SPAIN
19,200,000
(440)
370,000
Madrid
Barcelona
Valencia
41,403,000
61,362,000

PORTUGAL
5,960,000
(30)
Lisbon

Atlantic Ocean
Mediterranean Sea

Copyright by Rand McNally & Company, Made in U.S.A.

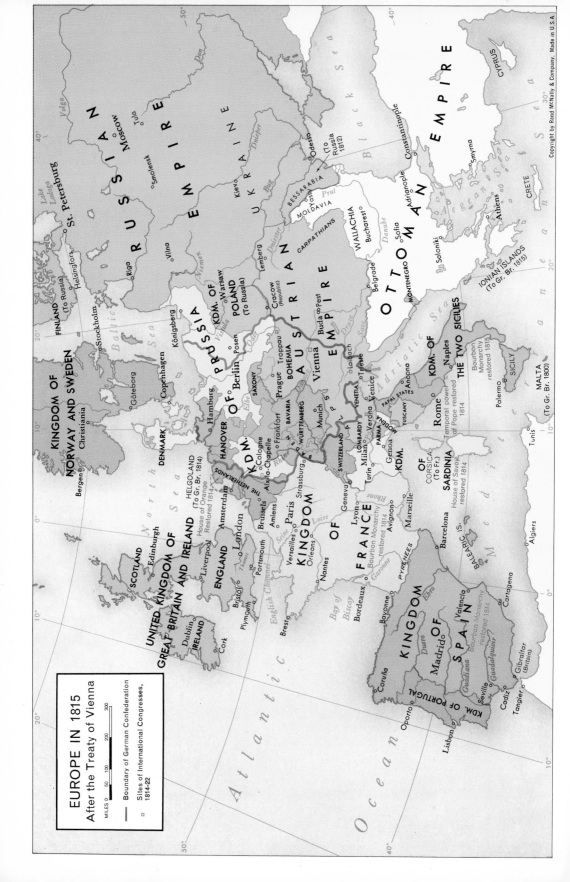

EUROPE IN 1815
After the Treaty of Vienna

——— Boundary of German Confederation

□ Sites of International Congresses, 1814-22

MILES 0   50   100   200   300

Copyright by Rand McNally & Company. Made in U.S.A.

RUSSIAN EMPIRE

OTTOMAN EMPIRE

AUSTRIAN EMPIRE

KINGDOM OF PRUSSIA

KDM. OF POLAND (To Russia)

KINGDOM OF NORWAY AND SWEDEN

UNITED KINGDOM OF GREAT BRITAIN AND IRELAND

KINGDOM OF FRANCE
Bourbon Monarchy restored 1814

KINGDOM OF SPAIN
Bourbon Monarchy restored 1814

KDM. OF PORTUGAL

KDM. OF THE TWO SICILIES
Bourbon Monarchy restored 1815

KDM. OF SARDINIA
House of Savoy restored 1814

PAPAL STATES
Temporal power of Pope restored 1814

HANOVER

KDM. OF THE NETHERLANDS
House of Orange Restored 1814

DENMARK

UKRAINE

BOHEMIA

BAVARIA

SAXONY

WÜRTEMBERG

SWITZERLAND

LOMBARDY

VENETIA

PARMA

MODENA

TUSCANY

WALLACHIA

MOLDAVIA

BESSARABIA (To Russia 1812)

FINLAND (To Russia)

SCOTLAND

ENGLAND

IRELAND

MONTENEGRO

BALEARIC IS.

CORSICA (To Fr.)

SICILY

SARDINIA

CRETE

CYPRUS

HELGOLAND (To Gr. Br. 1814)

MALTA (To Gr. Br. 1800)

IONIAN ISLANDS (To Gr. Br. 1815)

Moscow
Tula
Smolensk
St. Petersburg
Helsingfors
Riga
Vilna
Kiev
Odessa
Lemberg
CarpatianS
Warsaw
Cracow (Republic)
Posen
Königsberg
Stockholm
Göteborg
Copenhagen
Hamburg
Berlin
Prague
Troppau
Buda Pest
Vienna
Munich
Frankfort
Cologne
Aix-la-Chapelle
Strassburg
Geneva
Turin
Milan
Verona
Venice
Trieste
Loiben
Laibach
Ancona
Rome
Naples
Palermo
Genoa
Brussels
Amsterdam
London
Liverpool
Portsmouth
Plymouth
Bristol
Edinburgh
Dublin
Cork
Paris
Versailles
Amiens
Orleans
Nantes
Bordeaux
Bayonne
Lyon
Marseille
Avignon
Barcelona
Madrid
Valencia
Seville
Cadiz
Cartagena
Gibraltar (Britain)
Coruña
Oporto
Lisbon
Tangier
Algiers
Tunis
Constantinople
Adrianople
Salonika
Smyrna
Athens
Sofia
Bucharest
Belgrade
Jassy
Bergen
Christiania

Volga
Don
Dnieper
Bug
Dniester
Niemen
Vistula
Oder
Elbe
Rhine
Danube
Seine
Loire
Rhone
Garonne
Ebro
Duero
Guadiana
Guadalquivir
Prut
Drave

Lake Ladoga

Baltic Sea
North Sea
Atlantic Ocean
Bay of Biscay
English Channel
Mediterranean Sea
Adriatic Sea
Aegean Sea
Black Sea

PYRENEES
ALPS

21. LIBERTY LEADING THE PEOPLE. In this striking example of romantic painting, Eugène Delacroix reveals not only his talent for vivid and tumultuous use of color, but also his sympathy with the revolution of 1830 and the new political and social fervor that engendered it.

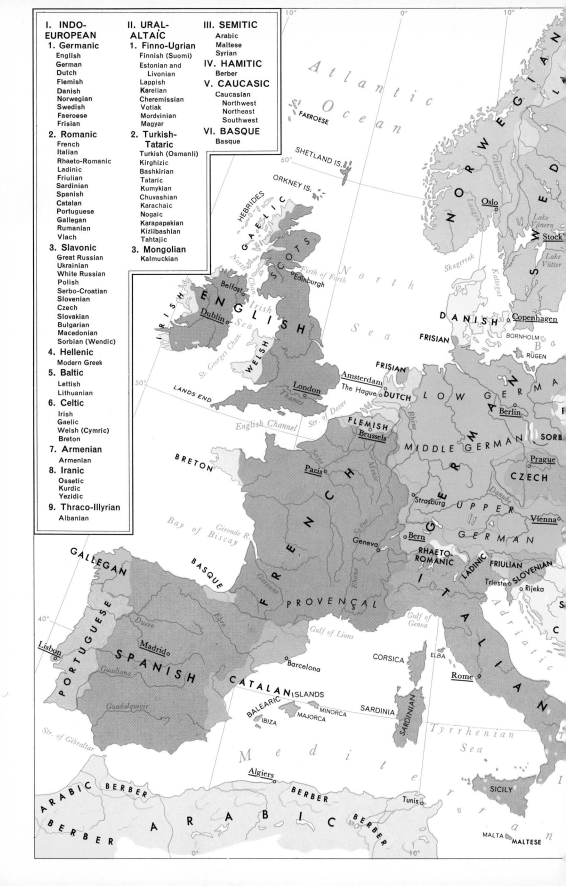

I. INDO-EUROPEAN
1. **Germanic**
   English
   German
   Dutch
   Flemish
   Danish
   Norwegian
   Swedish
   Faeroese
   Frisian
2. **Romanic**
   French
   Italian
   Rhaeto-Romanic
   Ladinic
   Friulian
   Sardinian
   Spanish
   Catalan
   Portuguese
   Gallegan
   Rumanian
   Vlach
3. **Slavonic**
   Great Russian
   Ukrainian
   White Russian
   Polish
   Serbo-Croatian
   Slovenian
   Czech
   Slovakian
   Bulgarian
   Macedonian
   Sorbian (Wendic)
4. **Hellenic**
   Modern Greek
5. **Baltic**
   Lettish
   Lithuanian
6. **Celtic**
   Irish
   Gaelic
   Welsh (Cymric)
   Breton
7. **Armenian**
   Armenian
8. **Iranic**
   Ossetic
   Kurdic
   Yezidic
9. **Thraco-Illyrian**
   Albanian

II. URAL-ALTAIC
1. **Finno-Ugrian**
   Finnish (Suomi)
   Estonian and Livonian
   Lappish
   Karelian
   Cheremissian
   Votiak
   Mordvinian
   Magyar
2. **Turkish-Tataric**
   Turkish (Osmanli)
   Kirghizic
   Bashkirian
   Tataric
   Kumykian
   Chuvashian
   Karachaic
   Nogaic
   Karapapakian
   Kizilbashian
   Tahtajic
3. **Mongolian**
   Kalmuckian

III. SEMITIC
   Arabic
   Maltese
   Syrian
IV. HAMITIC
   Berber
V. CAUCASIC
   Caucasian
   Northwest
   Northeast
   Southwest
VI. BASQUE
   Basque

LANGUAGES OF EUROPE
In the 19th Century

MILES 0   50   100   200   300

——— Boundaries after 1922.

22. THE UPRISING. Honoré Daumier, who began his career as a bitter political satirist, also depicted the harshness of lower-class existence with uncompromising realism; here he catches the power and brutal force, as well as the driving need, of the angry mob.

on methods of popular education and appeals to philanthropic sentiment for the realization of their schemes. Only occasionally would some hard-bitten conspirator like "Gracchus" Babeuf or Filippo Buonarotti secretly plot for the violent overthrow of existing society and the establishment of a communistic social order.

It was Karl Marx (1818–1883) who molded the diffuse visions of the early socialists into a disciplined system of thought. Member of a scholarly Jewish family in the Rhineland, eloquent, brilliant, and supremely self-confident, the radical publicist was contemptuous of the ideological fuzziness of utopian theorists like Saint-Simon or Fourier. They had spent their lives composing pleas, exhortations, sermons, and lectures. He based his views on rigidly logical argumentation, on what he himself called "science." Socialism, he maintained, was not only desirable; it was inevitable. It would be achieved not by dignified appeals to benevolent sentiments but through the process of history itself. For history was determined by the conflict of economic forces which shaped the character of human society. In ancient times the class struggle between slave and master had settled the fate of Greece and Rome. In the Middle Ages serf and lord became the protagonists in a titanic battle which gave birth to the Modern Age. At present it was the capitalist and the proletarian who were locked in combat for the mastery of the world. But the outcome was not in doubt. The laboring masses had to conquer; the entire course of the economic

KARL MARX. The gentleman with the formidable beard who spent his days in the British Museum studying economics and philosophy was one of the intellectual architects of the modern world.

development of the West guaranteed that. As for the individual, he could enlist on the side of destiny and help hasten its progress, or resist it and be crushed. In any case the capitalistic order would be overthrown to make way for the classless society of economic and social justice.

As a matter of fact, Marx maintained, capitalism was already digging its own grave. Through ruthless competition, through periodic financial crises, through merciless exploitation, the rich were becoming richer and fewer, the poor poorer and more numerous. The process of bourgeois self-destruction would culminate in a revolution toppling established governments which represented only the interests of the capitalists and preparing the ground for a new economy free from oppression. In the *Communist Manifesto,* which Marx and his friend Friedrich Engels published in 1848, the new "scientific" socialism threw down the gauntlet to the bourgeoisie of Europe: "Let the ruling classes tremble at a Communistic revolution. The proletarians have nothing to lose but their chains. They have a world to win. Workingmen of all countries, unite!" While for men of property Marxism preached only eternal warfare, to the proletariat it brought a gospel, a messiah, and a promise of a socialist paradise. Countless workers in all countries embraced the new faith, followed it, practiced it, and sometimes died for it.

CONSERVATISM

While liberal, democrat, and socialist vied for the allegiance of the new forces in European life, conservatism was vainly trying to protect the old order. But in grappling with the political and social effects of the French Revolution and the Industrial Revolution it was forced to seek a new ideological foundation. The familiar arguments of divine-right absolutism made less and less sense in an age which had seen anointed monarchs fleeing before republican armies and libertarian ideals. Something different was needed to defend established institutions like the throne and the altar, and that something was the doctrine of political romanticism. To the teachings of individual freedom which attracted the bourgeoisie, to the visions of a classless society which were held out before the proletariat, the Restoration replied with a new emphasis on history and tradition. The individual, it argued, cannot live by the paper schemes and perfectionist plans which the doctrinaire theorist never tires of spinning. He must have his roots in his country and in the unique national heritage of which he is a part. The proposition that all men are equal is meaningless, because as a matter of fact men differ in speech, in culture, in religion, in nationality, in property, in education, and in outlook. To pretend that these differences do not exist is to destroy the foundations of society and invite anarchy. The historic institutions of a people—its monarchy, its church, its aristocracy, its government—are living bonds between past and present. They cannot be up-

Rulers and Regimes of the Leading States
of Europe since 1815

AUSTRIA

Francis I, 1792–1835
Ferdinand I, 1835–1848
Francis Joseph, 1848–1916
Charles I, 1916–1918
Republican Regime, 1918–1938
Union with Germany, 1938–1945
Republican Regime, since 1945

ENGLAND

George III, 1760–1820
George IV, 1820–1830
William IV, 1830–1837
Victoria, 1837–1901
Edward VII, 1901–1910
George V, 1910–1936
Edward VIII, 1936
George VI, 1936–1952
Elizabeth II, since 1952

FRANCE

Louis XVIII, 1814–1824
Charles X, 1824–1830
Louis Philippe, 1830–1848
  (Orléanist Monarchy)
The Second Republic, 1848–1852
Napoleon III, 1852–1870
  (the Second Empire)
The Third Republic, 1870–1940
Pétain Regime, 1940–1944
Provisional Government, 1944–1946
The Fourth Republic, 1946–1958
The Fifth Republic, since 1958

GERMANY

William I, 1871–1888
Frederick III, 1888
William II, 1888–1918
The Weimar Republic, 1918–1933
The Third Reich, 1933–1945
Military Government, 1945–1949
The Federal Republic (West) and the
  Democratic Republic (East),
  since 1949

ITALY

Victor Emmanuel II, 1861–1878
Humbert I, 1878–1900
Victor Emmanuel III, 1900–1946
  (Mussolini Regime, 1922–1943)
Humbert II, 1946
Republican Regime, since 1946

PRUSSIA

Frederick William III, 1797–1840
Frederick William IV, 1840–1861
William I, 1861–1888
Part of United Germany, since 1871

RUSSIA

Alexander I, 1801–1825
Nicholas I, 1825–1855
Alexander II, 1855–1881
Alexander III, 1881–1894
Nicholas II, 1894–1917
Provisional Government, 1917
Communist Regime, since 1917

SARDINIA

Victor Emmanuel I, 1802–1821
Charles Felix, 1821–1831
Charles Albert, 1831–1849
Victor Emmanuel II, 1849–1878
Part of United Italy, since 1861

rooted with impunity, for on them depends the spiritual and physical well-being of the individual and the nation.

These views sounded eminently sensible to those who had a vested interest in the status quo. The landed nobility, the military caste, the aristocratic bureaucracy, and the established church agreed with the new conservatism, which differed from the old in its language but not in its objective. They found, moreover, important intellectual allies among romanticist political thinkers who sought a refuge from war and revolution in traditional institutions. The most important of them was Edmund Burke (1729–1797), who as early as 1790 had warned the world in his *Reflections on the Revolution in France* that a nation which destroyed its roots in the past in order to attempt to achieve some impossible ideal of constitutional perfection would end by drifting into chaos and then dictatorship. Under the restoration this argument was repeated over and over again by Louis de Bonald in France, Karl Ludwig von Haller in Switzerland, Adam Müller in Germany, and Friedrich Gentz in Austria. Yet although kings endorsed it, clergymen propounded it, and aristocrats defended it, romanticist conservatism failed to change history. As the years wore on, it grew progressively weaker, quietly expiring at last some time before 1914. Even afterwards coteries of intellectual reactionaries continued to dabble in its philosophy, and some of its spirit and vocabulary was taken over by the fascist movement. But by the early twentieth century it had ceased to exist as a vital political force in its own right.

2. The Restoration

THE MOST PRESSING TASK before the victorious statesmen of 1814–1815 who had defeated Napoleon was the reestablishment of a stable international order. This task meant more than simply dusting off the map of 1789. So many changes had taken place in the previous twenty-five years that a return to the status quo of the eighteenth century was out of the question. A new political balance had to be achieved which could provide the states of Europe with a period of tranquillity they badly needed. This was the great undertaking which the peacemakers set out to accomplish.

THE PEACE TREATIES

The men entrusted with the responsibility of achieving the restoration of Europe were conservatives who had grown up in the world of ideas of enlightened despotism. Yet they were not blind reactionaries resolved to oppose innovation as a matter of principle. They recognized that much of what had been done since the outbreak of the French Revolution could no longer be undone. Although acknowledging the theory of legitimacy, the theory that international treaties should ideally safeguard dynastic possessions based on legitimate historic claim, in practice they were prepared to modify the prewar territorial arrangements, provided that those whose rights were infringed received fair compensation. The result was a peace settlement involving a wholesale exchange of provinces and populations without regard for national sentiment or cultural cohesiveness. But it also introduced on the Continent a century of relative stability.

The peace settlement after the Napoleonic wars, as after the First World War and the Second, was essentially the work of the victorious great powers. Since the secondary states were also to be affected by its provisions, they naturally sought to make their influence felt at the conference table. Yet the basic decisions were made by the big four, later enlarged by the addition of France to the big five. The representative of England was Robert Stewart, Viscount Castlereagh (1769–1822), a highly gifted diplomat whose conservative policies earned him the hostility of English liberals. The great poet Shelley, for example, claimed in *The Masque of Anarchy* (1819) that

> I met Murder on his way,
> He had a mask like Castlereagh.

Yet the British foreign minister was a perceptive and moderate statesman. Tsar Alexander I of Russia (1777–1825), like President Wilson of the United States a hundred years later, exercised direct control over the foreign affairs of his country. Unstable, half-mystic and half-conniver, he combined a belief in his own destiny

METTERNICH. The famous English artist Sir Thomas Lawrence painted this portrait of the leading conservative statesman of Europe in the first half of the nineteenth century.

as the liberator of Europe with a hard-headed concern for the extension of his possessions. The interests of Austria were defended by Prince Klemens von Metternich (1773–1859), a grand aristocrat of the old school who sought above all to maintain the dominant position of the Habsburgs in central Europe. Prince Karl August von Hardenberg (1750–1822), an aged *bon vivant* hungry for power, was the leading statesman of the weakest of the four victor states, Prussia. Finally the brilliant but unscrupulous Charles Maurice de Talleyrand (1754–1838), who had served with impartial efficiency under Louis XVI, the Directory, and Napoleon, now emerged as the trusted adviser of Louis XVIII. It was a tribute to his skill that he succeeded in gaining for his defeated nation a voice in the determination of the future of the Continent equal to that of the other great powers.

The initial step in the establishment of peace was the First Treaty of Paris of May 30, 1814, concluded between France and the states allied against her. Its most notable feature was its leniency. While France had to renounce her claims to lands acquired during the wars of the French Revolution and Napoleon, she was permitted to retain the boundaries of 1792 including various enclaves which had formerly been under foreign sovereignty. She thus actually gained some 150 square miles with 450,000 inhabitants beyond what had been contained within her frontiers

TALLEYRAND. This unscrupulous but brilliant diplomat of the old school served France well during the Congress of Vienna.

under the Old Regime. There was not a word about indemnity or occupation. The victors chose to act on the theory that not the French nation but Napoleon had been responsible for the suffering inflicted on Europe in the previous fifteen years. Now that he was overthrown, it would be illogical to penalize the legitimate government of France for the misdeeds of a usurper. The hope of the allies expressed by Hardenberg was that "restored to its ancient frontiers, this kingdom will resume, among the powers of Europe, the place which belongs to it, without compromising the tranquillity of its neighbors and exercising over them a disastrous preponderance."

Following a summer of ceremonial visits and celebrations, the statesmen met next in September 1814 in the Austrian capital to consider the reconstruction of the rest of the Continent. The Congress of Vienna, which remained in session until the signing of the Final Act on June 9, 1815, was one of the great diplomatic conferences of European history. Although conducted in an atmosphere of balls, entertainments, deals, and intrigues, it produced a settlement which endured with important modifications until the Peace of Paris a hundred years later. The Habsburg monarchy regained its former possessions but surrendered the southern Netherlands to Holland in return for the territories of the Venetian Republic. In Italy there was a complete restoration of the status quo of the eighteenth century, except that the two city-states of Venice and Genoa became provinces of Austria and the Kingdom of Sardinia respectively. Prussia acquired new holdings in the Rhineland and Saxony, ceding to Russia in turn a part of her Polish provinces. No attempt was made to reestablish the old and discredited Holy Roman Empire. The new Germany consisted of thirty-nine states, ranging from the two giants, Austria and Prussia, to pygmy principalities like Waldeck or Schwarzburg-Sondershausen, all of them joined in a loose association known as the German Confederation. Russia emerged from the Napoleonic wars with gains in Poland, Finland, and Bessarabia. Finally Great Britain, who had no territorial ambitions on the Continent, acquired strategic overseas bases, for example, Malta in the Mediterranean, Mauritius in the Indian Ocean, Tobago in the Caribbean, Helgoland in the North Sea, and Capetown at the southern tip of Africa.

Before the Congress of Vienna had concluded its deliberations, Napoleon escaped from Elba and the brief tragedy of the Hundred Days took place. Once again allied troops marched into France, and now a new treaty had to be signed with the government of Louis XVIII. It was understandable that the Second Treaty of Paris of November 20, 1815, should display greater severity on the part of the victors toward a nation which had shown itself so impenitent. Yet even this peace was moderate, allowing France to remain a major power. A few small territorial losses reduced her to the boundaries of 1790, leaving her no worse off than she had been before the revolution. There was to be an army of occupation stationed in the fortresses of the north and east for not more than five years, and an indemnity of

$140 million would be paid to the allies, not an exorbitant amount for a prosperous country. A measure of the generosity of the treaty was the fact that the Parisians seemed to object most strenuously to the return of the works of art which Napoleon had assembled in his capital from all corners of Europe as spoils of war. A peace which offended esthetic sensibilities most of all could not be considered harsh by the normal standards of diplomacy.

THE CONGRESS SYSTEM

The restoration of Europe was not the only problem with which the peace-makers of 1814–1815 dealt. Like the victorious statesmen after the two world wars of the twentieth century, they were deeply concerned with the establishment of a stable order in international relations which could prevent future recourse to arms. The achievement of perpetual peace, a dream of men of goodwill since Isaiah and Micah, had aroused particular interest among publicists during the enlightened eighteenth century. The Abbé Charles de Saint-Pierre, for example, the great Jean Jacques Rousseau, and the eminent philosopher Immanuel Kant were among those who devoted their attention to this question. The experiences of the French Revolution and the Napoleonic era intensified the longing for tranquillity on the Continent. A generation which had fought and bled for more than two decades was now eager for repose. The leaders of Europe shared this feeling. Castlereagh, for example, had at one time contemplated the inclusion of a statement of pacific principles in the Final Act of Vienna, while even Napoleon in exile on Saint Helena insisted that he had wanted a compact establishing harmony among nations. The moment appeared favorable for a bold new experiment in the conduct of foreign affairs.

The first to seize the opportunity was Alexander I of Russia. For years he had been turning over in his mind the idea of an international agreement by which crowned heads would promise "to live like brothers, aiding each other in their need, and comforting each other in their adversity." The allied victory over Napoleon convinced him that the time had arrived to realize his grand vision. In a mood of religious exaltation he came to believe that he was the chosen instrument of providence for the establishment of a reign of peace for mankind, just as he had been summoned by the divine will to take the lead in the overthrow of the Corsican Antichrist. He was reinforced in this belief by Baroness Barbara Juliane von Krüdener, a lady who had turned from amatory adventures in her youth to transports of piety in her middle age, and who became for a time the spiritual comforter of the tsar. In September 1815 he composed a declaration of principles or intentions known as the Holy Alliance which he invited the rulers of Europe to sign. It asserted that international relations should be based "upon the sublime truths which the Holy Religion of our Saviour teaches" and should be governed by "the precepts of that Holy Religion, namely, the precepts of Justice, Christian Charity, and Peace, which, far from being applicable only to private concerns, must have an immediate influence on the councils of princes, and guide all their steps."

At first the tsar's allies found this declaration completely baffling. Nothing like it had ever been encountered in the chancelleries of Europe. Castlereagh considered it "a piece of sublime mysticism and nonsense," while Metternich described it as a "loud-sounding nothing." But once they had recovered from their surprise, they decided that there was no reason why they should not humor the Russian emperor by endorsing the document. It was after all nothing but a statement of lofty sentiments without specific commitments or binding obligations. A government could subscribe to it and still retain full freedom of action. Eventually all the sovereigns of Europe signed the declaration except the Pope, who was annoyed that a ruler of the Orthodox church should be expatiating on "the duties which the Divine Saviour has taught to mankind"; the prince regent of England, who explained that his signature would be invalid unless accompanied by that of a responsible minister; and the sultan of Turkey, who as a Mohammedan could not very well be expected to agree to rule in "Christian Charity." Yet since the Holy Alliance imposed no distinct duties, it could have no practical consequences. It remained a vague term used to describe the diplomatic collaboration of the three eastern autocracies, Russia, Austria, and Prussia.

The statesmen of Europe, however, succeeded in establishing a more practical instrument for the preservation of peace. On November 20, 1815, the same day on which they signed the Second Treaty of Paris, the representatives of the four victorious great powers concluded the Quadruple Alliance designed to enforce the settlement which had just been arranged. Most of the provisions dealt with the danger of new French aggression. The allies agreed to maintain the peace treaty and to prevent the return of Napoleon. If France should attack the army of occupation, the signatories would raise a force of sixty thousand men each to counter the move. But the most important article concerned the general question of stability on the Continent. It stated that "the High Contracting Parties have agreed to renew their meetings at fixed periods, either under the immediate auspices of the Sovereigns themselves, or by their respective Ministers, for the purpose of consulting upon their common interests, and for the consideration of the measures which at each of these periods shall be considered the most salutary for the repose and prosperity of Nations, and for the maintenance of the Peace of Europe."

What this diplomatic language meant was that the great powers would meet from time to time to consider all questions threatening the established order in international affairs. A directory of the leading states had thus come into existence for the purpose of maintaining the peace by mutual consultation and joint action. This experiment in international government has been variously called the congress system, the conference system, the concert of Europe, the confederation of Europe, or grandiloquently the Areopagus of Europe. It in effect entrusted the large countries with the responsibility of enforcing the settlement of disputes among governments. Such an arrangement was practicable as long as the great powers could agree among themselves on a common policy toward a disturbance of public tranquillity. But what if the great powers disagreed? The congress system had no answer for such an eventuality. Like the League of Nations or the United Nations, it was built on a system of international relations in which ultimate authority rested with independent sovereign states. It assumed that the more powerful of these states would be prepared to use their strength to police the community of nations. Yet, by the same token, if they began to work at cross-purposes, the structure of the peace was bound to crumble. Everything depended on the continuing harmony of the wartime allies.

THE END OF THE ALLIANCE

At first the congress system seemed to live up to the expectations aroused by its formation. A Europe tired of violence was apparently ready to accept the territorial and governmental arrangements introduced after the downfall of Napoleon. Even France had become reconciled to the restoration of the Bourbons, thereby providing an additional guarantee for the maintenance of the established order. To reward her willingness to abide by the terms of the peace, the allies met in 1818 in the city of Aachen in western Germany. They regulated the payment of the indemnity to which they were entitled and arranged for the withdrawal of the army of occupation. As a sign of their confidence, moreover, they admitted the government of Louis XVIII to their compact, transforming the Quadruple Alliance into a Quintuple Alliance. Never did the prospect for stability on the Continent look brighter. Yet within two years the congress system had to face a crisis which ultimately destroyed it. In January 1820 a revolution broke out in Spain; in July it spread to the Kingdom of the Two Sicilies, in August to Portugal, and in the following March to the Kingdom of Sardinia. All of these uprisings were motivated by the desire of liberals for constitutional government under a limited monarchy. The autocratic statesmen who had just been congratulating themselves on the final victory of conservatism began to tremble. Here was 1789 all over again. It was imperative, they insisted, that the great powers meet at once to suppress this danger to international tranquillity.

But proposals for intervention encountered stubborn resistance from the English government which maintained that, while it was prepared to collaborate with its allies in opposing aggression by one country against another, it would not support meddling in the internal affairs of foreign states. Public opinion in the British Isles was generally sympathetic to uprisings inspired to a large extent by the example of the United Kingdom. The world of business, moreover, feared that the defeat of the revolution in the Iberian Peninsula would encourage Spain to attempt to reconquer her possessions in the New World which had been in a state of insurrection since the days of Napoleon. Great Britain had developed a profitable trade with these rebellious Spanish colonies, a trade which would be threatened if Madrid succeeded in reasserting its sovereignty. A combination of ideological and material considerations thus led Castlereagh to issue on May 5, 1820, an important state paper which helped define Britain's foreign policy throughout the nineteenth century. It asserted that the Quintuple Alliance "never was, however, intended as an Union for the Government of the World, or for the Superintendence of the Internal Affairs of other States. . . . The fact is that we do not, and cannot feel alike upon all subjects. Our Position, our Institutions, the Habits of thinking, and the prejudice of our People, render us essentially different. . . . We shall be found in our Place when actual danger menaces the System of Europe; but this Country cannot, and will not, act upon abstract and speculative Principles of Precaution."

The absolutist governments of Russia, Austria, and Prussia would not accept this contention. They saw in revolution a contagious disease which might begin its course as a purely domestic disturbance but would soon begin to infect all of Europe. Was this not precisely what had happened in the French Revolution? The distinction between civil insurrection and military aggression, they maintained, was artificial, since one necessarily led to the other. Intervention in a country which was in a state of rebellion merely meant the timely suppression of a threat which would otherwise have to be faced at a later time and with a greater risk. A protocol of November 19, 1820, submitted by the three eastern autocracies rejected Castlereagh's arguments: "States which have undergone a change of government due to revolution, the results of which threaten other states, *ipso facto* cease to be members of the European Alliance, and remain excluded from it until their situation gives guarantees for legal order and stability. If, owing to such alterations, immediate danger threatens other states, the powers bind themselves, by peaceful means, or if need be, by arms, to bring back the guilty state into the bosom of the Great Alliance."

There could be no reconciliation between two so diametrically opposed views of the function of the congress system. The great powers met at Troppau in Bohemia in October 1820; they met again at Laibach in Slovenia in January 1821; they met for a third time at Verona in northern Italy in October 1822. It was in vain. The gulf separating them only grew deeper. Castlereagh, who was prepared to make one more attempt to achieve a compromise, suffered a nervous breakdown and committed suicide shortly before the congress of Verona. He was followed in the foreign office by George Canning (1770–1827), a statesman of an entirely different outlook. Insular, hardheaded, and cautious, he did not share his predecessor's willingness to pledge Great Britain to the maintenance of stability on the Continent. While it was proper to convoke international conferences for the purposes of concluding peace, "periodic reunions" could be highly dangerous. He might have been willing to agree to harmless expressions of "moral solidarity," but specific commitments or risky obligations were out of the question. His creed was: "Every nation for itself, and God for us all!" He was John Bull in a mood of splendid isolation.

After 1822 the congress system was finished. It failed because of the incompatible objectives of the states which had created it. For the next thirty years the great powers were divided into two loose alignments, each held together by a community of ideological and political interests. The three autocracies, acting in defense of conservative principles of government, exerted a dominant influence in the affairs of central and eastern Europe. In 1821 they authorized Austria to crush the revolution in Italy, and two years later they encouraged the French to cross the Pyrenees and suppress the uprising in Spain. England with her small standing army was powerless to resist the policy of intervention on the Continent, but on the high seas her position was unassailable. She was therefore able to frustrate all plans for the reconquest of the Spanish colonies in the western hemisphere. Although the European mainland was largely in the grip of absolutism, Canning could still boast that "I called the New World into existence to redress the balance of the Old." After 1830, moreover, France came to support Great Britain in most questions of foreign policy, and the combination of the two leading parliamentary states was usually able to assert its will in western Europe. This dualism in the diplomatic affairs of the Continent prevailed until the mid-century when new alliances began to form among the great powers. The bold but unsuccessful attempt to maintain peace by means of the congress system had given way to the more traditional practices of the balance of power.

3. Western Europe

IF THE NINETEENTH CENTURY was the heroic age of liberalism, western Europe was its land of promise. There nature and history had collaborated to create those conditions which are particularly conducive to the development of representative government. The factory system was raising the standard of living and improving the level of education. The political and social domination of the landed aristocracy had been weakened by revolution and industrialization. And a vigorous and courageous middle class was prepared to lead the struggle against absolutism. It was thus understandable that liberal institutions should find an especially favorable environment on the northeastern shores of the Atlantic.

GREAT BRITAIN

In the years after Waterloo Great Britain succeeded in gradually transforming herself from an oligarchy governed by the well-to-do into a democracy ruled by the people. What is more, she effected this change without bloodshed and without lasting bitterness. In the seventeenth century she had affirmed the principle that Parliament is supreme in the field of legislation. In the eighteenth century she had invented the device of responsible cabinet government, by which Parliament was also able to control the executive branch of government. In the nineteenth century she democratized her political institutions and achieved a new sense of social responsibility.

Even before the French Revolution a group of young reformers—Tories as well as Whigs—had begun to agitate for a thoroughgoing change in governmental policy. The younger William Pitt, Edmund Burke, and Charles James Fox among others were urging an expansion of the suffrage, a reduction of tariff rates, and the extension of full political rights to Catholics. But the war with France which broke out in 1793 put an end to the reform movement by enlisting all national energies in the defense effort and causing every demand for change to seem like the first step to revolution. In 1815 England emerged from her ordeal victorious and strong but completely dominated by the spirit of unbending conservatism which held sway among the Tory statesmen in control of Parliament.

The immediate postwar years were a period of bitter conflict between the masses clamoring for political and economic reform and a government determined to resist all innovation. A revolution led by the radicals and supported by the lower classes remained a distinct possibility, even after some of the more moderate Tories succeeded in lowering the import duties on grain, revising the harsh criminal code, and emancipating Roman Catholics and Nonconformists. It was only after the Whigs came to power in 1830 that the opposition to reform was finally forced back. In 1832 the most important English parliamentary enactment of the nineteenth century gave the vote and the political balance of power to the industrial middle class. The following year slavery was abolished throughout the British Empire, and the agitation of humanitarians like William Wilberforce was crowned with success. At the same time the government began to reduce illiteracy and combat radicalism among the masses by extending financial assistance to church schools. In 1834 the poor laws were revised; in 1835 municipal government was liberalized; and in 1836 the right of counsel in court proceedings was extended.

While the urban bourgeoisie was the chief beneficiary of this decade of reform, the industrial proletariat also won important concessions from a government anxious to maintain social stability. In 1833 the first measure to regulate successfully the employment of children in factories was adopted with the aid of conservative landowners and over the opposition of liberal industrialists. And in 1846 the corn laws—the tariff duties on imported grain which tended to inflate the cost of living—were finally repealed. Thereafter Great Britain was a stronghold of free trade for almost a century. Yet the demands of the worker for the right to vote remained unfulfilled another twenty years. Neither the Liberals nor the Conservatives, as the Whigs and Tories were now called, were ready to entrust their fortunes to the masses. In vain did the radicals in 1839, 1842, and 1848 present to Parliament the People's Charter, a petition calling for universal manhood suffrage, secret ballot, and equal electoral districts. Only after the middle of the century did the notion of admitting the lower classes to the franchise come to be seriously considered in well-to-do circles. The Liberals were the first to make a cautious effort in this direction. But it was the Conservatives who, refusing to be outdone by their rivals, took the leap in the dark. In 1867 they promulgated another great suffrage bill enfranchising the workers of the cities, and Great Britain crossed the dividing line between liberalism and democracy.

The years of reform at home were also years of prestige abroad. With a full treasury, a powerful navy, and a natural defense against invasion, the English government could play a vital role in the colonial affairs of the world and even on the European continent itself. After the collapse of the Quintuple Alliance in 1822, it managed to prevent an attempt to reconquer the Spanish colonies in the New World. In the 1830's the United Kingdom won a guarantee of the independence and neutrality of Belgium. She intervened time and time again in the Near East to protect Turkey against the ambitious designs of the Russians. She actively participated in diplomatic conflicts and settlements involving Spain, Portugal, Denmark, Germany, and Italy. The man who was most influential in the conduct of the foreign policy of Great Britain was Lord Palmerston (1784–1865), a Liberal statesman who personified those qualities of aggressive confidence and moral self-righteousness characteristic of the English public in the nineteenth century. The masses cheered "Old Pam," as he assured them that he would make the name of Briton mean in the modern world what the name of Roman had meant in the ancient. On the Continent, however, among princes and statesmen tired of the posturing and swaggering in London, there was a less complimentary view of the United Kingdom's leading diplomat:

> And if the devil have a son,
> Then his name is surely Palmerston.

Presiding over this age of British progress and prosperity was the figure of Queen Victoria. A woman of narrow outlook and limited understanding, she yet reflected perfectly the mood of the self-satisfied bourgeoisie who dominated her reign. In her middle-class respectability and simple piety the public recognized itself, and in singing the praises of the monarch it was extolling its own virtues. Ruler and people harmonized so completely that her name became permanently associated with her era. Her husband, the German Prince Albert, was less fortunate. The English always looked upon him with a jaundiced eye, because he was more interested in practical politics than seemed proper in a member of royalty, because he hoped to reassert a measure of monarchic influence over parliamentary

QUEEN VICTORIA AND PRINCE ALBERT. The English royal couple symbolized the domestic fidelity and respectability so important to the bourgeois society of their day.

life, and, worst of all, because he was a foreigner. But he died in 1861, and thereafter nothing stood between the ruler and her subjects. By the end of her long reign—which extended from 1837 to 1901—she had become a national institution, a motherly symbol to a people who could remember no other sovereign. For most Britons, the Victorian Era was a golden age in which their country advanced steadily toward greater economic well-being and diplomatic influence.

FRANCE

Across the English Channel in France political development was not as placid. The French Revolution had left physical and psychological wounds which even a century of national progress could not heal. It had made the aristocracy more reactionary, the lower classes more radical, the bourgeoisie more ambitious. Whereas behind Great Britain lay a long tradition of peaceful compromise, in France there were bitter memories of a profligate court and the revolutionary guillotine. Social antagonisms were greater and sharper, and a readiness to use force in order to achieve change was more widespread than in Great Britain. Yet France also had more verve, more reckless idealism than her neighbor. English political writers were always ready to sermonize about Gallic instability and lack of serious purpose, but they tended to overlook the profound belief of the French in political principle.

In 1814, however, many Frenchmen had been ready to compromise their principle and accept a restoration of the Bourbons. Exhausted by revolutions and wars, they saw in the stodgy Louis XVIII (1814–1824) a welcome change from the extravagant ambitions of Napoleon. The new king, brother of the unhappy Louis XVI and uncle of the uncrowned "Louis XVII" who had died in 1795 in a republican prison, had learned something from the misfortunes of his family. Behind an unimpressive exterior was a sharp mind which recognized that the past could not be brought back to life. He granted his subjects a constitutional charter establishing a legislature dominated by the well-to-do; he refused to revoke the legal equality of all citizens introduced by the Code Napoléon; he made no effort to restore the lands of the aristocracy which the peasantry had acquired after 1789; and he tacitly resolved to rule in the spirit of moderate constitutionalism. But his brother who succeeded him in 1824 as Charles X was made of sterner stuff. Determined to resurrect the France which he had known in his youth, he increased the authority of the church in education, dissolved the middle-class National Guard, generously compensated the nobility for their lost lands, and finally, in July 1830, attempted to silence the opposition by modifying the suffrage requirements so as to disfranchise the bourgeoisie. The result was a three-day uprising in Paris engineered by the liberals and executed by the mob, an uprising which led to the downfall of the king. In his place, the triumphant bourgeoisie selected as ruler Louis Philippe, duke of Orléans, and cousin of the Bourbons. As for the peasants of the countryside, they shrugged their shoulders and went on cultivating their fields.

The new king knew how to repay his political debts. His reign, which lasted until 1848, has been appropriately called the era of the bourgeois monarchy. He spoke, behaved, dressed, and looked like a prosperous merchant, banker, or certified public accountant. The constitutional charter of 1814 was retained in a slightly modified form, which safeguarded the competence of the legislature yet still restricted the suffrage to men of property. In François Guizot (1787–1874), moreover, Louis Philippe found a minister highly sensitive to the wishes of the middle class. At home the government encouraged the growth of factories, the construction of railroads, and the flow of investments. Abroad it followed a safe and sound policy of befriending everyone and antagonizing no one. And in dealing with the opposition in the parliament it displayed a "fatal dexterity," manipulating elections and corrupting voters in a fashion which would have warmed the heart of an American ward politician. The outcome of its efforts was an industrial bourgeoisie fat and sleek, but also a growing discontent among the other classes of the population. On the right were the legitimists, especially strong in the aristocracy, the army, and the church, who were still faithful to the memory of Charles X and who could not forgive Louis Philippe for his disloyalty to the Bourbons. On the left were the

THE LEGISLATIVE BELLY BY HONORÉ DAUMIER. A brilliant caricaturist depicts here a session of the French legislature, ridiculing the middle-class politicians who came to power under the parliamentary system of government.

republicans and utopian socialists supported by the urban proletariat, who dreamed of a democratic commonwealth and a controlled economy. And everywhere there was a growing nationalism, a dissatisfaction with the uninspiring foreign policy pursued by the king, and a yearning for the revival of Napoleonic glories.

The storm broke in February 1848 following a course which had become traditional in French politics. The Parisian mob rose in insurrection, built barricades, fought troops, forced Louis Philippe to abdicate, and proclaimed a republic. A National Assembly chosen by manhood suffrage was to prepare a constitution, but in the meantime a provisional government composed of republicans and socialists held the reins of power. The elections revealed, however, that the country as a whole was much more conservative than the capital, and in June hostility between the cautious bourgeoisie and peasantry on the one hand and the radical proletariat on the other led to another bloody conflict. The workers of Paris were defeated by the army, and the representatives of the nation then proceeded to publish a middle-of-the-road constitution. Yet civil chaos played into the hands of the nephew and heir of the great Napoleon, Louis Napoleon Bonaparte (1848–1870), who was elected president of the republic on a platform promising law and order to the upper classes, work and bread to the lower classes, and military and diplomatic prestige to all. Immediately after his inauguration he began to plot the overthrow of the republic, and three years later—on December 2, 1851—the president executed

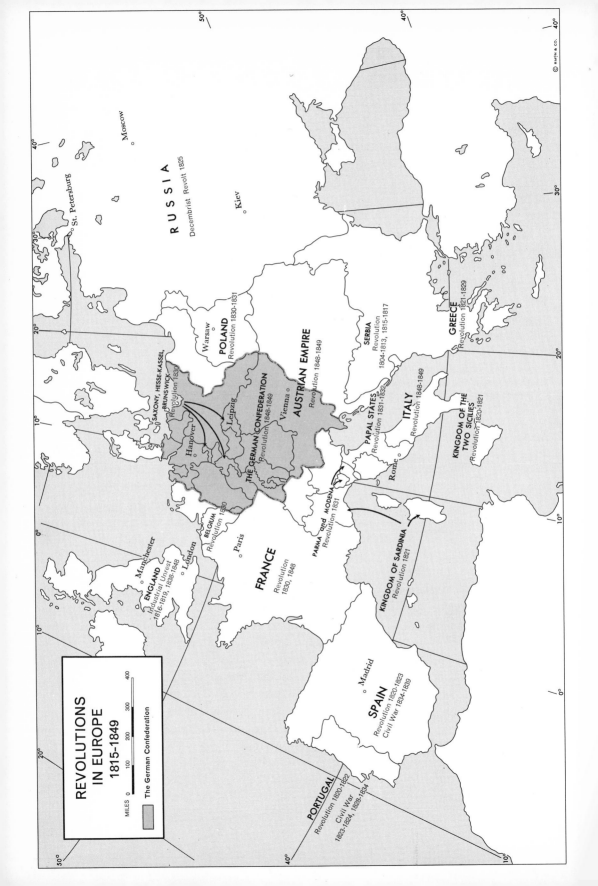

REVOLUTIONS
IN EUROPE
1815-1849

MILES 0 100 200 300 400

The German Confederation

© RAND & CO.

RUSSIA
Decembrist Revolt 1825

Moscow

St. Petersburg

Kiev

Warsaw

POLAND
Revolution 1830-1831

SAXONY, HESSE-KASSEL,
BRUNSWICK
Revolution 1830

Leipzig

THE GERMAN CONFEDERATION
Revolution 1848-1849

Hanover

Vienna

AUSTRIAN EMPIRE
Revolution 1848-1849

SERBIA
Revolution
1804-1813, 1815-1817

GREECE
Revolution 1821-1829

PAPAL STATES
Revolution 1831-1832

ITALY
Revolution 1848-1849

KINGDOM OF THE
TWO SICILIES
Revolution 1820-1821

Rome

BELGIUM
Revolution 1830

PARMA and MODENA
Revolution 1831

KINGDOM OF SARDINIA
Revolution 1821

Paris

FRANCE
Revolution
1830, 1848

Manchester

ENGLAND
Industrial Unrest
1816-1819, 1838-1848

London

Madrid

SPAIN
Revolution 1820-1823
Civil War 1834-1839

PORTUGAL
Revolution 1820-1822
Civil War
1823-1824, 1828-1834

a coup d'état which left him master of the state. One year more, and he crowned his triumph by announcing a revival of the empire and proclaiming himself Napoléon III.

The emperor had spent most of his life in exile, dreaming and scheming for a victory of the Bonapartist cause, often only one step ahead of the police, sometimes actually arrested and imprisoned. Now that he was in power he remained a political opportunist, living by expedients rather than principles. Among his contemporaries he soon won a reputation as a clever and unpredictable statesman, but behind the enigmatic expression and the strange blue eyes there was only an overwhelming desire to remain ruler. This desire led the country from one adventure to the next, until emperor and empire went down in tragic defeat. For the time being, however, the unscrupulous, the upstart, the corrupt gathered at the court where they found a ready welcome. France speculated on the stock exchange, gambled in commercial ventures, invested in industrial enterprises, danced the can-can, hummed the tunes of Offenbach, and transformed Paris into the world capital of fashion, luxury, and the arts sacred and profane. Over this carnival which lasted twenty years presided the monarch, smiling, genial, devious.

Although the empire always claimed to represent the will of the people, it was actually for the first half of its existence a thinly disguised dictatorship. The

NAPOLEON III. Until his regime collapsed in 1870, the emperor was the great enigma of Europe, mystifying the diplomats of other countries and sometimes of his own as well.

press was muzzled, the opposition suppressed, the vote rigged, the legislature intimidated. Yet as long as the government subsidized economic expansion and won military glory, the nation was ready to accept it as the only alternative to political anarchy. When after 1860, however, France began to suffer diplomatic reverses and to sink deeper into debt, the mood of the country changed ominously. Sensing his loss of popularity, the emperor attempted to recover lost ground by becoming the champion of liberal reform. The censorship was relaxed, the legislature received greater authority, parliamentary criticism became permissible, and finally, in 1869, the empire was transformed into a constitutional monarchy on the English model. Since he was obviously unable to fill the shoes of his illustrious uncle, Napoleon III decided to play Queen Victoria. But he could not escape his nemesis. In May 1870 the nation voted 7,358,000 to 1,571,000 in favor of the new policy of parliamentarianism. Four months later the emperor was a prisoner and the empire a shambles. The carnival had come to an end.

To a Bonaparte who had no legitimate historical claim to power success was the indispensable condition of survival. As long as he could parade victories before the people, all was well. But once the magic of his name failed to produce results, his only claim to allegiance vanished. During the 1850's he still managed to win wars which brought France prestige, if little else. Between 1854 and 1856 his armies, allied with Great Britain, defeated the Russians in the Crimea, and in 1859 he overcame the Austrians in Italy. Then came a succession of disasters. In 1863 a Polish revolution which he had supported diplomatically was crushed by Russia. His plan to create a satellite state in Mexico ruled by the Austrian Archduke Maximilian failed miserably when the United States forced the French to withdraw from the New World and Maximilian himself was executed by his enemies. And the defeat of Austria by Prussia in 1866 established a powerful new state on the eastern frontier of the French Empire.

Feeling the scepter slipping from his grasp, Napoleon liberalized the government. But then in July 1870 he blundered into a war with the Prussians. His hope was that a victory would bring the dynasty new prestige. Instead German armies defeated the imperial troops in one battle after another, until on September 2 at Sedan 104,000 Frenchmen, including the emperor himself, were captured. On the following day Paris read the telegram sent by Napoleon: "The army has been defeated and taken prisoner; I myself am a prisoner." It was the death knell of the empire. On September 4 an insurrection in the capital deposed the Bonaparte dynasty, and a defeated France returned to her republican tradition.

THE LOW COUNTRIES AND SCANDINAVIA

The Low Countries, strategically situated between France and England, followed the liberal example of their powerful neighbors. Both Belgium and Holland, with their high standard of living, their developing industrialism, their energetic bourgeoisie, and their tradition of sturdy self-government, were favorably disposed toward theories of constitutionalism. Yet their union in 1815 under the House of Orange had not been happy. The two peoples were separated by the religious antagonisms of Protestant and Catholic, by the cultural differences between Dutch and French, and by the economic conflicts of commercial and industrial interests. In 1830 there was a revolution in Belgium which led to her political independence, confirmed by an international guarantee of her perpetual neutrality. As their first ruler the Belgians chose a German prince, Leopold of Saxe-Coburg (1831–1865). The uncle of Queen Victoria and the son-in-law of Louis Philippe, he governed his small state in a spirit of sober bourgeois parliamentarianism, winning the respect of the great powers and the support of his subjects. As for Holland, King William I (1815–1840) had issued a cautious constitution in 1815, which was amended and democratized during the great revolution which overwhelmed Europe in 1848. Possessing valuable colonies in the Far East, important mercantile and marine establishments, prosperous factories and banks, and a well-to-do peasantry, the Dutch, like the Belgians, were naturally inclined to accept liberal theory and practice.

So were the Scandinavians. Among the mariners, fishermen, and independent farmers of the north there had developed a strong opposition to the political and economic claims of the nobility. Even in the age of enlightened despotism royal ambitions had met with hostility, and in the nineteenth century this tradition of independence led to the victory of constitutionalism. Denmark, reduced in size and importance by the Napoleonic Wars, adopted on June 5, 1849, a liberal constitution which was the first step in a far-reaching program of parliamentary and social reform. In Norway, which was bound by a personal union to Sweden, a representative assembly enjoyed extensive powers of government and constituted a check on the pretensions of the crown. In Sweden, on the other hand, King Charles XIV, formerly General Bernadotte, a friend of Napoleon, and his successor Oscar I exercised an authoritarian and militaristic rule supported by the aristocracy. Even after 1864, when a modern parliament replaced the antiquated Riksdag with its four estates, the monarch and the nobility retained extensive power. It was to be expected that the political union of Swedes and Norwegians would be turbulent, and before long a strong movement for separation developed among the latter.

4. Central and Southern Europe

BEYOND THE FRONTIERS OF FRANCE industrialism was slower and absolutism stronger. Liberal doctrines encountered the resistance of a powerful landed aristocracy, while nationalist slogans had to overcome a deep-seated tradition of localism. Yet although the armies of Napoleon had been expelled from central and southern Europe after only a few years of occupation, the revolutionary ideas they had brought with them could not be entirely suppressed. Throughout the nineteenth century Germans, Italians, Spaniards, and Portuguese sought with varying degrees of success to adapt their native political institutions to the new ideals of parliamentarianism and nationalism.

GERMANY

In Germany there was a brief reform movement in the period which followed the Napoleonic wars, when a number of idealistic academicians, publicists, and intellectuals dreamed of transforming the German Confederation into a united fatherland governed in accordance with parliamentary practice. But by 1819 the conservatives led by Metternich managed to suppress their opponents, and for the next thirty years Teutonic kings and princes ruled by divine right over submissive subjects. Some of the smaller states adopted more or less liberal constitutions, but the two giants of Germany, Austria and Prussia, remained opposed to any compromise with reformism. The only comfort liberal patriots could find in those years was the creation of the Zollverein, a customs union established in 1834 under Prussian auspices, which embraced most of Germany. Efforts to achieve political change, however, were answered by the censor and the jailer. "No power on earth," announced Frederick William IV of Prussia (1840–1861) in 1847, "will ever succeed in prevailing upon me to transform the natural relationship between prince and people, the relationship which by its inward truth has made us so powerful, into a contractual, constitutional one."

One year later he was eating his words. The revolution which broke out in France in February 1848 swept eastward across the Rhine, overthrew established authority in Germany, put in power men who for more than a generation had been clamoring for change, and gave central Europe a taste of liberal reform and national unification. In the spring demonstrations and riots in almost all the states forced the rulers of the German Confederation to agree to reform and led to the meeting of a representative national assembly in Frankfurt am Main to prepare a constitution for a united fatherland. But the Frankfurt Parliament was too preoccupied with transforming the country politically and economically into a liberal bourgeois state to retain the support of the masses who had made the spring uprising possible. Instead of helping the peasant become an independent farmer and protecting the artisan against the competition of the factory system, the parliamentarians prepared to create a new nation of mills and banks, dominated by the educated and the propertied. The result was a gradual decline in popular enthusiasm for the revolution.

By the time the Frankfurt Parliament completed its constitution in the spring of 1849, it stood isolated before a revived conservatism. Desperately seeking to save the national cause, it invited the ruler of Prussia to become the emperor of a united, liberal Germany. But Frederick William IV had had enough of parliaments, constitutions, and reforms. Rejecting what he called "the crown from the gutter," he helped disperse the Frankfurt Parliament. By the end of 1850 the old order had been completely reestablished, while thousands of liberals were languishing in prison or building new lives on the plains of Wisconsin and Missouri.

The effect of the failure of the revolution was a profound disillusionment with constitutionalism. German patriots increasingly came to favor a policy of *Realpolitik*, a policy of letting the ends justify the means and emphasizing success at the expense of principle. By the early 1860's they had found one of the greatest of all practitioners of Realpolitik in the person of a hard-bitten Prussian landed aristocrat, Otto von Bismarck (1815–1898). Always a conservative in his political philosophy, and at first violently opposed to national unification, he had gradually come to the conclusion that the triumph of nationalism was inevitable. It was therefore better that the Prussian monarchy rather than parliamentary politicians or Habsburg bureaucrats should receive the credit for what was bound to happen anyway. In 1862 he received an opportunity to put his ideas into practice when

BISMARCK. Despite his air of bold determination and his military costume, the "iron chancellor" was a complex personality often troubled by doubts and fears.

he was named prime minister of Prussia in the midst of a constitutional crisis.

Soon after the outbreak of the revolution Frederick William IV had reluctantly promulgated a constitution for his kingdom, and now some ten years later the liberals had managed to win a majority in the legislature. King William I, who had recently ascended the throne (1861), entrusted Bismarck with the task of taming the parliament, a task which the latter found congenial. For four years he governed in defiance of the chamber and in violation of the constitution. The policy he pursued was dangerous, but there was method in his madness. By creating a united German fatherland he hoped to conciliate the bourgeoisie and reconcile it to continued conservative influence in government. On September 30, 1862, he boldly described his theory of statecraft: "The great questions of the time are not decided by speeches and majority resolutions—that was the great mistake of 1848 and 1849—but by iron and blood."

The chance to use iron and blood came soon enough. Bismarck had long realized that Prussia could reorganize central Europe only after crushing her rival Austria, and as prime minister he worked tirelessly to arrange a day of reckoning with the Habsburgs. In 1864 he persuaded Vienna to join him in a war against Denmark for the possession of the two German duchies of Schleswig and Holstein. Immediately after their victory the recent allies found themselves involved in a bitter quarrel over the disposition of their conquest, a quarrel carefully fostered by the wily Prussian statesman. In 1866 it came to open hostilities. The Austrians could boast the best marching bands in Europe, but the Prussians had the very effective needle gun and a military genius in General Helmuth von Moltke. The Seven Weeks' War was a glorious triumph for Bismarck, who became the hero of all Prussia. He forced Austria to withdraw from German affairs and then proceeded to organize the states north of the Main River into the North German Confederation, dominated by the Hohenzollerns. As for his parliamentary opponents, he managed to compose his differences with them by promulgating a moderately liberal constitution for the new national union. He completed his mission four years later by skillfully provoking the Franco-Prussian War which proved to be a succession of German victories. On January 18, 1871, while the siege guns were booming around Paris, the princes of Germany met in Versailles to proclaim the formation of a united state and to acknowledge William I as their chief. The German Empire was born.

ITALY

If the creation of a unified Germany under Prussian auspices was the most momentous diplomatic development in Europe in the nineteenth century, the establishment of a united and liberal kingdom in Italy was not far behind in political significance. The French Revolution had awakened sentiments of na-

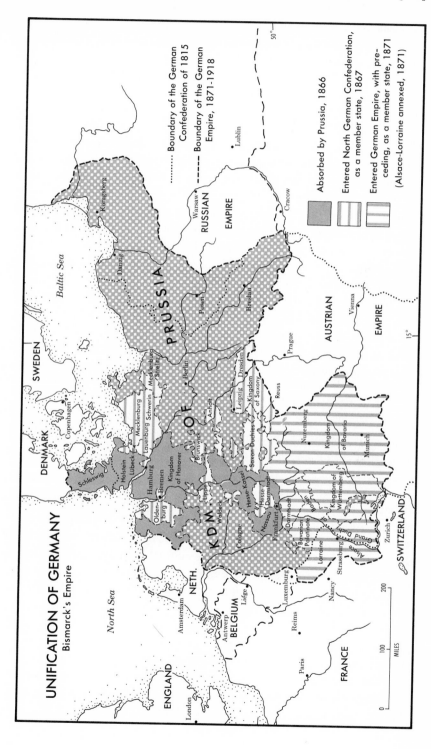

UNIFICATION OF GERMANY
Bismarck's Empire

Boundary of the German
Confederation of 1815

Boundary of the German
Empire, 1871-1918

Absorbed by Prussia, 1866

Entered North German Confederation,
as a member state, 1867

Entered German Empire, with preceding, as a member state, 1871
(Alsace-Lorraine annexed, 1871)

tionalism and liberalism among the Italians in opposition to the prevailing provincialism and absolutism. But during the restoration, Austria, in possession of the two northeastern provinces of Lombardy and Venetia, took the lead in maintaining the status quo. At first resistance to the policies of Metternich was the work of secret associations like the Carbonari, which were organized throughout the peninsula by the patriotic and the discontented. Yet after Carbonarist revolts failed in 1820–1821 and 1830–1831, three new schools of national thought arose to direct the revival of Italian political consciousness, known as the *Risorgimento*. Young Italy, founded by the enthusiastic but visionary Giuseppe Mazzini (1805–1872), urged an uprising of the masses led by the youth to establish a democratic, centralized republic. There was also the Neoguelph movement inspired by the gentle priest Vincenzo Gioberti who hoped that the Papacy would help create a loose confederation of Italian states, thus fulfilling national hopes without violence and bloodshed. Finally the party around Marquis Massimo d'Azeglio maintained that the rulers of the Kingdom of Sardinia should strive to organize a constitutional national monarchy with their dynasty at its head.

The revolution of 1848 put each of these solutions of the Italian problem to the test. Each failed, but one managed to survive defeat and achieve its purpose a decade later. At first, during the "springtime of nations" in 1848, the forces of Mazzini, of Pope Pius IX, and of King Charles Albert of Sardinia cooperated in a national war against Austria. But the tenacity of the Habsburg armies and the growing rivalry of republicans, monarchists, and clericals weakened the common effort. Pius IX, alarmed by the antipapal resentment of the Austrians—who were as loyal Catholics as the Italians—decided to avoid too close identification with the nationalist ideology. Thereupon Mazzini succeeded in establishing briefly a democratic republic in Rome in defiance of the Pope. The latter, however, soon regained control over his capital with the aid of troops dispatched by the new French president Louis Napoleon, who was seeking the support of the church for his political ambitions. Charles Albert attempted to continue the struggle with his own resources, risking his political future on the slim chance of a victory over the Austrians. But at the Battle of Novara in March 1849 that chance vanished, and even the royal plan to fall on the field of battle rather than endure defeat failed. Brokenhearted, the king abdicated in favor of his son, who became Victor Emmanuel II, and then withdrew into a humiliating retirement from which he was delivered before long by his premature death. The only lasting achievement of the movement on which he had gambled so heavily was the liberal constitution, the *Statuto*, promulgated in Sardinia early in the revolution.

Within a decade, however, the national cause managed to recover from its defeat and to open a new campaign for unification. The author of this remarkable transformation was Count Camillo di Cavour (1810–1861), the new prime minister of Sardinia. A grand aristocrat with the outlook and appearance of a bourgeois,

FRANCE

SWITZERLAND

AUSTRIAN EMPIRE

HUNGARY

Geneva

LOMBARDY
1859
Legnano · Milan
Novara · Magenta
Turin · Pavia
Chambéry
SAVOY

TRENTINO

CARNIOLA

VENETIA
1866
Verona
Custozza
Villafranca
Solferino
Mantua
Venice

Trieste
Fiume
CROATIA

To France
1860
PIEDMONT
Genoa
KINGDOM
1860
Parma
PARMA
MODENA
Modena
Bologna
ROMAGNA
Ravenna

OTTOMAN

Zara
DALMATIA
EMPIRE

NICE

To Tuscany
1847
Nice · Monaco

LUCCA
Pisa
Leghorn
1860
TUSCANY
Siena
Florence
San Marino
PAPAL
UMBRIA
STATES
1860

THE MARCHES

Adriatic Sea

Ragusa

OF

CORSICA
Ajaccio
To France

ELBA

— 42°

ABRUZZI

Rome
1870
PONTECORVO

SARDINIA

To Papal States
Naples
Salerno
CAMPANIA
BENEVENTO
KINGDOM
Bari
Brindisi
APULIA
Otranto

SARDINIA

Cagliari

*Tyrrhenian
Sea*

OF THE

CALABRIA

Mediterranean Sea

TWO

Messina
Reggio

Palermo
SICILY
SICILIES
1860 · Syracuse

◊ PANTELLERIA

UNIFICATION OF ITALY

MILES	0	50	100	150

TUSCANY	Independent states in 1815
- - - - - - - -	Northern boundary of Kingdom of Italy, 1866-1919
1859	Joined by plebiscite with Sardinia
1860	Joined by revolution and plebiscite with Sardinia, to form Kingdom of Italy, proclaimed 1861
1866, 1870	Joined with Kingdom of Italy

12°

Cavour recognized that only with the assistance of the liberal western powers could the Austrians be expelled from Italy. During the 1850's, therefore, he labored tirelessly to make his small mountainous state politically liberal and economically progressive. Carefully cultivating friendly diplomatic relations in the courts of Europe, he finally succeeded in concluding a treaty with Napoleon III which in 1859 led to a joint war against Austria. The outcome was Sardinian acquisition of Lombardy and of the small principalities of Tuscany, Modena, and Parma.

No sooner had Cavour completed this expansion in northern and central Italy than an unexpected stroke of good luck brought his work within sight of complete success. In 1860 the gallant adventurer Giuseppe Garibaldi with about a thousand followers organized a private expedition against the corrupt rule of the Neapolitan Bourbons in the south. Invading Sicily, he seized the island in a campaign of only a few weeks and then crossed to the mainland and promptly made himself master of the rest of the Kingdom of the Two Sicilies. In a remarkable display of selflessness he handed over his conquests to Victor Emmanuel II and retired to his farm to lead the life of a private citizen. Now only the Austrian province of Venetia and the papal possessions around Rome were lacking to complete the process of unification. The former was acquired when Italy allied herself with Prussia in the Seven Weeks' War. The latter required even less exertion, for when the French garrison in the Eternal City was withdrawn for service in the Franco-Prussian War, it was promptly replaced by the troops of the new Italian kingdom. By 1870 the Sardinian government had consummated the amalgamation of the peninsula, and a new nation joined the ranks of the great powers.

THE IBERIAN PENINSULA

While Italians were rejoicing in the revival of the political glories of their land, Spanish patriots could only mourn the contrast between a splendid past and the tragic present. Poor, backward, proud, deprived of her colonies, exploited by her aristocracy, dominated by her church, Spain struggled vainly throughout the nineteenth century to find a system of government appropriate to her needs and circumstances. The liberals sought to uphold the constitution of 1812 and the more moderate charter of 1845, while the conservatives found their champions in unscrupulous royal intriguers like King Ferdinand VII and his brother Don Carlos. The accession in 1833 of Queen Isabella II merely meant that the inefficient oppressiveness of the previous reign was replaced by the inefficient immorality of the new.

A revolution in 1868 resulted in the deposition of the queen whose private life had scandalized her pious subjects, but once again the new order was not much of an improvement over the old. For two years the Spaniards tried to find someone willing to risk becoming their king. When an Italian prince finally agreed in

1870 to ascend the throne as Amadeo I, they lived up to their reputation for political instability by forcing him to abdicate three years later. A brief experiment in a republican form of government proved even more disastrous, and in 1875 the son of Queen Isabella II was unenthusiastically invited to wear the crown as Alfonso XII. But the sham constitutionalism of the new regime could not deal effectively with the fundamental problems of Spanish political insecurity and social discontent.

Similarly, in neighboring Portugal declining economic fortunes and bitter class antagonisms made satisfactory adjustment to the liberal era difficult. True, there was the constitution of 1821 which had introduced a measure of individual freedom and parliamentary government, but there was also a strong conservative party which staunchly adhered to the traditions of the past. Its leader Dom Miguel plunged the country into a civil war which raged from 1828 to 1834, but even his defeat and the moderate reigns of Queen Maria II and her two sons, Pedro V and Luiz I, failed to end the widespread corruption in public life, the heavy burden of taxation, the low level of popular education, and the steady migration of thousands of persons to Brazil. Besides, the huge colonial empire of some eight hundred thousand square miles, which Portugal proudly insisted on retaining, was an expensive luxury for a state which financially had enough difficulty keeping its own head above water. While western liberals sometimes spoke optimistically of Portugal as an Iberian Belgium or Holland, as a matter of fact deep-seated social ills and economic weaknesses were undermining the political structure of the country.

5. Eastern Europe

THE HEART OF CONSERVATISM lay on the other side of Europe among the great estates and ancient castles of the east, where proud aristocrats lorded over a cowed peasantry. The lands of the Habsburgs and the Romanovs were still governed in the spirit of royal absolutism which had been destroyed in western Europe by the French Revolution. On the plains which extend beyond the Vistula and the Alps factories and railroads were few and middle-class entrepreneurs and politicians timid. Faint echoes of the liberal ideas which were on the march elsewhere did manage to penetrate the walls of censorship surrounding the eastern autocracies, but their effect was limited. Theories of divine-right monarchism, on the other hand, found a favorable reception in Vienna and St. Petersburg, and the poverty-stricken populace of village and town remained respectfully obedient to the throne. For what did high-flown talk about individual rights and representative government mean to the masses who barely managed to keep body and soul together?

THE AUSTRIAN EMPIRE

The Austrian Empire remained essentially a conservative anachronism throughout the nineteenth century. Its social structure made it conservative, its political organization made it anachronistic. Not only did the governing aristocracy oppose constitutional reform, but the irreconcilable demands of opposing nationalities within the state engendered a mounting civic tension. Throughout the Habsburg crownlands peoples of different languages and traditions began to clamor for recognition and self-determination. In Bohemia it was Czech against German, in Galicia Ukrainian against Pole, in Hungary Slovak, Romanian, and Croat against Magyar, and in Istria Italian and Slovene against German.

At first the claims of the oppressed peoples did not go beyond a defense of the local culture against the prevalent Germanism, but gradually this linguistic nationalism changed into a political consciousness seeking autonomy within the empire. The Bohemian historian Francis Palacky sang the past greatness of the Czech nation and demanded administrative freedom for his nation. In Hungary the Magyars, hard pressed by the Habsburg authorities in Vienna, bullied in turn the minorities in their midst and embarked on a loud campaign for cultural and governmental autonomy. Among the Croats, Slovenes, and Serbs of the south there developed an Illyrian nationalism which maintained that they all had a common political and linguistic tradition. Even some of the dominant Germans, attracted to their brothers farther north, began to advocate a united Teutonic fatherland in which the Germanic Austrians could take their place. Despite the most strenuous efforts of the bureaucracy, these conflicting patriotisms continued to gain strength in the years after the Congress of Vienna.

Habsburg fortunes reached their nadir in 1848. The news of the downfall of Louis Philippe in France led to the outbreak of revolutions throughout the Austrian Empire. In Vienna itself the aged Metternich was forced to resign and escape incognito to England, while a national assembly went to work to prepare a liberal constitution. In Hungary the radical politician Louis Kossuth forced the government to accept the March Laws establishing a parliamentary and autonomous Magyar state. In Bohemia the Czechs won a promise of self-government; in Lombardy-Venetia the Austrian garrisons were driven out of Milan and Venice; and in Galicia the Poles demanded political concessions. But the proverbial luck of the Habsburgs did not desert them in the hour of their greatest need. The army and the bureaucracy, still loyal to the dynasty, were able to exploit the differences which arose among the revolutionaries on the morrow of their triumph. Moreover, in the reactionary new emperor Francis Joseph (1848–1916) and his reactionary new prime minister Felix zu Schwarzenberg they found leaders with determination and nerve. In the summer of 1848 Prince Alfred zu Windischgrätz suppressed the uprising in Bohemia by playing off German against Czech, while Field Marshal

Joseph Radetzky was able to defeat the Italians, who were torn by the rivalry between liberals and democrats. Revolutionary Vienna was captured by the imperial forces in the fall; and the Hungarians, fighting with stubborn courage, were finally crushed the following summer by the armies of the Austrians, the Croatians, and the Russians, who were sent by the tsar to help his fellow autocrat. Within less than two years the Habsburg Empire was restored in all its uncompromising conservatism.

The 1850's were years of reaction in Austria. Revolutionaries were imprisoned, voices of criticism were silenced, local rights of self-government were abolished. The administration was completely centralized in Vienna. Yet the Bach System, as this iron regime was called after Minister of the Interior Alexander Bach, did not eliminate national dissatisfactions. It merely sat on them. At the first sign of weakness in the government they were bound to rise to the surface again. When the Austrian armies were defeated in 1859 by the combined forces of France and Sardinia, the myth of the military invincibility of the state was shattered, and the subject peoples immediately began to revive their demands for political concession. The ministry tried to satisfy them by promulgating the October Diploma of 1860 and the February Patent of 1861, constitutional decrees establishing a half-hearted parliamentarianism in the empire. But the Hungarians, the most vigorous of the oppressed nationalities, refused to settle for anything less than the March Laws of 1848. Francis Joseph was at first inclined to engage in a test of strength with Magyar nationalism, but when his troops were defeated once again in the Seven Weeks' War (1866) he realized that he could not risk a new revolution. In 1867, therefore, he concluded the *Ausgleich*, a constitutional compromise between Austria and Hungary which remained the political foundation of the state until 1918.

The Habsburg lands were divided into two distinct national entities, the Austrian Empire and the Kingdom of Hungary. The former was to be ruled by a constitution based on the February Patent of 1861, the latter by the March Laws of 1848. A few functions of government such as military affairs and foreign policy were to be exercised by common ministries, but in most cases the partners in the Dual Monarchy acted as entirely separate and independent countries. They were held together, however, by a common fear of the other nationalities, for even in combination the Germans in Austria and the Magyars in Hungary constituted less than half of the total population of the state. Surrounded by a Slavic sea, they were willy-nilly obliged to maintain their alliance against the subject peoples whom they were jointly dominating. Of course, they might have been able to solve the problem of the national minorities by a federalist reorganization of the government giving autonomy to the oppressed. But then they would have had to surrender their monopoly of political and economic influence. Neither the bureaucrats in Vienna nor the magnates in Budapest were capable of such magnanimity. They preferred instead to delude themselves that the grumblings about them were only the work of a few malcontents who refused to accept their proper station in life. "The situation is critical but not serious" became the credo of a ruling class marching blithely to destruction.

RUSSIA

Russia, too, had her national minorities. Within her borders lived millions of Poles, Lithuanians, Latvians, Estonians, Finns, Ukrainians, and Jews, as well as a bewildering variety of Caucasian and Asiatic peoples, all restive under tsarist oppression. But whereas in Austria the dominant national elements were a minority of the total population, in the possessions of the Romanovs the Russians proper comprised about half of all inhabitants, and the state could therefore better afford to ignore the wishes of the subject peoples. Still it had to wrestle with the equally serious difficulties created by a rapid transformation in the social and economic structure of the country. Russia in the nineteenth century was a land bewildered and frightened by the sudden transition from an age of serfdom and autocracy to one of industrialism and liberalism. Confronted by the political strains arising out of the need to adjust to swiftly changing material conditions, Russian rulers introduced alternately policies of stern repression and moderate reform, failing to stem popular discontent with either. Revolutionary ideas could not be exiled to Siberia, and imperial concessions were too little and too late to prevent the collapse of the monarchy. The final act of the tragedy of Russian absolutism was played out on a terrible July day in 1918 when the last of the tsars and his entire family were slaughtered by the soldiery of a new and even more pitiless regime.

At the time of the Congress of Vienna, however, it looked as if a new era of civic progress were opening for the colossus of the north. Tsar Alexander I (1801–1825), a well-intentioned neurotic who had been educated in the political theories of the French philosophes, acceded to the throne determined to win a place in history as a philosopher-king. In conversation with his intimates over a cup of tea in some luxurious salon he could discourse tirelessly about the need for reform, but he somehow always managed to find a reason for postponing the execution of his philanthropic plans. Perhaps the poet Lord Byron was not far from the truth, when he portrayed the emperor

> With no objection to true liberty,
> Except that it would make the nations free.

In any case the Russian peasant continued to groan in serfdom, and the Russian nobleman continued to play God, while Alexander fought first against Napoleon, then for Napoleon, and then against Napoleon again. In 1813 he became the liberator of Europe, and two years later the end of the war with France freed his hands for the work of domestic reform. He appeared, however, to be in no hurry to renounce his prerogatives. True, he gave Poland an autonomous status and a liberal constitution; he maintained friendly relations with parliamentarians in England and France; he even gave a measure of encouragement to revolutionaries in Greece plotting an uprising against the Turks. Yet the reforms which he granted to the Russians themselves were few and unimportant, and after the Congress of Troppau in 1820 he listened with growing interest to the conservative theories of Metternich. By the time of his death in December 1825 he had turned into an out-and-out reactionary—moody, restless, resentful, haunted by visions of the murder of his father in which he himself had been implicated.

His brother and successor, Nicholas I (1825–1855), was cast in a different mold. He was blessed with a simple and unquestioning faith in royal absolutism which was never troubled by the doubts which had assailed his predecessor. Trained as a soldier, he approached the problems of statecraft with a drill sergeant's insistence on blind obedience. His natural inclination toward conservatism, moreover, was intensified by the unsuccessful uprising organized upon the death of Alexander I by a handful of liberal army officers and Francophile aristocratic intellectuals. This Decembrist Revolt of 1825 was easily suppressed, but the tsar never forgot that the reformers had planned to introduce a constitutional regime by replacing him with his brother Constantine. Throughout the thirty years of his reign he remained the foremost opponent in Europe of the principle of popular sovereignty. In 1830–1831 he crushed an uprising of the Poles and revoked their right of self-government; in 1849 he helped the Austrians defeat the rebellion in Hungary; and in 1852–1853 he opposed Napoleon III because of the revolutionary origin of the authority of the Bonapartes. The autocrat who was prepared to help destroy liberalism abroad was certainly not going to tolerate it at home. Critics of the government were jailed, the press was censored, schools were supervised, and radical agitation was stifled by the Third Section, an early example of that long series of secret police organizations which have become a tradition in Russia. Autocracy, orthodoxy, and nationalism were the articles of faith of a militant tsarism.

Most Russians seemed to look upon the unbending conservatism of their monarch with fatalistic resignation. There were a few opponents of the established order like Michael Bakunin and Alexander Herzen who, from a safe distance beyond the Russian frontier, continued to condemn the political and economic institutions of their native land. But their denunciations made a deeper impression on radicals in London and Paris than on the benighted muzhiks of the eastern steppes. Even the educated classes learned to accept what they could not change, consoling themselves with the thought that while Nicholas I ruled his possessions with an iron hand he also inspired great respect in foreign countries. If liberalism suffered under his rule, national pride flourished. Tsarist troops invaded the Balkans and terrorized the sultan in Constantinople; they defeated Polish and Hungarian revolutionaries; they threatened to intervene in Germany in defense of the Habsburgs; they subjugated tribal princes and nomad chieftains in the Caucasus and in Siberia. Russia loomed over the European horizon like a giant bestriding the world.

Yet the giant had feet of clay. In 1853 the tsar overplayed his diplomatic hand by provoking hostilities with Turkey, who promptly received assistance from France and England. The Crimean War resulted in a resounding defeat for Russia, a defeat seriously weakening the autocratic principle. The state was shown to be corrupt and backward, and public opinion, which for more than a generation had venerated an unconquerable absolutism, turned against the fallen idol.

Nicholas I died in the midst of the war, a disappointed and broken man, so that his son Alexander II (1855–1881) was left to reap the whirlwind. Like his uncle Alexander I, he was eager to conciliate his subjects without relaxing his hold over them. Although in 1861 he finally decreed the abolition of serfdom, the aristocrats retained the most fertile fields, while the peasants were obliged to pay a heavy price for the modest allotments of land which they acquired. Three years later the emperor established district and provincial *zemstvos,* elective councils enjoying jurisdiction over schools, roads, hospitals, and orphanages; but he would not even hear of the creation of a national representative legislature. In 1864 he promulgated a progressive judicial system; in 1870 he reformed municipal government; and in 1874 he modernized the army. Having shown himself so magnanimous to his subjects, he confidently expected to be hailed as the Solon of the age. Instead the Poles rose in revolution, the peasants clamored for more land, and the newspapers demanded further political concessions. Once the tsar realized that nothing less than a parliamentary system of government would satisfy the liberal opposition, his enthusiasm for change left him. By the early 1870's he showed himself to be a true son of Nicholas I by abandoning the policy of reform and setting out on the familiar road to reaction.

THE OTTOMAN EMPIRE

South of Russia lay the sick and dying Ottoman Empire. The religious fervor and military zeal which once made the Turks invincible had long since evaporated, leaving behind them sultans who won their victories in the harem rather than on the battlefield, and pashas who plotted against their own government more than they prepared for war with foreign enemies. What is more, with the rise of nationalism throughout Europe the subject Orthodox Christian peoples in the Balkans grew increasingly restless under the corrupt rule of Constantinople. Greeks, Bulgarians, Serbs, and Romanians began first to develop pride in their cultural tradition, then to remember a great historical past, then to form secret patriotic societies, and then to raise the banner of rebellion. Finally the great powers found themselves more and more attracted by diplomatic complications in the Balkans. Whereas elsewhere in Europe firmly established states had become the rule, in the southeast political conditions were unsettled enough to tempt diplomats to fish in troubled waters. Economically the region was backward, but its strategic location at the crossroads of three continents gave it major importance. Two powers especially found themselves deeply involved in the complexities of the Near Eastern question. Russia, convinced that the disintegration of Turkey was inevitable, had resolved to gain the vital straits connecting the Black Sea with the Aegean and to assert her influence over the Christian nationalities in the Balkan peninsula. England, on the other hand, unwilling to see Russian naval might established in the eastern Mediterranean and anxious to retain the rich Turkish markets, became the champion of the Sublime Porte. The conflicting influences and policies of St. Petersburg and London with regard to the Ottoman Empire made of it an international problem of the first magnitude.

At first the Russians seemed to be gaining the upper hand. Revolutions in Serbia in 1804–1813 and 1815–1817 and in Greece in 1821–1829 weakened the Turkish government and provided the tsar with an excellent pretext for an invasion of the Balkans. Although the British cabinet was forced by public opinion at home to intervene halfheartedly in the Near East in order to persuade the sultan to make concessions to his Christian subjects, it was Russia who, by the brief war of 1828–1829 against the Ottoman Empire, won independence for Greece and autonomy for Serbia. The Turks, deciding that resistance against their powerful neighbor was useless, entered into a close alliance with Russia by the Treaty of Unkiar Skelessi of 1833.

For a few years Romanov influence was paramount in Constantinople, but then the balance began to shift in favor of the British. In 1841 Britain encouraged the sultan to replace the unwelcome alliance with the tsar by an international convention barring all foreign warships from the straits. And before long the English ambassador, Stratford Canning, was inciting the Sublime Porte to resist the demands of St. Petersburg by intimating that Queen Victoria's navy would help defend the Ottoman Empire. Nicholas I confidently decided in 1853 to call the Turkish bluff, only to end up much to his chagrin with a war on his hands against England, France, and Sardinia, as well as Turkey. Hostilities were largely confined to the siege of the great naval base of Sevastopol in the Crimea. Upon its fall Alexander II was forced to sign the Treaty of Paris in 1856, promising to abstain from intervention in Ottoman affairs and to destroy all Russian military installations on the Black Sea as a pledge of good behavior. Great Britain and Palmerston had won a hard-fought victory, although most of the glory had been earned by the French army.

The Crimean War proved only a temporary check to Russian designs. As soon as his empire had recovered from the shock of defeat Alexander II began to plan for a revision of the Treaty of Paris. His opportunity arrived in 1870. While the rest of Europe was absorbed in the Franco-Prussian War, the tsar repudiated the demilitarization clauses of the treaty and proceeded to rebuild naval installations on the Black Sea. In the meantime one more autonomous Christian nation had been established in the Balkans. A political union of the two Danubian principalities of Moldavia and Wallachia took place in 1858; and the new state of Romania chose as its ruler first a native aristocrat, Alexander Cuza, and then the Hohenzollern Prince Charles. The Sublime Porte during the 1850's and 1860's made a determined effort to strengthen its position by a policy of liberal modernization. Early in 1856 the *Hatt-i Humayun*, a reform edict inspired by English and French influence, granted the Christian subjects of the sultan security of life and property and equality of legal and political status. Five years later, with the accession of the enlightened Abdul Aziz (1861–1876), Turkey entered on a period of rapid Westernization designed to protect the empire against rebellion within and aggression without.

The most important development in the Orient, however, was the completion in 1869 of the Suez Canal connecting the Mediterranean with the Red Sea. The work of the French diplomat and promoter Ferdinand de Lesseps, the canal gave a new economic and strategic importance to the lands of the Ottoman Em-

THE OPENING OF THE SUEZ CANAL, 1869. Sovereigns and statesmen from all over the world attended the ceremonies marking the completion of a vital new waterway.

pire. By intensifying the rivalries of the great powers, it helped set off a new round of plotting, scheming, intriguing, manipulating, and wirepulling in the Balkans which culminated in the summer of 1914 in the outbreak of a world war.

Yet for optimistic liberals around the middle of the nineteenth century every prospect was rosy. Wherever they turned they could see their ideas on the march; they could see the growth of parliamentarianism, the expansion of industrialism, the rise of middle-class influence, the unfolding of freedom. Human bondage was being abolished along the Volga and in the British West Indies; representative institutions were being introduced in Vienna and Berlin; freedom of worship was being proclaimed in Rome and Constantinople; factories were rising in St. Petersburg and Madrid. Hereditary class privileges were being abolished, arbitrary governmental practices were being abandoned, religious discriminations were disappearing, protective tariff walls were falling, man's inhumanity to man was abating. It was good to be a bourgeois liberal. The enlightened and benevolent man of property was on the side of the angels; he fought for a cause that was invincible. As he contemplated the forces of injustice and oppression in flight before his righteousness, he sang with the poet Alfred Tennyson (*Morte d'Arthur*, 1842):

> The old order changeth, yielding place to new,
> And God fulfills himself in many ways,
> Lest one good custom should corrupt the world.

Further Reading

Among the many general accounts of the political development of Europe in the years between Metternich and Bismarck two deserve mention: *F. B. Artz, *Reaction and Revolution, 1815–1832* (New York, 1934); and *R. C. Binkley, *Realism and Nationalism, 1852–1871* (New York, 1935). For the dominant ideologies of the early nineteenth century see *G. De Ruggiero, *The History of European Liberalism* (New York, 1927); and H. Cecil, *Conservatism* (New York, 1913). Penetrating accounts of revolutionary theoreticians and traditions are to be found in *I. Berlin, *Karl Marx* (New York, 1948); and *E. Wilson, *To the Finland Station* (Garden City, 1953).

There are many works dealing with the reconstruction of Europe after the fall of Napoleon, but none is more readable than *H. Nicolson, *The Congress of Vienna: A Study in Allied Unity* (New York, 1946). *C. K. Webster, *The Congress of Vienna, 1814–1815* (London, 1950) presents a sound brief account. The standard book on Britain's diplomatic role is C. K. Webster, *The Foreign Policy of Castlereagh*, 2 vols. (London, 1925–1931). The policy of the Austrian foreign minister has been examined by H. Kissinger, *A World Restored: Metternich, Castlereagh and the Problem of Peace, 1812–1822* (London, 1957). The slippery Talleyrand is the protagonist of a number of good studies, among them G. Ferrero, *The Reconstruction of Europe: Talleyrand and the Congress of Vienna* (New York, 1941). For the congress system see W. A. Phillips,

The Confederation of Europe: A Study of the European Alliance, 1813–1823 (London, 1920); and H. G. A. V. Schenck, *The Aftermath of the Napoleonic Wars: The Concert of Europe—An Experiment* (New York, 1947).

E. Halévy, *A History of the English People in the Nineteenth Century,* 5 vols. (Gloucester, Mass., 1949–1952) has become a classic. For sheer biographical brilliance nothing surpasses L. Strachey, **Queen Victoria* (New York, 1921) and **Eminent Victorians* (Cape Town, 1947). There are learned and lively accounts in F. B. Artz, *France under the Bourbon Restoration, 1814–1830* (Cambridge, Mass., 1931); **J. M. Thompson, *Louis Napoleon and the Second Empire* (Oxford, 1954); and G. Wright, *France in Modern Times, 1760 to the Present* (Chicago, 1960).

J. G. Legge, *Rhyme and Revolution in Germany* (London, 1919) is a collection of source materials illustrating the rise of liberalism and nationalism in central Europe. For the events of 1848 there is V. Valentin, *1848: Chapters of German History* (New York, 1940), a drastically abridged translation of a major work in German. Perhaps less profound but certainly more readable is **P. Robertson, *Revolutions of 1848* (Princeton, 1952). O. Pflanze, *Bismarck and the Development of Germany: The Period of Unification, 1815–1871* (Princeton, 1963) presents the best portrait of the Iron Chancellor available in English. Of the older accounts C. G. Robertson, *Bismarck* (New York, 1919) is still instructive. A. J. B. Whyte, *The Evolution of Modern Italy, 1715–1920* (Oxford, 1944) describes the Risorgimento. Among the noteworthy biographies of the political leaders of Italy are W. R. Thayer, *The Life and Times of Cavour,* 2 vols. (Boston, 1914); and S. Barr, *Mazzini: Portrait of an Exile* (New York, 1935).

H. du Coudray, *Metternich* (New Haven, 1936) and J. Redlich, *Emperor Francis Joseph of Austria* (New York, 1929) deal with the Austrian Empire through the lives of two outstanding public figures. **M. Karpovich, *Imperial Russia, 1801–1917* (New York, 1932) provides a useful introduction to more specialized works like **A. G. Mazour, *The First Russian Revolution, 1825* (Berkeley, 1937). R. W. Seton-Watson, *The Rise of Nationality in the Balkans* (London, 1917) examines political developments in the Ottoman Empire, while V. J. Puryear, *England, Russia, and the Straits Question, 1844–1856* (Berkeley, 1931) is the best account of the origin and course of the Crimean War.

CHAPTER 17

Nationalism
and Democracy
1871–1914

Never did the sun shine more brightly over Europe than in the years from 1871 to 1914. For almost half a century no war among the great powers disturbed the tranquillity of the West. For almost half a century there was a swift increase in population and a steady expansion of industrial production. Seeking new fields to conquer, the leading states embarked on a course of imperialism. They colonized and modernized; they carried the blessings of technological progress to the four corners of the earth. Among colored peoples, restless under the white man's domination, there was bitter resentment, but before the Occidentals stretched an endless vista of political strength and economic prosperity. To be sure, bright young men who gathered in arty drawing rooms suffered from a feeling of cynicism and boredom, the feeling of *fin de siècle*. And in the cities of Asia and Africa native nationalists were denouncing the cupidity of the foreign master. But to the average citizen of England or France or Germany times were good and bound to get better.

1. The Indian Summer of the European Age

SUCH OPTIMISM was not unjustified. European society had created a better life for its growing population; and it had developed a civic philosophy which came to grips with the problems created by the Industrial Revolution. After 1871 laissez-faire liberalism, with its emphasis on the rights of property, slowly gave way before a popular democracy preaching the primacy of the general welfare over individual prerogative. Middle-class constitutionalists had at first been so determined to destroy the power of royal despotism that they refused to consider any compromise with personal freedom, but once the battle against absolutism was won, they were in a better position to adapt their social theories to proletarian needs. Recognizing factory labor as a political force which in the hands of radicalism could turn against established authority, they gradually began to strengthen the civic and economic position of the masses.

BOURGEOIS REFORMISM

Libertarian doctrines which in 1815 had reflected only the narrow self-interest of an ambitious social class became by 1914 instruments for the advancement of society as a whole. A new humanitarian impulse broadened the outlook of bourgeois parliamentarianism. John Stuart Mill (1806–1873), a political theorist who in his intellectual development had progressed from individualistic liberalism to egalitarian democracy, spoke for militant reform in his *Principles of Political Economy* (1848):

> Each person should have power to dispose by will of his or her whole property; but not to lavish it in enriching some one individual, beyond a certain maximum, which should be fixed sufficiently high to afford the means of comfortable independence. The inequalities of property which arise from unequal industry, frugality, perseverance, talents, and to a certain extent even opportunities, are inseparable from the principle of private property, and if we accept the principle, we must bear with these consequences of it: but I see nothing objectionable in fixing a limit to what any one may acquire by the mere favor of others, without any exercise of his faculties, and in requiring that if he desires any further accession of fortune, he shall work for it.

The achievements of middle-class democracy were considerable. Everywhere in Europe there was an extension of the franchise to the masses. The Third French Republic and the German Empire introduced universal manhood suffrage at the time of their formation during the Franco-Prussian War. The United Kingdom admitted virtually every adult male to the polls by the parliamentary reform bill of 1884. In 1905 the Russian government agreed to give the proletariat the right to vote. Austria followed in 1907, and Italy in 1912. Some of the smaller states were even more daring, and by the time of the First World War Norway and Denmark had introduced female suffrage.

The problems of industrial labor were also attracting sympathetic attention in governmental circles. During the 1880's Germany pioneered in the establishment of social insurance against sickness, disability, and old age. In 1911 England went still further by protecting its working population against unemployment as well as illness. Italy prescribed a weekly day of rest for labor and nationalized private insurance companies. Austria experimented with the municipal ownership of public utilities. Opportunities for academic training and social advancement also improved, as one government after another hastened to educate its masses through free and compulsory elementary schooling. The result was a decline of proletarian illiteracy and an increasing influence of the lower classes in public life.

PROLETARIAN RADICALISM

The improvement in the lot of the proletariat took the wind out of the sails of radicalism. Since social progress under an enlightened capitalism was becoming a reality, political extremism lost much of its appeal. In the first half of the nineteenth century the ruling classes of Europe had lived in constant fear of revolution. They could remember the widespread popular uprisings of 1820–1821, 1830–1831, and 1848–1849. But after 1871 the only serious insurrection to affect a major state outside chronically unstable Turkey occurred in Russia in 1905. There, moreover, it merely reemphasized the lesson that sedition was the alternative to reform. Similarly the rise of Marxian parties on the Continent was not a symptom of the aggravation of class conflicts, but rather a sign of the growing political consciousness of the masses. The workers joining the socialist movement did so in order to attain a higher standard of living, to win a higher wage and a shorter work day. They emphasized more and more bread-and-butter objectives, immediate gains in daily economic life. Almost imperceptibly, the proletarian had ceased to be a civic outcast. He was becoming part of an organized social force capable of achieving an important position within the capitalistic system.

The great European federation of socialist parties reflected this decline of revolutionary militancy. In 1864 Marx had founded the First International Workingmen's Association, a radical organization established to direct the struggle against the established order in all countries and on all continents. Yet despite its grandiose pretensions, it was never more than a feeble hodge-podge of diverse political tendencies. Torn by factionalism and persecuted by the police, it collapsed after twelve years of agitation. The Second International, founded in 1889, had better luck. Less concerned with doctrinal subtleties, even prepared at times to sacrifice dogma for practical advantage, it grew and prospered. By the time of the First World War its following ran into the millions. It still continued to deliver blood-and-thunder sermons about the evils of capitalism, but in spirit it was steadily drawing closer to middle-class democracy. As it acquired offices, newspapers, housing developments, clinics, administrators, bureaucrats, and employees of its own, it became less violently opposed to the established order. At times it was actually prepared to enter into an alliance with democratic parliamentarianism. In England the socialist James Keir Hardie helped organize the middle-of-the-road Labor party. In France Alexandre Millerand agreed to enter a cabinet composed of representatives of the progressive bourgeoisie. In Germany Gustav Noske came out in favor of colonial expansion and against a reduction in armaments. It was becoming obvious that socialism's bite was not nearly as bad as its bark.

Some socialists even argued that the theory of the class struggle should be modified in accordance with changing economic conditions. In the 1890's Eduard Bernstein in Germany began to preach revisionism, maintaining that the teachings of Marx must be interpreted in the light of practical experience. Specifically he stressed the improvement of the conditions of labor under capitalism and urged the abandonment of the doctrine of the irreconcilability of social conflicts:

> Socialism will come . . . not as the result of the ever increasing oppression, misery, and degradation of the workers, but as the result of their growing social influence and the relative improvements, of an economic, political, and general social (ethical) nature, which they have achieved. I see socialist society arising not out of chaos, but out of the union of the organizational accomplishments of workers in the realm of the free economy with the accomplishments of militant democracy in state and community. Despite all the convulsions and the flailing about of the forces of reaction, I still see the class struggle itself assuming more and more civilized forms. And it is precisely in this civilizing of political and economic struggles that I perceive the best guarantee for the realization of socialism.[1]

At its congress in Amsterdam in 1904 the Second International condemned revisionism as heresy. Most of the great Marxian theoreticians—among them August Bebel, Karl Kautsky, and Jules Guesde—declared that it represented an unacceptable departure from ideological orthodoxy. But no amount of dialectical sleight of hand could overcome the mood of gradualism which had become dominant among their followers. When 1914 came, each socialist party urged the worker to support his government against his fellow worker across the frontier. The great crisis of bourgeois society thus created an irreparable breach in the ranks of socialism.

For those who did not want their radicalism diluted there was anarchism. Convinced that all government was based on oppression, anarchism insisted that all government was evil. Society should ideally be built on voluntary cooperation, on the free consent of men and women ready to subordinate their private interests to the common good. Not the policeman on the street corner, not the bureaucrat behind his desk, but the natural human impulse to work for the welfare of mankind should become the bulwark of a new social order. Yet how could the existing coercive system of rule be overthrown? Some anarchists agreed with the gentle

---

[1] Eduard Bernstein, *Von der Sekte zur Partei* (Jena: Eugen Diederichs, 1911), p. 76. Trans. by Theodore S. Hamerow.

Prince Peter Kropotkin who taught that a moral regeneration of the individual must precede the establishment of a better society. Others, acting on the advice of Michael Bakunin, waged a war of terror against the representatives of established authority. They threw bombs and fired revolvers, assassinating Empress Elizabeth of Austria, King Humbert I of Italy, President Sadi-Carnot of France, and President William McKinley of the United States. Still others, accepting the anarchosyndicalism of Georges Sorel's *Reflections on Violence* (1908), believed that trade unions would become the shock troops of revolution and destroy capitalism through a general strike.

Despite its promises of Utopia, however, anarchism did not prove a serious threat to the ruling classes of the West. In the popular mind the anarchist always remained the familiar caricature that peered out of the pages of the newspapers, wild-eyed and black-bearded, hurling dynamite at the world.

Here and there in France, Italy, and Spain anarchosyndicalism did manage to win a following in militant proletarian circles, but generally it could not compete successfully with the socialists for the support of the masses. The anarchist movement attracted the intellectual and the bohemian, not the rank and file of labor, and in the early years of the twentieth century it entered a period of decline.

THE RISE OF NATIONALISM

Since socialism was growing more powerful but less aggressive, and anarchism more aggressive but less powerful, bourgeois society was safe against its critics. The danger which it faced came from its avowed defenders. The great crisis of 1914 was not the work of a proletariat rising against the middle class, but of forces which established authority had created and nourished. It was the product of an irresponsible, aggressive nationalism.

In its simplest form, nationalism preached that all men of common culture and common history properly constituted a single political organism. Its origins could be traced back to antiquity, to the Hebrew notion of the chosen people and the Roman concept of municipal citizenship. In the Middle Ages there had been vague stirrings of national feeling among the states of Europe. The Renaissance and the Reformation weakened the unifying force of religious life and encouraged the rise of national monarchies. In his *Defense and Illustration of the French Language*, published in 1550, the Frenchman Joachim du Bellay proclaimed "my natural affection toward my fatherland," and thirty years later the Englishman John Lyly was assuring his countrymen that they held a special place in the sight of God: "So tender a care hath He alwaies had of that England, as of a new Israel, His chosen and peculiar people."

But it was a German clergyman educated in the enlightened teachings of the eighteenth century who first advanced a systematic theory of nationalism. For

Johann Gottfried Herder (1744–1803) each people possessed a historic heritage in the form of a distinct culture which separated it from every other people. By identifying himself with his national culture the individual became a link in the spiritual bond which connected the present with the past and the future. Yet he also belonged to humanity, within which each nation had its unique mission:

> Nature has distributed its gifts differently according to climate and culture. How could they be compared to one another? Rather we should rejoice, like Sultan Suleiman, that there are such varied flowers and peoples on the gay meadow of this earth, that such different blossoms can bloom on both sides of the Alps, and that such varied fruits can ripen.

The cultural nationalism of Herder became political in the course of the French Revolution and the Napoleonic era. During the restoration nationalism continued to grow, especially among those peoples which were politically disunited. The Germans recalled the glory of the Holy Roman Empire, the Italians remembered the grandeur that was Rome, the Magyars sang the deeds of Janos Hunyadi, the Czechs of Jan Ziska, the Poles of Vladislav Jagiello, the Greeks of Pericles, the Irish of Hugh O'Neill. Everywhere enthusiastic young men were joining patriotic organizations like the Burschenschaften, the Carbonari, the Young Ireland party, and the Hetairia Philike. Their purpose was to reconstruct Europe on the principle of nationalism. Once each people was free to determine its own form of government, they maintained, men would live peacefully in mutual respect. Giuseppe Mazzini (1805–1872) was their most eloquent spokesman:

> Nationalities are sacred, and providentially constituted to represent, within Humanity, the division or distribution of labor for the advantage of the peoples, as the division and distribution of labor within the limits of the state should be organized for the greatest benefit of all citizens. If they do not look to that end, they are useless and fall.

Yet there were also indications that nationalism might in the end prove to be a Frankenstein monster. During the revolution of 1848 John Stuart Mill noted sadly: "In the backward parts of Europe and even (where better things might have been expected) in Germany, the sentiment of nationality so far outweighs the love of liberty that the people are willing to abet their rulers in crushing the liberty and independence of any people not of their race and language." In the hands of the practitioners of *Realpolitik* who governed Europe after 1871 nationalism became a weapon in the struggle for diplomatic hegemony. There was less and less regard for the aspirations of other states, less and less concern for the welfare of humanity. Nationalism turned into an obsession, stimulating the spread of militarism and racialism. In that poisonous atmosphere the German General Friedrich von Bernhardi asserted in all earnestness that war "is not only a necessary element in the life of people, but also an indispensable factor in culture, indeed the highest expression of the strength and life of truly cultured peoples." The London *Saturday Review* stated bluntly, "England has awakened to what is alike inevitable and her best hope of prosperity. *Germaniam esse delendam* [Germany must be destroyed]." The Russian diplomat Alexander Izvolski exulted, when the shooting finally began: "*C'est ma petite guerre* [This is my little war]." The age which had begun with the great voyages of discovery in the fifteenth century came to an end in 1914 in the trenches of Flanders.

2. *Western Europe*

GREAT BRITAIN

For England the closing decades of the reign of Victoria were a golden sunset. Never before had the country been so prosperous, never again was it to be so self-confident. As the indestructible queen grew older, the ministers who had guarded the throne in the early years of her rule—Melbourne, Russell, Palmerston, Peel, Derby—began to pass from the scene. Their place was taken by the second generation of Victorian statesmen. After 1870 the Liberal party was guided by the sincere, long-winded William Ewart Gladstone (1809–1898). His great opponent was Benjamin Disraeli (1804–1881)—intellectual, dilettante, and fop of Jewish birth—who emerged as the dominant figure in a party which had come to represent the interests of the proudest aristocratic families. The landed nobility willy-nilly accepted his leadership, for he alone seemed capable of saving it from defeat. Convinced that the old shibboleths of throne and altar had lost their meaning in an age of industrialism, he transformed the Conservative party into the champion of imperialism. To middle-class insistence upon domestic reform he replied with the call for a bold foreign policy.

It was fitting that the two great Gladstone ministries of 1868 to 1874 and 1880 to 1885 should be devoted to an improvement of political and social institutions. In 1870 a new education law laid the foundation for a system of universal elementary schooling, and an order in council introduced the merit principle into the civil service. In 1871 the practice of purchasing commissions in the armed forces was ended; in 1872 the ballot was made secret; in 1883 corruption at the polls was suppressed; and in 1884 the extension of the suffrage to agricultural laborers established virtually universal manhood suffrage. During the Disraeli ministry from 1874 to 1880, on the other hand, the British lion roared. In 1875 the prime minister cleverly engineered the purchase by his government of a controlling share in the management of the Suez Canal Company. In 1876 he fired the imagination of the country by sponsoring a bill conferring upon the queen the title Empress of India. In 1878

MOSÉ IN EGITTO!!! The cartoon shows Disraeli, who has just acquired control of the Suez Canal, exchanging meaningful glances with the sphinx.

he checked Russian expansion in the Near East, obtaining Cyprus from Turkey in return for promises of military assistance which did not cost a single pound. Even after his death Conservative statesmen like Lord Robert Salisbury, Arthur Balfour, and Joseph Chamberlain remained exponents of an energetic diplomacy. In the years from 1885 to 1905, when the Conservatives were usually in power, Downing Street continued to acquire overseas possessions and wave the Union Jack.

The Liberals finally managed to win a major parliamentary victory as a result of economic difficulties at home. By the early twentieth century British industry was encountering growing competition from Germany, America, and Japan. At first the urban proletariat sought to improve its position through unionization and strike activity. But then in 1900 the Labor Representation Committee, which soon became the Labor party, began to attract the working class by its advocacy of democratic socialism. A growing demand for protective tariffs added to the difficulties of the Conservative party, and in 1905 King Edward VII (1901–1910) called on the leader of the opposition, Sir Henry Campbell-Bannerman, to form a new ministry.

For the next ten years the Liberals were at the helm, introducing innovations which would have shocked such earlier stalwarts of the party as Lord Russell and John Bright. The moving spirit behind this reform movement was David Lloyd

George (1863–1945), a fiery Welshman of lower-class background who attacked the rich with a hatred nurtured by his early poverty. In 1906 labor unions were declared immune against the damage suits of employers; in 1909 pensions were granted to workers over seventy; in 1911 the masses were insured against sickness and unemployment; and in 1912 a minimum-wage law for the coal industry was promulgated. Moreover, when the conservative aristocrats who dominated the House of Lords protested against new taxes on wealth by rejecting the budget of 1909, the ministry took the issue to the country, won two bitter electoral campaigns, and with the Parliament Bill of 1911 deprived the upper chamber of the right to veto measures approved by the House of Commons.

The colonial possessions of Great Britain were the indirect beneficiaries of the growth of democracy in the mother country. The status of a self-governing dominion obtained by Canada in 1867 proved so successful an instrument of imperial administration that it was soon extended to other overseas territories inhabited by a European population. In 1901 New South Wales, Victoria, Queensland, South Australia, Western Australia, and Tasmania were united in the Commonwealth of Australia. In 1907 New Zealand was elevated from a colony to a dominion. And in 1910 Cape Colony, Natal, Transvaal, and Orange River Colony in South Africa formed a federal state in which Briton and Boer ruled jointly over the native Negro masses.

But what England managed to accomplish in distant lands she failed to do only a few miles from her shores. For Ireland remained an insoluble problem throughout the nineteenth century. Separated by religion, by occupation, and by political sentiment from their British masters, the Irish rebelled time and time again against their position within the United Kingdom. In London one cabinet after another attempted in vain to end sedition on the Emerald Isle. In 1829 Catholics were given the right to hold public office, and in 1869 the Irish Episcopal Church was disestablished. Between 1870 and 1903 a series of land-purchase laws enabled the tenant to buy his farm from the landowner and transformed Ireland into a country of independent peasant proprietors. Finally in 1914 a bill giving the island political autonomy was adopted, only to create the danger of a civil war between the Protestant minority concentrated in the north and the Catholic majority of the south. But a national tragedy in Ireland was temporarily averted by the international tragedy of Europe. When hostilities began on the Continent, both sides in the Irish dispute agreed to conclude an armistice and support the government in its hour of need.

FRANCE

In France, in the meantime, democratic republicanism was helping a defeated country recover from military disaster. Yet when the Third French Republic was born in 1870, it looked as if it would not last even as long as the ill-fated Second French Republic of 1848. The war continued to go badly, Paris was forced to surrender early in 1871, and the general elections held two weeks later produced a national assembly dominated by monarchists. That spring an insurrection of the Parisian radicals was suppressed only with the help of the army; and the harsh peace treaty surrendering Alsace-Lorraine to Germany and providing for an indemnity of a billion dollars weakened the position of the government still further.

If the royalists had been able to compose their differences, they would have had little difficulty in destroying this republic without republicans. The champions of the grandson of Charles X, however, were at loggerheads with the supporters of the grandson of Louis Philippe, and in the meantime republicanism was gaining strength. President Adolphe Thiers, a lifelong monarchist, finally came out in favor of it. Although he was forced out of office for this temerity, his countrymen increasingly tended to agree with him that a republic was "the government which divides us least." In 1875 a series of constitutional laws created a republican form of political organization based on a chamber of deputies elected by universal manhood suffrage, a senate chosen by a complicated system of indirect elections, and a president appointed by the legislature. When four years later the royalist president M. E. P. M. de MacMahon resigned in the face of a hostile parliamentary majority, the victory of the republicans was complete.

Aided by a swift political recovery and steady economic expansion, the republic was now in a position to settle old scores. In France the Catholic church, never forgetting the bitter days of Jacobin persecution in the French Revolution, was traditionally opposed to democracy. During the 1880's it paid the price of defeat. In 1880 the Jesuit Order was ordered dissolved; in 1882 a system of free, secular education was established to train a generation of loyal republicans; in 1884 divorce—prohibited during the restoration—once again became permissible. At the same time the government attempted to reconcile the proletariat and the bourgeoisie by issuing an amnesty to the participants in the Parisian uprising of 1871 and by legalizing labor unions. It even made an effort to enlist nationalist sentiment through a policy of colonial expansion in Africa and Asia.

Nevertheless the enemies of the republic refused to give up hope. The monarchists, the clericals, the aristocrats, the chauvinists continued to dream of a royalist restoration. By chronic venality, moreover, democratic politicians played into their hands. In 1887 a shocked country learned that the son-in-law of President Jules Grévy was selling membership in the Legion of Honor, and in 1893 the failure of the Panama Company led to the revelation that legislators had been in the habit of receiving lavish gifts from the managers of the unlucky enterprise. The result was a sudden rise of political discontent on the left as well as the right. Radical doctrines gained new strength as the trade unions formed the General Confederation of Labor to work for the overthrow of capitalism. And conservative malcontents found their hero in the dashing General Georges Boulanger, who preached a war of revenge against Germany and issued thundering pronouncements about the need for political change. Had his nerve been as strong as his language, he might perhaps have made himself master of France. But when in 1889 the government prepared to try him for treason, his courage evaporated. The brave soldier fled abroad, and in a supremely Gallic gesture committed suicide on the grave of his mistress.

The great crisis in the history of the republic, however, was still to come. In 1894 Captain Alfred Dreyfus, a Jewish army officer serving on the general staff, was convicted by a court-martial of selling military secrets to Germany and was sentenced to lifelong imprisonment on Devil's Island. Yet, when two years later a reexamination of the evidence suggested that not Dreyfus but a Major Charles Esterhazy was the traitor, the military authorities decided to suppress the new findings. Why compromise the army's reputation for infallibility for the sake of a confirmed republican and a Jew at that? Still, the news that an innocent man had been unjustly imprisoned leaked out. Before long the nation was involved in a bitter struggle during which the fate of one individual became a symbol of the conflict of political ideologies. Against Dreyfus were the enemies of the government who saw in him the personification of all the evils of democracy. For him were intellectuals like Émile Zola, republicans like Georges Clemenceau, and socialists like Jean Jaurès.

The scales of public opinion slowly shifted in his favor, and by 1906 the affair had reached a denouement which not even a Hollywood scenario could have improved. Of his foes, General Le Mouton de Boisdeffre resigned, Esterhazy went into exile, and Colonel Hubert Henry killed himself. Dreyfus, on the other hand, was exonerated and promoted to major, and his champion, Colonel Georges Picquart, became minister of war. As for Zola, he died too soon to enjoy all the spoils of victory, but his spirit must have rejoiced at the splendid state funeral and the ceremonial interment in the Pantheon. The government could now also insist on a strict reckoning with the opposition. The armed forces were purged of conservative extremists, known monarchists were dismissed from the civil service, most religious orders were suppressed, and in 1905 church and state were separated. France continued to be plagued by proletarian discontent and labor unrest, and inefficiency and corruption remained the incubus of public life. Yet the republic had at last crushed its enemies.

THE LOW COUNTRIES AND SCANDINAVIA

The Low Countries were also exposed to the economic and social consequences of industrialization and democratization. In Belgium the reigns of Leopold II and Albert I witnessed the rise of socialism and a wave of labor unrest. Proletarian demands for an extension of the franchise to the lower classes led to the establishment of universal manhood suffrage in 1893, but the urban masses were still resentful of the system of plural voting which clearly favored the aristocracy and the bourgeoisie. Finally, the school problem remained a source of contention between the Liberals and the Clericals, the former in favor of a public and secular organization of education, the latter demanding financial support from the government for church institutions of learning.

In Holland political developments under King William III and Queen Wilhelmina followed a similar pattern. Radical influence among the masses resulted in the adoption of social legislation. Lower-class agitation led to extensions of the right to vote in 1887 and 1896, although universal manhood suffrage was not achieved until 1917. And differences of opinion regarding religious instruction continued to divide the freethinking Liberals from the Calvinist Conservatives and the Catholic Clericals.

The Scandinavian countries, too, pursued a policy of democratic reform. Denmark succeeded in improving her agricultural system by fostering rural cooperatives, encouraging dairy farming for the British market, and creating a class of peasant proprietors. During the 1890's an old-age pension law and a health insurance measure were adopted. Early in the twentieth century universal manhood suffrage was introduced, the right to vote was given to most women, and the cabinet became responsible to the lower chamber of the legislature. At the same time Sweden was undergoing an industrialization accompanied by the usual effects: the rise of radicalism, the introduction of social legislation, the adoption of protective tariffs, and finally in 1907 the establishment of practically universal manhood suffrage. Yet political and economic progress was not enough to reconcile the Norwegians to the union with their eastern neighbors. The traditional grievances which troubled relations between the two peoples were further aggravated by the development of a cultural nationalism in Norway. Impatience with the slow pace of constitutional reform in Stockholm and the feeling that Norwegian commercial interests were ineffectively represented by the consular service of Sweden strained political ties to the breaking point. In 1905 the parliament in Oslo declared the union dissolved, and upon its invitation Prince Charles of Denmark became King Haakon VII of Norway.

3. Central and Southern Europe

GERMANY

From 1871 to 1918 the German Empire remained the most powerful of the states of Europe. Militarily it possessed an efficiently organized army which conscripted its soldiers from a population of some sixty million, second only to Russia. Politically it formed a federal union of twenty-five states, governed with the consent of a parliament elected by universal manhood suffrage, but dominated by an energetic, conservative Prussia. Economically it prospered in the struggle for international markets. Its factories and mines in the Ruhr constituted one of the greatest concentrations of industrial might in the world. Its optical goods, chemical products, electrical appliances, and precision instruments enjoyed an international reputation. In the hunt for profits it pursued tactics which envious competitors called "ungentlemanly," meaning that they were imaginative and successful. German salesmen traveled to Asia and Africa, they learned Turkish and Arabic, they adjusted the designs of their wares to the tastes of the Chinese and the Persians. By the time of the First World War the industrial output of Germany had left France far behind, and it was slowly but surely passing Great Britain.

As long as Bismarck was master in Berlin, the political resources of the state were employed to maintain the diplomatic equilibrium. Convinced that with the achievement of national unification the legitimate aspirations of Germany had been satisfied, he practiced his statecraft for the benefit of the status quo. But in his domestic policies he was less moderate. Throughout the 1870's he was engaged in the futile *Kulturkampf*, a struggle against the political influence of Catholicism. His motive was the desire to stimulate patriotic sentiment and please his liberal allies. Yet the effort to supervise the religious education and the secular activity of the clergy resulted only in the rise of the Catholic Center party which fought the Iron Chancellor to a standstill. Realizing at last that a victory was impossible, he arranged an orderly retreat, and in the 1880's he turned against an even more dangerous foe, Marxism. His new campaign was a skillful blend of blandishment and repression. To win the loyalty of the workingman, Germany became the world's pioneer in social legislation, insuring the urban masses against illness in 1883, accident in 1884, and old age in 1889. To overcome the threat of revolution, socialist newspapers were suppressed and socialist leaders imprisoned. But neither the velvet glove nor the mailed fist could destroy radicalism. The Social Democratic party continued to grow, until Bismarck in despair began to think about the abrogation of the liberal constitution which provided the enemies of the government with a measure of protection.

His opportunity to put these plans into effect never arrived. After 1888 there developed a growing coolness between him and the new young emperor, William II (1888–1918). Both were ambitious, both were unbending. There was simply not enough room in public life for two such colossal egoists. In 1890 the grand old man of Germany was curtly dismissed and the country prepared to follow a new course. The Iron Chancellor had made bombastic speeches as well as any super-patriot; he had boasted on one occasion that "we Germans fear God and nothing else in the world." But as a matter of fact there were many things of which he was afraid, and caution had become a habit with him. The emperor, on the other hand, actually believed with all his heart such nationalistic nonsense as "our Lord God would not have taken such great pains with our German fatherland and people, if

He did not have still greater things in store for us." The result was a reign of tub-thumping and saber-rattling which antagonized the world.

Bismarck had practiced colonialism with reserve; William II became a loud and aggressive imperialist. Bismarck had carefully avoided any challenge to British supremacy on the seas; William II, influenced by the jingoistic Admiral Alfred von Tirpitz, launched a naval race which drove England into alliance with his enemies. Bismarck had consistently avoided involvement in the Near East, which he considered of little importance for central Europe; William II actively fostered German influence in the Ottoman Empire, arousing resentment in St. Petersburg and London. The emperor's disastrous foreign policy led to an international isolation of his government which provoked political discontent at home. In 1912 the last general election held before the outbreak of hostilities gave a third of all votes to the socialists and strongly endorsed the parties in opposition to the regime. Demands for a restriction of the prerogatives of the crown became more insistent, until the coming of the war put a halt to the rising movement for constitutional reform.

ITALY

Italy was the weakest of the great powers. A country without the natural resources essential to industrial greatness, rich only in classical ruins and bumper crops of babies, she had achieved national unification against heavy diplomatic odds. Once this goal was reached, however, there was a violent reaction against the idealistic mood of the Risorgimento. Many who had sacrificed all in the struggle against the foreign enemy were now determined to enjoy the material benefits of victory. And since there were not enough benefits to go around, too often those with the sharpest elbows rose to the top.

The masses continued to live amid a poverty which was bearable in the progressive north, total and appalling in the barren south. Politics became a game of musical chairs played by a small minority of the well-to-do who alone possessed the right to vote. Now the right would be in power, wrestling with chronic deficits, imposing new taxes, distributing patronage, manipulating elections. Then the left would profit from the delinquencies of its rivals, win a parliamentary majority, form a cabinet, and proceed to commit precisely the same sins.

Civic and economic shortcomings were intensified by the Italian ambition to play the role of a major power. Statesmen eager for reelection could always make political capital with rabble-rousing speeches about the imperative need to acquire overseas colonies and to conquer regions like the Trentino and Istria, which were inhabited by Italians but ruled by Austria. While they fired the public with patriotic oratory, the taxpayer was forced to support an army and a navy out of all proportion to the size of his pocketbook. Lastly, the church problem complicated national affairs still further. The Papacy, refusing to accept the loss of its temporal possessions, persisted in urging the faithful to adopt a policy of passive resistance toward their government. Thereby it created a crisis of conscience for millions of Italians torn between piety and patriotism.

From the establishment of the Italian kingdom in 1861 until 1876 the politicians of the right dominated the national government. Cautious bourgeois liberals from the north, they ruled in the spirit of Cavour. They encouraged industrialism and strengthened the army, but also levied taxes ruthlessly. Managing at last to balance the budget, they were voted out of office by a financially exhausted electorate. For the next twenty years the country was in the hands of the parties of the left, composed largely of underpaid professionals and small businessmen from the south. These were radical and anticlerical in speech, cynical and rapacious in deed. Their leaders, Agostino Depretis and Francesco Crispi, attacked the church, condemned poverty, and insisted that only an aggressive foreign policy could win for the nation its rightful place. Yet despite their promises the standard of living remained miserably low. Moreover, corruption in high places came to be accepted as normal, and political criticism was met with stuffed ballot boxes and with the panacea of *transformism*, a high-flown euphemism for the practice of buying off dangerous opponents. As for colonial aspirations, Tunisia was snatched from under Italian noses by France in 1881, and Abyssinia inflicted a humiliating defeat on Italian arms in the war of 1895–1896. Only the hot and unhealthy wastes on the east coast of Africa known as Eritrea and Somaliland were left to salve national pride.

By the beginning of the twentieth century political ineffectualness had led to the rise of socialism and anarchism. While liberals, democrats, and nationalists followed each other in office, the peninsula was swept by an epidemic of labor strikes and political assassinations which took the life of King Humbert I himself. The government's answer was to try to reach an understanding with the church, to promulgate a modest program of social legislation, to introduce universal manhood suffrage, and to wage a successful war against Turkey in 1911–1912 which brought the country another half-million square miles of desert sand in Tripoli. Yet civic and social antagonisms continued to mount. By 1914 Italy was a frightened country, disillusioned with parliamentarianism and haunted by the specter of revolution. The coming of a world war seemed to her leaders to offer a way out of a hopeless impasse.

THE IBERIAN PENINSULA

Economic and social weaknesses also blocked civic progress in the Iberian peninsula. In Spain the moderate constitution of 1876 maintained a parliamentary system of government in which the conservatives, under Antonio Cánovas del Castillo, and the liberals, under Práxedes Mateo Sagasta, rotated in office without significant differences in policy. While they were alternately enjoying the spoils of bureaucratic power, the endemic political discontent of the country mounted. The Carlist reactionaries and Catholic ultraroyalists accused the authorities of doctrinaire liberalism. The republicans and the socialists charged them with blind conservatism. The anarchists were opposed to all government as a matter of principle. And the particularists in Catalonia demanded cultural and administrative autonomy for their region. The war with America in 1898, which cost the Spaniards Cuba and the Philippines, turned an outraged patriotism against the national leadership, while the hatred between clerical and anticlerical added to the embitterment of public life. Under the circumstances there was nothing for the crown to do but steer a middle course amid conflicting ideologies.

The Braganzas in Portugal, like the Bourbons in Spain, tried to follow a policy of political opportunism. But they were less successful. As long as Luiz I was on the throne, the government was by turns in the hands of two cliques of professional politicians—the Regenerators and the Progressives—about as different as tweedledum and tweedledee. Such an artificial parliamentarianism was open to the attacks of the republicans. Still, with the support of the army and the bureaucracy, the king managed to keep the opposition in check. The scandals and extravagances surrounding his successor, Carlos I, however, played into the hands of the enemies of the monarchy. The new ruler, moreover, had no patience with the intricacies of party politics, preferring to govern with an iron hand through his prime minister, João Franco. Yet the Portuguese were in no mood for a game of divine-right absolutism. In 1908 their sovereign was assassinated in broad daylight while driving through the streets of Lisbon. Two years later his son, Manuel II, was deposed and a republic was proclaimed. Turning against the church, which was considered a stronghold of royalism, the new order adopted a series of anticlerical decrees. Monastic orders were suppressed, religious instruction in elementary school was prohibited, and church and state were separated. A national assembly in the meantime promulgated a constitution designed to transform the country into a model democracy. But more than a sheet of paper was needed to overcome the civic tradition of a people. The conservatives continued to plot for a monarchist restoration, and the socialists went on organizing strikes, until the nation finally sought relief from strife in a succession of gingerbread dictators.

4. Eastern Europe

THE AUSTRIAN EMPIRE

As the nineteenth century drew to a close the three great autocracies of the east still presented the appearance of substantial solidity. In the Austrian capital there was a superficial gaiety which disguised the fact that the state was suffering

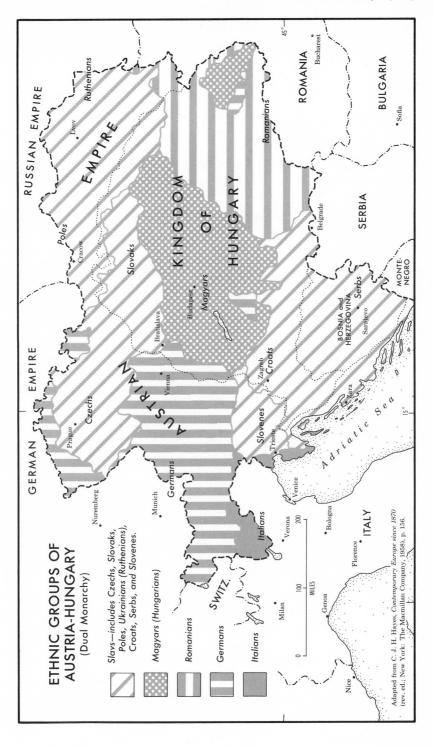

ETHNIC GROUPS OF
AUSTRIA-HUNGARY
(Dual Monarchy)

Slavs—includes Czechs, Slovaks,
Poles, Ukrainians (Ruthenians),
Croats, Serbs, and Slovenes.

Magyars (Hungarians)

Romanians

Germans

Italians

Adapted from C. J. H. Hayes, *Contemporary Europe since 1870*
(rev. ed.; New York: The Macmillan Company, 1958), p. 156.

from serious weaknesses. For the Ausgleich of 1867 had failed to solve the problem of nationalism which was destroying the unity of the Habsburg crownlands. The Czechs, the Slovaks, the Poles, the Ukrainians, the Italians, the Romanians, the Croats, and the Slovenes grew more insistent in their demands for regional autonomy, while the Germans and the Hungarians were more determined than ever to maintain their dominant position. Emperor Francis Joseph was a fitting symbol of the tragedy of his realm. Morose, lonely, and tired, his brother Maximilian executed in Mexico, his wife Elizabeth assassinated in Switzerland, his son Rudolf a victim of his own suicidal impulse, his nephew Francis Ferdinand a sacrifice to Serbian fanaticism, the old man silently carried the heavy burden of dynastic responsibility.

In the western half of the Dual Monarchy public affairs at first followed the familiar pattern of bourgeois constitutionalism. Conservatives, liberals, democrats, and socialists competed for the favor of a propertied electorate. But with the intensification of particularist sentiment political parties came to represent more and more national groups rather than civic ideologies. Ultimately the legislature degenerated into a bedlam of ethnic factions screaming epithets and hurling inkwells. The adoption of universal manhood suffrage in 1907 failed to relieve the tension, and in view of the irresponsible conduct of the parliamentary representatives the government was forced to rule by bureaucratic decree.

In Budapest, on the other hand, all was decorum. The Liberals and the Independents deliberated in a dignified fashion, although the apparent stability of Hungarian politics was built on a policy of repression. Only Magyars could sit in parliament, and while they were promulgating laws which served their special interests, the oppressed nationalities encouraged by their brothers across the border conspired against the state. By 1914 the inward disintegration of the empire had advanced so far that a group of influential government leaders, among them Foreign Minister Leopold von Berchtold and Chief of Staff Conrad von Hötzendorff, decided that only a successful war against Slavic nationalism could save their country from ruin.

RUSSIA

The Russian monarchy was also entering a critical period. Pursued with determination, the reform program of Alexander II might have prepared the country for the transition from agrarian feudalism to industrial capitalism. But the Tsar Liberator was not a man to compromise and conciliate. Since his subjects failed to display proper appreciation of the favors conferred on them, he would show them that he was still the Autocrat of all the Russias. The policy of reaction pursued after 1870, however, only drove the opposition underground. At first the radicals organized a populist movement to arouse revolutionary ardor among the peasantry.

Yet when the muzhik remained deaf to slogans of civic justice and economic emancipation, the populists turned to terror. In a state in which the public expression of political dissatisfaction was prohibited, violence was the only weapon at the disposal of the critics of the established order. Alarmed by the campaign of assassination against prominent officials, the emperor finally resolved to adopt once more a program of moderate concession. In 1881, acting on the advice of Minister of the Interior Michael Loris-Melikov, he agreed to establish a representative council to advise the government in the adoption of needed legislation. But it was too late for a reconciliation with the enemies of autocracy. On March 13, the day he gave his assent to the reform plan, the tsar fell under a terrorist bomb.

If Alexander II resembled Alexander I in his good intentions and weak will, his son Alexander III (1881–1894) seemed to inherit the inflexible conservatism of Nicholas I. All projects of constitutional reform were tossed into the wastepaper basket, all thoughts of compromise with the opposition were suppressed. For thirteen years Russia was ruled with an iron hand. Terrorism was crushed by the ruthless Viacheslav Plehve, who commanded the secret police, while ideological warfare against subversion was directed by Constantine Pobiedonostsev, the chief administrative officer of the national church. Bureaucratic controls over education, research, and writing multiplied, and the government organized a systematic persecution of religious and ethnic minorities. The Protestants in the Baltic provinces and the Catholics in Poland were exposed to official harassment, but the harshest treatment was reserved for the Jews. They became the scapegoats for all the ills besetting the nation. The economic and social disabilities under which they lived were made more rigorous, and the authorities encouraged the oppressed peasantry to vent its resentments in pogroms directed against a frightened and helpless people. At the same time, however, the state was unwittingly preparing the ground for a revival of radical thought. Not only did the reign of injustice win recruits for the opponents of tsarism, but in order to maintain the political and military strength of the country the emperor—under the influence of his minister of finance, Sergei Witte—fostered the growth of industrialism. And with industrialism came a factory proletariat and the socialist ideology.

The storm finally broke over the last of the Romanovs. The handsome Nicholas II (1894–1917) was an overbearing but weak man, governing his possessions with a stubbornness born of fundamental insecurity. Determined to maintain his father's policy of unbending autocracy, he lacked his father's iron will. While he continued to imprison political malcontents and to oppress national minorities, the opposition was secretly winning new strength. In 1898 the Russian Marxists, inspired by the teachings of George Plekhanov, organized the Social Democratic party. Five years later it divided into the militant Bolsheviks under the leadership of V. I. Lenin and the moderate Mensheviks whose spokesman was Julius Martov. In 1901 the radical agrarians founded the Social Revolutionary party, which preached a rural social-

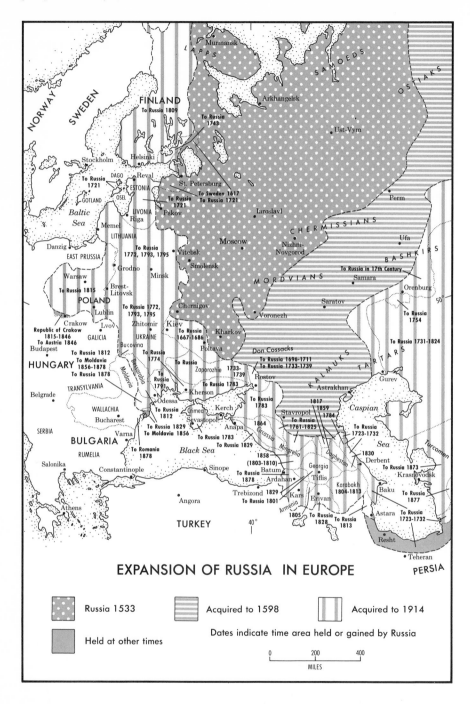

EXPANSION OF RUSSIA IN EUROPE

Russia 1533   Acquired to 1598   Acquired to 1914

Held at other times

Dates indicate time area held or gained by Russia

0   200   400
MILES

ism adapted to the needs of the peasant masses. Finally in 1903 the democratic bourgeoisie formed the Union of Liberation, a party of moderate constitutionalists.

At first the enemies of tsarism made little progress in the face of official perseçution, but the military fiasco of the government in the Russo-Japanese War opened the way for insurrection. Having come into conflict with the Land of the Rising Sun over Manchuria and Korea, Nicholas II in 1904 provoked a war with the Nipponese. The outcome was a succession of disasters on land and sea which forced the Russians to sign the Treaty of Portsmouth on September 5, 1905, establishing Japan as the dominant power on the eastern coast of Asia.

By this time Russia was in the throes of revolution. The news of military reverses combined with an accumulation of economic grievances to produce a wave of political murders, demonstrations, and strikes. Hoping to stem the tide, the tsar in the fall of 1905 issued the October Manifesto, promising to promulgate a democratic constitution, to restrict the prerogatives of the crown, to set up a representative assembly or Duma elected by a generous franchise, and to guarantee civil rights and liberties. His strategy was successful, because to bourgeois moderates these concessions were enough, while to proletarian radicals they were only the beginning. Having split the opposition, the government further strengthened its hand by recalling the army from the Far East and floating a huge loan in France.

The first Duma, which assembled in 1906, was under the influence of the liberals, but by now the authorities felt confident enough to order its dissolution. When in the following year the second Duma proved even more hostile toward absolutism, it met a similar fate. The reactionary prime minister, Peter Stolypin, won the support of the peasantry by introducing rural reform legislation. At the same time he published a new electoral law increasing the representation of the propertied classes. Hence the third Duma, elected in 1907, and the fourth, meeting in 1912, were submissive, and conservative statesmen at court began to rub their hands in satisfaction at the clever way in which they had tamed subversion. But they were mistaken. The day of reckoning had only been postponed. The outbreak of hostilities in 1914 was the first step toward another and even more terrible revolution.

THE OTTOMAN EMPIRE

The forces of democracy and nationalism were also undermining the political structure of the Balkans. For one thing, the oppressed Orthodox peoples of the peninsula—the Greeks, the Serbs, the Romanians, and the Bulgarians—worked ceaselessly for the dismemberment of the Ottoman Empire. Yet each in turn regarded the ambitions of its neighboring coreligionists with suspicion. Secondly, among educated patriotic Turks there was a growing realization that their country faced the alternative of reform or collapse. In an age of parliamentary government and industrial production, they argued, there was no place for theocratic absolutism. Thus a struggle between traditionalists and modernizers, complicated by the antagonism between Christian separatism and Ottoman centralism, divided the empire. Even more important, the roles which the great powers had customarily assumed at the Sublime Porte began to change. Toward the end of the nineteenth century Great Britain, long the defender of Constantinople, resolved to reduce her commitments in the Balkans. Control of the Suez Canal and possession of Egypt provided sufficient protection for her life line to India. The German Empire under William II, on the other hand, developed a growing interest in the Near East. It advised the Turkish government, reorganized the Turkish army, bolstered the Turkish economy, and planned direct rail communication between Berlin and Baghdad. Austria, driven out of Italy and Germany, also turned southward, partly to recoup her political losses, partly to counter the appeal of Serbian nationalism. And Russia never ceased to dream of the conquest of the Straits.

The 1870's opened in the Balkans on a familiar note. Christian nationalism and Moslem maladministration provoked an uprising against Ottoman rule first in Bosnia and Herzegovina and then in Bulgaria. Both sides conducted their military operations to the accompaniment of the customary atrocities. Europe as usual closed her eyes to Slavic excesses and grew indignant at Turkish barbarity. Once again the Russians had a perfect pretext for intervention in the peninsula. Charging in from the north like St. George about to slay the dragon, Alexander II defeated the armies of the sultan in 1877, and early the following year he forced the Sublime Porte to sign the Treaty of San Stefano. The tsar won full possession of Bessarabia in Europe and Ardahan, Kars, and Batum in Asia; Serbia and Romania gained recognition as independent states; Montenegro acquired the port of Antivari; and a large autonomous Bulgarian state was established, nominally under the suzerainty of the Sublime Porte, actually as an outpost of Russian influence.

But the congratulations which the diplomats in St. Petersburg were exchanging proved a little premature. The great powers had no intention of leaving the sultan at the mercy of his ambitious neighbor. Once again a coalition of major states led by Great Britain stepped in between Russia and Turkey. Remembering the unpleasant outcome of the Crimean War, Alexander II reluctantly agreed to a new settlement of the Near Eastern question. The Berlin Congress, meeting from June 13 to July 13, 1878, allowed the English to occupy Cyprus, authorized the Austrians to administer Bosnia and Herzegovina, encouraged the French to seize Tunisia, and made vague suggestions to the Italians about expansion into Albania. As for the minor states in the Balkans, most of them were delighted to see tsarism's pet Bulgaria reduced in size, but their satisfaction turned to chagrin when their own claims were also largely ignored.

The Berlin Congress introduced a period of relative stability in the Near East. Tsarist hopes of expansion into the Ottoman Empire had been frustrated twice

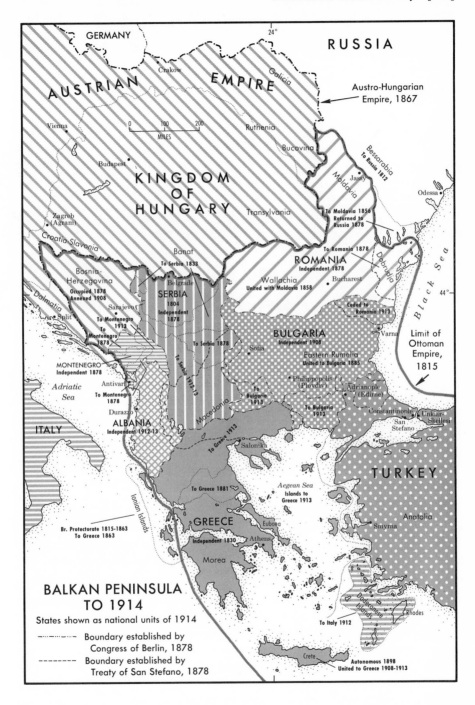

GERMANY

24°

RUSSIA

AUSTRIAN EMPIRE

Austro-Hungarian
Empire, 1867

Crakow

Galicia

Vienna

0   100   200
MILES

Ruthenia

Bucovina

Budapest

Jassy

Moldavia

Bessarabia
To Russia 1812

Zagreb
(Agram)

Transylvania

To Moldavia 1856
Returned to
Russia 1878

Odessa

KINGDOM
OF
HUNGARY

Croatia-Slavonia

Banat
To Serbia 1833

Belgrade

To Romania 1878

ROMANIA
Independent 1878

Dobrudja

Bucharest

Black Sea

44°

Dalmatia

Bosnia-
Herzegovina
Occupied 1878
Annexed 1908

SERBIA
1804
Independent
1878

Wallachia
United with Moldavia 1858

Ceded to
Romania 1913

Sarajevo

Split

To Montenegro
1913
To
Montenegro
1878

To Serbia 1878

BULGARIA
Independent 1908

Sofia

Varna

Limit of
Ottoman
Empire,
1815

MONTENEGRO
Independent 1878

To Serbia 1912-13

Eastern Rumelia
United to Bulgaria 1885

Adriatic
Sea

Antivari

To Montenegro
1878

Macedonia

To
Bulgaria
1913

Philippopolis
(Plovdiv)

Adrianople
(Edirne)

Durazzo

ALBANIA
Independent 1912-13

To Greece 1913

To Bulgaria
1913

Constantinople
San
Stefano

Unkiar
Skellesi

ITALY

Salonika

TURKEY

Ionian Islands

To Greece 1881

Aegean Sea
Islands to
Greece 1913

Euboea

Anatolia

Smyrna

Br. Protectorate 1815-1863
To Greece 1863

GREECE
Independent 1830

Athens

Morea

Dodecanese
Islands

Rhodes

To Italy 1912

BALKAN PENINSULA
TO 1914

States shown as national units of 1914

—·—·—·— Boundary established by
Congress of Berlin, 1878

——————— Boundary established by
Treaty of San Stefano, 1878

Crete
Autonomous 1898
United to Greece 1908-1913

THE CONGRESS OF BERLIN. This picture shows the leading statesmen of Europe gathered in 1878 to settle the troublesome problem of the Balkans.

within twenty-five years, and Russia therefore turned eastward to the Pacific. Without the support of the big brother of all the Slavs the Balkan peoples could do little more than cast poisonous glances in the direction of Constantinople. Security from foreign attack, moreover, relieved the Sublime Porte of the need to adopt domestic reform. In 1876, confronted by the danger of revolution, Sultan Abdul Hamid II had accepted a constitution granting political equality, religious freedom, and parliamentary representation. Within a year, however, he decided that there was no longer any reason to play the liberal. Dismissing his progressive advisers, he returned to the tradition of absolutism.

In the decades which followed the sultan ruled by cruelty and deception, living up to the popular view of how an Oriental despot behaved. By the beginning of the twentieth century his tyranny had led to the rise of a secret opposition party, the Young Turks, composed of westernized bureaucrats and officers. Convinced that only a modernization of the political institutions of the state could save it from destruction, they prepared for the overthrow of the authoritarian regime. In 1908 the banner of revolution rose in Macedonia, and when the troops sent to suppress the insurrection joined it, Abdul Hamid II decided that once again the time had come to be enlightened. The constitution of 1876 was dusted off and reissued, and for a few weeks there was wild jubilation throughout the empire, as Moslem and Christian celebrated the arrival of the millennium.

Then the first outburst of enthusiasm began to subside. The Young Turks made the discovery that good intentions and eloquent speeches were not enough to solve the complexities of the Near Eastern question. To begin with, the emancipated minorities within the country preferred to seek union with their brothers beyond the frontier rather than become good Ottomans. Secondly, imperialistic foreign governments closed in around Turkey. In 1908 Austria annexed Bosnia and Herzegovina which she had been administering for thirty years. In 1911–1912 Italy made war on the Ottoman Empire, seizing Tripoli in northern Africa and occupying the Dodecanese Islands off the coast of Asia Minor. And late in 1912 a Balkan coalition composed of Bulgaria, Greece, Serbia, and Montenegro attacked the armies of Sultan Mohammed V, and within a few months conquered all of his remaining European possessions except the region around Constantinople.

Embittered by this succession of disasters, the Young Turks decided to forget the fine words about civic equality and save what they could from the general debacle by a suppression of political discontent. Reviving the same dictatorial methods of government against which they had recently rebelled, they employed the army to oppose all demands for local autonomy. In Enver Pasha they found a leader who in 1914 took them into war on the side of Germany, hoping that a military victory would restore the vitality of the state.

5. The New Imperialism

EARLY IN THE NINETEENTH CENTURY there had been a reaction in Europe against overseas expansion. The successful revolutions of the English colonies in North America and of the Spanish colonies in South America apparently demonstrated that the acquisition of dependencies was in the long run a fruitless enterprise. While the mother country fought wars and incurred debts to win colonial possessions, as soon as these acquired sufficient political experience they seceded and formed their own states. Moreover, once the nations of the West began to industrialize their economies, their interest in overseas acquisitions waned. The conquest of new lands in Asia and Africa seemed less attractive when there were factories and railroads to build at home. Finally, since economic liberalism and free trade were on the march, there appeared to be no advantage in the possession of colonial sources of raw materials or captive markets for manufactured goods. Even Benjamin Disraeli maintained in 1852: "These wretched colonies will all be independent too in a few years and are a millstone around our necks."

THE WHITE MAN'S BURDEN

In the second half of the nineteenth century the attitude toward imperialism changed once more. Industrial capitalism began to seek new fields to conquer, as the demand for raw materials and customers continued to grow. And since after 1870 the movement for free trade gave way before protectionist policies, colonies again assumed commercial importance. The advocates of expansionism armed themselves with the economic theories of scholars like Paul Leroy-Beaulieu, who maintained that colonial dependencies were essential to national might. They seized on the naval theories of writers like Alfred T. Mahan to prove that national greatness was impossible without overseas possessions. They employed the language of scientists like Charles Darwin to assert that the laws of nature made inevitable the domination of the earth by the white man. They even made God Himself an imperialist, arguing that colonialism meant the Christianization of the heathen.

Karl Pearson, a professor of mathematics at University College, London, expressed a widespread attitude in his evaluation of imperialistic policies:

> History shows me one way, and one way only, in which a high state of civilization has been produced, namely, the struggle of race with race, and the survival of the physically and mentally fitter race. . . . This dependence of progress on the survival of the fitter race, terribly black as it may seem to some of you, gives the struggle for existence its redeeming features; it is the fiery crucible out of which comes the finer metal. You may hope for a time when the sword shall be turned into the ploughshare, when American and German and English traders shall no longer compete in the markets of the world for their raw materials and for their food supply, when the white man and the dark shall share the soil between them, and each till it as he lists. But believe me, when that day comes mankind will no longer progress.[2]

THE INTERACTION OF EAST AND WEST

Who could resist the common appeal of profit, patriotism, and religion? Once the process of national unification in Europe was completed with the Franco-Prussian War, a new imperialism began to conquer the rest of the world. By 1914 Africa had been explored and partitioned by the great powers; Asia had been divided into spheres of influence which retained the shadow of native independence without its substance; Oceania had become a conglomeration of naval bases, coaling stations, and trading posts. The economy of the West entered a period of rapid expansion based on the exploitation of overseas resources. Rubber from the Belgian

---

[2] Karl Pearson, *National Life from the Standpoint of Science* (London: Adam and Charles Black, 1901), pp. 19, 24.

Congo, oil from Persia, tin from Malaya, jute from India, all contributed to the increasing well-being of the Occidental. Not only the industrialist and the financier but also the factory worker and the farmhand profited from the creation of a complex international financial structure controlled by the stock exchanges of the West. True, even without colonialism there would in all probability have developed a close economic interdependence among the various regions of the earth. For scientific technology and rational production tended to establish a single global market regardless of diplomatic developments. Yet the fact that the leading states of Europe gained political control over distant sources of raw materials meant that the formation of a world-wide economy took place under conditions highly advantageous to them. The Occidentals became the beneficiaries of the armed authority which their governments exercised over alien peoples in distant lands. Their high standard of living was made possible because the Chinese, the Indians, and the Egyptians were not free to tax the profits of foreign companies or interfere with their export policies. In effect the West was acting in accordance with the old Scottish maxim: "Thou shalt starve ere I want."

Exploitation, to be sure, had been familiar among colonial peoples long before the European came. The colored masses which in the nineteenth century began to serve the needs of the Occident were as a rule exchanging one master for another. The government bureaucrat and plantation overseer simply replaced the tribal chieftain and provincial aristocrat. What is more, the white man brought with him standards of official conduct which represented a significant improvement over native institutions. He suppressed cannibalism, murder, slavery, and brigandage. He improved medical care, public sanitation, agricultural methods, manufacturing techniques. He built schools and orphanages, factories and railroads.

Still, the material benefits which followed westernization were purchased with the political subjection and social subordination of colonial peoples. The Occidental was willing to educate them, but he was resolutely opposed to their admission to a status of equality within his own community. The apologists of imperialism tended to overlook the psychological effect which the domination of an alien civilization had on indigenous populations. With the technological and cultural advances introduced by Europeans came spiritual bewilderment for the natives. While the Spaniards were establishing the first universities in the western hemisphere, the Aztecs became bondsmen. Under the rule of Great Britain the Zulu, the terror of the African veld, settled in the slums of Capetown. Materially his position was probably better than before, for the colonial authorities transplanted to the tropics humanitarian ideals which had slowly matured in the more favorable environment of the temperate zone. Yet although they did much for the physical improvement of the colored man, they failed to realize that he also needed a sense of dignity and worth. Here lay the great weakness of western expansion.

THE SCRAMBLE FOR COLONIES

The forms of imperialism varied from region to region, depending on the level of civilization and form of government in the indigenous society. In North Africa, the part of the Dark Continent most familiar to Westerners, foreign rule was exercised sometimes indirectly through native figureheads, at other times directly through colonial administrators. At the beginning of the nineteenth century the vast territory stretching from the Red Sea to the Atlantic was almost entirely under the suzerainty of the Ottoman Empire, but in practice most of it was ruled by local potentates who enjoyed virtual independence. The first European power to acquire sizable possessions in this area was France, who began her conquest of Algeria in 1830, although some forty years were to elapse before all resistance had been crushed. By then the new imperialism was on the rise, and other occidental nations were beginning actively to seek overseas colonies. The Italians had their eyes on Tunisia, but in 1881 a French expeditionary force suddenly seized the prize. The following year Great Britain occupied Egypt, thereby gaining political and military control over the lifeline of her empire, the Suez Canal. In 1912 the French compelled the sultan of Morocco to place himself under their protection, while at the same time Italy after bitter fighting wrested Tripoli from Turkey. All of the southern coast of the Mediterranean was now under European control.

Below the Sahara foreign supremacy was maintained by outright annexation. Until the mid-century the interior of Africa was only a blank on the map, but then came a period of some thirty years when a group of intrepid explorers like the Scotsman David Livingstone, the Englishman Henry M. Stanley, the Frenchman Pierre Savorgnan de Brazza, and the German Karl Peters opened up the Dark Continent. The explorers were followed by missionaries and traders in search of converts and profits, and they in turn by soldiers and administrators. At an international conference which met in Berlin in 1884–1885 the great powers agreed on the rules to be followed in the establishment of colonies, and the race was on. By 1914 Central Africa had been completely partitioned. The French had gotten the lion's share in the great western bulge which protrudes into the Atlantic, but the English had also done well in acquiring Nigeria and the Gold Coast as well as British East Africa. During the 1880's Bismarck's Germany laid claim to Togoland, the Cameroons, German South West Africa, and German East Africa. The Portuguese succeeded in extending the footholds in Angola and Mozambique which they had originally won during the sixteenth century. Even a private company, the International Association of the Congo, managed to carve out for itself what was in theory an independent state, but in actuality a business venture for the production of rubber with forced native labor. Its treatment of the Negro population became so scandalous that in 1908 the Belgian government annexed the Congo

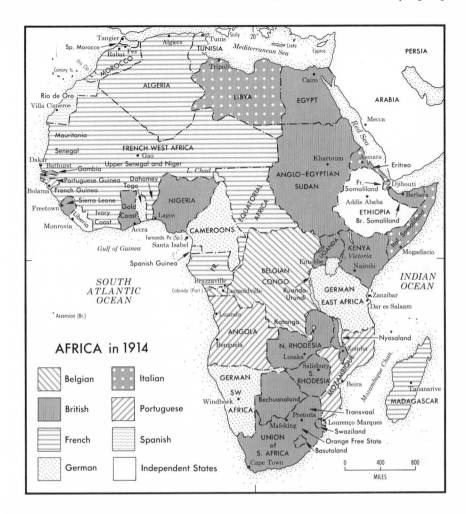

AFRICA in 1914

Belgian · Italian · British · Portuguese · French · Spanish · German · Independent States

Free State. But while the worst abuses were thereby remedied, the fact remained that throughout Central Africa the black man was totally and irremediably subservient to the white.

In South Africa the familiar pattern of European rule over colored natives was complicated by a bitter conflict among the Europeans themselves. The original white settlers of the Cape of Good Hope were Dutch farmers, the Boers, a pious and industrious people leading a pastoral existence. When Great Britain acquired the colony from Holland at the end of the Napoleonic wars, friction developed between the English and the Boers. Thousands of the latter moved northward into unclaimed lands where they ultimately established the South African Republic or Transvaal and the Orange Free State. Here they might have gone on pursuing their traditional way of life undisturbed, had not the discovery of diamond deposits in their country during the late 1860's created new political and economic problems for them. Expansionists in Capetown as well as London began to agitate for annexation, and between 1899 and 1902 there was a war whose outcome could not be in doubt. Although the free republics became colonies, Great Britain proved a generous victor. In 1910 the Boer provinces were joined with the English to form the self-governing Union of South Africa. Yet for the great majority of the population war or peace among white men made little difference. The Negro masses remained poor, ignorant, and unenfranchised.

In Asia, whose great empires and high civilizations were older than Greece and Rome, the great powers tended to impose their control through protectorates and spheres of influence. In most cases the existence of a developed native system of administration made it unnecessary for them to assume the burden of direct rule. The Arab possessions of the Ottoman Empire, for example, felt the might of the West through the economic concessions which the sultan granted to European entrepreneurs rather than by direct contact. Neighboring Persia also preserved nominal independence, although in 1907 England and Russia divided the country into spheres of influence without so much as consulting the government of the shah. British domination of India had begun in the eighteenth century, but it was not consolidated until the nineteenth. The last great effort of the native Indian population to throw off the foreign yoke was the Sepoy Mutiny of 1857–1858, after which the East India Company came to an end, and the crown in London began to govern the subcontinent directly. By the end of the century, moreover, the English had moved eastward into Burma and Malaya, while the French had established protectorates over the states of Indo-China. Further north the Russians completed their overland expansion across Siberia in 1860, the year in which they acquired the Maritime Province on the Pacific and founded the port of Vladivostok.

The vast Chinese Empire lived in blissful ignorance, confident of its superiority over the foreign barbarians, until wars with England in 1841–1842 and with England and France in 1857–1858 revealed to the world its innate weakness. After that a race began among the European powers for political and economic concessions. The British sphere of interest lay in the valley of the Yangtze River, the French in the provinces of Kwangsi and Kweichow, the German in Shantung, and the Russian in Manchuria. Conservative patriots sought to save their ancestral way of life by the Boxer Rebellion of 1900–1901, but an international expeditionary force equipped with the latest weapons of modern technology demonstrated the military preponderance of the Occident. It was now more obvious than ever that the country could be saved only by a process of thoroughgoing modernization. In 1911 a group of reformers led by Sun Yat-sen carried out a revolution which overthrew the monarchy. But the proclamation of a republic was no more than the first step in a long and difficult process of national rejuvenation. Another thirty-five years were to elapse before the last vestiges of foreign rule in China came to an end.

Of all the lands in the Far East only Japan succeeded in withstanding the pressure of western imperialism. Yet in 1853, when Commodore Matthew C. Perry of the United States opened the country to occidental influence, it was backward and isolated, still living in an age of feudalism. But then during the reign of Emperor Mutsuhito from 1867 to 1912 a revolution from above took place. Realizing that the choice before it was westernization or defeat, the crown reformed the constitution, reorganized the administrative system, modernized the armed forces, and encouraged the industrialization of the economy. Within a single generation Japan completed the transition from a medieval society to modern times. In 1894–1895 she displayed unexpected strength in winning a war against China, and in 1904–1905 she astounded the world by defeating Russia and asserting her claim to Korea. For the first time an Asiatic state had clearly and decisively triumphed over a European power. To colonial peoples throughout the world who had become resigned to the domination of the white man the Japanese victory brought hope that some day they too would be able to defy the Occident.

THE REACTION AGAINST COLONIALISM

The response of native peoples to alien domination assumed several forms. The first was a resolve to use sheer force in order to drive out the foreigners. Throughout the nineteenth century there was a struggle between native traditionalism and European imperialism. The Sepoy Mutiny in India in 1857–1858 was one example; the Zulu War of Cetshwayo in South Africa in 1879 was another; the Boxer Rebellion in China in 1900–1901 was a third. Rallying behind their ancestral gods, the colored masses of the world fought the white man time and again. But the end was always the same. He was simply too strong for them. He had cannon, railways, steamships, and factories. More important, he had civic discipline and a rational view of nature. There could be no question about who would emerge victorious in a contest of force.

The obvious futility of armed resistance encouraged the growth of an assimilationist tendency among the subject peoples. Since the old gods had failed, the new ones must be better. Important groups in the indigenous community, especially the educated and propertied, succumbed to the impulse for cultural identification with the conqueror. In every major colonial city of Asia and Africa could be found a class of native inhabitants assiduously cultivating occidental manners. Politicians, lawyers, doctors, and clerks worked tirelessly at being Anglo-Saxon or Gallic. They imitated the English spoken at Oxford or the French heard at the Sorbonne. They wanted to have nothing to do with the traditional ceremonies and beliefs of their forefathers. Their one consuming ambition was to win acceptance as completely westernized. Their tragedy was that they could not escape from themselves. The Occidental treated them with a show of cordiality to encourage their conforming zeal, but behind their backs he often poked fun at their efforts to show themselves better than their fellows. As for inviting them to his club or his home, that was out of the question. Alienated from their countrymen, patronized by the Westerners, the assimilated natives usually found themselves in a world of make-believe which offered them neither peace of mind nor sense of belonging.

Finally, out of the interaction of Orient and Occident arose a political movement which sought to oppose the imperialism of the West with the weapons of the West. Recognizing that uncritical imitation was as self-deluding as blind rejection, it advocated a program of civic reform which would enable native society to put an end to foreign rule without destroying its cultural tradition. An adjustment of convention to progress was necessary, it conceded, but that adjustment must not restrict the political independence or debase the social dignity of the colored man. The ideas of Herder, exported from central Europe to the banks of the Yangtze and the Nile, proved a powerful weapon in the struggle against colonialism. The language of the Indian patriot Chitta Ranjan Das had an unmistakably Mazzinian ring:

> What is the ideal which we must set before us? The first and foremost is the ideal of nationalism. Now what is nationalism? It is, I conceive, a process through which a nation expresses itself and finds itself, not in isolation from other nations, not in opposition to other nations, but as part of a great scheme by which, in seeking its own expression and therefore its own identity, it materially assists the self-expression and self-realization of other nations as well: Diversity is as real as unity. And in order that the unity of the world may be established it is essential that each nationality should proceed on its own line and find fulfilment in self-expression and self-realization. . . . I contend that each nationality constitutes a particular stream of the great unity, but no nation can fulfil itself unless and until it becomes itself and at the same time realizes its identity with Humanity. The whole problem of nationalism is therefore to find that stream and to face that destiny. If you find the current and establish a continuity with the past, then the process of self-expression has begun, and nothing can stop the growth of nationality.[3]

Once native peoples became acquainted with the traditions of the West, they began to apply that knowledge to the solution of their own national problems. The struggle against colonialism was thus in a sense not the struggle of Orient against Occident, but of one complex of occidental theories and practices against another. Although by the time of the First World War the white man's political domination of the earth was beginning to draw to a close, his ideological influence was stronger than ever. The question was no longer whether the hegemony of Europe would end, but what would take its place.

---

[3] P. C. Ray, *The Life and Times of C. R. Das* (Bombay: Oxford University Press, 1927), p. 265.

6. *The Coming of the War*

IN 1914 THE NINETEENTH CENTURY came to an end. A strong, prosperous Europe entered into a ruinous war which weakened conquered and conqueror alike. As they took the fatal step, the participants tried to persuade themselves that they were at Armageddon, engaging in a battle between the forces of right and wrong. But, as a matter of fact, the antagonists were brothers, children of the same culture and the same history. Nothing demonstrated their fundamental identity of interest more clearly than the military struggle itself which, in defeating some, crushed them all.

In the long run the only victors in that struggle were some businessmen who profited from the economic boom of the war years, the communists who came to power amid the ruins of tsarism, and colonial peoples who began to press their demands for political concession against the exhausted states of the West. The ultimate irony was that with greater wisdom the outbreak of hostilities might have been avoided altogether. The conflict of political objectives arising out of nationalism, imperialism, and capitalism was not irreconcilable. The great imperialistic powers like England and France fought not against but for each other. The captains of industry in Germany and Italy had no valid motive for disrupting the international business community. Even national interests were injured rather than served by the military contest. It was essentially human pride and human weakness which caused the First World War.

EUROPEAN ALLIANCES AND ALIGNMENTS

Throughout the nineteenth century there had been international conflicts in Europe, but these had been of short duration and for limited objectives. The Russians had fought the Turks in 1828–1829 to help liberate Greece; the English and the French had taken up arms against Russia in 1854–1856 to defend the Ottoman Empire; the French had defeated the Austrians in 1859 to further Italian unification; the Prussians had attacked the Austrians in 1866 to gain domination over Germany. Yet the alliances which had preceded these wars did not persist after the return of peace, because until 1870 the European balance of power established by the Congress of Vienna was not seriously threatened. A new era in diplomatic relations opened, however, with the outbreak of the Franco-Prussian War. First of all, the German Empire emerged out of that struggle as the greatest political and military state on the Continent. Second, France refused to accept the loss of Alsace and Lorraine as permanent and continued to dream of retaliation against the Teutons. As long as Bismarck stood at the helm in Berlin the international equilibrium remained undisturbed. The Iron Chancellor was convinced that his country had reached its logical dimensions and that the maintenance of peace was therefore the best guarantee of its national security. He knew well enough that the French would welcome a war of revenge, but by their own unaided efforts they could hardly hope for success. Consequently, his objective became to keep his western neighbor isolated and therefore peaceful. England would follow her traditional policy of splendid isolation unless her vital interests were imperiled. Italy was too busy trying to pull herself up by her bootstraps into the ranks of the great powers to risk involvement in a dangerous military adventure. Autocratic Russia and Austria would normally be reluctant to enter into a partnership with republican France. The political outlook was thus distinctly favorable to Germany.

Germany's greatest asset was the brilliant statecraft of Bismarck, who patiently built one diplomatic dike after another to maintain the status quo by segregating France. A meeting of William I, Francis Joseph, and Alexander II held in Berlin in September, 1872, led to the formation of the Three Emperors' League, an informal agreement among the conservative monarchies of the east to work together for the preservation of peace. Unfortunately the conflicting aims of St. Petersburg and Vienna in the Balkans made lasting cooperation between them impossible, and during the crisis of 1878 which culminated in the Berlin Congress the two courts fell out. One year later Bismarck concluded a defensive treaty with Austria directed against Russia and France. In 1882 this Dual Alliance became a Triple Alliance, as the Italians, outraged by the French seizure of Tunisia which they themselves had long planned to occupy, decided to seek revenge with the assistance of the Teutonic powers.

Still the Iron Chancellor had too much respect for the armed might of Russia to accept a permanent estrangement between the Romanovs and the Hohenzollerns. In 1881 he revived the Three Emperors' League, and when six years later tension in the Near East once again disrupted this uneasy collaboration, he executed one of his most daring maneuvers. By the secret Reinsurance Treaty of 1887, William I and Alexander III each agreed to maintain neutrality if the other were attacked by a third power. Had this arrangement become known in Vienna, there would have been bitter recriminations among the members of the Triple Alliance. But the sorcerer of the Wilhelmstrasse in Berlin spun his fine web of diplomacy with consummate skill.

Bismarck's successors were less deft. Arguing that the German government had entered into too many incompatible commitments, William II refused to renew the Reinsurance Treaty in 1890. He was confident that the Autocrat of all the Russias would never agree to an association with the ideological heirs of the Jacobins. He underestimated, however, the force of national self-interest. Early in 1894 Russia and France concluded a defensive pact directed against the Triple Alliance. All the major powers of Europe except Great Britain were thus mem-

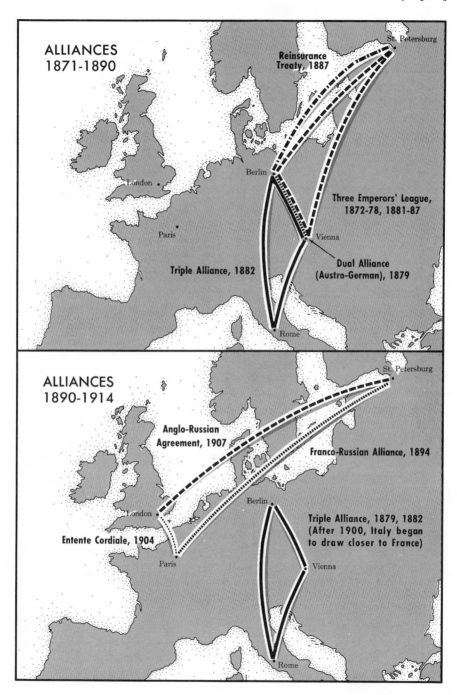

ALLIANCES
1871-1890

Reinsurance
Treaty, 1887

St. Petersburg

London

Berlin

Three Emperors' League,
1872-78, 1881-87

Paris

Vienna

Triple Alliance, 1882

Dual Alliance
(Austro-German), 1879

Rome

ALLIANCES
1890-1914

St. Petersburg

Anglo-Russian
Agreement, 1907

Franco-Russian Alliance, 1894

London

Berlin

Triple Alliance, 1879, 1882
(After 1900, Italy began
to draw closer to France)

Entente Cordiale, 1904

Paris

Vienna

Rome

bers of one or the other of two great alliance systems, and the Court of St. James's did not straddle the fence long either. The reckless policies pursued by the Kaiser drove England into the arms of his enemies. From the point of view of the British, it was bad enough that their markets were gradually being conquered by German businessmen. But then the aggressive imperialism practiced by Berlin, the growing Teutonic influence in the Near East, and the ambitious program of naval construction advocated by Admiral Tirpitz intensified the feeling of alarm on Downing Street. In 1904 the United Kingdom and France signed a colonial agreement settling their differences regarding Egypt, Siam, Newfoundland, and Madagascar which had embittered the relations of the two countries in the past. On paper it seemed to have only a remote bearing on the continental diplomatic situation, but in practice it introduced a period of close political and military cooperation between London and Paris, popularly known as the *Entente Cordiale*, the friendly understanding.

The treaties of 1894 between France and Russia and of 1904 between France and England led logically to the completion of the triangle by a treaty between England and Russia. In 1907 their governments agreed to adjust conflicting claims in Persia, Afghanistan, and Tibet, thereby clearing the way for a new policy of

WILLIAM II. The photograph shows the emperor on the left, reviewing his troops, while behind him marches an impressive array of plumes and boots.

collaboration between these traditional enemies. The Triple Alliance and the Triple Entente now became mutually opposed armed camps. Their role in bringing on the war was accurately described by the German diplomat Arthur Zimmermann on August 1, 1914, when he realized that the bullets were about to start flying: "It all came from this damned system of alliances, which was the curse of modern times."

A DECADE OF CRISES

Like gamblers playing for such stakes that they cannot afford to withdraw from the game, the great powers clashed in a series of crises which gradually prepared Europe for the idea of a recourse to arms. Neither side wanted a test of strength, but pride, ambition, and resentment made compromise ever more difficult. Before they fully realized what was happening, they had passed the point of no return.

The first encounter took place in 1905, when France prepared to end, and Germany to defend, the independence of Morocco. William II won an early tactical victory by forcing Paris to submit the issue to an international conference meeting in Algeciras in Spain. Yet his jubilation soon turned to chagrin, as all the major states except Austria voted to give France a dominant voice in the internal affairs of the sultanate. In 1908 the decision of Vienna to annex Bosnia and Herzegovina, which it had been administering since the Berlin Congress, brought the Continent once again to the brink of disaster. Russia, the champion of Slavic Orthodox nationalism, was supporting Serbian claims to the two provinces, when to the assistance of the Austrians came Germany "in shining armor"—to use the Kaiser's exuberant figure of speech. With bitterness in its heart the court of St. Petersburg was forced to back down. In 1911 there was another crisis, as France moved to complete her conquest of Morocco, and Germany once more began to rattle the saber. England rushed to support her ally, but the danger of an open clash was averted when Berlin agreed to settle for two bits of French Equatorial Africa. Finally in 1913 the outcome of the hostilities between the Ottoman Empire and the Balkan coalition of Bulgaria, Greece, Serbia, and Montenegro again threatened to involve the major countries in a world war. The Serbians backed by the Russians were determined to acquire the Turkish province of Albania, while the Austrians were resolved to keep their sworn enemies from the Adriatic shore. Moreover, the Italians, who had their own designs on the coastland, seconded the efforts of Francis Joseph. Only the readiness of Vienna to employ military means to decide the question compelled the government of the tsar to agree to the creation of an independent Albanian state. It secretly vowed, however, that this would be its last retreat.

THE OUTBREAK OF HOSTILITIES

By the summer of 1914 Europe had run out of diplomatic miracles. On June 28 Archduke Francis Ferdinand, the heir to the Austrian throne, was assassinated in Sarajevo, the capital of Bosnia and Herzegovina, by the fanatical Serbian nationalist Gavrilo Princip. For weeks important officials in Belgrade had known of his intentions and had even given him material assistance, although the police authorities in Vienna could only guess at such connivance. For the statesmen of Austria the murderous deed provided an opportunity to settle accounts with the Serbians, who had long fanned political unrest among the Slavic subjects of the Habsburgs. On July 23 the imperial government dispatched an ultimatum made deliberately so harsh as to be unacceptable. Five days later, after the expected rejection, Austria declared war. The advisers of Francis Joseph felt sure that they would be left free to crush their weak opponent while the great powers growled at each other without daring to risk involvement in hostilities.

But they had not reckoned with Russia's determination to avoid another political defeat. On July 30 the tsar after some hesitation ordered the general mobilization of his armies, thereby unintentionally forcing the hand of the military leaders in Berlin. For the German strategic plan, prepared nine years before by

THE ARCHDUKE FRANCIS FERDINAND AND HIS WIFE ON JUNE 28, 1914. A few minutes after this photograph was taken, the imperial couple was assassinated and a world war became imminent.

General Alfred von Schlieffen, provided that in the event of a Russian mobilization the Kaiser's forces were to engage at once in war with Russia and France. They were to turn first against the latter in overwhelming strength and achieve a swift victory in the west by an unexpected thrust through Belgium. Then a strong, united front could be established against the slowly assembling tsarist forces. The decision of Nicholas II to call up the army reserves thus panicked the Germans, forced them to declare war against Russia on August 1, drove them to commence hostilities against France on August 3, and a day later drew Great Britain into the struggle. The English cabinet had thus far been unable to decide on neutrality or participation, but the invasion of Belgium tipped the scale in favor of the advocates of aiding France. On August 4 the United Kingdom entered the conflict, and the First World War was under way.

Yet far from seeking hostilities, most of the leaders of Europe had been desperately anxious to avoid them. Certainly among the crowned heads there was little pugnacity. George V wrung his hands; Francis Joseph shrank from a struggle in which he saw little chance of victory; William II sent pleading telegrams to St. Petersburg; Nicholas II worried about the "thousands and thousands of men who will be sent to their death." The mood of the diplomats was even more despairing. The German chancellor, Theobald von Bethmann-Hollweg, broke down; the English ambassador in Berlin, Sir Edward Goschen, cried; the foreign secretary of Great Britain, Sir Edward Grey, lamented; the Austrian ambassador to the United Kingdom, Albert von Mensdorff, was crushed by sorrow; the German ambassador in London, Prince Karl Max Lichnowsky, was on the verge of a collapse; the Russian minister of foreign affairs, Sergei Sazonov, and the German ambassador in St. Petersburg, Friedrich von Pourtalès, embraced in tears before separating; the German ambassador in Paris, Wilhelm von Schön, sobbed as he delivered the declaration of war to the French government. There was not a dry eye in the government offices of the great powers during those early days of August. Not even the military men displayed much enthusiasm at the prospect of taking the field. The German chief of staff, General Helmuth von Moltke, became ill; the German secretary of the navy, Admiral Alfred von Tirpitz, was frightened; the Russian minister of war, General Vladimir Sukhomlinov, appeared nervous and depressed.

Only the sheep being led to the slaughter found it all very exciting. While bands played and girls waved their handkerchiefs, countless young men paraded gaily through towns and villages away from humdrum routine to a glorious adventure. Before long, millions of them would lie beneath a vast field of white crosses stretching from the English Channel to the Black Sea. And on the evening of August 4, as his world was coming to an end, Sir Edward Grey in London addressed the approaching tragedy: "The lamps are going out all over Europe; we shall not see them lit again in our lifetime."

Further Reading

*C. J. H. Hayes, *A Generation of Materialism, 1871–1900* (New York, 1941) is a thoughtful account of the last decades of the nineteenth century, critcizing the secular outlook of the period. The development of political radicalism is analyzed in G. D. H. Cole, *Socialist Thought: Marxism and Anarchism* (New York, 1954). W. A. Mc-Conagha, *The Development of the Labor Movement in Great Britain, France, and Germany* (Chapel Hill, 1942) and *P. Gay, *The Dilemma of Democratic Socialism: Eduard Bernstein's Challenge to Marx* (New York, 1952) are important studies of the socialist movement. Of the numerous works dealing with nationalism the following merit special attention: C. J. H. Hayes, *The Historical Evolution of Modern National-ism* (New York, 1948); L. L. Snyder, *The Meaning of Nationalism* (New Brunswick, 1954); and *B. C. Shafer, *Nationalism: Myth and Reality* (New York, 1955).

R. C. K. Ensor, *England, 1870–1914* (New York, 1936) and *G. M. Young, *Victorian England* (Garden City, 1954) depict the golden age of Great Britain. *G. Dangerfield, *The Strange Death of Liberal England* (New York, 1935) deals with the decline of laissez faire before the First World War. The standard biography of Gladstone is J. Morley, *The Life of William Ewart Gladstone,* 3 vols. (New York, 1903), which should be supplemented with W. F. Monypenny and G. E. Buckle, *The Life of Benjamin Disraeli,* 6 vols. (New York, 1910–1920). J. O'Connor, *History of Ireland, 1798–1924,* 2 vols. (Garden City, 1926) describes the Irish struggle for self-government. For a brilliant account of the Third French Republic, see D. W. Brogan, *The Development of Modern France, 1870–1939* (London, 1940). Another sound introduction is *D. Thomson, *Democracy in France Since 1870* (New York, 1952). M. Josephson, *Zola and His Time* (New York, 1928) and G. Bruun, *Clemenceau* (Cambridge, Mass., 1943) portray two republican heroes of France, while H. Goldberg, *The Life of Jean Jaurès* (Madison, 1962) describes an eminent socialist leader.

W. H. Dawson, *The German Empire, 1867–1914,* 2 vols. (New York, 1919) is a work of substantial scholarship, although on social and cultural developments it should be supplemented with K. S. Pinson, *Modern Germany* (New York, 1954). The economic growth of Germany has been examined in such books as W. F. Bruck, *Social and Economic History of Germany, 1888–1938* (New York, 1938) and G. Stolper, *German Economy, 1870–1940* (New York, 1940). For military developments see *G. A. Craig, *The Politics of the Prussian Army, 1640–1945* (New York, 1955), while for the German socialists there is the detailed study by *C. E. Schorske, *German Social Democracy, 1905–1917* (Cambridge, Mass., 1955). B. Croce, *A History of Italy, 1871–1915* (New York, 1929), written by an eminent philosopher, criticizes the policies of the Italian kingdom. D. M. Smith, *Italy: A Modern History* (Ann Arbor, 1959), is a well-known solid account.

*O. Jaszi, *The Dissolution of the Habsburg Monarchy* (Chicago, 1929) and A. J. May, *The Hapsburg Monarchy, 1867–1914* (Cambridge, Mass., 1951) present the best histories of the Dual Monarchy. On the nationality problem in Austria-Hungary, see R. W. Seaton-Watson, *Racial Problems in Hungary* (London, 1908) and *German, Slav, and Magyar* (London, 1916). *H. Seton-Watson, *The Decline of Imperial Russia, 1855–1914* (London, 1952) is a first-rate work describing the last years of tsarism. *B. D. Wolfe, *Three Who Made a Revolution* (Boston, 1955) vividly portrays Lenin, Trotsky, and Stalin before their rise to power. The diplomacy of Russia is treated in A.

Lobanov-Rostovsky, *Russia and Asia* (Ann Arbor, 1951). For the Near East see W. Miller, *The Ottoman Empire and Its Successors, 1801–1927* (New York, 1936); J. A. R. Marriott, *The Eastern Question* (New York, 1940); and E. M. Earle, *Turkey, the Great Powers and the Bagdad Railway* (New York, 1923).

The two most influential books on imperialism are J. A. Hobson, *Imperialism: A Study* (New York, 1948) and *V. I. Lenin, *Imperialism: The Highest Stage of Capitalism* (New York, 1939), both of them highly critical interpretations. For less rigid analyses see R. Maunier, *The Sociology of Colonies,* 2 vols. (London, 1949); and *J. A. Schumpeter, *Imperialism and Social Classes* (New York, 1955). *F. S. C. Northrop, *The Meeting of East and West* (New York, 1946) and *A. J. Toynbee, *Civilization on Trial* (New York, 1958) describe the cultural interaction of diverse peoples. The most readable general work on European imperialism is still P. T. Moon, *Imperialism and World Politics* (New York, 1926). It should be supplemented, however, with sound regional accounts like J. S. Keltie, *The Partition of Africa,* 2nd ed. (London, 1895); and B. Lasker, *Peoples of Southeast Asia* (New York, 1944). For the Arab world there is the excellent study by H. A. R. Gibb, *Islamic Society and the West* (New York, 1951).

R. J. Sontag, *European Diplomatic History, 1871–1932* (New York, 1933) is less smooth but more judicious than A. J. P. Taylor, *The Struggle for Mastery in Europe, 1848–1918* (New York, 1954). W. L. Langer, *European Alliances and Alignments, 1871–1890* (New York, 1950) and *The Diplomacy of Imperialism, 1890–1902,* 2 vols. (New York, 1935) are model diplomatic histories. Of the major works dealing with the outbreak of the First World War *S. B. Fay, *The Origins of the World War,* 2 vols. (New York, 1928) defends the Triple Alliance; B. E. Schmitt, *The Coming of the War, 1914,* 2 vols. (New York, 1930) champions the Triple Entente; and L. Albertini, *The Origins of the War of 1914,* 2 vols. (New York, 1952–1953) occupies a middle position. Among the studies of the underlying causes of the crisis of 1914 are E. M. Carroll, *Germany and the Great Powers, 1866–1914* (New York, 1938); R. J. S. Hoffman, *Great Britain and the German Trade Rivalry, 1875–1914* (Philadephia, 1933); and E. L. Woodward, *Great Britain and the German Navy* (New York, 1935).

CHAPTER 18

The Passing of
the European Age
1914–1945

The international conflict which began in 1914 was not really a world war. It was essentially a contest among European states, by European means, for European objectives. That some of the campaigns were fought on other continents did not alter the fact it was first and last Europe which was going through a crisis. Lands overseas were concerned in the hostilities, to be sure, but only to the extent that their national development depended on the political and economic condition of the great powers. They did not sacrifice their population; they did not waste their wealth. It was European society alone which destroyed the foundations of its stability.

When the twentieth century began, the Continent was still a going concern, suffering perhaps from some of the early symptoms of middle age, but still basically vigorous. True, its industrial supremacy was no longer beyond challenge, and its grip on colonial possessions was weakening. Yet these changes were gradual enough to be tolerable. In a period of peace and prosperity the West would in all likelihood have been able to adjust to them with relatively little social tension. What the First World War did was to hasten and intensify a process of decline which was probably unavoidable but not necessarily catastrophic. As it was, in the course of a few years a sound civic order was bled white and left spiritually exhausted. The European Age had passed.

1. The First World War

THE OUTCOME OF THE WAR was in a sense determined within a few weeks after its beginning. Given the human and the material resources of the opponents, the only chance of a Teutonic victory lay in a swift success. The Schlieffen plan had recognized this truth, and that is why immediately following the declaration of hostilities the armed might of Germany turned westward to achieve a rapid conquest of France. At first all went on schedule, and on August 25 General Moltke informed the Kaiser: "In six weeks the whole story will be concluded." But his optimism was premature. The French finally took a stand along the Marne River from which they could not be dislodged, and on September 9 the German commander confessed: "It goes badly—the first hopes have been utterly belied. . . . Bitter disillusionment is already upon us." Both forces now tried to outflank the enemy by moving to the west, and both succeeded in reaching the sea at about the same time. By the end of 1914 the war of maneuver had become a war of attrition, as millions of men faced each other across no man's land from two long lines of trenches extending six hundred miles from the English Channel to Switzerland.

THE PERIOD OF STALEMATE

For the next three years there was a complete stalemate on the western front. The Entente Powers vainly tried to break the deadlock by such desperate offensive actions as the Battle of Champagne in 1915, the Battle of the Somme in 1916, and the Battle of Ypres in 1917. The Germans, on the other hand, sought to save their manpower by confining themselves by and large to defensive operations, especially after the attack against Verdun, which they launched in 1916, proved a costly failure. But time was on the side of France and England, for they had greater access to raw materials and world trade than the Central Powers. The limited success of the German navy at the Battle of Jutland in 1916 was not enough to break the British blockade, while the effort to starve the United Kingdom into submission in 1917 by unrestricted submarine warfare only provided the United States with one more reason for joining the Entente Powers. The bleak outlook for the Teutonic cause eventually brought Italy, Japan, and more than twenty other states into the war on the side of the western allies, while Berlin and Vienna could find comfort only in the accession of weak Turkey and weaker Bulgaria.

TRENCH WARFARE. The horror of modern war is suggested by this photograph of British infantrymen during the First World War awaiting an enemy attack.

Yet the high command of the Central Powers was convinced that there was still an alternative to defeat. When the war began it had expected a quick victory in the west and a test of endurance in the east. Instead there was a total impasse on the western front and a succession of brilliant German victories in the eastern theater of operations. The common soldier serving in the armies of the tsar faced the enemy with courage, but his leadership was usually unintelligent and sometimes corrupt, while his equipment was totally inadequate. Even so, the Russian forces succeeded in inflicting serious reverses upon the Austrians, but they were no match for the best military organization in Europe. Skillfully directed by General Paul von Hindenburg and General Erich von Ludendorff, the Kaiser's forces won impressive successes in 1914 at the battles of Tannenberg and the Masurian Lakes, and in 1915 they occupied Poland and Lithuania.

The Entente Powers, anxious to bolster the tottering tsarist regime, made determined efforts to open a direct line of communication between east and west through Turkish territory. But the surprisingly strong resistance of Ottoman troops trained by German officers proved too much for them. In 1915 a campaign against the Straits, designed to secure free passage from the Mediterranean to the Black Sea, failed miserably, and in 1916 an attempt to establish contact between England and Russia in the Middle East resulted in the capitulation of a British garrison at

The Belligerents in the First World War*

(In the order of their participation)

I. The Central Powers

Austria-Hungary: July 28, 1914

Germany: August 1, 1914

Turkey: November 3, 1914

Bulgaria: October 11, 1915

II. The Allied and Associated Powers

Serbia: July 28, 1914

Russia: August 1, 1914

Luxemburg: August 2, 1914

France: August 3, 1914

Belgium: August 4, 1914

British Empire: August 4, 1914

Montenegro: August 9, 1914

Japan: August 23, 1914

Italy: May 25, 1915

San Marino: June 1, 1915

Portugal: March 9, 1916

Romania: August 27, 1916

Greece: November 24, 1916

United States: April 6, 1917

Cuba: April 7, 1917

Siam: July 22, 1917

Liberia: August 4, 1917

China: August 14, 1917

Brazil: October 26, 1917

Panama: November 10, 1917

Guatemala: April 22, 1918

Nicaragua: May 6, 1918

Costa Rica: May 24, 1918

Haiti: July 15, 1918

Honduras: July 19, 1918

III. New States recognized by the Allies which became involved in the war and signed some of the peace treaties

Hejaz: March 19, 1917

Czechoslovakia: June 30, 1918

Poland: November 2, 1918

IV. States which broke relations with some of the Central Powers and signed some of the peace treaties

Bolivia: April 14, 1917

Peru: October 6, 1917

Uruguay: October 17, 1917

Ecuador: December 17, 1917

* Not all Allied and Associated Powers were at war with all of the Central Powers, and declarations of war by one member of a coalition against different members of the other coalition did not occur at the same time. For example, Italy declared war against Austria-Hungary on May 24, 1915, Turkey August 21, 1915, Bulgaria October 19, 1915, and Germany August 28, 1916. Reference is made only to the first declaration of war in this table, from *Twentieth Century Europe,* by C. E. Black and E. C. Helmreich; copyright 1950 by Alfred A. Knopf, Inc.; reprinted by permission of the publisher. The chart was adapted from *A Study of War* by Quincy Wright by permission of The University of Chicago Press. Copyright 1942 by The University of Chicago. All rights reserved.

Kut-el-Amara. The dismissal of Grand Duke Nicholas as supreme commander of the Russian armies and the assumption of direct leadership by Nicholas II himself in September 1915 only made matters worse. The Central Powers were by now gambling on a decisive victory against the tsar's forces, which would enable them to dictate a peace settlement in the east and then organize an offensive by their combined armies against the weary Entente Powers in the west.

THE TURNING POINT OF THE WAR

The year 1917 was the turning point of the war, for new political and military developments enabled the belligerents to break the deadlock which had prevailed on the western front for more than three years. For one thing Russian resistance finally began to collapse, as a revolution in March forced the tsarist order to give way to a provisional government dominated by democratic reformers. The new regime tried for a few months to continue hostilities against the Central Powers, but in November it in turn fell before an insurrection led by the Bolsheviks. The latter agreed at once to the conclusion of an armistice with the enemy, and on March 3, 1918, Russia signed under protest the Treaty of Brest-Litovsk. She was forced to surrender virtually all her European acquisitions since the days of Peter the Great, leaving Germany free to transform the eastern borderlands into a Teutonic sphere of influence. The Kaiser's high command could at last plan for a major attack in the west, which would complete its triumph by defeating the French and English armies.

But in the meantime the Entente Powers had found a new ally whose enormous resources proved in the long run decisive. From the beginning of the war public opinion in the United States had favored them, as cultural ties, economic interests, and military considerations made a victory of the western democracies seem desirable. Early in 1917 the opening of a submarine campaign against neutral trade with Great Britain supplied the immediate justification for American participation in the conflict, and on April 6 Congress voted for a declaration of war on Germany.

By the time General Ludendorff opened his great offensive in the west in March 1918, the last chance of a German success had vanished. Although at first he made important gains, the tide slowly began to turn, and by July the initiative had passed to the other side. The Kaiser's armies were forced into an orderly but uninterrupted retreat, and on October 2 the high command admitted: "We can carry on the struggle for an appreciable time yet and can cause severe losses to the enemy; we can, however, no longer win." Military operations came to an end at last on November 11, after William II had abdicated in the face of insurrection and disorder. The new republican government of Germany accepted an armistice under conditions which in effect precluded a resumption of hostilities.

FIT FOR ACTIVE SERVICE. The well-known artist George Grosz portrays with savage irony the injustices of German society during and after the First World War.

BEHIND THE LINES

The First World War opened a new period in the conduct of armed conflict among states, the period of total national effort. Its significance lay not only in the magnitude of the struggle: the thirty-odd governments involved; the sixty-five million men in uniform; the twenty-nine million wounded, captured, or missing; the eight and a half million dead; the direct costs of two hundred billion dollars; and the indirect costs of a hundred and fifty billion more. It was the complete subordination of every aspect of public and private life to the demands of the struggle which distinguished this new mode of warfare. Gone were the days when campaigns were fought by professional soldiers under universally respected rules, while the civilian went about his usual business. After 1914 the difference between soldier and civilian became one of degree rather than kind, as both were subjected to the rigid discipline made necessary by the conditions of modern war.

For the first time in the history of Great Britain the government of Prime Minister Herbert Asquith introduced military conscription, which Englishmen had traditionally considered incompatible with personal freedom. In the United States Bernard Baruch regulated factory production in violation of the sacred principles of free enterprise. In Germany Secretary of the Interior Karl Helfferich prepared the National Service Law which put into operation a system of forced labor and provided for the compulsory arbitration of industrial disputes. In France Premier Georges Clemenceau was merciless toward those suspected of defeatism, imprisoning some like Joseph Caillaux, exiling others like Louis Malvy. The rights for which liberals had fought for more than a hundred years were sacrificed to Mars. Worst of all, the belief in the fundamental decency of man which western society in its better moments had upheld was drowned in a sea of hatred fed by governments seeking to counteract war-weariness. Frenchmen and Americans were told that "the Huns" amused themselves by impaling babies with their bayonets, while the Germans bolstered up their morale with such pieces of "poetry" as:

> Hate by water and hate by land;
> Hate of heart and hate of the hand;
> We love as one and hate as one;
> We have but one foe alone—England.

Unlimited means of warfare led logically to unlimited objectives of warfare. In the course of the hostilities each side sought to convince public opinion that it wanted nothing more than international justice. The English writer H. G. Wells coined the phrase, "the war to make the world safe for democracy," which became the unofficial slogan of the western allies. A more systematic statement of political aims came from President Wilson of the United States, who in his Fourteen Points spoke of the freedom of trade and navigation, the reduction of armaments, the adjustment of colonial claims, the right of oppressed peoples to national self-determination, and the formation of a league of nations. In the Teutonic camp the lower chamber of the German legislature announced: "The Reichstag strives for a peace of understanding and lasting reconciliation of nations. Such a peace is not in keeping with forcible annexations of territory or forcible measures of political, economic, or financial character." And Emperor Charles, who in 1916 succeeded Francis Joseph as ruler of the Dual Monarchy, made known his longing for a peace of compromise and moderation.

Yet it was too much to expect that nations which were sacrificing their bravest sons on the battlefield should renounce all thought of compensation. While publicly parading their virtue, they were privately preparing for a division of the booty. In a series of secret treaties the Entente Powers agreed on a partition of enemy territories, England claiming Mesopotamia and Palestine, France the Rhineland and Syria, Russia the Straits and East Prussia, and Italy the Trentino and Istria. Nor were the Central Powers less grasping. In December 1917 Hindenburg declared: "Belgium will continue to exist and will be taken under German military control until she is ripe politically and economically for a defensive and offensive alliance with Germany. . . . Nevertheless, for reasons of military strategy, Liége and the Flemish coast, including Bruges, will remain permanently in Germany's possession." A few weeks later Count Ottokar Czernin, the Austrian foreign minister, was on his way to Brest-Litovsk to participate in the spoliation of Russia. Whichever side won the war, the peace settlement was bound to be based on coercion.

THE PEACEMAKERS AND THE PEACE

The statesmen who gathered in Paris in January 1919 to draft the treaties to be imposed on the defeated enemy acted by and large as might have been expected under the circumstances. Although they represented thirty-two "allied and associated" states, the task of peacemaking became essentially the responsibility of the leaders of the victorious great powers, the Big Four. President Wilson was there, with the mind of a university professor and the soul of a Presbyterian elder, lecturing, preaching, exhorting. He could be an inspiring idealist at his best, a tiresome phrasemonger at his worst. And during the conference, unfortunately, he was not at his best. The economist John Maynard Keynes said about him: "He had no plan, no scheme, no constructive ideas whatever for clothing with the flesh of life the commandments which he had thundered from the White House. He could have preached a sermon on any of them or have addressed a stately prayer to the Almighty for their fulfillment; but he could not frame their concrete application

VERSAILLES, 1919. Orlando, Lloyd George, Clemenceau, and Wilson, exhausted by the years of war and troubled by their serious political differences, posed for this picture during the peace conference in Paris.

to the actual state of Europe." Prime Minister Lloyd George of England, on the other hand, was a clever politician anxious to maintain himself in power by any expedient. The radical firebrand of prewar years had become a shrewd demagogue. Having won an election in December 1918 with slogans like "Hang the Kaiser!" "Make Germany pay!" and "Squeeze the German lemon until the pips squeak!" he now found himself embarrassed by promises which he knew could not be kept. Georges Clemenceau of France was a hardheaded, hard-bitten old man, determined to make his nation secure against its traditional enemy. Instinctively distrustful of political sentimentality and verbal posturing, he thought in terms of nineteenth-century Realpolitik: "Mr. Wilson bores me with his Fourteen Points; why, God Almighty has only ten!" The least influential member of this diplomatic quartet, the Italian prime minister Vittorio Orlando, was also the least complicated. His purpose was simply to defend his country's "sacred egoism" by getting as much Austrian territory as possible.

Given the temper of the western allies, given the wishes of their voters and the illusions of their taxpayers, the Central Powers could expect nothing but a Carthaginian peace. The Treaty of Versailles, signed on June 28, 1919, deprived Germany of Alsace and Lorraine in the west, of Posen and part of West Prussia in the east, and of all her colonies in Africa and Asia. Her army was reduced to one hundred thousand professional soldiers, and her armaments and fortifications were rigidly restricted. For damage done to the civilian population of the victors she was to make financial reparations which were eventually fixed at thirty-two billion dollars. And she was to support an allied army of occupation in the Rhineland for fifteen years. To rub salt into her wounds, Article 231 asserted: "The Allied and Associated Governments affirm and Germany accepts the responsibility of Germany and her allies for causing all the loss and damage to which the Allied and Associated Governments and their nationals have been subjected as a consequence of the war imposed upon them by the aggression of Germany and her allies." Of the idealistic Fourteen Points little was left except the Covenant of the League of Nations, which became a constituent part of the treaty with Germany. As for the Dual Monarchy, immediately after the defeat of the Central Powers it disintegrated into its component national elements. Most of the Habsburg possessions were divided among new countries like Czechoslovakia, Poland, and Yugoslavia, or among old ones like Italy and Romania. Only the two diminutive states of Austria and Hungary remained. Their union of four hundred years was now dissolved, and they had to adjust to new humble circumstances formalized by the treaties of St.-Germain and Trianon. Finally the Treaty of Neuilly made small Bulgaria even smaller, while the Treaty of Sèvres deprived the Ottoman Empire of all its territories except the interior of Asia Minor and the city of Constantinople.

The diplomats responsible for these settlements were tired men wrestling with problems of the greatest complexity under conditions which made constructive statesmanship exceedingly difficult. Their mistakes were understandable and

TERRITORIAL DIVISION
of the
AUSTRO-HUNGARIAN EMPIRE
after the First World War

Based on Saucerman, *International Transfers of Territory in Europe*, U.S. Government Printing Office, 1937.

Austrian territory prior to division.

Hungarian territory prior to division.

In addition, Fiume and its immediate environs, formerly Hungarian, became a free city in 1920; it was ceded to Italy in 1924.

perhaps excusable, but it would be hard to argue that they produced a good peace. To begin with, the terms which they imposed upon the defeated enemy were such that he could not reconcile himself to their permanent acceptance. The conservative statesmen who met in Paris at the beginning of the nineteenth century had made it possible for their foe to retain his self-respect by negotiating a treaty which was stern but not unfair. The democratic statesmen who met in Paris a hundred years later were less generous. True, self-interest rather than generosity is the dominant principle in international relations, but when the world desperately needed a period of peaceful reconstruction, self-interest demanded generosity. The humiliating conditions dictated to the Central Powers sowed the seeds of future wars by breeding bitterness and defiance.

To make matters worse, the western allies intensified the effects of their ill-advised harshness by an even more ill-advised weakness. Having decided on a settlement sure to arouse the opposition of the vanquished, they should have upheld it with sufficient resolution to overcome that opposition. For to adopt a policy of repression without the means for its enforcement was to invite disaster. As it turned out, the democracies demanded strict observance of the peace treaties only while there was no determined resistance to them. As soon as the losers found themselves in a position to take a strong stand, the resoluteness of the victors vanished. They hastened to concede under threats of violence what they had denied to pleas for justice. Appeasement, however, only invited aggression. By their exclusive concern with narrow partisan advantage, the peacemakers of 1919 gained no more than a breathing spell of twenty years. Then the West plunged once again into a catastrophic world war.

2. *The Rise of Communism*

THE FIRST WORLD WAR marked the end of the European Age. Throughout the nineteenth century occidental society had lived in a mood of optimism inspired by a succession of scientific discoveries and imperialistic conquests. Hence it could afford the luxury of benevolence. It abolished personal servitudes, ended religious discriminations, eliminated economic evils, and composed political differences. The tragedy of 1914 closed the heroic era of the middle class of the West. Politically it fostered an extremism of the right as well as the left; economically it destroyed the popular belief in the efficacy of a laissez-faire capitalism; socially it aggravated traditional class differences; ideologically it encouraged attitudes hostile to the fundamental assumptions of liberalism.

Whereas before the war experience seemed to indicate that in the long run liberty contributed to the welfare of mankind, after the war it began to teach that individualism led to an anarchic struggle of all against all. Forced to decide between freedom and security, many chose security. Until Sarajevo the masses of Europe did not have to make the choice. Thereafter they could no longer escape it. Especially in countries where economic hardship was greatest and national resentment deepest there arose out of the military ordeal a reaction against the doctrines of bourgeois liberalism and a search for new authoritarian means of achieving political objectives.

THE RUSSIAN REVOLUTION

Communism was one form of this reaction. Ideologically, it evolved out of the left wing of the prewar socialist movement, but its growth was made possible by the experiences of the war itself. It won its first victories in Russia, a land which had suffered more than any other from the effects of the military conflict. After the Revolution of 1905 tsarism had taken the first hesitant steps toward parliamentary government, but at the time of the First World War representative institutions were still only a thin veneer over a tradition of authoritarianism. Reverses at the front and privations at home destroyed the remnants of popular loyalty to the crown, and in March 1917 there was a bloodless insurrection which forced the abdication of Nicholas II.

He was replaced by a provisional government representing cautious liberals like Paul Miliukov and moderate socialists like Alexander Kerensky. The provisional government immediately proceeded to democratize the political institutions of the country, but by its failure to make peace and to introduce economic reform it played into the hands of the Bolsheviks. The latter, directed by Vladimir Ilyich Lenin (1870–1924) and Leon Trotsky (1870–1940), began to agitate for a conclusion of the war, a division of the land among the peasantry, and a seizure of the factories by the workers. The Bolsheviks soon won the support of the soviets, labor councils representing the organized industrial proletariat. Although at no time more than a minority, they made up in disciplined militancy what they lacked in numbers. Like the Jacobins in 1792, they were the only ones who in the face of confusion and despair had a clear program of action. On November 6, 1917,

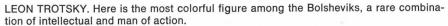

LEON TROTSKY. Here is the most colorful figure among the Bolsheviks, a rare combination of intellectual and man of action.

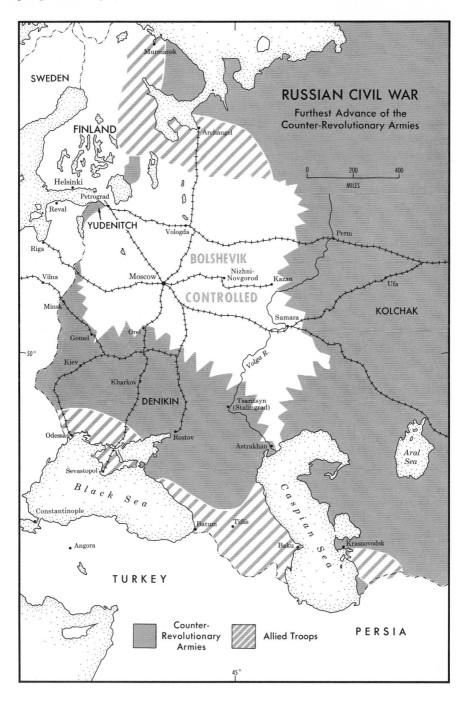

SWEDEN

Murmansk

FINLAND

RUSSIAN CIVIL WAR
Furthest Advance of the
Counter-Revolutionary Armies

Archangel

Helsinki

```
0        200        400
         MILES
```

Petrograd

Reval

YUDENITCH

Riga

Vologda

Perm

BOLSHEVIK

Vilna

Moscow

Nizhni-
Novgorod

Kazan

Ufa

Minsk

CONTROLLED

Samara

KOLCHAK

Gomel

Orel

Kiev

Volga R.

—50°

Kharkov

DENIKIN

Tsaritsyn
(Stalingrad)

Odessa

Rostov

Astrakhan

*Aral
Sea*

Sevastopol

B l a c k   S e a

C a s p i a n   S e a

Constantinople

Baku

Krasnovodsk

Batum

Tiflis

Angora

TURKEY

| Counter-Revolutionary Armies | Allied Troops |

PERSIA

45°

they led an insurrection against the provisional government, seized the reins of power, and formed a radical regime resolved to destroy the capitalistic order.

The communist victory opened a period of civil and foreign wars which continued for more than four years. First, conservative groups in opposition to the new government took up arms under such leaders as General Anton Denikin, General Nikolai Yudenitch, and Admiral Alexander Kolchak. Second, the western allies, frightened by the specter of radicalism, offered military and financial assistance to the counterrevolutionary forces. Finally, a secession movement developed in the borderlands, where Poland, Finland, Lithuania, Latvia, Estonia, the Ukraine, Georgia, Armenia, and Azerbaijan declared their independence from Russia.

Assailed by a thousand dangers, the Bolsheviks acted with a ruthless determination. Against civilian enemies they introduced a reign of terror under the Cheka, a political police organization headed by Felix Dzerzhinsky, which boasted of its role as the "unsheathed avenging sword of the Revolution." Against armed opponents they formed the Red Army, commanded with unexpected skill by Commissar of War Trotsky. To retain the support of the masses they partitioned large estates among the peasants and gave workingmen control over industrial plants, although at the same time they ordered the forcible requisitioning of grain and prohibited strikes in the nationalized factories. The struggle between the Reds and the Whites dragged on, with neither side asking or receiving quarter. But through sheer willpower the Soviet government succeeded in defeating its enemies one by one, until by 1922 it had overcome all the forces of the opposition. The critics at home had been silenced; the armies of the monarchists had been dispersed; the halfhearted intervention of the western allies had come to an end. The new regime had survived the first great test of its claim to power.

THE COMMUNIST IDEOLOGY

The political and social theory by which the Bolsheviks sought to justify their program was derived from the teachings of Karl Marx. But in their emphasis on uncompromising revolutionary action they differed from the moderate socialist movements which had emerged in the states of western Europe by the beginning of the twentieth century. They considered parliamentary government nothing more than an instrument of capitalistic domination. To renounce the use of force under existing conditions, they argued, meant to play the game according to the enemy's rules. For the propertied classes would always manage by one trick or another to mislead the masses, especially in the villages and on the farms, into voting against their own interests. The system of so-called free election was a fraud, since the established order had at its disposal all the means for controlling public opinion such as newspapers, journals, books, the movies, and the radio. The communists must therefore reject parliamentarianism. They should sit in bourgeois legislative bodies only in order to oppose the government, to publicize revolutionary ideas and appeal to the lower classes. The victory of the proletariat was not likely to be achieved by peaceful means, since capitalism would fight tooth and nail to defend its dominant position. The conflict between the haves and have-nots could therefore in all probability be resolved only by revolution.

The function of the communist parties in capitalistic countries, as they themselves defined it, was to prepare the working class for that revolution. They should use the "army, rifle clubs, citizen guard organizations, etc., for the purpose of giving the workers military training for the revolutionary battles to come." They should consider "every member of the party and every revolutionary worker as a prospective soldier in the future revolutionary army." Tactics of violence, to be sure, were not always applicable. The strength of the Bolsheviks lay in their flexibility. Lenin explained that "a Marxist . . . must not continue clinging to the theory of yesterday, which, like every theory, at best only outlines the main and the general, only approximately embracing the complexity of life." At times he urged his followers "to be cautious, to retreat, to wait, to go slowly, . . . to compromise with the bourgeoisie," while under more favorable circumstances they were "to be meticulously rigorous" in their strategy. The ultimate goal of communism remained constant, but the means to be employed in the achievement of that goal would have to vary in accordance with different historical conditions.

Once capitalism had been overthrown, the working class could proceed to establish the dictatorship of the proletariat as a transitional stage preceding the creation of a classless society. During this period the state must be controlled by the communist party. Leon Trotsky insisted that "the revolutionary supremacy of the proletariat presupposes within the proletariat itself the political supremacy of a party, with a clear program of action and a faultless internal discipline. . . . The Party includes in its ranks only the most class-conscious and devoted; and only in careful selection does it widen its ranks." The dictatorship of the proletariat, moreover, should be ruthless in suppressing the enemies of the revolution. "No organization except the army has ever controlled man with such severe compulsion as does the state organization of the working-class in the difficult period of transition. . . . The state, before disappearing, assumes . . . the most ruthless form" and "embraces authoritatively the life of the citizens in every direction." But while authority was the instrument of communism, its final objective was a free community of men. The Bolsheviks proclaimed that "state power, which is the embodiment of class rule, vanishes in proportion to the vanishing of classes. . . . The proletariat only needs the state temporarily." In their future utopia, as in most utopias, humanity would live in eternal love, liberty, and justice.

ECONOMIC RECOVERY

The price of the Bolshevik triumph was enormous. War, revolution, terror, hunger, and disease had created a population loss of more than twenty million people. The value of imports fell from four hundred million dollars in 1917 to thirty million dollars in 1918 to less than two million dollars in 1919. Between 1913 and 1920 the output of agricultural products declined 50 per cent, of manufactured consumer articles 87 per cent, of cotton goods 95 per cent, of pig iron 97.6 per cent, and of iron ore 98.4 per cent. Economic recovery became essential for the survival of the Soviets. In order to achieve it they prepared to end the system of complete governmental direction of production known as War Communism. In characteristically blunt fashion, Lenin admitted the failure of the wholesale adoption of socialistic practices: "We have eighteen People's Commissariats. Of these at least fifteen are absolutely no good."

In 1921, therefore, came the New Economic Policy, a compromise with capitalism which permitted the establishment under close official supervision of private commercial and industrial enterprises and which legalized the sale of a part of the farmer's crop for profit. This "temporary retreat" from Marxian orthodoxy was followed in 1928 by the First Five-Year Plan and in 1933 by the Second Five-Year Plan, carefully organized national campaigns to increase productive capacity, especially in heavy industry. At the same time the authorities introduced a program of rural socialization, forcing the peasants to give up their individual holdings and form huge collective farms. The result of these strenuous efforts was a remarkable revival of Russian economic strength, although in comparison with most capitalistic states the standard of living remained low. In its haste to carry out industrialization and collectivization, the government ignored the interests of the consumer, insisting that advances in production which the bourgeois democracies had needed a hundred years to achieve must be attained in the Soviet Union in ten. By the time of the Second World War the country had become a major manufacturing power, but it had paid for its accomplishments with the physical privation of an overworked, impoverished people.

THE STALIN DICTATORSHIP

Meanwhile an autocracy more despotic than tsarism had fastened its grip on Russia. From its beginning the Soviet regime had preached the rule of the proletariat, but at first it had tolerated such socialistic opposition groups as the Mensheviks and the Social Revolutionaries. Even when it turned the weapon of terror against them, it continued to permit freedom of discussion within the Communist party. After the death of Lenin in 1924, however, the march to complete authoritarianism became inexorable. For a few years the state was torn by the contest for leadership between Leon Trotsky and Joseph Stalin (1879–1953). The former urged an unceasing emphasis on revolutionary uprisings throughout the world; the latter maintained that for the time being communism must concentrate on consolidating its hold on the Soviet Union. By 1927 Stalin had won control of the party and, through the party, of the government. An ambitious, unscrupulous bureaucrat, he began to transform the political structure of the country into an out-and-out personal dictatorship.

By 1929 Trotsky had been expelled from the land he had helped win for the Bolsheviks, but before long a more tragic fate befell other communist officials prominent enough to constitute a possible threat to the autocrat. Between 1935 and 1938 such famous leaders of the revolution as Gregory Zinoviev, Leo Kamenev, Karl Radek, and Nikolai Bukharin were tried on fantastic charges of treason, conspiracy, and sabotage. Even more fantastic, they confessed without a word of defense to crimes of which they were obviously innocent. The purge trials presented a mystery which will probably remain unsolved until the secret archives of the Kremlin are opened, but their effect was clear. The last potential sources of opposition in the government, the army, and the party had been suppressed. It was a piece of irony that in 1936, while the judicial murder of the most brilliant sons of Russian Marxism was in progress, a new constitution was promulgated providing for universal suffrage, secret voting, and freedom of speech, assembly, and the press. An obsequious assembly of communist delegates heard from Stalin that "the constitution of U.S.S.R. is the only thoroughly democratic constitution in the world." In fact, he had forced on his country a tyrannical cult of the leader.

THE DIPLOMACY OF THE SOVIET UNION

The diplomatic position of the Soviet government had gained strength since those days following the revolution when it was an outcast among nations. After the failure of the allied intervention in Russia the statesmen of the western democracies had sought to encircle the Bolsheviks with a "sanitary cordon" of hostile countries consisting of Romania, Poland, the Baltic States, and Finland. The communists, confident that their revolution was only the first in a series of imminent anticapitalistic uprisings, responded with a propaganda campaign directed at the proletarian masses of Europe. Their agitation did inspire futile insurrections in Hungary, Germany, and Finland, but by 1920 it had become obvious that bourgeois society had regained its equilibrium and that a world upheaval was not around the corner after all. That was when Lenin turned to the East. Perhaps colonial peoples struggling against bourgeois imperialism would prove to be natural allies of the working class of the West. In the early 1920's the Soviet Union began to pay court to Turkey, Persia, and China. Still, while these countries welcomed Russian military and economic support, they stubbornly refused to accept the doctrines of Marxism.

Admitting reluctantly, therefore, that for the time being neither could destroy the other, communism and capitalism prepared to reestablish the commercial and diplomatic connections severed by the revolution. In 1924 and 1925 Great Britain, Italy, France, and Japan recognized the Soviet Union, although resentments and suspicions continued to trouble their relations. With the rise of fascism in the 1930's, however, middle-class democracy and proletarian dictatorship were willy-nilly forced into closer collaboration. Both feared the totalitarianism of the right; both wanted to reinforce their political position. In 1933 Russia exchanged ambassadors with the United States; in 1934 she entered the League of Nations; in 1935 she concluded a defensive alliance with France. Right up to the eve of the Second World War Stalin went on frantically seeking security for his regime in the popular-front policy, advocating cooperation between bourgeois parliamentarianism and Soviet radicalism against fascist aggression.

Yet despite Russian protestations of goodwill there could be no lasting reconciliation between communism and democracy. For the ideology by which the leaders of the Soviet Union justified their policy assumed a fundamental conflict of interest between the bourgeoisie and the proletariat. The revolution of 1917, they believed, was only the initial victory in a struggle which would not end until capitalism had been extirpated. That was why the Bolsheviks established the Third International to encourage and direct communist organizations throughout the world. In 1921 they boldly proclaimed their plan of action:

> The working class and the Communist Parties of all countries prepare themselves not for a period of quiet agitation and organization, but for prolonged struggle which capital will now force upon the proletariat, in order to beat it into submitting to all the burdens of capitalist policy. In this fight the Communist Parties must develop the highest militant discipline. Its Party leaders must coolly and deliberately consider all the lessons of the fight, they must prudently review the battlefield, uniting enthusiasm with the greatest deliberation. They must forge their militant plans and their tactical course in the spirit of collective thinking of the entire Party, giving due consideration to all criticism by comrades of the Party. But all the Party organizations must unhesitatingly carry out the course adopted by the Party. Every word and every step of every Party organization must be subordinated to this purpose. The Parliamentary factions, the press of the Party, the Party organizations must unwaveringly obey the order given by the Party leadership.[1]

The distrust between the capitalistic states and communist Russia was too strong to be overcome by trade agreements or alliance treaties. The political, economic, and intellectual differences separating them were too great. They remained divided by mutual fears until the Second World War drove them into an uneasy friendship.

3. Fascism on the March

FASCISM, LIKE COMMUNISM, was a twentieth-century reaction against the nineteenth-century libertarian ideal. But whereas communism had its roots in the socialist

---

[1] Third (Communist) International, *Theses and Resolutions Adopted at the Third World Congress of the Communist International, June 22nd–July 12th, 1921* (New York: Contemporary Publishing Association, 1921), p. 198.

thought of the prewar days, fascism was an expression of the ideological chaos created by the war itself. To nations exhausted by military sacrifices and economic exactions it offered an alternative to revolution. It promised to save the traditional institutions of property and status, but only within a framework of dictatorial control. While democracy had insisted that the freedom of the citizen was essentially in harmony with the welfare of society, the new authoritarianism taught that the individual had to submit to a bureaucratic regulation of his activity to protect the vital interests of the state. Such submission meant the suppression of the instrumentalities of popular representation and the surrender of the freedoms of speech, religion, and assembly. In place of these liberties were to come obedience and discipline. For only by sacrificing his independence to social stability and national might could the citizen defend himself against anarchy. In 1923 the German political theorist Artur Moeller van den Bruck voiced the mood of bitter disillusionment with the liberal faith: "It is the disintegrating atmosphere of liberalism which spreads moral disease amongst nations and ruins the nation whom it dominates."

THE THEORY OF FASCISM

The fascist movement saw in parliamentary government the rule of the weak and incompetent. It argued that at a time when society needed bold and vigorous leadership, the traditional party system offered a rehash of outworn liberal slogans. Only a dictatorship of dedicated patriots could provide the nation with a new sense of purpose. Benito Mussolini (1883–1945), the founder of Italian fascism, boasted that his party "combats the whole complex system of democratic ideology, and repudiates it, whether in its theoretical premises or in its practical application. Fascism denies that the majority, by the simple fact that it is a majority, can direct human society; it denies that numbers alone can govern by means of a periodical consultation, and it affirms the immutable, beneficial and fruitful inequality of mankind, which can never be permanently leveled through the mere operation of a mechanical process such as universal suffrage." Behind the facade of democracy lurked the hidden but powerful influence of selfish interests. Representative institutions, by encouraging the free expression of political and economic differences, aggravated class conflicts and fostered the growth of radicalism. An authoritarian regime was the only safeguard of the established social order against plutocracy or communism.

The dictatorship which fascism preached would subordinate class distinctions to the greatness of the state. It would not destroy differences in economic position and social status but would regulate them in the interest of the nation at large. Private voluntary organizations like industrial associations, labor unions, professional societies, and scholarly groups should be transformed into institutions for increasing the collective strength of the country. Discipline was seen as more important than liberty, obedience more useful than inquisitiveness. "The state is born out of the necessity of ordering the community . . . in accordance with certain laws," taught the National Socialist party in Germany. "Its characteristic attribute is power over every branch of the community. . . . Whoever violates the laws of the state will be punished. The state has officials to execute its laws and regulations. . . . The state embodies power!" Fascism, in other words, was willing to sacrifice freedom for the sake of stability. It proposed to maintain social differences by suppressing political differences. Its ultimate objective was not the classless society of socialist theory, but the preservation of class distinctions through the creation of a totalitarian regime. In effect it was trying to defend the established system of property relations by abandoning the humanitarian hopes and aspirations of the West.

The glorification of national might led logically to aggressiveness in dealing with foreign states.The fascists scorned the liberal ideal of perpetual peace as a symptom of weakness and decadence. They announced that "a doctrine which is founded upon this harmful postulate of peace is hostile to Fascism. And thus hostile to the spirit of Fascism, though accepted for what use they can be in dealing with particular political situations, are all the international leagues and societies which, as history will show, can be scattered to the winds when once strong national feeling is aroused by any motive—sentimental, ideal, or practical. This anti-Pacifist spirit is carried by Fascism even into the life of the individual." In central and eastern Europe, moreover, fascism adopted racialist doctrines which taught that the native population was biologically superior to alien ethnic groups. These doctrines were directed primarily against those classic scapegoats for the ills of European society, the Jews. The latter were portrayed as both capitalists and communists, liberals and Marxists, cowardly and impudent, clannish and pushing. The entire complex of fascist ideas, for that matter, was often illogical and inconsistent. It was a hodgepodge of slogans and attitudes rather than a rigorously systematic philosophy of politics and economics. But to those who were embittered by the tragedy of a ruinous war or frightened by the danger of economic decline it seemed to offer a way out of the chaos of the postwar world. Only another global conflict and untold human suffering would show how wrong they were.

FASCIST ITALY

Nowhere was the disillusionment with liberalism deeper than in Italy where the First World War had aggravated all the ills of the country. At the peace conference her government got only 9,000 square miles of territory and 1,600,000 new subjects, not much of a compensation for some 460,000 dead and nearly 1,000,000 wounded. Moreover the demobilization of the armed forces and the end of the war boom led to spreading unemployment. The result was a radicalization of the masses. In 1919 the socialists became the largest single party in parliament; in 1920 a wave of strikes and lockouts resulted in the seizure of many factories by workers; in 1921 a communist party was formed with the blessings of the Third International.

As for the authorities, they seemed incapable of coping with the danger of a political upheaval. One prime minister followed another in rapid succession, first Vittorio Orlando, then Francesco Nitti, then Giovanni Giolitti, then Ivanoe Bonomi, and then Luigi Facta, none of them able to win public confidence. Out of this confusion of ideologies and factions arose Benito Mussolini and his Fascist party. Originally an ardent socialist, he had become during the war an even more ardent nationalist. After hostilities came to an end he began to preach the subordination of all party differences to the cause of Italian greatness. Around his banner rallied frightened businessmen, unemployed veterans, disgruntled superpatriots, restless adventurers, all who saw in the black shirt of fascism the only defense against the communist hammer and sickle. Although its representation in parliament did not exceed thirty-five deputies, the party demanded full executive power. In October 1922 a march on Rome by some thirty thousand of its members frightened King Victor Emmanuel III into forcing the resignation of the Facta cabinet and appointing Mussolini as prime minister.

Once in a position of authority, the Fascists proceeded to assume autocratic power. The parties of the opposition were dissolved, and their leaders imprisoned or even murdered, as was the Socialist deputy Giacomo Matteotti. No one was surprised when in 1924 the supporters of Mussolini increased their representation in parliament to 375 seats, more than ten times the number they had won in the last free election three years before. After all, who wanted to risk a beating by a strong-arm squad for criticizing the actions of the government?

Having manufactured a popular endorsement of its policies, fascism went to work reorganizing the constitutional and social structure of the state. The prime minister was authorized to rule by decree, the principle of manhood suffrage was abrogated, and the electorate was reduced by about three million persons. The ruling party was given the right to name official candidates for the legislature. At the same time labor unions and trade associations were replaced by syndicates and corporations, organizations in theory representing the interests of employers and employees, in fact subservient to the bureaucracy. Thereafter strikes and lockouts became illegal.

The Duce also did his best to encourage patriotic enthusiasm. Resplendent in black shirt and military tunic, he harangued wildly cheering crowds from the balcony of his palace in Rome, proclaiming the birth of a new Italy, disciplined and aggressive. Young men were enrolled in the ranks of the Fascist militia where they received training in the arts of war. Boys between the ages of eight and fourteen learned obedience and combativeness in the *Balilla*. For that matter, children from six to eight were not considered too young to learn how to stand at attention in the Sons of the Wolf. Mussolini meant it when he thundered: "Above all fascism . . . believes neither in the possibility nor the utility of perpetual peace. It thus repudiates the doctrine of pacifism—born of a renunciation of the struggle and an act of cowardice in the face of sacrifice. War alone brings up to its highest tension all human energy and puts the stamp of nobility upon the peoples who have the courage to meet it."

Then there were the ambitious programs of land reclamation, industrial expansion, military modernization, and naval improvement. The government practiced aggrandizement in Europe and colonialism in Africa. Its talent for dealing with political opponents, moreover, improved with time. In 1924 the dictator won 4,800,000 votes and his foes 2,250,000; in 1929 the figures were 8,500,000 and 136,000. Even the Papacy seemed to fall in step. By the Lateran Treaties of 1929, church and state composed the differences which had troubled their relations for more than fifty years. The former received sovereign rights in Vatican City and financial compensation for its territorial claims; the latter won recognition as the legal source of political authority in the country. Many foreigners, impressed by the ostentatious vigor of the new regime, conceded that at least "the trains are running on time." Only the Second World War revealed the moral bankruptcy behind the achievements of the sawdust Caesar.

NAZI GERMANY

In Germany parliamentarianism held out a little longer before it too succumbed to the combined effects of military collapse and economic privation. The fall of the empire had brought to the helm the parties of moderate socialism, bourgeois democracy, and progressive Catholicism, which before the war had advocated civic reform. Yet the tasks facing them after 1918 proved beyond their strength. The republic proclaimed by the national assembly meeting in Weimar had to cope first with widespread communist uprisings inspired by economic hardship. No sooner were these suppressed, than the reactionaries attempted to seize power and establish an authoritarian form of rule. While engaged in the struggle against its enemies on the left and the right, the government was forced to sign the Treaty of Versailles, a millstone around the neck of German liberalism. And, as if all this were not enough, the precarious financial situation led to a catastrophic inflation which in November 1923 reduced the value of the currency to the point where one dollar was worth two and a half trillion marks.

The middle class, traditionally the backbone of constitutionalism, was thus impoverished and demoralized. The economic recovery which began a year later proved no more than a brief respite. By 1929 the great depression which descended on the entire capitalistic world brought new unemployment and despair to the masses of central Europe. The end of the Weimar Republic was at hand. President Paul von Hindenburg, the hero of the war years, was a bewildered, tired old man. Chancellor Heinrich Brüning fought frantically but vainly to stem the rising tide of totalitarianism. The democratic parties in parliament, paralyzed by indecision, debated endlessly whether to support the cabinet because of its good intentions or criticize it for its lack of accomplishment. In this atmosphere of confusion, amid rumors, fears, plots, and counterplots, the senile president was persuaded by his conservative advisers to dismiss Brüning. A few months later, in January 1933, Adolf Hitler (1889–1945), the leader of the National Socialist party, was invited to become head of the government.

The new chancellor was the embodiment of all the demonic forces which the ordeal of war and depression had unleashed. He had grown up in the Dual Monarchy during the years of its political decline before 1914, and had fallen under the spell of the virulent chauvinism which seemed to infect everything it touched in that doomed empire. The disasters which followed the First World War created a favorable environment for his gospel of hate. In the 1920's he began to preach in Germany a doctrine of national regeneration through the overthrow of parliamentarianism and the persecution of the Jews. At first the undisguised brutality of his views repelled all but a handful of fanatics, so that as late as the election of 1928 his party won only 12 seats in parliament out of 491. The economic crisis which began a year later, however, destroyed popular confidence in liberalism. In their bewilderment millions began to clutch at ideological straws. The one worker out of every three who was unemployed, the small businessman sinking into bankruptcy, the wealthy industrialist afraid of a communist revolution, the patriot seeking to avenge the humiliating defeat, the aristocratic landowner contemptuous of democratic government—each for his own reasons was ready to acclaim the messiah in the brown shirt. Yet at no time was Hitler able to win a popular majority through a free vote. Only the control over the state apparatus which he acquired as chief minister made possible his establishment of a dictatorship.

Within a year after taking office he had transformed the republic into an autocracy by methods which Mussolini had used with success in Italy. The chancellor received the right to rule by decree; adverse opinions were suppressed; rival parties were dissolved; political opponents were packed off to concentration camps. Every enterprise and every interest was brought under the supervision of the state. The Labor Front directed the activities of the worker; the Hitler Youth provided patriotic recreation for the young; the Evangelical church amalgamated the Protestant communities under the leadership of so-called *German Christians;* the Ministry of Church Affairs kept a sharp eye on the doings of Catholic clergymen; and the Strength through Joy supplied cheap vacations to the lower classes. There were National Socialist associations of writers, actors, motorcyclists, athletes, housewives, aviators, students, and scientists. And looking down on this vast system of totalitarian regimentation from a million posters was the stern face of the Führer.

Most Germans accepted the authoritarian regime gladly, even enthusiastically. Under the new order the economic depression came to an end, as the government program of military rearmament and industrial expansion solved the problem of unemployment. Trade unions were abolished, but at the same time production was stimulated by public works and secret remilitarization. The establishment of youth labor camps, the reintroduction of conscription, and the world-wide economic recovery of the middle 1930's also helped restore social stability in central Europe.

Why then should the man in the street have opposed National Socialism? True, he had to be careful about what he said, but in return he got bread and circuses. The former he earned in factories manufacturing airplanes and tanks; the latter were provided by the splendid congresses of the party and the parades of its special armed units, the S.A. and the S.S. Everywhere flags were flying and drums were rolling; everywhere arms were raised in the Nazi salute; everywhere could be heard the greeting "Heil Hitler!" The western democracies which had been deaf to the pleas of the republic now listened attentively to the wishes of the Third Reich. As for the masses, they would read now and again about some socialist "shot while trying to escape" or see a Jew beaten by a uniformed bully. Usually they turned the other way and tried not to notice what was happening.

"DAY OF REJOICING," 1936. This photograph of a Nazi ceremonial gathering in Berlin suggests fascism's characteristic glorification of power.

THE SPREAD OF FASCISM

The successes of fascism in two of the major powers encouraged autocratic tendencies among those secondary states which had never wholeheartedly accepted liberalism. In Spain King Alfonso XIII tried to deal with political discontent by conferring dictatorial powers on General Miguel Primo de Rivera. But in 1930 the prime minister resigned in the face of mounting popular unrest, and the following year a republic was proclaimed. Then came a confused period of conflict between the radicals and the conservatives, until the election of 1936 resulted in a decisive victory for the parties of the left advocating land redistribution, industrial regulation, labor welfare measures, and anticlerical legislation. Defeated at the polls, the forces of the right representing the army, the aristocracy, and the church resorted to arms. Led by General Francisco Franco and assisted by Germany and Italy, they defeated the republican government after a savage civil war which raged until 1939. In its place they established a regime based on the principles of fascism. The dictatorship in Spain was warmly welcomed by the dictatorship in Portugal formed early in the 1930's under the leader of the National Union party, Antonio de Oliveira Salazar. By the time of the Second World War the Iberian peninsula was completely dominated by a traditionalist, clerical authoritarianism.

In eastern Europe, amid the Balkan nations carved out of former Turkish possessions and the succession states built on the ruins of Russia and Austria, the rule of force was an ancient tradition. The teachings of parliamentarianism were meaningless to the exploited peasant masses, and authority passed easily into the hands of the propertied classes. Most of the countries in this region boasted liberal constitutions promising representative government and personal freedom. But they were politically too inexperienced and economically too backward to translate democratic words into democratic deeds. Some were simply old-fashioned dictatorships ruled by strong men with the support of the army and the bureaucracy, like Poland under Marshal Joseph Pilsudski and Yugoslavia under King Alexander I. Others flirted with the theories of reactionary totalitarianism without succumbing to them entirely, like Romania under King Carol II and Hungary under Admiral Nicholas Horthy. And a few openly announced their adherence to fascist policies, like Austria under Chancellor Engelbert Dollfuss and Lithuania under President Antanas Smetona.

For fascism seemed strong and confident. While democratic nations were torn by doubts, the Italian political theorist Alfredo Rocco preached that only the authoritarian principle of statecraft could save the world from class war:

Fascism therefore not only rejects the dogma of popular sovereignty and substitutes for it that of state sovereignty, but it also proclaims that the great mass of citizens is not a suitable advocate of social interests, for the reason that the capacity to ignore individual private interests in favor of the higher demands of society and of history is a very rare gift and the privilege of the chosen few. Natural intelligence and cultural preparation are of great service in all such tasks. Still more valuable perhaps is the intuitiveness of rare great minds, their traditionalism and their inherited qualities.[2]

4. Democracy on the Defensive

FOR THE LIBERAL STATES the interwar years were a time of ordeal. The conflict which was supposed to make the world safe for democracy had instead weakened the foundations on which European democracy had rested. It had encouraged the growth of industrialism on other continents; it had destroyed the dream of free trade by intensifying economic nationalism; it had stimulated the opposition to imperialism among colonial peoples; it had led to the establishment in America of barriers to immigration; it had shaken popular belief in bourgeois parliamentarianism; it had aggravated social insecurities and resentments. Worst of all, it had caused liberalism to lose faith in itself. Not only the masses of the West but its leaders as well were seized by a moral panic. Teachers and writers, convinced that war was the work of munitions manufacturers and international financiers, "the merchants of death," urged the young never again to bear arms for their country. Economists and sociologists, shocked by the widespread sufferings which accompanied the economic depression of 1929, began to condemn capitalism as an exploitative system of production. Even those statesmen and businessmen who attempted to defend established institutions did so with little conviction. The bourgeois political order faced a terrible crisis.

FRANCE

After struggling against the enemy for four ruinous years, France emerged from the First World War a broken, sick nation. More than half of her male inhabitants who were between the ages of twenty and thirty-two when hostilities began had fallen on the battlefield. The hundreds of destroyed towns and thousands of wrecked factories were eventually restored by the expenditure of eighty billion francs. But the one and a half million dead could not be brought back to life, nor could the half a million maimed be made whole again. The hope that Germany would be forced to pay the costs of the war proved to be no more than wishful thinking, for not even the seizure of the rich Ruhr by French troops in 1923 succeeded in squeezing much money out of the impoverished Weimar Re-

---

[2] Alfredo Rocco, "The Political Doctrine of Fascism," *International Conciliation*, 223 (October 1926), 405.

public. The loss of investments in Russia and the high price of reconstruction produced a financial crisis which did not come to an end until 1928, when Prime Minister Raymond Poincaré devalued the franc from nineteen cents to four. This repudiation of almost 80 per cent of the liabilities of the state, the spread of communism among the lower classes, the chronic instability of the postwar cabinets, and the involvement of important politicians in the peculations of the shady financial manipulator Serge Stavisky produced an outburst of antirepublican sentiment. Royalist and fascist organizations like the *Action Française,* the *Solidarité Française,* the *Jeunesses Patriotes,* and the *Croix de Feu* proliferated, and in February 1934 a wave of political disorder swept over the country threatening to topple the government. A hastily-formed coalition cabinet under Gaston Doumergue representing the middle-of-the-road parties managed to weather the storm, but not before the republic had come closer to collapse than at any time since the Dreyfus affair.

To counter the danger of a reactionary coup, the parties of the center and the left, the Radical Socialists, the Socialists, and the Communists, formed in 1935 a parliamentary alliance known as the Popular Front. The following year they won a major electoral victory on a platform urging the defense of political democracy and the advancement of social welfare. The new cabinet headed by the socialist intellectual Léon Blum went to work at once to revive the confidence of the proletariat in the republic. The forty-hour work week was proclaimed, paid vacations were guaranteed to all factory employees, labor disputes were subjected to compulsory arbitration, the munitions industry was nationalized, the Bank of France was placed under public control, and fascist organizations were dissolved or at least restrained.

Yet measures which conciliated the worker alienated the businessman, and before long the coalition of bourgeois liberalism and proletarian radicalism began to encounter serious financial difficulties. Anxious to halt the continuing decline in the value of the franc, the government announced a temporary suspension of further plans for social reform. But differences of opinion among the parties supporting it grew steadily, and in 1938 the Popular Front came to an end. The cabinet of Edouard Daladier which followed moved farther and farther to the right. Labor attempted to resist this conservative tendency by organizing a strike campaign, but its opposition only led to stern government action against trade unions. While important industrialists were muttering among themselves that Hitler was better than Blum, while millions of workers were announcing that their allegiance belonged not to Daladier but to Stalin, France marched to disaster.

GREAT BRITAIN

In England political differences were less intense, but economic difficulties were even greater. The most serious effect of the First World War was not the loss of two million casualties nor the expenditure of eight billion pounds, but the increased industrial rivalry of other states which had expanded their productive capacity during the hostilities. Trade was a matter of life and death to a country which had to purchase almost two-thirds of its food supply abroad. Yet between 1913 and 1929 Great Britain's share of the world's exports fell from almost 14 per cent to less than 11, while her population was steadily growing. The result was chronic unemployment and social unrest which culminated in 1926 in an unsuccessful general strike involving some two and a half million workers.

Hard times also brought mounting criticism of the theories of freedom of trade and freedom of enterprise which had been unquestioningly accepted in the nineteenth century. The Liberal party, traditionally identified with economic and political individualism, was especially vulnerable to attacks on the teachings of laissez faire. In 1922 it was replaced by the Labor party as the chief parliamentary opponent of the Conservatives. While on the American stock exchange investors were engaging in wild speculation, while even among the defeated Germans there was an appearance of confidence after the stabilization of the currency in 1923, in the United Kingdom newspapers were full of stories about strikes and lockouts, about workers without work and families on the dole.

The depression beginning with the Wall Street crash of 1929 was the climax of a series of economic reverses which staggered Great Britain. The number of unemployed, never less than a million throughout the 1920's, rose to two and a half million in 1930. At the same time exports were shrinking and profits falling. Faced by a national emergency, Prime Minister J. Ramsay MacDonald decided to introduce a program of recovery which would have scandalized the statesmen of the prewar years. On September 21, 1931, the country went off the gold standard, and the expression "sound as sterling" lost its historic meaning. In the following year a century of free trade came to an end, when protective duties of 10 per cent ad valorem were imposed on most imports. Before long the government adopted almost all of the other practices of economic nationalism which the hard times were encouraging everywhere in Europe. It controlled foreign exchange, manipulated paper currencies, made public appeals to "buy British," and established a system of preferential tariffs within the empire at the Ottawa Imperial Economic Conference of 1932.

These measures succeeded little by little in alleviating the worst effects of the depression. But they also represented an abandonment of cherished economic beliefs. Fascism and communism made little headway among the masses, yet the exuberant self-confidence of the days of Palmerston and Disraeli had vanished. The prime ministers of the 1930's, MacDonald, Stanley Baldwin, and Neville Chamberlain, expressed the subdued mood of the nation in their policies. Honest, sincere, hard-working, and well-meaning, they labored in an unimaginative, plodding way to restore financial prosperity and maintain diplomatic influence. They lived in times, however, which demanded more than the sober virtues of the certified public accountant. For opposed to them were ruthless fanatics. The silk umbrella and the black Homburg reflected the middle-class respectability of one side, just as the steel helmet and hobnailed boot expressed the militant authoritarianism of the other. Only in 1939 did the English government recognize at last the serious danger to its position as a major power. By then it was almost too late.

The decline in the authority of Downing Street encouraged greater independence on the part of the dominions. Their contribution to the war effort of the Entente Powers had been considerable, and with the coming of victory they received their reward in the form of a new freedom of action in international affairs. Represented at the peace conference by their own statesmen rather than those of the mother country, they succeeded in vindicating their claims to the spoils of conquest. The Union of South Africa gained control of German South West Africa, Australia acquired most of the German Pacific colonies south of the equator, and New Zealand was entrusted with the administration of German Samoa. As befitted the dignity of full-fledged states, moreover, they obtained admission to the League of Nations as sovereign members. Before long they were establishing diplomatic relations with foreign countries and concluding political and commercial treaties. The English government agreed at the imperial conference of 1926 that dominions "are autonomous Communities within the British Empire, equal in status, in no way subordinate one to another in any respect of their domestic or external affairs, though united by a common allegiance to the Crown, and freely associated as members of the British Commonwealth of Nations." This view was given formal sanction in the Statute of Westminster of 1931, which substituted free cooperation for historic right as the basis of the imperial union.

Under this arrangement relations between the crown and the dominion governments were harmonious everywhere except in Ireland. The end of the First World War opened a period of civil war in the island which continued until the signing of a treaty in 1921 establishing the Irish Free State. Even then the uncompromising nationalists under Eamon de Valera would not accept the exemption of Protestant Ulster in the north from the jurisdiction of the new state. In 1937, a few years after winning a parliamentary majority, they promulgated a new constitution severing virtually all remaining ties between Dublin and London. Yet neither diplomatic negotiations, nor financial inducements, nor deeds of terrorism succeeded in overcoming the obstacles to a reunification of the Emerald Isle.

THE SMALL DEMOCRACIES

The small democracies also had their difficulties in coping with the political and economic problems of the interwar period. Belgium, whose neutrality had been violated during the First World War, sought security from aggression in an alliance with France which remained in force until 1936. But then the German military revival persuaded the government in Brussels to seek better relations with the Third Reich. Holland, on the other hand, consistently pursued a policy of strict diplomatic nonalignment which had served her so well since the end of the Napoleonic wars. Yet events were to show that neither country could escape the horrors of the next global conflict. Both of them, moreover, were seriously affected by the great depression which forced them to adopt drastic economic measures. Progressive social legislation could not prevent the rise of popular discontent reflected in the growth of radicalism on the left and fascism on the right. The democratic tradition, however, was strong enough to withstand the effects of hard times. The great threat to the Low Countries was the approach of a new world war in which there could be no room for neutrals. In both Belgium and Holland 1940 was to prove an even more fateful year than 1914.

The Scandinavian states, after a century of almost uninterrupted peace, were generally confident that any future conflict would leave them untouched. While the war clouds were beginning to gather on the European horizon, they proceeded with ambitious programs of popular welfare under the auspices of a moderate socialism. By limiting the size of their armed forces, they were able to concentrate their financial resources on improving the standard of living of the population. Even the depression did not affect their economy as seriously as in most countries of the West. In Sweden, for example, a system of unemployment insurance introduced in 1934 helped offset the effects of hard times, while in Norway a year later social security legislation was promulgated which proved valuable in combating the financial crisis. Scandinavian socialism, which played such an important role during the interwar period, believed in parliamentary government and tolerated the capitalistic system. It sought to modify rather than revolutionize, and its achievements often served as a model for liberal reformers in other parts of the world. But not far away Hitler's airplane factories were working twenty-four hours a day, and millions of young men were receiving instruction in the use of the rifle and the bayonet. The good fortune of Scandinavia in escaping the wars of the Continent would not last much longer.

In the east Finland and Czechoslovakia were two small islands of democracy threatened by a rising tide of authoritarianism—communist in one case, fascist in the other. Finland, after achieving independence from Russia during the First World War, led an uneasy existence as a parliamentary republic, fearful of Bolshevik armies abroad and reactionary forces at home. Yet she succeeded in following a middle-of-the-road course like that of her Scandinavian neighbors. Czechoslovakia was in an even more vulnerable position. Surrounded on three sides by unfriendly states, Germany, Austria, and Hungary, she had to cope in addition with the problem of discontented minorities within her borders, mostly Teutonic and Magyar. To make matters worse, the two dominant nationalities of the country, the Czechs and the Slovaks, were often at loggerheads. During the presidency of the highly

respected Thomas G. Masaryk the government was by and large successful in defending its political interests, but with the rise of National Socialism in Germany
a period of acute danger opened for the republic. As long as France was prepared to
uphold the alliance with Prague concluded in 1924, the latter could defy its foreign
and domestic enemies. Once the great powers of western Europe decided to pursue
a policy of appeasement, however, Czechoslovakia's days were numbered.

5. The Pipe Dream of Peace

NOT ONLY DID THE FIRST WORLD WAR betray the promise "to make the world safe
for democracy"; it also failed to live up to the expectation that it was "the war to
end war." While hostilities were still in progress, the problem of peacemaking
seemed simple enough. Justice would be done, no more and no less; and justice
meant the punishment of the warmongers on the other side and the rewarding of
the peace-loving states on this side. Translated into diplomatic practice in Paris in
1919, this view led to the imposition upon the vanquished of a punitive peace which
was bound to arouse resentment among them. But their protests were ignored as
long as they lacked the military means to obtain redress.

The statecraft of the western allies proved in the long run to be self-defeating.
No major power could fashion permanent security for itself out of the permanent
insecurity of another major power. The victims of an international diplomatic
order based on the lasting subordination of some of its members were sure to work
with all means at their disposal for the overthrow of that system. It did no good to
charge them with bad faith and call them aggressors. Having been compelled by
force to accept what they considered an unfair arrangement, they had no hesitation
about using force to compel its revision. The treaties on whose sanctity the victor
states insisted throughout the interwar period were for the defeated states nothing
more than a piece of legalized extortion to be denounced at the earliest possible
moment. In 1815 the duke of Wellington had warned the conquerors of that day
that "if peace and tranquillity for a few years is their object, they must make an
arrangement which will suit the interests of all the parties to it, and of which the
justice and expediency will be so evident that they will tend to carry it into execution." The wisdom of his views was demonstrated a hundred years later.

A DECADE OF INTERNATIONAL STABILITY

At first there was nothing to make the victors doubt the correctness of their
policy. Before them was the prospect of an enduring peace based on their preponderance of power. The League of Nations provided an instrument for the pacific set-

tlement of international differences and for the prompt defeat of all unilateral attempts to alter the peace treaties. The desire to avoid future armed conflicts, moreover, led to the Washington Conference of 1922 and the London Conference of 1930 limiting naval armaments. The Permanent Court of International Justice was established at The Hague in 1922 to adjudicate diplomatic disputes, and by the Kellogg-Briand Pact of 1928 sixty-three states solemnly announced that "they condemn recourse to war for the solution of international controversies, and renounce it as an instrument of national policy in their relations with one another."

Not content with pacific declarations, the Quai d'Orsay in Paris also succeeded in creating a system of defensive alliances designed to guarantee France's dominant position on the Continent. The reestablishment of the prewar connection with Russia was out of the question, for to the bourgeoisie of the Third Republic communism was the work of Satan. But might not the succession states of eastern Europe prove a satisfactory substitute for the tsarist regime? After signing a military convention with Belgium in 1920, France proceeded to negotiate political agreements with Poland in 1921, with Czechoslovakia in 1924, with Romania in 1926, and with Yugoslavia in 1927. Finally the French and the German foreign ministers, Aristide Briand and Gustav Stresemann, initiated a policy of reconciliation between their governments which led to the Locarno Pact of 1925. Berlin renounced all efforts to obtain a revision of its western frontier, and the following year it was rewarded with admission to the League of Nations.

THE DISINTEGRATION OF THE PEACE

The coming of the depression destroyed the illusion that the danger of war had vanished, because the fears and tensions which accompanied hard times played into the hands of political extremists. Among nations with authoritarian leanings the belief grew that armed might could rectify longstanding civic and economic grievances. The first major break with the system of security established at Paris came in 1931–1932, when the Japanese seized Manchuria and organized it as a vassal state. The attempts of the League of Nations to mediate in the conflict were met by Japan's withdrawal from the world organization. The weakness of the postwar diplomatic structure was now revealed, convincing a bold opportunist like Hitler that the moment was ripe for a one-sided revision of the Treaty of Versailles. In 1935 Germany announced the reintroduction of military conscription, and the following year it remilitarized the Rhineland. As for England and France, they sent protest notes which the Führer promptly buried in the files of the foreign office.

At the same time Mussolini was avenging the defeat of Italian arms forty years before by conquering Ethiopia. Emperor Haile Selassie appeared in Geneva to plead before the great powers for assistance against fascist tyranny, but the weary democracies were in no mood to become involved in a war over the wastes of East Africa. They went through the motions of introducing economic sanctions against the attacker, yet when to no one's surprise these failed to stop the armies of the Duce, they acquiesced in his aggression. In 1936 the two triumphant dictators formed an alliance which came to be known as the Rome-Berlin Axis, and soon thereafter they were joined by Japan in the Anti-Comintern Pact directed ostensibly against communism.

The diplomats of the western democracies sought to counter totalitarian expansionism with a policy of appeasement. Struggling against unemployment and poverty, they were ready to make almost any sacrifice in order to avoid another world war. They had an uneasy feeling, moreover, that the Treaty of Versailles had not really been fair, and that demands for its revision were in principle reasonable. Finally at least some of them hoped that after a few concessions from London and Paris the Rome-Berlin Axis would turn eastward against Russia, and the authoritarians of the right and the left would destroy each other to the advantage of the liberal states.

During the Spanish civil war, while Germany and Italy were giving assistance to the insurgent forces and the Soviet Union was providing supplies for the republican government, England and France followed a course of nonintervention, seeing no evil, hearing no evil, doing no evil. They looked hard the other way when in 1937 Japan embarked on a new campaign against China. They contented themselves with halfhearted reproofs when in the spring of 1938 the Third Reich engineered the incorporation of Austria, a step which enjoyed popular support among the Germans and the Austrians, but which was also a clear violation of the Treaty of Versailles. Six months later, when the Führer began to press Czechoslovakia for the cession of the Sudetenland, a region inhabited largely by a German population, Chamberlain and Daladier prepared to sell out their democratic friends in Prague. Chamberlain in particular was pathetically anxious to find a peaceful settlement of the dispute. His airplane trips to confer with the Nazi dictator inspired one wit to comment: "If at first you don't concede, fly, fly again." On September 29, 1938, the two chief statesmen of liberal Europe met in Munich with Hitler and Mussolini to accept all the demands of the totalitarian powers, thereby averting the danger of an international conflict through the sacrifice of the Czechs. Great Britain was now "the lion of least resistance," her authority as a victor in the First World War undermined, her prestige as a founder of the League of Nations dissipated. Yet so great was the prime minister's relief that hostilities had been avoided, so great was his faith in the sanctity of a tyrant's signature, that after returning to London with one of the most humiliating treaties in his country's history he triumphantly announced to a crowd of well-wishers: "There has come back from Germany to Downing Street peace with honour." And his listeners interrupted their singing of "For He's a Jolly Good Fellow" to cheer this colossal piece of self-deception.

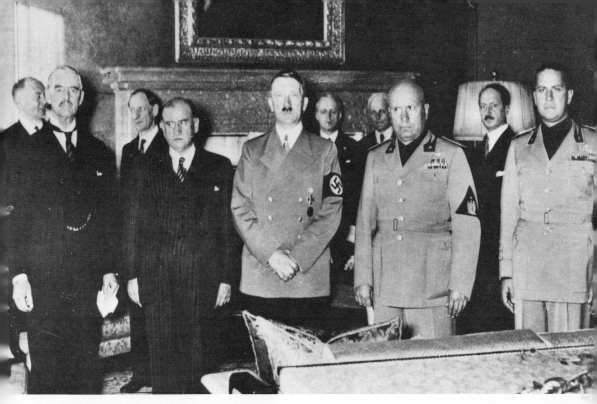

MUNICH CONFERENCE, 1938. Chamberlain and Daladier, soberly dressed in civilian clothes, pose with Hitler and Mussolini to whom they sacrificed the Czechs as the price of a peace which could not be maintained.

THE OUTBREAK OF THE SECOND WORLD WAR

They were disabused soon enough. Less than a month after he had made his promises to the western statesmen Hitler issued a secret directive to his military advisers informing them that "the armed forces must be prepared at all times for . . . the liquidation of the remainder of Czechoslovakia." The blow fell in March 1939, when the Czech state which had been rendered defenseless by the Munich Agreement was completely dismembered by Germany. Even Chamberlain, no longer able to delude himself regarding the ambitions of National Socialism, admitted that "public opinion in the world has received a sharper shock than has ever yet been administered to it, even by the present regime in Germany." Recognizing at last that the policy of appeasement was a costly failure, the democracies resolved to take a strong stand in the next international crisis, regardless of the consequences. They announced this intention through a pact of mutual assistance with Poland, and sought to strengthen their military position by a program of rapid rearmament.

As the Führer began to send threatening notes to Warsaw regarding the Polish Corridor which separated East Prussia from the rest of the fatherland, England and France entered into negotiations with Russia for the establishment of a united front against fascist encroachment. Stalin, however, had just decided that nothing was to be gained from a policy of collaboration with the liberal states. Instead, on August 23, 1939, he executed a complete about-face by concluding a nonaggression treaty with Germany. The Führer was thus freed from the danger of a war on two fronts. "The Soviet Union has joined the Anti-Comintern Pact" was a quip circulating in the capitals of Europe. But there was nothing amusing about the consequences of the Kremlin's astounding reversal of diplomacy, because the outbreak of hostilities had now become inevitable. For about a week the Third Reich played a game of cat-and-mouse with Poland, until on September 1 the German armies crossed the frontier to attack a weak, isolated opponent. Two days later, grimly resolved to stand up to the fascist menace, London and Paris dispatched declarations of war to Berlin. Another world conflict was under way.

6. The Second World War

IN PREPARING FOR THE SECOND WORLD WAR the military leaders of the western democracies had relied on the experiences of the First World War, just as in planning for the First World War they had studied the lessons of the Franco-Prussian War. In both cases the actual course of events caught them by surprise. In 1914 what had been expected to be a contest of maneuver turned out to be a trial of endurance, and in 1939 what had been expected to be a trial of endurance turned out to be a contest of maneuver.

The French army, still reputed to be the strongest on the Continent, had defeated the enemy once by means of trench warfare, and it proposed to defeat him again with the same technique. During the 1930's it had constructed along the eastern frontier a chain of powerful fortifications known as the Maginot Line, complete with running water, electric light, and central heating, and there it expected to sit out any future war until victory arrived. This emphasis on defense, both as a concept of strategy and as a state of mind, reflected the effects of the terrible ordeal which the country had undergone twenty years before. The Germans, on the other hand, having been on the losing side in 1918, applied themselves thereafter to the invention of new tactics designed to counter the process of attrition which had been the undoing of the Kaiser. They found what they were looking for in the application of armored force closely supported by air power in sufficient strength to break through a fixed entrenched position. Bold and original methods of attack developed by a group of capable general officers and executed by well-trained troops made the Wehrmacht the best military organization in the world when hostilities began in 1939.

The Belligerents in the Second World War*
(In the order of their participation)

I. The Axis and Satellite States

Germany: September 1, 1939
Italy: June 11, 1940
Hungary: April 10, 1941
Bulgaria: April 24, 1941
Romania: June 22, 1941
Finland: June 25, 1941 (Previously at war with the U.S.S.R. Nov. 30, 1939 to March 12, 1940)

Japan: December 7, 1941
Manchukuo: December 8, 1941
Slovakia: December 12, 1941
Croatia: December 14, 1941
Albania: December 17, 1941
Thailand: January 25, 1942
Nanking government of China: January 9, 1943

II. The Coalition Against the Axis

Poland: September 1, 1939
United Kingdom: September 3, 1939
France: September 3, 1939
India: September 3, 1939 (Action taken by government in London)
Australia: September 3, 1939
New Zealand: September 3, 1939
Union of South Africa: September 6, 1939
Canada: September 10, 1939
Norway: April 8-9, 1940
Belgium: May 10, 1940
Luxemburg: May 10, 1940
Netherlands: May 10, 1940
Greece: October 28, 1940
Yugoslavia: April 6, 1941
Union of Soviet Socialist Republics: June 22, 1941 (Previously invaded Poland Sept. 17, 1939; at war with Finland Nov. 30, 1939 to March 12, 1940; declared war on Japan August 8, 1945)
United States: December 7, 1941
Philippine Commonwealth: December 7, 1941
Panama: December 7, 1941
Costa Rica: December 8, 1941
Dominican Republic: December 8, 1941
Nicaragua: December 8, 1941
El Salvador: December 8, 1941
Haiti: December 8, 1941
Honduras: December 8, 1941
Guatemala: December 9, 1941
Cuba: December 9, 1941
China: December 9, 1941 (Chinese-Japanese incident had begun July 7, 1937)

Czechoslovakia: December 9, 1941 (Government-in-Exile)
Brazil: May 2, 1942
Mexico: May 22, 1942
Ethiopia: December 1, 1942
Iraq: January 16, 1943
Bolivia: April 7, 1943
Iran: September 9, 1943
Colombia: November 26, 1943 (State of Belligerency with Germany)
Liberia: January 27, 1944
Ecuador: February 2, 1945
Paraguay: February 8, 1945
Peru: February 11, 1945 (State of Belligerency with Germany and Japan)
Chile: February 12, 1945 (State of Belligerency with Japan)
Venezuela: February 14, 1945 (State of Belligerency with Germany and Japan)
Uruguay: February 22, 1945
Turkey: February 23, 1945
Egypt: February 26, 1945
Syria: February 26, 1945
Lebanon: February 27, 1945
Saudi Arabia: March 1, 1945
Argentina: March 27, 1945 (Declared war against Germany and Japan, but not a signatory to Declaration by United Nations)
Mongolian People's Republic: August 9, 1945 (Declared war against Japan, but not a signatory to Declaration by United Nations)

III. Axis satellites which subsequently declared war against the Axis

Italy: October 13, 1943
Romania: August 24, 1944
Bulgaria: September 8, 1944

Finland: September 15, 1944
San Marino: September 21, 1944
Hungary: January 20, 1945

* From *Twentieth Century Europe*, by C. E. Black and E. C. Helmreich. Copyright 1950 by Alfred A. Knopf, Inc. Reprinted by permission of the publisher. Compiled from Katherine E. Crane, "Status of Countries in Relation to the War, August 12, 1945," *Department of State Bulletin* 13 (1945), 230–241; Royal Institute of International Affairs, *Chronology of the Second World War* (London, 1947).

THE AXIS IN THE ASCENDANT

The first weeks of the war provided an impressive display of Germany's offensive power. Throughout the summer which preceded the outbreak of the conflict there had been optimistic comment in western newspapers about Poland's capacity to resist attack, about the bravery of her army and the impenetrability of her mud. Yet within a month the Germans had overrun the country and divided it with the Russians in accordance with a secret protocol appended to their nonaggression treaty. There followed half a year of deceptive inactivity, and then in the spring of 1940 the Wehrmacht marched forth to its greatest triumphs. In April it seized neutral Denmark and Norway in order to safeguard its flank in the north, easily defeating an Anglo-French expeditionary force sent to the defense of Scandinavia. One month later it invaded the Low Countries, and then broke through the French position at Sedan. Fanning out to the west and the south, it took the Maginot Line from the rear against little opposition, for the guns of the fortifications had been constructed to face immovably toward the Rhine. On June 10 Mussolini, anxious to participate in the division of the spoils, declared war against the democracies. Four days later Paris fell, and on June 22 the new head of the government of France, Marshal Henri Philippe Pétain, agreed to an armistice which left most of his country occupied by the enemy. Early the following month the Third Republic came to an end, as the legislature voted by an overwhelming majority to establish an authoritarian regime.

Meanwhile, the British by heroic efforts managed to evacuate more than three hundred thousand men from the beaches of Dunkirk, men who were later used in better planned and more successful operations against the fascist powers. For the time being, however, western Europe lay prostrate before the jubilant Führer. Winston Churchill, who on May 11 had replaced Chamberlain as prime minister of England, was facing up to the hard truth when he warned his countrymen that "I have nothing to offer but blood and toil and tears and sweat."

For an entire year the government in London stood alone against the totalitarian assault. Since Britain's navy still controlled the seas, Hitler decided to prepare the way for an invasion of England by massive air raids which would destroy the opponent's will to resist. From August 1940 until May 1941 the Royal Air Force and the Luftwaffe met day after day in roaring battles in the sky, until the German high command decided to abandon temporarily the plan for a landing in England. For one thing, its losses in airplanes and in airmen were heavy enough to make the outcome of an amphibious military operation uncertain. Second, the Führer was once again beginning to look to the east. Hungary, Romania, and Bulgaria had been bribed or bullied into joining the Axis, but Greece and Yugoslavia stubbornly clung to their political independence. In April 1941, therefore, the last lightning campaign of the Wehrmacht completed the subjugation of the Balkans.

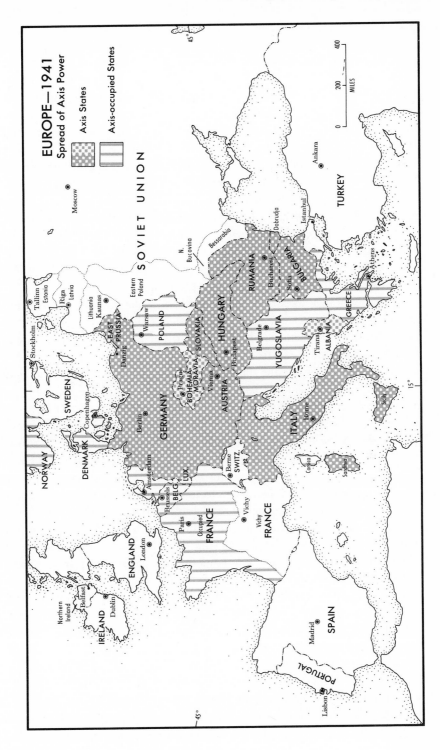

EUROPE—1941
Spread of Axis Power

Axis States

Axis-occupied States

THE TURNING OF THE TIDE

Two months later, on June 22, Germany attacked Russia in one of the fateful developments of the war. The ideological differences between the two dictatorships had been aggravated to the breaking point by conflicts of interest in the Baltic Sea and in the Balkan peninsula. Convinced that the Red Army could be crushed before the onset of winter, Hitler dispatched a force of more than three million Germans, Italians, Romanians, Hungarians, and Finns against the Soviet Union. It was 1812 all over again. Again the invaders won important early successes; again they advanced deeper and deeper into hostile territory; again they encountered burned villages and guerrilla bands. Yet, unlike the emperor of France, the leader of the Third Reich was never to enjoy a triumphal entry into the Kremlin. The swastikas came within forty miles of Moscow, but on December 6 a Russian counterattack over the frozen plains drove them back for the first time. The following day came the electrifying news that the Japanese had bombed Pearl Harbor, and that the United States was finally in the war.

The American attitude had been sympathetic to the democratic cause from the beginning of hostilities, although at first Washington would not go beyond moral encouragement to England and France. After the great German victories in western Europe, however, it began to extend military and economic aid to the British. Indeed, in order to ensure the uninterrupted flow of supplies across the Atlantic, it sent troops to Greenland, Iceland, and Ireland and provided merchantmen with naval protection against submarines. The difference between antifascist neutrality and antifascist belligerency was rapidly melting away when developments in the Far East created the immediate occasion for the final transition from one to the other.

Japan, engaged since 1937 in military operations against China, had taken advantage of the defeat of France to win control over Indochina. Her war machine, however, depended heavily on imports from the New World of strategic materials, mainly oil, steel, scrap iron, copper, and lead. In the summer of 1941 President Franklin D. Roosevelt cut off the shipment of goods to the Japanese in order to curb their imperialistic ambitions, leaving them no choice but to abandon their colonial conquests or acquire new economic resources. Their answer came on December 7, "a date which will live in infamy," when a surprise air raid on the Hawaiian Islands crippled the United States navy and exposed the western Pacific to the attack of the expansionists in Tokyo. Four days later Germany and Italy declared war on America, and the campaign in eastern Europe, in the Mediterranean, and in Asia merged in one great global conflict.

The spring and summer of 1942 were the high-water mark of Axis success. In the Soviet Union a new offensive was swiftly carrying the Germans toward the rich oil fields of Caucasia; in North Africa General Erwin Rommel, "the desert fox," was leading the fascist forces deep into Egypt to within seventy miles of Alexandria; in the Far East the Japanese were seizing the Netherlands East

THE SINKING OF THE U.S.S. *CALIFORNIA*. The Japanese attack on Pearl Harbor on December 7, 1941, the results of which are shown here, brought the Second World War to the Pacific.

Indies, the Philippines, Hong Kong, Malaya, and Burma. Then the tide began to turn. The Red Army succeeded in pushing back the Wehrmacht in a series of savage battles, of which the most important took place at Stalingrad. In the Pacific the mikado's warships were stopped in the Coral Sea and at Midway Island, while his troops got their first taste of defeat when the United States marines landed on Guadalcanal in the Solomon Islands. And in the Mediterranean theater of operations a concerted advance by the British from the east and the Americans from the west closed in on the German Afrika Korps, capturing its last strongholds of Tunis and Bizerte in May 1943.

The next campaign against the Axis was an invasion of Italy, designed to topple the shaky regime of Mussolini. The swift conquest of Sicily did lead to the fall of the Duce, but Hitler rushed enough troops south to gain control of most of the peninsula. For nearly another two years hard fighting continued amid the Apennines. By the beginning of 1944, however, the grand coalition against fascism was winning the upper hand on all fronts. In eastern Europe the Russians were crossing their prewar frontiers, carrying the fight to the enemy. In the Italian boot the Allied armies were slowly advancing northward toward Rome. In the Far East the forces of General Douglas MacArthur, having occupied strategic points in the Gilbert and the Marshall islands, were sending their bombers closer and closer to the Japanese homeland. Everywhere the struggle was financed by America, who was producing vast quantities of war materials and shipping them to the four

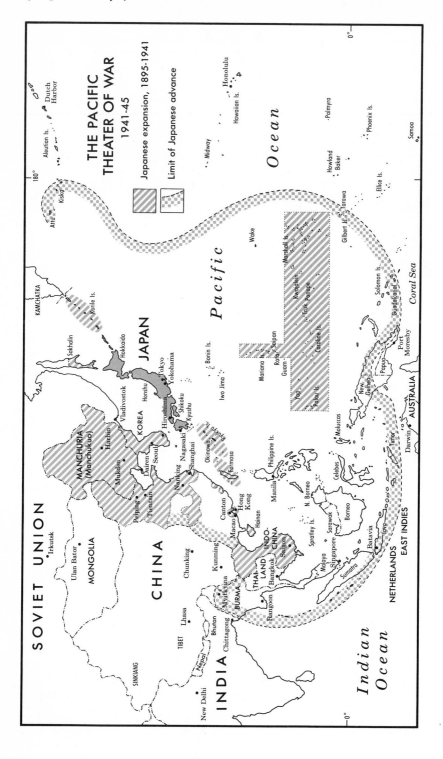

THE PACIFIC
THEATER OF WAR
1941-45

Japanese expansion, 1895-1941

Limit of Japanese advance

corners of the earth. The New World, protected by its oceans against air attack and military invasion, had become the arsenal of democracy.

THE VICTORY OF THE GRAND COALITION

The last phase of the war opened on June 6, 1944, with the invasion of western Europe by Allied troops under General Dwight D. Eisenhower. They succeeded by the end of the summer in driving the enemy out of France and Belgium, while the Red Army was making itself master of eastern Europe and approaching the frontiers of East Prussia. Recognizing the hopelessness of the military situation, a group of German officers attempted to assassinate Hitler in order to facilitate peace negotiations. But their effort failed, and the struggle went on to the bitter end. Late in 1944 the Wehrmacht launched a last desperate offensive against the western Allies in the Forest of Ardennes. When that failed, the Third Reich was left incapable of further effective resistance.

In the spring of 1945 a coordinated attack by the Russians in the east and the Americans in the west culminated in the meeting of their forces along the Elbe on April 25. Five days later, as his capital was falling to the troops of the Soviet Union, the Führer committed suicide, and on May 7 in Reims General Alfred Jodl accepted the instrument of unconditional surrender for Germany. Japan con-

SURRENDER, 1945. The end of the Second World War in Europe came with the German capitulation on May 7, 1945, in Reims, France. In this picture the surrender document is about to be signed.

tinued to fight alone for another few months, although the Allies had in the meantime retaken the Philippines and were now in a position to raid Japanese cities from air bases on Iwo Jima and Okinawa only a thousand miles from Yokohama and Nagasaki. What finally forced the mikado's government to agree to lay down its arms was first the destruction of the city of Hiroshima by an atomic bomb on August 6, and then two days later the entry of Russia into the conflict in the Far East. In the middle of the month Japan announced her readiness to meet the demands of the grand coalition, and on September 3 her civilian and military leaders signed the terms of capitulation on board the U.S.S. *Missouri*. Hostilities which had begun in the summer of 1939 on the road to Danzig came to an end six years later on the other side of the world in Tokyo Bay.

The agony of total conflict made familiar by the First World War recurred on an even more tragic scale in the Second World War. Those killed on the battlefield numbered some fifteen million men, while civilian losses were at least equally great. One out of every twenty-two Russians, one out of every twenty-five Germans, one out of every forty-six Japanese was dead or missing. The bitter quip that during hostilities the safest place is the front proved to be almost literally true. In England 20 per cent of all homes were damaged or destroyed; in Germany close to 25 per cent of the buildings were reduced to rubble; cities like Stalingrad, Warsaw,

LONDON, 1944 *(opposite page)*, and BERLIN, 1945 *(this page)*. The juxtaposition of these pictures of the destruction of the capitals of two of the principal belligerents of the Second World War suggests the tragedy of total war.

Kassel, and Rotterdam were in ruins; in Hiroshima a single atomic explosion took the lives of more than seventy thousand people and leveled four square miles. The financial costs of the conflict were estimated at from two to four trillion dollars, but what currency could express human suffering and sorrow? The Axis treated conquered countries with a ruthless brutality. It even organized a systematic, cold-blooded extermination of ethnic minorities which brought death to six million Jews. Yet the democracies were not entirely above reproach either. Their mass bombing of enemy countries made no distinction between the good and the bad, the innocent and the guilty. How many Americans felt uneasy in March 1945 about the great air raid on Tokyo which caused almost 125,000 civilian casualties? How many Britons protested two months later against the sack of Berlin by the Red Army? Amid the hatred and cruelty which had become instruments of modern warfare there was little room for such unpatriotic sentiments as compassion for the other side.

Seen in historical perspective the Second World War was part of a vast political process, the passing of the European Age. It weakened still further the civic and material bases on which the Old World had built its greatness, for it intensified the reaction of the Orient against imperialism, strengthened the economic position of America, and established the military preponderance of Russia. But for those who in 1945 had to face the future from the ruins of their civilization it was also a crushing personal tragedy. Now their only source of strength was an instinctive faith in the ultimate value of life, like that of the fifteen-year-old Jewish girl, Anne Frank, who wrote in her diary shortly before she was deported to her death in a wartime concentration camp:

> That's the difficulty in these times: ideals, dreams, and cherished hopes rise within us, only to meet the horrible truth and be shattered. . . . Yet I keep them, because in spite of everything I still believe that people are really good at heart. I simply can't built up my hopes on a foundation consisting of confusion, misery, and death. I see the world gradually being turned into a wilderness, I hear the ever approaching thunder, which will destroy us too, I can feel the sufferings of millions and yet, if I look up into the heavens, I think that it will all come right, that this cruelty too will end, and that peace and tranquillity will return again.[3]

Further Reading

The best military histories of the First World War are C. R. M. Cruttwell, *History of the Great War, 1914–1918* (New York, 1934); and B. H. Lidell Hart, *A History of the World War, 1914–1918* (Boston, 1935). *B. W. Tuchman's eminently readable *The Guns of August* (New York, 1962) describes the first weeks of hostilities. For events behind the lines see F. P. Chambers, *The War behind the War, 1914–1918* (New York, 1939). *J. W. Wheeler-Bennett, *Brest-Litovsk, The Forgotten Peace, March 1918* (London, 1939) is a brilliant treatment of Russia's withdrawal from the war. On the surrender of the Central Powers there is H. R. Rudin, *Armistice, 1918* (New Haven, 1944). The standard account of the peace conference is H. W. V. Temperley, ed., *A History of the Peace Conference of Paris*, 6 vols. (New York, 1920–1924). H. Nicolson, *Peacemaking, 1919* (New York, 1939) and P. Birdsall, *Versailles Twenty Years After* (New York, 1941) are important briefer works, while J. M. Keynes, *The Economic Consequences of the Peace* (New York, 1920) presents a shrewd estimate by a well-known economist.

*W. H. Chamberlin, *The Russian Revolution, 1917–1921*, 2 vols. (New York, 1935) is a balanced history of the Bolshevik seizure of power. Sympathetic eyewitness accounts may be found in L. Trotsky, *The History of the Russian Revolution*, 3 vols. (New York, 1936) and *J. Reed, *Ten Days That Shook the World* (New York, 1926). E. H. Carr, *A History of Soviet Russia*, 7 vols. (New York, 1950–1964), is also favorable to the revolutionary cause. M. Fainsod, *How Russia Is Ruled* (Cambridge, Mass., 1953) offers a solid analysis. *L. Fischer, *The Life of Lenin* (New York, 1964) is a graphic portrait of the Bolshevik leader. The best biography of Stalin is *I. Deutscher,

---

[3] From *The Diary of a Young Girl* by Anne Frank. Copyright 1952 by Otto H. Frank. Reprinted by permission of Doubleday & Co., Inc., and Vallentine Mitchell & Co., Ltd.

Stalin (New York, 1949), which should be complemented with the same author's **Trotsky,* 3 vols. (New York, 1954–1963). M. Beloff, *The Foreign Policy of Soviet Russia, 1929–1941,* 2 vols. (New York, 1947–1948) and L. Fischer, *The Soviets in World Affairs* (Princeton, 1951) deal with the diplomacy of the Kremlin. For the ideology of the Soviet Union see J. Somerville, *Soviet Philosophy* (New York, 1946); M. T. Florinsky, *World Revolution and the U.S.S.R.* (New York, 1933); and M. Ebon, *World Communism Today* (New York, 1948).

H. Holborn, *The Political Collapse of Europe* (New York, 1951) is a penetrating analysis of the interwar period. On the development of fascism there are A. Rossi, *The Rise of Italian Fascism, 1918–1922* (London, 1938); and H. W. Schneider, *Making the Fascist State* (New York, 1928). B. King, *Fascism in Italy* (London, 1931) and G. A. Borgese, *Goliath: The March of Fascism* (New York, 1937) describe the regime of Mussolini. The soundest treatment of the Weimar Republic is **S. W. Halperin, *Germany Tried Democracy* (New York, 1946). **A. Rosenberg, *The Birth of the German Republic, 1871–1918* (New York, 1931) examines its origin, while A. Brecht, *Prelude to Silence* (New York, 1944) deals with its fall. A thoughtful account of National Socialism is presented in **F. L. Neumann, *Behemoth: The Structure and Practice of National Socialism* (New York, 1942). J. W. Wheeler-Bennett, *Wooden Titan: Hindenburg in Twenty Years of German History, 1914–1934* (New York, 1936) and **A. L. C. Bullock, *Hitler: A Study in Tyranny* (New York, 1958) are important biographical works. **J. W. Wheeler-Bennett, *Nemesis of Power* (New York, 1954) traces the relationship between militarism and totalitarianism in Germany. **T. F. Abel, *Why Hitler Came into Power* (New York, 1938) is an enlightening study of the social environment out of which National Socialism rose.

The background and course of the civil war in Spain are treated in **H. Thomas, *The Spanish Civil War* (New York, 1961); and **G. Brenan, *The Spanish Labyrinth* (New York, 1943). **H. Seton-Watson, *Eastern Europe between the Wars, 1918–1941* (New York, 1945) is an outstanding study of authoritarianism in eastern Europe.

The effects of the great depression are discussed by P. Einzig, *The World Economic Crisis, 1929–1931* (New York, 1931); and H. V. Hodson, *Slump and Recovery, 1929–1937* (New York, 1938). E. J. Knapton, *France since Versailles* (New York, 1952) and A. Werth, *The Twilight of France, 1933–1940* (New York, 1942) deal with the last years of the Third French Republic. See also C. A. Micaud, *The French Right and Nazi Germany, 1933–1939* (Durham, 1943); and A. Maurois, *Tragedy of France* (New York, 1940). **R. Graves and A. Hodge, *The Long Week End: A Social History of Great Britain, 1918–1939* (New York, 1941) depicts the decline of England. For imperial problems there is E. A. Walker, *The British Empire* (New York, 1943).

G. M. Gathorne-Hardy, *A Short History of International Affairs, 1920–1939* (New York, 1942) is a useful introduction to interwar diplomacy. For a challenging interpretation see **E. H. Carr, *The Twenty Years' Crisis, 1919–1939* (London, 1939). F. P. Walters, *A History of the League of Nations,* 2 vols. (New York, 1952) and **F. Gilbert and G. A. Craig, eds., *The Diplomats, 1919–1938* (Princeton, 1953) are valuable for an understanding of international affairs in the twenties and thirties. The weaknesses of the democratic powers become apparent from a reading of **A. Wolfers, *Britain and France between Two Wars* (New York, 1940), while the alliance of the authoritarian states is scrutinized by E. Wiskemann, *The Rome-Berlin Axis* (New York, 1949). On the policy of appeasement the following works are of major importance: F. L. Schuman, *Europe on the Eve: The Crisis of Diplomacy, 1933–1939* (New York, 1939); *J. W. Wheeler-Bennett, *Munich: Prologue to Tragedy* (New York, 1948); and L. B. Namier, *Diplomatic Prelude, 1938–1939* (New York, 1948). For the Second World War see W. P. Hall, *Iron Out of Calvary: An Interpretative History of the Second World War* (New York, 1946); and *C. Wilmot, *The Struggle for Europe* (New York, 1952). *W. S. Churchill, *The Second World War,* 6 vols. (Boston, 1948–1953) is a vast, stirring narrative by a leading statesman. For an informative account of diplomatic developments see *J. L. Snell, *Illusion and Necessity: The Diplomacy of Global War, 1939–1945* (Boston, 1963).

CHAPTER 19

New Patterns
of Culture

The great political and economic transformation which followed
the French Revolution brought with it important cultural innovations. Even amid
the wars which overthrew benevolent despotism there were those who realized that
the outlook of their society was undergoing a fundamental change. And only ten
years after Waterloo the aging poet Johann Wolfgang von Goethe complained to
the musician Karl Zelter of the restlessness of the new age:

> Wealth and speed are the things the world admires and for which all men strive.
> Railways, express mails, steamboats, and all possible means of communication are
> what the educated world seeks. . . . Actually this is the century of clever minds, of
> practical men who grasp things easily, who are endowed with a certain facility, and
> who feel their own superiority to the multitude, but who lack talent for the most
> exalted tasks. Let us as far as possible retain the ideals in which we were raised.
> We and perhaps a few others will be the last representatives of an era which will
> not soon return.[1]

With an old man's conviction that in his youth everything had been better, the
great writer grumbled about the advent of industrialism which was changing the

---

[1] *Goethes Briefe*, 50 vols. (Weimar: H. Böhlaus, 1887–1912), XXXIX, 216. Trans. by Theodore S.
Hamerow.

familiar landscape of Europe. For regardless of the material benefits which the progress of technology promised, it was destroying the placid world of enlightened princely absolutism in which he had grown up.

1. The Scientific Image of Nature

THE CULTURE OF THE NEW CENTURY was bound to be affected by the common experiences of its society. The temper of ancient Hellas had been shaped by the tradition of the Greek city-state with its fierce municipal loyalty. In the Middle Ages the constant preoccupation with the problem of salvation, the constant admonition *memento mori* ("remember that you must die") reflected the harshness of life on this earth. The confidence in the perfectibility of man and society characteristic of the Age of Enlightenment arose out of the stable political conditions of the eighteenth century. As for the intellectual climate of opinion which prevailed after 1815, it was influenced by two major historic experiences, the growth of industrialism (which was discussed in Chapter 15) and the progress of science. One created new cultural problems and demands; the other provided a new interpretation of nature and of man. Formerly the arts and letters developed in an atmosphere of religious certainty and aristocratic patronage. Now they had to adjust to a world in which the scientist rather than the theologian answered questions about the cosmos, and in which the masses rather than the patriciate determined the canons of taste. Revolutionary changes in the production and distribution of material goods were thus accompanied by a revolutionary change in the form of culture.

THE PROGRESS OF SCIENCE

The scientific image of the universe was completed in the nineteenth and twentieth centuries. To the astronomical discoveries of the age of Copernicus and the physical discoveries of the age of Newton was added a new understanding of force and matter. In the nineteenth century Hermann von Helmholtz and James Joule analyzed the relationship between heat and energy. Michael Faraday demonstrated that the rotation of a metal core within a magnetic field produced a flow of electricity. James Maxwell and Heinrich Hertz advanced the view that a fundamental unity existed between the waves of light and electricity. The examination of the chemical composition of matter by scientists like Jöns Berzelius and Dmitri Mendeleev showed that there is a fixed number of elements out of which all substance is created, and that the atom is the smallest unit of each element possessing its basic characteristics. Toward the end of the nineteenth century a new field of research was opened when Wilhelm Röntgen, Henri Becquerel, and Pierre and Marie Curie initiated the study of radiation, the emission of rays by such rare substances as radium and actinium. Finally, in the years preceding the First World War physicists like J. J. Thomson, Ernest Rutherford, and Niels Bohr provided evidence that the atom itself is composed of electrical particles, some with positive, others with negative charges, all revolving about each other at enormous speed and held together with vast force.

While chemistry and physics were discovering the cosmic forces underlying the behavior of matter, geology was advancing new theories about the origin of the world. When in the seventeenth century Archbishop James Ussher concluded that the earth had been created in the year 4004 B.C., his system of chronology was accepted and reprinted in the margins of the Authorized Version of the English Bible. Although even in his own day there were skeptics who scoffed at his views, it was not until two hundred years later that a systematic study of the evolution of the world was undertaken. To be sure, as early as 1785 James Hutton in his *Theory of the Earth* emphasized the importance of observation in geological research, and insisted that in the investigation of such phenomena as plant fossils and rock strata "no powers are to be employed that are not natural to the globe, no action to be admitted except those of which we know the principle." Yet geology achieved recognition as a science only after the appearance in 1830–1833 of the *Principles of Geology* by Sir Charles Lyell. A work of popularization designed for the general public as well as the savant, it presented a naturalistic account of the formation of the earth. Contemporaneously scholars like Alexander von Humboldt and Karl Ritter were laying the foundation of physical geography. By the time Henry M. Stanley wrote his famous account of how in 1871 he found David Livingstone in darkest Africa, the prevalent view of the geological and geographical environment of man had become completely transformed. After 1900 even the frozen wastes of the Arctic and the Antarctic were explored and charted.

The study of the nature of life aroused even greater popular interest. Perhaps the most important advance in the field of biology was the demonstration of the cellular structure of organisms in the 1830's by Theodor Schwann and Matthias Schleiden. Out of it developed modern medical science, which in the course of a century almost doubled life expectancy in the West. The germ theory of disease owed its acceptance to the work of two brilliant bacteriologists, one a Frenchman, the other a German, united in a common dedication to the progress of knowledge. Louis Pasteur contributed to the growth of preventive medicine by analyzing the nature of microscopic organisms and demonstrating their relationship to human illness. Robert Koch proved that the same kind of microbe invariably caused the same sickness and devised a technique for preparing pure cultures of bacteria which could be used for experimental study. The first effective use of an anesthetic was made in 1846 by the Boston dentist William T. G. Morton, and about twenty years later Joseph Lister introduced the practice of antiseptic surgery. Meanwhile, the studious monk Gregor Mendel was discovering the basic laws of heredity and publishing his findings in an obscure scientific journal in Brno in Moravia. The embryologist Johann F. Meckel propounded the challenging hypothesis that the development of the organism during the period of gestation recapitulates the biological history of the species, a hypothesis which proved to be only partially true. And the outstanding botanist of the century, Wilhelm Hofmeister, conducted important investigations into the development of plant life and the process of its reproduction.

THE THEORY OF EVOLUTION

The scientific theory which made the deepest impression on the nineteenth century was the achievement of the retiring, hard-working naturalist Charles Darwin (1809–1882), who applied himself to the study of the evolutionary growth of living species. The notion that organic existence developed from the simple to the complex in the course of adaptation to a changing environment had long been familiar. Aristotle in the ancient world, Albertus Magnus in medieval times, and Francis Bacon and Gottfried Wilhelm von Leibnitz in the early modern period

CHARLES DARWIN. This portrait of the great scientist captures the quality of selfless dedication which was an important part of his character.

had suggested that the forms of life were not immutable. More recently the philosopher Immanuel Kant, the morphologist Georges de Buffon, and the zoologist Jean de Lamarck had advanced the doctrine of biological evolution. What Darwin therefore did was not to propound a new theory, but to present a new explanation of the way in which that theory operated.

From the demographic teachings of Thomas Malthus, Darwin concluded that in the animal kingdom as in human society the expansion of population invariably tended to exceed the increase in food supply, and that there was consequently a constant struggle for existence in nature by which the fit triumphed and the unfit perished. The gradual accumulation of those characteristics which enabled the survivors to adjust to changing conditions produced in time new species. In what was to become perhaps the most influential book of the nineteenth century, *On the Origin of Species by Means of Natural Selection* (1859), Darwin expressed his views in a language which must have sounded formidable even to dedicated scholars:

> If under changing conditions of life organic beings present individual differences in almost every part of their structure, and this cannot be disputed; if there be, owing to their geometrical rate of increase, a severe struggle for life at some age, season, or year, and this certainly cannot be disputed; then, considering the infinite complexity of the relations of all organic beings to each other and to their conditions of life, causing an infinite diversity in structure, constitution, and habits, to be advantageous to them, it would be a most extraordinary fact if no variations had ever occurred useful to each being's own welfare, in the same manner as so many variations have occurred useful to man. But if variations useful to any organic being ever do occur, assuredly individuals thus characterised will have the best chance of being preserved in the struggle for life; and from the strong principle of inheritance, these will tend to produce offspring similarly characterised.

Darwin himself was forced to admit that "my volume cannot be mere light reading, and some part must be dry and even rather abstruse"; while his publisher stated in confidence that he found the theory of evolution "as absurd as contemplating the fruitful union of a poker and a rabbit." Yet the work turned out to be a huge success not only among biologists but also with the general educated public. What accounted for this popularity more than its scientific validity was its implication for economic and political life. To a generation of rugged individualists it offered a justification of the ethic of competition which supposedly insured the survival of the fittest. Indeed, in the hands of an astute systematizer like Herbert Spencer the doctrine of the struggle for existence became part of a civic faith. Industrialists could invoke it to oppose governmental regulation. Chauvinists found in it a divine endorsement of aggressive diplomacy. Imperialists and racialists were delighted with what they interpreted to be a vindication of the inherent superiority of the white man over the yellow and the black. And militarists were now more convinced than ever that only through war would the manly virtues triumph over sloth and decrepitude.

For the traditional theological outlook of the Occident, however, the theory of evolution was a serious challenge. By maintaining that in the course of countless millennia man had evolved from lower forms of life, Darwin contradicted the orthodox view that he had been created in the image of God at some fixed point in time. The struggle between science and religion, or rather between Darwinians and anti-Darwinians, raged furiously for about fifty years. Proselytizing naturalists, notably Ernst Haeckel and Thomas H. Huxley, preached the evolutionary gospel with an apostolic zeal. Opposed to it were eminent clergymen, among them Bishop Samuel Wilberforce of the Church of England, who once in the course of a public debate with Huxley coolly asked his learned opponent whether he was descended from an ape on his grandmother's or his grandfather's side. The opposition's strictures, moreover, were endorsed by devout laymen like the American statesman William Jennings Bryan, widely known for his espousal of such lost causes as free silver, anti-imperialism, and fire-and-brimstone theology. Still, the weight of biological evidence was on the other side, and little by little the churches began to accept new interpretations of the origin of man. Catholicism allowed its communicants to construe the Book of Genesis figuratively, provided that they accepted the doctrine that at a specific moment in the process of gradual creation man was endowed with an immortal soul. Protestantism divided into a modernist and a fundamentalist wing, the former ready to make peace with science by an allegorical exegesis of the Bible, the latter insisting on the literal truth of every word of the Good Book.

THE NEW VIEW OF THE UNIVERSE

Even among the theological bitter-enders opposition to the theory of evolution became less rigid after the opening of the twentieth century. For scientific teachings were now increasingly regarded with the unquestioning respect which had formerly been reserved for religious doctrines. As a matter of fact, the laboratory probably inspired an even greater faith than the church, since its miracles were occurring in the present and its promises were being fulfilled in this world. Not only was it producing in ever greater abundance such necessities of life as food, clothing, and shelter, but through devices like the radio, the automobile, the motion picture, and the television set it was revolutionizing the way of life of human society. There seemed to be no end to the wonders emerging out of the test tube. The enlistment of the techniques of science in the service of economic progress was making possible a swiftly rising level of material welfare. And the scientist himself was no longer a lonely genius experimenting in the attic of his home with primitive apparatus which he had bought at his own expense. In most cases he had become a highly trained, well-paid technician, hired by some great corporation to produce a tonic for the removal of dandruff or a fuel for guided missiles. The disciplined application of talent in physics, chemistry, and biology had in effect created an assembly-line method of experimentation by which invention could be made to order.

There was a growing gap in science between practical invention and theoretical investigation. The former continued to turn out new products and new models until the appetite of the consumer had to be stimulated by the mumbo-jumbo of the advertising profession. The latter, however, presented a picture of a cold, frightening universe in whose enormous vastness the individual dwindled into nothingness. The earth on which he lived became a mere speck floating through space around a star called the sun, which was only one of billions of stars constituting a galaxy named the Milky Way, itself only one of perhaps a million or more galaxies whose distances from each other were too great to envision. The matter with which man came in contact every moment of his life was not really the familiar solid substance it appeared to be, but rather an agglomeration of countless tiny particles known as electrons, protons, and neutrons. These in turn were nothing more than blobs of congealed energy which under certain conditions could assume a completely incorporeal form. Even the laws of atomic physics proved to be only statements of statistical probability. Finally, in 1905 Albert Einstein advanced the bewildering theory that such fundamental categories as time, space, and mass were merely relative, so that a voyager in a rocket moving away from the solar system at a very high velocity would never grow old, while the weight of an athlete running at a sufficiently great speed would reach a ton.

The man in the street was clearly incapable of understanding the evidence supporting this image of the cosmos. For that matter, the average scientist in industry looking for some new detergent in which the housewife could wash dishes without roughening her hands was not always familiar with the findings of theoretical investigation. Indirectly, however, the world became conscious of the wild forces ruling its destiny and sensed their implication for human existence. Medieval man, sunk in poverty and ignorance, could find a source of strength in the knowledge that he was the greatest achievement of creation. God and Satan were locked in eternal combat for the possession of his soul. He mattered. But there was no such comforting certainty for man in the twentieth century. He had to contemplate a universe which was neither friendly nor hostile but simply indifferent, a universe in which his own position had become insignificant. He had to wrestle with the doubts aroused by science, which the empiricist thinker Bertrand Russell described:

> That man is the product of causes which had no prevision of the end they were achieving; that his origin, his growth, his hopes and fears, his loves and his beliefs, are but the outcome of accidental collations of atoms; that no fire, no heroism, no intensity of thought and feeling can preserve an individual life beyond the grave;

that all the labours of all the ages, all the devotion, all the inspiration, all the noon-day brightness of human genius are destined to extinction in the vast death of the solar system, and that the whole temple of man's achievement must inevitably be buried beneath the debris of a universe in ruins—all these things, if not quite be-yond dispute, are yet so nearly certain that no philosophy which rejects them can hope to stand.[2]

2. The Scientific Image of Society

THE EFFECTIVE APPLICATION of the scientific method to natural phenomena sug-gested its value for a study of social institutions. Why could not the accumulation and classification of data lead to as precise an understanding of the community as of the universe? The achievements of the laboratory technique in the manipulation of inanimate matter seemed to promise equally impressive results in the reorganiza-tion of human society. Before long there arose a widespread demand for the crea-tion of a science of man. Its most influential spokesman was the philosopher Auguste Comte (1798–1857), who had received his education in a polytechnical institute in Paris and had then become a teacher of mathematics. Yet the task which was closest to his heart was the improvement of humanity. A true son of the nine-teenth century, he shared its passion for philanthropic reform and its respect for scientific investigation. Out of the basic cultural impulses of his age he formed a new philosophy of civilization known as positivism.

POSITIVISM

Essentially Comte believed that in the course of its development every science, including the science of man, had to pass through three distinct cultural levels. In the first, which he described as theological, natural events were explained in terms of the unpredictable actions of mythical gods and spirits. Then came the meta-physical state, when the questions posed by human experience were analyzed in abstract theories divorced from constructive action. Finally thought entered the scientific or positivistic phase, in which observation and experimentation led to the discovery of fundamental laws. The world now stood on the threshold of the third stage. But while physicists, chemists, and biologists were solving the riddles of nature, the systematic study of civic problems was lagging behind. It was this deficiency which the founder of positivism proposed to make good:

---

[2] Bertrand Russell, "A Free Man's Worship," *Mysticism and Logic* (London: George Allen & Unwin, Ltd., 1936), p. 44.

Though involved with the physiological, Social phenomena demand a distinct classi-fication, both on account of their importance and of their difficulty. They are the most individual, the most complicated, the most dependent on all others; and there-fore they must be the latest,—even if they had no special obstacle to encounter. This branch of science has not hitherto entered into the domain of Positive philosophy. Theological and metaphysical methods, exploded in other departments, are as yet exclusively applied, both in the way of inquiry and discussion, in all treatment of Social subjects, though the best minds are heartily weary of eternal disputes about divine right and the sovereignty of the people. This is the great, while it is evi-dently the only gap which has to be filled, to constitute, solid and entire, the Posi-tive philosophy. Now that the human mind has grasped celestial and terrestrial physics,—mechanical and chemical; organic physics, both vegetable and animal,—there remains one science, to fill up the series of observation,—Social physics.[3]

For Comte himself positivism offered a blueprint of the good society. Tem-poral power would be concentrated in the hands of industrialists, bankers, and landlords, while a priesthood composed of social scientists rather than orthodox clergymen was to minister to the spiritual needs of mankind. He even worked out in detail a new religious cult complete with theologians, saints, sacraments, and sacred writings, a kind of "Catholicism without Christianity." While few were ready to embrace this manufactured faith, the summons to study society with the same dispassionate precision as nature found a sympathetic hearing in scholarly circles.

THE SOCIAL SCIENCES

Positivism contributed directly to the development of the social sciences. These represented an attempt to examine the structure of society by means of statistical and comparative techniques. For more than two thousand years efforts to analyze civic institutions had been made in such works as Plato's *Republic*, Aristotle's *Politics*, Machiavelli's *Prince*, Jean Bodin's *Republic*, and Hugo Grotius' *Law of War and Peace*. What distinguished the new school was its methodology borrowed almost bodily from the natural sciences. Behind it stood the assumption that the universe of matter and the community of man were essentially similar, so that the means employed to achieve an understanding of one could be applied with minor modifications to the other in order to discover constant laws of development.

Out of positivistic doctrines there arose late in the nineteenth century the discipline known as sociology, concerned with an analysis of the forces governing human society through the examination of social data. Frédéric Le Play was the author of more than thirty monographs dealing with the way of life of the working

---

[3] *The Positive Philosophy of Auguste Comte*, trans. by Harriet Martineau, 2 vols. (London: Kegan Paul, Trench, Trübner & Co., 1893), I, 6.

class of Europe; Charles Booth undertook a voluminous study of the *Life and Labour of the People in London* (1903); and Herbert Spencer in England, Paul von Lilienfeld in Russia, Albert Schäffle in Germany, and Ludwig Gumplowicz in Poland applied biology and especially the theory of evolution to the process of civilization. At the same time anthropology was initiating the comparative study of cultures in an attempt to define the influence of heredity and environment on community institutions. In 1871 Edward Burnett Tylor, the first professor to teach the new subject at Oxford University, published his *Primitive Culture: Researches into the Development of Mythology, Philosophy, Language, Art, and Custom*, which for more than a generation remained the standard textbook in the field. Throughout the nineteenth century scholars like Jacques Boucher de Perthes, Sir John Lubbock, Lewis H. Morgan, and William Graham Sumner were gathering and classifying primitive artifacts or conducting investigations into the the development of human beliefs. In economics the champions of laissez faire had for a century been preaching the primacy of natural law. But by the turn of the century their theories, which were basically a compound of logic and metaphysics, had begun to retreat before the empirical method of Alfred Marshall, the evolutionary approach of Gustav von Schmoller, and the statistical technique of William Stanley Jevons, who went so far as to maintain that a mathematical connection could be demonstrated between sunspots and business depressions. As for the traditional study of political philosophy, it came to be replaced by the new political science, whose students produced analytical accounts of national life like James Bryce's *American Commonwealth* (1888) or systematic examinations of corporate associations like Otto von Gierke's *Natural Law and the Theory of Society* (1913).

Under the influence of positivism the traditional ties between the study of history on the one hand and literature, philosophy, and theology on the other began to weaken. As early as 1824 Leopold von Ranke, perhaps the greatest of modern historians, expressed the credo of a new historiography in the preface to his *Histories of the Romance and Teutonic Peoples:* "History has had assigned to it the task of judging the past, of instructing the present for the benefit of the ages to come. To such lofty functions this work does not aspire. Its aim is merely to show what actually occurred." Ranke himself was too discriminating a scholar not to perceive the fundamental difference between the historical and the natural disciplines. But after the middle of the nineteenth century historians began to create a science of history. They examined source materials, studied archaeological remains, gathered statistical data, weighed conflicting evidence, and published their findings in detailed monographic works buttressed by voluminous footnotes and vast bibliographies which only the specialist could appreciate. The result, they believed, was pure truth free from the personal prejudices and social predispositions which had marred scholarship in the past. Their attitude was that of the eminent medievalist,

N. D. Fustel de Coulanges, who told an enthusiastic audience during one of his lectures: "Do not applaud me. It is not I that speak to you but history that speaks by my mouth." The employment of rigorous standards of judgment did, as a matter of fact, destroy many of the superstitions which earlier ages had accepted without question. Yet it also helped create a myth of its own, the myth that history can be apprehended directly by dispassionate study rather than indirectly through the mind of the historian. The will-o'-the-wisp of total objectivity could not transform the analysis of the past into an exact science, but it was to a large degree responsible for the growing gulf between the intelligent reading public and professional learning.

Even deeper was the effect of scientific progress on theology. Not only did scholarly hypotheses like the theory of evolution challenge ecclesiastical doctrines, but the technique of empirical investigation could be turned against religion itself by means of the so-called higher criticism. The comparative study of supernatural beliefs tended to encourage a theological relativism. James Frazer in his study of primitive superstitions and ceremonies entitled *The Golden Bough* (1890) shocked the devout by boldly asserting: "It is now easy to understand why a savage should desire to partake of the flesh of an animal or man whom he regards as divine. By eating the body of the god he shares in the god's attributes and powers. And when the god is a corn-god, the corn is his proper body; when he is a wine-god, the juice of the grape is his blood; and so, by eating the bread and drinking the wine, the worshipper partakes of the real body and blood of his god." David Friedrich Strauss subjected the Bible to a critical analysis, concluding that an account is self-contradictory "when one relation of events says what the other denies, as when one narrative makes Jesus appear definitely only after the arrest of the Baptist in Galilee, but the other, after Jesus had already worked for some time in Galilee as well as in Judea, remarks that John has not yet been thrown into prison." Ernest Renan who had at one time studied for the priesthood lost his professorship at the Collège de France because his *Life of Jesus* (1863) portrayed the founder of Christianity as a saintly but human figure. Such attacks were bound to weaken the fabric of theology. A sensitive poet like Matthew Arnold, lonely in a world suddenly deprived of religious certitude, could only mourn the loss of his belief (*Dover Beach*, 1867):

> The Sea of Faith
> Was once, too, at the full, and round earth's shore
> Lay like the folds of a bright girdle furl'd.
> But now I only hear
> Its melancholy, long, withdrawing roar,
> Retreating, to the breath
> Of the night-wind, down the vast edges drear
> And naked shingles of the world.

PSYCHOLOGY AND PSYCHOANALYSIS

The methodology of science was applied to man himself. Within twenty years after the enunciation of the evolutionary hypothesis Wilhelm Wundt was initiating the experimental study of the mind in a laboratory in Leipzig and publishing his pioneer work, *The Principles of Physiological Psychology* (1873–1874). Not long thereafter Ivan Pavlov began the observation of the behavior of dogs which enabled him to stimulate in his subjects conditioned reflexes, that is, forms of physical reaction independent of the reflective will. The investigation of such automatic physiological activities contributed late in the century to the rise of the school of behaviorism led by John B. Watson, who argued that mental processes can be understood solely in terms of the structure and activity of the body. On the other hand, members of the Gestalt school like Wolfgang Köhler and Kurt Koffka maintained that living organisms respond primarily not to simple physical stimuli but to total patterns of experience.

The most important advance toward an understanding of the mind, however, was made by the Viennese physician Sigmund Freud (1856–1939). In the last years of the nineteenth century he developed a technique known as psychoanalysis for dealing with emotional disturbances. From his clinical observations he gradu-

SIGMUND FREUD. The founder of psychoanalysis is shown here in the spring of 1938, a few months before he was forced to seek refuge from Nazi bigotry in England.

ally arrived at a radically novel explanation of the mechanism of human behavior. At the heart of his theory was the view that the conduct of the individual is vitally affected by irrational impulses of which he is unaware because they are to a large extent subconscious. The repression of these instinctive drives, if severe enough, could lead to a psychological breakdown. More commonly it resulted in such maladjustments as phobias, compulsions, and complexes. In any case the basic problem of the morbid personality was the conflict between conscience and desire, a conflict which the trained diagnostician could help resolve:

> We come to the conclusion, from working with hysterical patients and other neurotics, that they have not fully succeeded in repressing the idea to which the incompatible wish is attached. They have, indeed, driven it out of consciousness and out of memory, and apparently saved themselves a great amount of psychic pain, *but in the unconscious the suppressed wish still exists*, only waiting for its chance to become active, and finally succeeds in sending into consciousness, instead of the repressed idea, a disguised and unrecognizable surrogate-creation . . . to which the same painful sensations associate themselves that the patient thought he was rid of through his repression. This surrogate of the suppressed idea—the symptom—is secure against further attacks from the defenses of the ego, and instead of a short conflict there originates now a permanent suffering. We can observe in the symptom, besides the tokens of its disguise, a remnant of traceable similarity with the originally repressed idea; the way in which the surrogate is built up can be discovered during the psychoanalytic treatment of the patient, and for his cure the symptom must be traced back over the same route to the repressed idea. If this repressed material is once more made part of the conscious mental functions—a process which supposes the overcoming of considerable resistance—the psychic conflict which then arises, the same which the patient wished to avoid, is made capable of a happier termination, under the guidance of the physician, than is offered by repression.[4]

The image of man presented by psychoanalysis was essentially a secularized version of the view of orthodox Christianity. Both saw in the human spirit dark passions threatening to drown out the voice of reason. Both saw in intelligence only a thin veneer disguising "the submarine jungle of the half-conscious" with its wild, mysterious yearnings. For Freud as for Calvin, the curse of original sin and the total depravity of the soul were terrible realities. The sense of guilt found by scientific study to be at the root of so many mental disorders had been familiar to religion for two thousand years. The medical description of amoral drives at grips with the sense of propriety suggested the theological account of the struggle between will and intellect, instinct and morality. And was there really a great deal of difference between the psychoanalyst's couch and the priest's confessional?

As a therapeutic technique in the treatment of emotional illness psychoanalysis proved valuable. Although many of the theories advanced by its founder

---

[4] Sigmund Freud, "The Origin and Development of Psychoanalysis," *American Journal of Psychology*, XXI (1910), 195–196.

were eventually rejected even by his own disciples, in particular Carl C. Jung (1875–1961) and Alfred Adler (1870–1937), psychoanalysis has remained fundamental for an understanding of the disordered personality. Yet by a curious irony the rational investigation of the mind proved only its irrationality. Gone was the hope that the progress of knowledge would subdue passion and create a brave new world of universal understanding. For two hundred years it had inspired great /achievements in science, until science revealed that the road to truth eventually led back to the starting point. With Freud the circle was completed. In the spiritual universe of phobias and neuroses which the earnest young doctor uncovered St. Augustine and Martin Luther would have felt perfectly at home.

CULTURAL PESSIMISM

Similarly the psychological effect of the scientific study of society was not certainty but doubt. The questioning of accepted beliefs weakened the moral axioms which had provided the community with its scale of values. The sexual taboos recognized in Europe as universally valid were found to be ignored with impunity in Samoa. The competitive drive which the rugged individualism of America had assumed to be inherent in mankind could not be discovered among the Pueblo Indians. Standards of conduct thus lost their traditional meaning, and the result of an examination of established social norms without reference to a subjective system of truth was the rise of emotional insecurity.

Perhaps that was why so many of the attempts to synthesize the mass of information which scholarship had adduced concerning culture were conceived in a spirit of pessimism. During the French Revolution the philosopher Condorcet, outlawed and in hiding, could rise above his personal misfortune to announce in *The Progress of the Human Mind* (1793) that "nature has placed no bounds on the perfecting of the human faculties." For the twentieth century such a faith in the capacity of man for self-improvement became impossible. In Italy Vilfredo Pareto was emphasizing the irrational sources of political conduct in *The Mind and Society* (1916). In Germany Oswald Spengler's *Decline of the West* (1918–1922) was one long jeremiad about the imminent disintegration of the civilization of the Occident. In England Arnold Toynbee thought he saw a chance of salvation for modern society in a new dedication to religious truth, although his monumental *Study of History* (1934–1954) did not sound very hopeful about the likelihood of such a conversion. Even in America, the most prosperous of nations, the sociologist David Riesman, writing during and after the Second World War, was warning his countrymen that their hunger for social approbation had largely displaced the inner strength which their ancestors had possessed. And the world in the meantime anxiously continued to search for some new statement of values which could give an ethical meaning to the social truths discovered by the scientific method.

3. *Philosophic Thought*

FOR ABOUT FIFTY YEARS after his death in 1804 Immanuel Kant dominated philosophic thought in the West. The bookish little professor from provincial Königsberg led a successful revolution against the empiricism which had ruled metaphysics for more than a century. To the argument that only physical experience could provide the raw material of thought he replied by drawing a sharp distinction between two categories of knowledge. He was prepared to render unto Caesar the things which are Caesar's by conceding that scientific investigation was an effective instrument for the establishment of truth in the realm of natural phenomena. But he also insisted on the existence of another realm, the realm of feelings, judgments, and values, in which an instinctive understanding or "practical reason" supported the validity of religious and ethical principles.

IDEALISM

Essentially idealism, as Kant called his system of philosophy, sought to create a universe of spiritual meaning lying beyond the reach of the critical weapons which the empiricists had used with devastating effect against traditional moral and theological assumptions. It translated into a cardinal doctrine the sentiment expressed by Blaise Pascal over a hundred years before: "The heart has its reasons, which reason knows nothing of." Thereby it helped release a torrent of intuitive, even mystical speculation in all branches of thought. And hence to his admirers the author of the *Critique of Pure Reason* (1781) remained "the presiding genius of the spiritual life," while his critics went on arguing that "he was a mere misfortune."

There could be no gainsaying, however, that in the early years of the nineteenth century his authority was enormous. All the powers of faith and imagination which had been held in check by the rigidity of empiricism were suddenly liberated in a great outpouring of idealistic thought. Johann Gottlieb Fichte depicted life as an endless struggle for perfection in which the individual rose to new heights of moral strength by overcoming the forces of evil. F. W. J. von Schelling saw man and nature united in a common process of growth from lower to higher forms, from the unconscious to the conscious, from the amoral to the moral. Friedrich von Schlegel maintained that the ultimate aim of philosophy must be to perfect the inward life of the individual by the development within his mind of a sense of the divine. Nor were the Germans the only ones to rebel against the mechanical formulas of the Age of Enlightenment, although central Europe did gain a deserved reputation as the classic land of metaphysical speculation. In England such eminent writers as Samuel Taylor Coleridge and Thomas Carlyle fell under the spell of the new idealism. In France political writers like Louis de Bonald and Benjamin Constant questioned the doctrines of rationalism. Even on the other side of the Atlantic in far-off New England the transcendentalists—among them Ralph Waldo Emerson and Henry David Thoreau—preached that "within man is the soul of the whole; the wise silence; the universal beauty, to which every part and particle is equally related; the eternal one."

Idealism achieved its most lasting influence through the work of G. W. F. Hegel (1770–1831). Before the crowds of students who flocked to his lectures at the University of Berlin the brilliant philosopher expounded his analysis of political and social development in the light of an intuitive metaphysic. History to him was not a sum of discrete chance events but the concrete expression of a logical process originating in the divine will. It could be comprehended in terms of opposing spiritual principles whose dialectical progression would continue until the end of time. Meanwhile it was evolving the ideals of justice, freedom, and virtue. As for the state, it was the institution which made possible and gave form to the forces of morality. Indeed, it was itself the embodiment of ethical values through which the individual could achieve union with the realm of eternal truth: "The State is the Divine Idea as it exists on earth. . . . It is the Idea of Spirit in the external manifestation of human will and its Freedom."

The bureaucracy of Prussia, delighted to learn that it was only one step removed from the angels, bestowed honors on the eminent scholar who defended its authority with such fervor. Yet it would be a mistake to consider Hegel simply a defender of the status quo. His emphasis on the rational foundation of existing political institutions was pleasing to a conservative ruler like Frederick William III. But his view that the essential characteristic of the historical process was change had progressive connotations. In the hands of Karl Marx it was even turned into a philosophic defense of revolutionary violence. In the final analysis, Hegel's thought was neither reactionary nor radical but authoritarian. The young men who hung on every word which the master uttered in the classroom did not understand the full meaning of what they were hearing. Only a hundred years later did the fascists reveal the implications of his doctrine that the heroic leader must bend the masses to his will:

> World-historical men—the heroes of an epoch—must, therefore, be recognised as its clear-sighted ones; their deeds, their words are the best of that time. Great men have formed purposes to satisfy themselves, not others. Whatever prudent designs and counsels they might have learned from others, would be the more limited and inconsistent features in their career; for it was they who best understood affairs; from whom others learned, and approved, or at least acquiesced in—their policy. For that Spirit which had taken this fresh step in history is the inmost soul of all individuals; but in a state of unconsciousness which the great men in question aroused. Their fellows, therefore, follow these soul-leaders; for they feel the irresistible power of their own inner spirit thus embodied.[5]

---

[5] G. W. F. Hegel, *Lectures on the Philosophy of History*, trans. by J. Sibree (London: George Bell, 1890), p. 32.

THE CRISIS IN PHILOSOPHY

Hegel was the last of the philosophic giants like Plato or St. Thomas Aquinas or Descartes who attempted to create a vast, all-embracing system of thought. Those who came after him were less daring because they were less confident. Bewildered by the complexity of the image of the universe which science was forming, they tended more and more to exalt emotion over reason, instinct over intellect. Since in the realm of nature they encountered only a cold immensity, their interest turned inward to the contemplation of their own consciousness. While idealism still reigned supreme in the universities, Arthur Schopenhauer (1788–1860) was propounding the gloomy doctrine that man was the victim of an irrational will which drove him to incur suffering in a vain search for happiness. In his delusion he could not perceive that his lot on earth was simply "a striving without rest and without respite, a willing and a striving that may well be compared to an unquenchable thirst."

Before the century was over, Friedrich Nietzsche (1844–1900) had launched his attack on conventional ethics in such works as *Beyond Good and Evil* and *Thus Spoke Zarathustra,* strange mélanges of mystical vision and poetic insight with a pinch or two of philosophy. The sickly erudite who spent the last years of his life in a state of complete mental collapse prophesied the destruction of the accepted standard of values which protects the weak against the strong and anticipated the reorganization of society by a new race of ruthless supermen free from the shackles of a slave morality: "What is good?—Whatever augments the feeling of power, the will to power, power itself, in man. What is evil?—Whatever springs from weakness. What is happiness?—The feeling that power *increases*—that resistance is overcome. Not contentment, but more power; *not* peace at any price, but war; not virtue, but efficiency. . . . The weak and the botched shall perish: first principle of *our* charity. And one should help them to it. What is more harmful than any vice?—Practical sympathy for the botched and the weak—Christianity."[6]

That the retreat from rationalism in philosophy did not necessarily lead to a pessimistic outlook was demonstrated by Henri Bergson, whose lectures at the Collège de France cast a spell over an entire generation of French students at the beginning of the twentieth century. His view that the *élan vital,* the instinctive life urge implanted in the human subconscious, dominated the activity of man was not far removed from Schopenhauer's assertion of the primacy of will over reason. He was even ready to subordinate scientific knowledge to intuitive truth, because "we cannot sacrifice experience to the requirements of any system." Yet he found hope in his belief in "creative evolution," a mysterious elemental force carrying mankind onward to more perfect forms of existence. It was a poetic rather than a philosophic concept, and the language in which he described it had an appropri-

---

ately lyrical quality: "The animal takes its stand on the plant, man bestrides ani-
mality and the whole of humanity, in space and in time, is one immense army gal-
loping beside and before and behind each of us in an overwhelming charge able
to beat down every resistance, and clear the most formidable obstacles, perhaps
even death."

At the same time a group of American thinkers, among them Charles S.
Peirce, William James, and John Dewey, were elaborating in a more prosaic mood
the main tenets of pragmatism or instrumentalism. Making a virtue of necessity,
they rejected as impracticable the search for absolute value. For them the true was
not some eternal, immutable essence enthroned in the empyrean. It was variable;
it was temporary; it was relevant to a practical human situation. Hence, the test of
an idea or an institution was the effect which it produced in actual experience, in
other words, whether it worked. The mind had to create and shape its own truth,
because "to bid the man's subjective interests be passive till truth express itself from
out the environment, is to bid the sculptor's chisel be passive till the statue express
itself from out the stone."

Still, pragmatism was a faith for the bold. What most men wanted from philosophy was what philosophy had traditionally given them, a sense of certainty. In
the world of the twentieth century, however, it could no longer satisfy their need.
The fault was not entirely the philosophers', who were as active and contentious as
ever, perhaps more so. Among them were Neo-Aristotelians and Neo-Kantians,
Platonists and Thomists, Phenomenologists and Fictionists, mystical idealists and
logical positivists. But the clearest symptom of the philosophic distemper was the
vogue of existentialism, a doctrine of despair which began to flourish after the
Second World War. Assuming that the primary experience of life was frustration
in an alien environment, it preached a standard of conduct in accordance with an
inner sense of right. Through it man could at least face the hostile universe proudly,
although in the struggle against destiny he was doomed to defeat. There was a
good deal of pretentiousness about the youths who gathered in the arty Parisian
cafés on the left bank of the Seine, drank cognac, grew beards, and played at being
existentialists. Yet even their attitudinizing was a manifestation of the crisis of
conscience through which their age was passing.

4. Religion

THE DILEMMA OF PHILOSOPHY was bound to have a direct effect on theology. The
great religions of the East—Hinduism, Islam, and Buddhism—had always exalted
faith over reason. For them, therefore, the problem of understanding a changing
universe in terms of a traditional belief was not critical. Besides, the masses of

23. SUNRISE WITH SEA MONSTER. The work of the Englishman Joseph Mallord William Turner is representative of the new concern with the natural world which was one of the effects of the romantic revolution. Many of Turner's paintings, like this fairly late one in oil, were studies in the effects of light and water on color, and in many ways Turner's interests coincide with those of the impressionists half a century later.

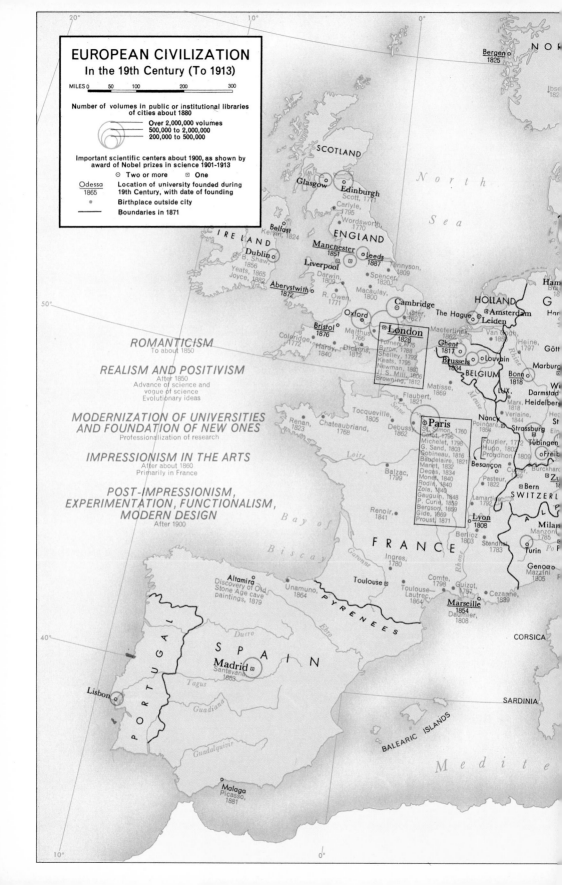

Sibelius,
1865

Helsinki
1828

St. Petersburg

Bjornson,
1832

Upsala ○

Stravinsky,
1882

Rimsky Korsakov,
1844

Gorki
1868

□ Stockholm
1878
Strindberg,
1849

Mussorgsky,
1835

Bakunin,
1814

Dorpat
1802

Moscow ○
Pushkin, 1799   1821
Dostoievsky,
Kropotkin, 1842

□ Copenhagen
Kierkegaard,
1813

Niemen

Mickiewicz,
1798

R U S S I A

Tolstoy,
1828

Lenin,
1870
(200 miles
east)

Danzig ○
Schopenhauer,
1788

Turgeniev,
1818

Tchaikovsky,
1840
(In the Urals)

M A N Y

Berlin
1809

Tieck,
1773

Fichte, 1762,

Warsaw ○
Chopin, 1810
Mme. Curie,
1867

Freytag,

Kharkov
1804

Halle □
Leipzig
Wagner,
1813

Breslau ○

Hauptmann,
1862

Gogol,
1809

Dvorak,
1841

Dresden ○

Cracow ○

Dnieper

Prague ○

Freud,
1856

Dniester

A U S T R I A

C A R P A T H I A N S

Dniester

Jassy
1860

Odessa
1865

nube

Vienna
Schubert, 1797
J. Strauss, 1825

Budapest ○

Cluj
1872

B l a c k

H U N G A R Y

R U M A N I A

S e a

ice ○

Belgrade
1863

ologna

Rossini,
1792

Leopardi,
1798

S E R B I A

Danube

Sofia
1888

d'Annunzio,
1863

A d r i a t i c

O T T O M A N

Croce,
1896

Constantinople
Robert College
(American)
1863

ome

S e a

—40°

Naples ○

rrhenian

I o n i a n

Excavations at
Troy, 1871 ff.

E M P I R E

S e a

S e a

G R E E C E

Athens
1837
Schools of Classical
Archeology:
French, 1846
German, 1874
American, 1881
British, 1886
Italian, 1910

Palermo ○

S I C I L Y

S e a

CRETE

20°

30°

Copyright by Rand McNally & Company, Made in U.S.A.

24. THE LUNCHEON OF THE BOATING PARTY. This painting by Pierre Auguste Renoir exhibits clearly the interest in the visual effects of color and of light central to impressionism, but perhaps no other impressionist delighted in glowing colors and dazzling vivacity as much as did Renoir.

25. HOUSE ON THE RIVER. The landscapes of Paul Cézanne, in which objects are beginning to be reduced to their essential geometric forms, mark a transition in art from impressionism to twentieth-century expressionism.

ICELAND
Reykjavik

30°   10°   0°   10°   20°   Arctic

THE FAEROES

SHETLAND
ISLANDS

Tornio

HEBRIDES   ORKNEY
IS.

Bergen   N   Vaasa
(Vasa)

Stavanger   O   Helsingfors
ALAND IS.   (Helsinki)

Aberdeen   Oslo   S   Uppsala
Glasgow   SCOTLAND   Edinburgh   W   Stockholm   EST

GREAT   North   Uppsala   GOTLAND   LAT
Belfast   Aalborg   Göteborg   E   Annexed by

IRISH FREE   Sea   DENMARK   Hälsingborg   D   OLAND   Memel   LITHUAN
Dublin   STATE   Liverpool   Leeds   Hull   Occupied by   Copenhagen   E   Kovno   Annexed
Cork   Manchester   Germany 1940   N   BORNHOLM   Königsberg   (Kaunas)   USSR 19
BRITAIN   Sheffield   HELGOLAND   Aalborg   Kiel   Lübeck   MEMELAND   EAST   V
Cardiff   Oxford   WALES   THE NETHERLANDS   Hamburg   Stettin   Danzig   PRUSSIA   Gre
Bristol   Birmingham   Bremen   Hanover   Tannenberg   Nazi-Soviet Pact Annexed
Plymouth   Portsmouth   ENGLAND   Amsterdam   Magdeburg   Posen   by Germany 1939   Brest
London   Rotterdam   GERMANY   Berlin   WARSAW   POLA   Litovsk
CHANNEL   Dover   BEL.   Essen   Cologne   Potsdam   Dresden   Breslau   SILESIA   Lublin
IS.   Havre   Dunkirk   Brussels   LUX.   Frankfurt   Leipzig   Cracow
Brest   Amiens   Lille   LORRAINE   Weimar   Cassel   Prague   To Pol. 1938
St. Nazaire   Caen   Reims   Verdun   SAAR   Mainz   Nuremberg   CZECHOSLOVAKIA   Przemysl
Rennes   FRANCE   Paris   Versailles   Fontainebleau   Plebiscite   Mannheim   BAVARIA   To Ger. at Munich 1938   Tesin
Nantes   Orleans   Occupied by   1935   Strassburg   Stuttgart   Pilsen   Curzon
Limoges   Lyon   Germany 1940   ALSACE   Basle   Munich   Vienna   Bratislava   Tarno
La Rochelle   Dijon   Berne   Zürich   LIECH.   AUSTRIA   (Pressburg)   RUTHENIA
Bordeaux   Loire   SWITZERLAND   Innsbruck   Anschluss 1938   Košice
Corunna   VICHY FRANCE   Geneva   ALPS   Graz   HUNGARY   Annexed by
Oporto   Bayonne   1940   Grenoble   TRENTINO   Ljubljana   Budapest   Oradea   Hungary
Coimbra   Burgos   PYRENEES   Montpellier   Milan   Verona   Zagreb   Mohacs   1940   TRANSYLVAN
Santander   Toulouse   Avignon   Turin   Venice   Trieste   CROATIA   Temisoara   RUM
Valladolid   ANDORRA   Marseille   Nice   Parma   Genoa   Fiume   YUGOSLAVIA   Sibiu
Lisbon   Saragossa   Toulon   San Remo   Bologna   Ravenna   BOSNIA   Belgrade   WALL
Madrid   Barcelona   SAN   Florence   Ancona   Zara   Sarajevo   SERBIA   Bucha
PORTUGAL   SPAIN   Toledo   BALERIC ISLANDS   MARINO   Split   DALMATIA   Nish   Sistove
Cordoba   (To Spain)   MINORCA   Ajaccio   CORSICA   Rome   LAGOSTA   MONTE-   Novi   BUL
Cadiz   Seville   Granada   Valencia   (To France)   (To Italy)Dubrovnik   NEGRO   Pazar   Sofia
Tangier   Gibraltar   Almeria   MAJORCA   ITALY   Antivari   (Ragusa)   ALBANIA   Philippopolis
(To Great Britain)   Cartagena   SARDINIA   Naples   Durazzo   Adrie
SPANISH AREA   (To Italy)   Bari   Tirana   MACEDONIA   Dede-A
Robat   Cagliari   Tyrrhenian Sea   Taranto   Brindisi   Kavala
MOROCCO   Oran   Algiers   Palermo   Messina   Valona   CORFU   Salonika
ATLAS   MOUNTAINS   Tunis   SICILY   Syracuse   CEPHALLENIA   IONIAN ISLANDS   GREECE   LES
MALTA   Mediterranean   Yannina   Messolongi   Athe
(Br.)   Ionian Sea   Patras   Sparta
Tripoli   CRETE
ALGERIA   A   TRIPOLITANIA   Bengazi   CYRENAICA
To France   To Italy   Gulf of   To Italy
F   Sidra   C
LIBYA   A

Copyright by Rand McNally & Company, Made in U.S.A.

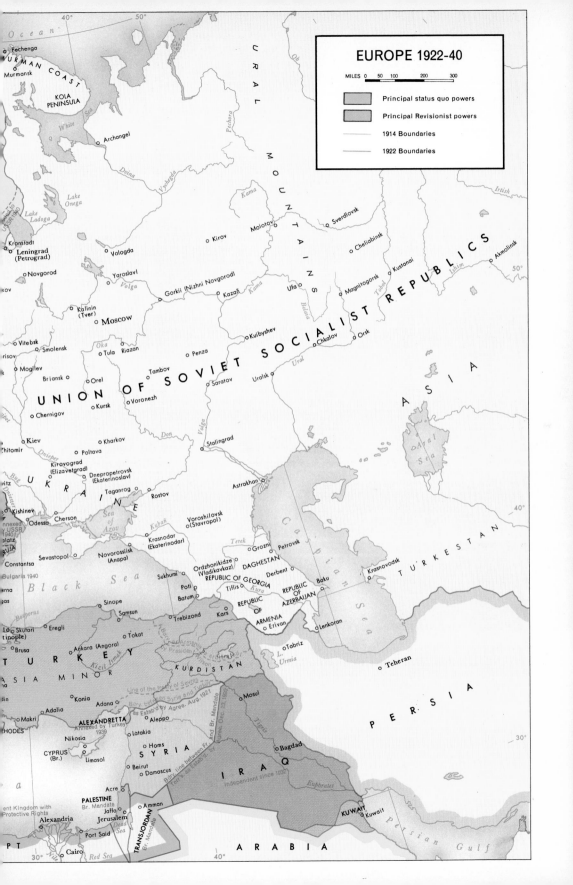

MILES 0 50 100   200   300

Principal status quo powers

Principal Revisionist powers

1914 Boundaries

1922 Boundaries

Ocean

Pechenga

MURMAN COAST
Murmansk

KOLA
PENINSULA

White
Sea

Archangel

Lake
Onega

Lake
Ladoga

Kronstadt
Leningrad
(Petrograd)

Novgorod

Vologda

Yaroslavl

kov

Vitebsk
Smolensk

Kalinin
(Tver)
Moscow

Oka

Gorkii (Nizhni Novgorod)

Kirov

Molotov

Sverdlovsk

Cheliabinsk

Kustanai

Akmolinsk

ASIA

Magnitogorsk

Ufa

Kazañ

Kama

Kama

Pechora

Dvina

Vychegda

MOUNTAINS

URAL

Volga

Lishim

Tobol

Irtish

U N I O N   O F   S O V I E T   S O C I A L I S T   R E P U B L I C S

risov

Mogilev

Briansk

Orel

Tula Riazan

Tambov

Penza

Kuibyshev

Chkalov
Orsk

Uralsk

Ural

Chernigov

Kursk

Voronezh

Saratov

Kiev

Poltava

Kharkov

Stalingrad

hitomir

Kiravograd
(Elizavetgrad)

Dnepropetrovsk
(Ekaterinoslavl)

Dnieper

Don

Volga

Astrakhan

Aral
Sea

itz

Kishinev

Odessa

Cherson

Taganrog

Rostov

UKRAINE

Bug

Sea
of
Azov

Kubañ

Voroshilovsk
(Stavropol)

nnexed
USSR
1940

alatz

Sevastopol

Novorossiisk
(Anapa)

Krasnodar
(Ekaterinodar)

Terek

Grozni

Petrovsk

DAGHESTAN

Derbent

Krasnovodsk

TURKESTAN

ARIA

Bulgaria 1940

Constantsa

Black   Sea

Sukhumi

Ordzhonikidze
(Vladikavkaz)

REPUBLIC OF GEORGIA

Caspian Sea

Baku

REPUBLIC
OF
AZERBAIJAN

arna

gas

Sinope

Poti

Batum

Tiflis

Kura

Lenkoran

Bosporus

Skutari

tinople)

Log

Eregli

Samsun

Trebizond

Kars

REPUBLIC
OF
ARMENIA

Erivan

L. Tabriz

Urmia

Teheran

PERSIA

TURKEY

Brusa

Ankara (Angora)

Tokat

Kizil Irmak

KURDISTAN

Armenia
Pres. Presiden

Archangel

ASIA   MINOR

din

Konia

Adana

Line of the Treaty of Sèvres

Mosul

RHODES

Adalia

Makri

ALEXANDRETTA
Annexed by Turkey
1939

Aleppo

Bdry. between Syria and Turkey
as Estab'd by Agree. Aug. 1921

Bdry. and Br. Mandate

Tigris

Bagdad

IRAQ

Independent since 1932

Euphrates

Nikosia

Latakia

CYPRUS
(Br.)

Limasol

SYRIA

Homs

Beirut

Damascus

Bdry. line between Fr.
and Br. as Estab'd by
Agree. Dec. 23, 1920

Acre

PALESTINE
Br. Mandate

Jaffa

Jerusalem

TRANSJORDAN
Br. Mandate

Amman

Dead
Sea

KUWAIT

Kuwait

Persian   Gulf

ent Kingdom with
Protective Rights

Alexandria

Port Said

a

PT

Cairo

Nile

Red Sea

A R A B I A

26. VIEW OF THE INDIAN SUBCONTINENT AND CEYLON. The exciting achievements of modern science and technology and man's increasing power over his universe are suggested by this photograph of India and Ceylon taken from a Gemini flight in 1966.

their followers continued to live in a social environment which was relatively stable, so that they did not have to grapple constantly with the moral uncertainty arising out of sudden political and economic innovation. But since the West had committed itself to a new way of life built on technological progress, Christianity was forced to adapt its ancient doctrines to a fundamentally altered order of society. The task was not unfamiliar to a theological system which had matured in the world of antiquity, which had learned to exercise a strong influence over medieval institutions, which had even succeeded in reaching an accommodation with absolute monarchy. In the age of science and industry, however, it had to face a greater challenge than any of the past. Now its opponents were not barbaric chieftains like Attila the Hun or ambitious emperors like Henry IV, but secular ideologies like nationalism, socialism, fascism, and materialism. What made these new opponents so formidable was their reliance on spiritual rather than physical force, on those same techniques of moral suasion and logical demonstration which the church had previously employed with such success. In other words they were basically new religions with a morality and salvation of their own, competing with older creeds for men's souls.

THE REVIVAL OF FAITH

In 1815, when peace finally returned to a Europe exhausted by twenty years of war and revolution, the climate of opinion was distinctly favorable to a religious revival. A generation of thinkers brought up in the theological indifference of the Age of Enlightenment had gone through a terrible experience which had shaken its confidence in human reason. In a chastened mood it began under the restoration to preach a return to ancient beliefs. Philosophic idealism provided a theoretical foundation for this renaissance of faith, while political conservatism encouraged a spirit of piety which made the task of reactionary government easier.

True, there were some liberal theologians like Friedrich Schleiermacher who criticized accepted formulas, maintaining that "the usual conception of God as a single being outside of the world and behind the world, is not the beginning and end of religion, but only a way of expressing it that is seldom entirely pure and never adequate." But far more typical were the traditionalists seeking to recapture a departed medieval spirituality. They included Friedrich von Hardenberg, better known by his pen name as Novalis, Joseph de Maistre, Louis de Bonald, Samuel Taylor Coleridge, and, a little later, Friedrich Julius Stahl and John Henry Newman. In Catholicism many of them became ultramontanes, champions of papal influence over secular as well as spiritual affairs. In Protestantism their emphasis was usually on the political and ecclesiastical status quo, on altar, throne, and caste. For all of them religion was intimately associated with a sense of wonder before the mysteries of nature. "God of Christians!" exclaimed François René de

Chateaubriand in the midst of a description of a sea voyage. "It is on the waters of the abyss, and on the expanded sky, that thou hast particularly engraven the characters of thy omnipotence! Millions of stars sparkling in the azure of the celestial dome; the moon in the midst of the firmament; a sea unbounded by any shore; infinitude in the skies and on the waves! . . . Never did thy greatness strike me with profounder awe than in those nights when, suspended between the stars and the ocean, I had immensity over my head, and immensity beneath my feet!"[7]

Among the masses, however, religious feeling was different. The man in the street did not rhapsodize about nature, because his efforts were devoted almost entirely to the task of physical survival in a world of factories and banks. Most churchmen were too busy heaping ridicule on the theory of evolution, like Bishop Samuel Wilberforce, or defending the dogma that the sovereign pontiff was infallible in questions of faith and morals, like Pope Pius IX, to concern themselves with conditions in city slums. Radicalism, therefore, increasingly became the religion of the urban proletariat of Europe, while Christianity was left to the well-to-do, to peasants, and to women and children.

Here and there, to be sure, isolated efforts were made in the nineteenth century to divert missionary zeal from the conversion of the heathen to the improvement of the believer. Robert de Lamennais sought to equate Catholicism with political democracy and economic reform, yet his views led only to his condemnation by the Holy See. Charles Kingsley incurred the resentment of the respectable by his advocacy of labor associations within the framework of what was called Christian Socialism. The usual attitude was that of the popular American clergyman Henry Ward Beecher, who in 1877 assured fashionable churchgoers: "God has intended the great to be great and the little to be little. . . . I do not say that a dollar a day is enough to support a workingman. But it is enough to support a man! Not enough to support a man and five children if a man insists on smoking and drinking beer. . . . But the man who cannot live on bread and water is not fit to live." Similarly, the *Syllabus of the Principal Errors of Our Time*, which the Papacy issued in 1864, had little to say about the social problems created by the advance of technology. It simply lumped together in a single category "Socialism, Communism, Secret Societies, Biblical Societies, Clerico-Liberal Societies," warning the faithful that "plagues of this variety are reprobated in the strongest terms in various Encyclicals."

CHRISTIANITY AND INDUSTRIALISM

It took Christianity about a hundred years to recognize the moral implications of industrial capitalism, but by the end of the nineteenth century the work of such

---

[7] Viscount de Chateaubriand, *The Genius of Christianity*, trans. by Charles I. White (Baltimore and New York: John Murphy Co., 1856), pp. 171–172.

pioneer reformers as Bishop Wilhelm Emmanuel von Ketteler and Franz Hitze in Germany, Antoine Frédéric Ozanam and Philippe Joseph Buchez in France, and Frederick D. Maurice and Thomas Hughes in England was finally acknowledged as a valid expression of the spirit of the Holy Scriptures. Pope Leo XIII stated in 1891 in his famous encyclical *Rerum novarum:* "Religion teaches the rich man and the employer that their working people are not their slaves; that they must respect in every man his dignity as a man and as a Christian; . . . and that it is shameful and inhuman to treat men like chattels to make money by, or to look upon them merely as so much muscle or physical power." The practical application of this pronouncement became the concern of civic organizations like the *Action Libérale Française,* of labor unions like the *Christliche Gewerkschaften,* and of prominent politicians like Count A. A. M. de Mun and Monsignor Ignaz Seipel. Within Protestantism Friedrich Naumann, Bishop Charles Gore, Josiah Strong, and Richard T. Ely were among the many who sought to alleviate economic strife through the ideals of the Sermon on the Mount. Their point of view was epitomized by George Bernard Shaw in the quip that "the only trouble with Christianity is that it has never yet been tried." The churches voiced their views regarding social problems with particular firmness during the geat depression, when bourgeois society found itself in the midst of a crisis which threatened to result in class warfare. In 1931 Pope Pius XI affirmed in the encyclical *Quadragesimo anno:* "The immense number of propertyless wage-earners on the one hand, and the superabundant riches of the fortunate few on the other, is an unanswerable argument that the earthly goods so abundantly produced in this age of industrialism are far from rightly distributed and equitably shared among the various classes of men." Similarly, in 1937 a Protestant World Ecumenical Conference held at Oxford asserted: "The existing system of property rights and the existing distribution of property must be criticized in the light of the largely nonmoral processes by which they have been developed."

Closely related to theological criticism of economic injustice was the movement popularly known as the social gospel. Essentially it was an attempt to translate the ethical teachings of Christianity into a program of civic reform. Distrustful of dogmatic formalism, it identified the essence of religion with the impulse to do good. It often found expression in philanthropic organizations like the Salvation Army, founded in 1878 by William Booth to combat alcoholism, immorality, and godlessness among the lower classes. In a more sophisticated form it left its impress on the so-called Advanced Modernism which retained only a shadowy belief in the supernatural, substituting service to humanity for faith in God. Even eminent European theologians like Albrecht Ritschl and Ernst Troeltsch endorsed its emphasis on the spirit rather than the letter of the New Testament. And in America Walter Rauschenbusch preached: "The Kingdom of God is a collective conception, involving the whole social nature of man. It is not a matter of saving human atoms,

A SALVATION ARMY HALL. The tired and homeless were offered food and shelter by the Salvation Army as an expression of the social gospel.

but of saving the social organism. It is not a matter of getting individuals to heaven, but of transforming the life on earth into the harmony of heaven."

THE SPREAD OF SECULARISM

The effect of the social gospel was greatest in the Anglo-Saxon countries where it did much to loosen the bonds of rigid orthodoxy. But it also tended to transform the church from an instrumentality of salvation into an agency for the performance of charitable works or sometimes into little more than the locale of neighborhood social functions. Indeed that was the danger which theological conservatism saw in the deification of the human and the humanization of the divine. For would not the progressive abandonment of such traditional concepts of religion as sin, penitence, and redemption lead to a slow erosion of belief? The Vatican thought so and attempted to buttress ecclesiastical authority by encouraging the revival of scholastic philosophy and condemning the teachings of Modernism in the encyclical *Pascendi gregis* (1907). Among Protestants the opposition to liberal doctrine assumed several forms. In the United States its stronghold was the fundamentalism of the South and the Middle West with its insistence on an uncompromising adherence to religious orthodoxy. In Great Britain it was the Anglican "high" church which maintained that the historic doctrines of Christianity constituted a living body, no part of which could be destroyed without injuring the whole. On the Continent the neo-orthodox movement under the leadership of Karl Barth preached a return to tradition in theology. Especially after the First World War had demonstrated how blind the confidence of the liberals in human reasonableness had been, Europe began to rediscover the God of Calvin, stern but just, sitting in judgment on man's depravity.

In the final analysis, the dilemma of modern faith was the dilemma of modern man. It involved the search for a spiritual meaning in a mechanized world. Modernism and fundamentalism, liberalism and orthodoxy, each attempted to adapt a traditional belief to a changing environment. The account of the struggle of the church against the forces of secularism which Professor John Herman Randall, Jr., presented was based on the experience of America, but indirectly it also described the problem facing every religious institution affected by the advance of industrialism:

> We are apt to overlook the real religious revolution . . . , the crowding of religion into a minor place by the host of secular faiths and interests. For every man alienated from the Church by scientific ideas, there are dozens dissatisfied with its social attitudes, and hundreds who, with no intellectual doubts, have found their lives fully occupied with the other interests and diversions of the machine age. What does it matter that earnest men have found a way to combine older beliefs with the spirit of science, if those beliefs have ceased to express anything vital in men's experience, if the older religious faith is irrelevant to all they really care for? . . . Even when the Church embraces the new interests, it seems to be playing a losing game. There is little of specifically religious significance in the manifold activities of the modern institutional church; a dance for the building fund is less of a religious experience than a festival in honor of the patron saint. And any minister knows that his "social activities" spring less from real need than from the fervent desire to attract and hold members. The church itself has been secularized. Its very members continue a half-hearted support, from motives of traditional attachment, of personal loyalty to the minister, of social prestige, because they do not want to live in a churchless community.[8]

5. The Arts and Letters

THE FRENCH REVOLUTION overthrew not only an outworn system of government but also a traditional standard of value in aesthetics. Benevolent despotism had become so closely associated with rationalistic philosophy, deistic theology, and classical art that its fall had a far-reaching effect on accepted canons of thought and

---

[8] John Herman Randall, Jr., "The Forces That Are Destroying Traditional Beliefs," *Current History* (June 1929), pp. 361–362.

taste. As a matter of fact, even before the storm broke there were signs of an impending cultural crisis. As early as 1781 Immanuel Kant ushered in a new intellectual age with his *Critique of Pure Reason,* and John Wesley initiated a great religious revival built on faith rather than reason with the establishment of Methodism. In literature and art the reaction against the Age of Enlightenment was already in full swing. The reading public wept over the suicide of the hero of Goethe's *Sorrows of Young Werther* (1774) and thrilled to the synthetic medieval flavor of poems like *Bristowe Tragedie or the Dethe of Syr Charles Bawdin* (1777) by Thomas Chatterton. The composition of music was still governed by moderation and restraint, but in the work of Joseph Haydn or Wolfgang Amadeus Mozart could be heard an impatience with classicism. As for painting, even before the turn of the century William Blake and Francisco Goya represented the growing scorn for the artificiality of such subjects as well-fed little cupids shooting arrows at pretty ladies or shepherds and shepherdesses who had never been near a real flock gamboling on meadows whose greenness had never been defiled by real livestock. In short, the revolution against formalism in culture began in the last years of enlightened absolutism, and the great political upheaval which soon followed merely hastened its victory.

ROMANTICISM

The name applied to this aesthetic revolution was romanticism. Rejecting the elegant lucidity of the classical tradition, it exalted sentiment and instinct. The protagonist of Goethe's *Faust* (1808) gave up a life of academic study for the sake of direct experience:

> Gray and ashen, my friend, is every science,
> And only the golden tree of life is green.

And in William Wordsworth's *The Tables Turned* (1798) the same preference appeared in different words:

> One impulse from a vernal wood
> May teach you more of man,
> Of moral evil and of good,
> Than all the sages can.

> Sweet is the love which Nature brings;
> Our meddling intellect
> Mis-shapes the beauteous forms of things:
> —We murder to dissect.

This emancipation of feeling led the writer to seek new literary themes. Sir Walter Scott and Victor Hugo found beauty in a medieval past which the Age of

Enlightenment had condemned as barbaric. Samuel Taylor Coleridge and François René de Chateaubriand sought the exotic in distant lands, the former in the Xanadu of Kubla Khan, the latter among the noble savages of the New World. Giacomo Leopardi and Adam Mickiewicz were inspired by a faith in the mission of their people. Lord Byron's Childe Harold, like Alexander Pushkin's Eugene Onegin, was a turbulent hero driven by an inward restlessness from adventure to adventure, from unhappiness to unhappiness. What tied together this great variety of subjects and forms in literature was their common rejection of the well-bred conventionalism of the previous age.

Romanticism inspired an outpouring of literary creativity which has never been surpassed. Moods and feelings held in check by the classical restraints of the eighteenth century were suddenly liberated in a great release of artistic energy. In the fifty years which followed the outbreak of the French Revolution every country in Europe exulted in the birth of a new epoch in its national literature. Poetry was the dominant form of expression of the romanticist spirit, but prose also became more emotional, more intense. The revolt against restrictive rationality which was at the heart of romanticism glorified the mysterious, the picturesque, the instinctive, the unique; it admired the free man following his destiny in defiance of moral conventions or social restraints; it exalted spontaneity and naturalness. The emancipation of feeling represented by the new literary movement appealed to a generation whose belief in tradition had been shaken by wars and revolutions. The romanticist writers were expressing in their work the sense of animation and wonder which the fall of the Old Regime had aroused in European society. The old certainties no longer seemed to fit a world in which new political and social ideals were in the ascendant. A feeling of participation in the great crisis of its time stimulated the sensibilities of the generation which had witnessed the fall of the Age of Enlightenment, and the decorous reasonableness of the past began to appear hopelessly outmoded. It was a new mood of ecstatic discovery of life which found voice in romanticist literature.

The change taking place in painting was equally profound. Théodore Géricault's "Raft of the Medusa" (1819), portraying the agonized survivors of a shipwreck, and Eugène Delacroix' "Liberty Leading the People" (1830), with its glorification of the spirit of popular insurrection, were worlds removed from the pictures of Socrates drinking the hemlock or Adonis embracing Venus which had been popular fifty years before. Even the landscapists of the early nineteenth century, like John Constable and J. M. W. Turner, saw in nature more than an idealized background for frisking satyrs and nymphs; in the natural world the romanticist found his own passions reflected, and nature herself became an appropriate subject for artistic endeavor.

In music the invention of new instruments and the improvement of existing ones made possible radical innovations in the technique of composition. Ludwig van Beethoven (1770–1827) was a lonely titan whose observance of traditional musical forms still reflected a conservative influence. But the next generation of musicians lacked his respectful attitude toward esthetic authority. The works of the composers of the first half of the nineteenth century, Felix Mendelsohn-Bartholdy, Robert Schumann, Franz Schubert, Frédéric Chopin, and Hector Berlioz on the concert stage, and Karl Maria von Weber, Gioacchino Rossini, and Gaetano Donizetti in the opera house, finally put an end to the reign of classicism. To a perceptive observer like the statesman Wilhelm von Humboldt it seemed that "there never was an epoch in which everywhere and at all points the old and the new stages appeared in such sharp contrast."

Yet romanticism was too intense, too theatrical a movement to exercise a lasting influence on the culture of the West. It tended to magnify and distort human experience, to make it seem bigger than life. There was an element of truth in the popular caricature of the romanticists as pale, artistic young men, living in a feverish agony of creativity, given to fits of coughing and spitting blood, and finally succumbing in their early thirties to tuberculosis, the fashionable disease of the restoration. The age too was short lived. It suffered from a penchant for the melodramatic, and sooner or later a reaction against it was sure to come, for the nineteenth century was an age of cities and machines, not picturesque Gothic castles.

THE RAFT OF THE MEDUSA. This masterpiece of the early romantic movement by Théodore Géricault, with its agonized theme and dramatic composition, represents a sharp break with the classical style of the eighteenth century.

BERLIOZ CONDUCTING ONE OF HIS OWN WORKS. This cartoon suggests the shock and scorn aroused in traditionalist circles by the advent of romanticism in music.

REALISM

By the middle of the nineteenth century the public had grown tired of the cult of feeling. It was all very well to criticize the primness of classicism, but could not an aggressive emotionalism be just as artificial? Industrial society began to look for an art which could mirror its own experiences, and it found what it was looking for in realism. The American novelist William Dean Howells described this new theory of esthetics in the injunction that "we must ask ourselves before we ask anything else, Is it true?—true to the motives, the impulses, the principles, that shape the life of actual men and women." Of course, to argue that the function of the artist is to portray the truth which determines "the life of actual men and women" is to beg the question, since the classicists as well as the romanticists had been convinced that they were dealing with precisely that kind of truth. But the realists met the difficulty by equating social reality with the average and the prosaic. For them a great talent was one "robust enough to front the everyday world and catch the charm of its work-worn, care-worn, brave, kindly face."

If romanticism found its supreme literary form in poetry, realism soberly turned to prose, especially to the novel. Its pioneers were Honoré de Balzac, whose *Human Comedy,* composed of more than a hundred novels, presented a monumental account of life during the reign of Louis Philippe, and Charles Dickens, who won an immense popularity in the Victorian era with his books compounded of just the right proportions of social criticism and old-fashioned sentimentality. Gustave Flaubert's *Madame Bovary* shocked the Second Empire with its portrayal of the moral impoverishment of French provincial life, while Émile Zola and Guy de Maupassant were the outstanding representatives of the realistic school in the early years of the Third Republic. In the meantime William Makepeace Thackeray, Thomas Hardy, and George Gissing in England, Gustav Freytag, Theodor Storm, and Theodor Fontane in Germany, and Ivan Turgenev, Feodor Dostoevski, and Leo Tolstoy in Russia were depicting the virtues of the bourgeoisie, or pondering the problems of morality.

The drama too was brought down to earth, and the mythological heroes and dashing outlaws who had populated the stage began to give way before more mundane protagonists. The younger Alexandre Dumas blazed a new trail with his *La Dame aux Camélias,* whose central character was a courtesan. But the greatest playwright of the century was the Norwegian Henrik Ibsen. Dealing with such themes as the subordination of women in *The Doll's House* (1879) and the weakness of democracy in *An Enemy of the People* (1882), he transformed the theater into a platform for the discussion of social and political issues. Before long writers like August Strindberg, George Bernard Shaw, Gerhart Hauptmann, and Anton Chekhov had firmly established the new realistic tradition in drama. The art of the essay also revived in an age which wanted to understand more than it wanted to believe. The writings of Thomas Carlyle, Thomas Babington Macaulay, Matthew Arnold, John Ruskin, C. A. Sainte-Beuve, Hippolyte A. Taine, Ernest Renan, and Georg Brandes displayed a belletristic skill of the highest order. Even the poets responded to the prevailing intellectual currents, Robert Browning in his sensitive psychological portraits executed in verse form, and Alfred Tennyson in his songs in praise of industry, peace, and patriotism.

The reaction against romanticism in art was foreshadowed before the mid-century in the social satire of Honoré Daumier and the reverence for lowly labor of Jean François Millet. Yet it did not become a full-fledged school of painting until the rise of impressionism. Arguing that the task of the artist was not to impose his own sense of symmetry upon nature but simply to depict what the eye saw, the impressionists became intoxicated with the qualities of light and color. They were prepared to sacrifice form and design for the sake of what was sometimes called "pictorial stenography." At their first exhibition held in Paris in 1874 they shocked the orthodox by their indifference to the accepted rules of composition. Edouard Manet was the leader of this movement for a new esthetic realism, although his own work was less revolutionary than that of many of his followers. Claude Monet with his strangely misty landscapes, Pierre Auguste Renoir and the radiant women and children whom he liked to portray, the ballet dancers of Edgar

Degas, the street scenes of Camille Pissarro, the outdoor etchings of James McNeill Whistler, whose artistic reputation fell victim to an unfortunate portrait of his mother—these were the best representatives of the impressionistic movement. Still, the view that the painter must record optical effects without intruding anything of himself did not go unchallenged. Paul Cézanne helped found postimpressionism by his renewed emphasis on form and dimension in painting. The half-mad Vincent van Gogh filled canvas after canvas with brilliantly burning suns and fields of grain emanating an unearthly luminosity. Paul Gauguin during his stay in the South Seas developed a style which was deliberately primitive in the use of color and the approach to composition. And Henri de Toulouse-Lautrec pictured the night life of Montmartre, the singers, the dancers, the roués, the harlots.

Since music could not by its nature give literal expression to everyday experience, its break with romanticism was less abrupt. Johannes Brahms seemed to be resuming where Beethoven had left off. The piano pieces of Franz Liszt revealed the influence of Chopin. Giuseppe Verdi wrote in the melodic tradition of his great compatriots Rossini and Donizetti. The composer, however, could not remain completely immune to the social thought of his age. The sense of nationality which so powerfully affected political developments was stimulated in the last decades of the century by the work of Edvard Grieg in Norway and Anton Dvořák in Bohemia. The emphasis on the actual appeared in such examples of program music as Peter Ilich Tchaikovsky's overture *The Year 1812,* which commemorated the defeat of Napoleon in Russia, and Paul Dukas' orchestral rendering of one of Goethe's ballads in his *Sorcerer's Apprentice.* The passion and sorrow of lower-class life formed the theme of those inseparable operatic twins, Pietro Mascagni's *Cavalleria Rusticana* and Ruggiero Leoncavallo's *I Pagliacci.* Even Richard Wagner, who arranged the shotgun wedding of all the art forms in his grandiloquent *Gesamtkunstwerke,* was voicing the self-satisfied mood of the bourgeois Philistine. Behind the medieval subject matter of his musical dramas could be heard all the ostentation of a parvenu Germany. Leo Tolstoy saw through this sham and left a devastating description of a performance of *Siegfried:* "When I arrived, an actor in jersey and tights was seated in front of an object intended to represent an anvil; his hair and beard were false; his hands, white and manicured, had nothing of the workman's; the carefree air, the bulging stomach, and the absence of muscle betrayed the actor. With an incredible hammer he struck, as no one ever struck, a sword that was no less fanciful. It was easy to see he was a dwarf because he bent the knee as he walked. He shouted for a long time, his mouth strangely open."

THE RISE OF ESTHETIC SUBJECTIVISM

After the opening of the twentieth century two divergent tendencies developed in the arts and letters. One, an outgrowth of realism, continued to define the function of the artist as the interpretation of a socially shared experience. Among those subscribing to this view were writers like Thomas Mann, who in his *Buddenbrooks* (1900) described the decline and fall of a patrician merchant family in Germany; Jules Romains, who in the nearly thirty interrelated novels of *The Men of Good Will* (1932–1946) presented a brilliant picture of the spiritual crisis of France; John Galsworthy, whose *Forsyte Saga* (1922) depicted the growing insecurity of the middle class in England; and Sinclair Lewis, whose *Babbitt*, also published in 1922, was a portrait of the desiccating shallowness of small-town life in America. Also within this tradition and working at about the same time were painters like George Grosz and Diego Rivera, concerned with themes of social injustice, and even Henri Matisse and Georges Rouault, with their unconventional techniques in the use of form and color. As for music, the works of Jean Sibelius, Richard Strauss, and Sergei Prokofiev revealed an approach to the problems of composition not radically different from that which had been traditionally taught in the conservatories.

At the source of the aesthetic principle of such artists was the need to communicate. Still conscious of the society about them, still eager to express some objective truth, they sought to remain within the framework of the accepted canons of art. The difficulty facing them, therefore, lay in the attempt to articulate a new truth in an old language. In a sense, of course, that was the dilemma which every theory of aesthetics in the past had had to resolve. But the process of artistic readjustment had become particularly arduous in a period of rapidly changing cultural values.

There was, however, an alternative. Why not ignore the environment of the artist and stress his inner world of emotion? Such a procedure involved the substitution of a psychological state for social reality as the object of creative enterprise. It led to the erection of an often insuperable barrier between the connoisseur's ideal and public taste. For once the communication of universal experience ceased to be the main concern of art, the way was clear for the aesthetic assertion of purely individual feelings which the rest of the world often found incomprehensible.

The roots of this radical subjectivism reached back into the late years of the nineteenth century, when in the decadent atmosphere of the *fin de siècle* writers like Stéphane Mallarmé, Paul Verlaine, Algernon Swinburne, and Oscar Wilde shocked their contemporaries with unconventional literary themes and imageries. Their countless imitators, striking artistic poses and reverently carrying the lily as the symbol of aesthetic purity, spread the cult of introspection. Its influence was felt in stream-of-consciousness novels like Marcel Proust's *Remembrance of Things Past* (1913–1927) or James Joyce's *Ulysses* (1922), and in the poetic obscurities of Gertrude Stein or E. E. Cummings.

Among artists the rejection of anything resembling literal representation culminated in such movements as cubism and surrealism. It led to the melting watches and weird, spindly crutches of Salvador Dali and to Marcel Duchamp's "Nude Descending a Staircase," in which there is neither a nude nor a staircase nor any

THE NAME OF DANTE GABRIEL ROSSETTI IS HEARD FOR THE FIRST TIME IN THE WESTERN STATES OF AMERICA: TIME: 1882: LECTURER: MR. OSCAR WILDE. The caricaturist Max Beerbohm is poking fun at the precious affectations of the esthetes of the late nineteenth century.

other identifiable object. In music the revolution against melody and harmony began with the haunting, sensuous dissonances of Claude Debussy who opposed "the stifling of emotion under the head of motifs and superimposed designs." It progressed with the highly original orchestral devices, or perhaps merely "cacophonic outrages and deviltries and tomfooleries," of Igor Stravinsky. And it assumed its most uncompromising form in the twelve-tone compositions of Arnold Schönberg. As for the artistic merit of these musical innovations, a moderate critic like Howard Taubman cautiously concluded that "the best atonal composers do say something." But others agreed with the unequivocal condemnation by R. O. Morris: "This complete upsetting of all traditional values, this disdain of all previously accepted melodic and harmonic relationships, suggests to me, not so much courage and sincerity, as an inflated arrogance of mind that can only be described as megalomania—a dreary wilderness of cacophony that somehow contrives to be pedantic and hysterical at the same time."

Aside from the question of whether esthetic modernism was good or bad, the fact remained that it represented a prevalent attitude. If the arts refused to speak an intelligible language, that was because the artists felt themselves estranged from their social surroundings. It did no good to scold them for failing to interpret the universe about them; it would be more useful to know why they were seeking artistic truth within themselves, within their own consciousness or subconsciousness.

NUDE DESCENDING A STAIRCASE (1912) BY MARCEL DUCHAMP. After a half century of non-representational art this painting no longer seems daring, for it can be recognized as an experimental effort to portray a figure in motion, in this instance, walking down a staircase.

GUERNICA BY PABLO PICASSO. This famous picture, inspired by a bombing incident during the Spanish civil war, suggests kaleidoscopically the horror of modern military conflict.

In all probability a feeling of insecurity lay at the root of their subjectivism. Shakespeare, Goethe, even Tolstoy could feel in essential harmony with society because basically they subscribed to its standard of private and public virtue. That sense of belonging vanished, however, when the artist found himself unable to perform the traditional function of his calling, the description of a universally recognizable reality. Once he lost his footing amid the shifting values of the modern world, all that was left for him to do was voice the indefinable anxiety of his age. His rejection of the material environment was an expression of a general escapist impulse. Besides, even when he decided to look for ultimate truth, how could he be sure what it was? Perhaps it was the elemental scientific process which Edgar Varèse tried to describe in a conglomeration of strange sounds entitled *Ionisation* (1931). Perhaps it was the horror of total war portrayed with painful vividness in Pablo Picasso's "Guernica" (1937). Or perhaps it was simply the deadly monotony of a dehumanized urban existence suggested by the *Preludes* (1917) of T. S. Eliot:

> The morning comes to consciousness
> Of faint stale smells of beer
> From the sawdust-trampled street
> With all its muddy feet that press
> To early coffee-stands.

> With the other masquerades
> That time resumes,
> One thinks of all the hands
> That are raising dingy shades
> In a thousand furnished rooms.[9]

6. *Changing Ideals of Learning*

THE CULTURAL CRISIS arising out of industrialism was aggravated by a basic change in the social function of learning. With the growth of material welfare which accompanied technological progress came new problems of education. Until the nineteenth century intellectual training had been by and large a monopoly of the well-to-do whose interests and attitudes shaped the form of instruction. The masses were too absorbed in the daily struggle for survival to exert any influence over culture. Primitive sagas, folk tales, popular ballads, and village dances provided the artist with material, but his creative talents were exercised for the benefit of a public which was essentially aristocratic in character. The paintings of Velásquez glorified the court of Spain; the plays of Molière were staged before the nobility of France; Haydn wrote his music to entertain the guests of a powerful Hungarian magnate.

Similarly the substance of education mirrored the stratified, hierarchical social order maintained by monarchic absolutism. There was no system of general elementary instruction, because the peasant did not need to read in order to plow the lord's land. As a matter of fact, too much knowledge could be a bad thing for the lower classes; it could spoil them and make them dissatisfied with their station in life. All they needed was piety, which taught them obedience and resignation. Did not even the great Voltaire announce despite his religious skepticism that "it is a very good thing to make men believe that they have an immortal soul and that there is an avenging God who will punish my peasants when they steal my wheat and my wine"?

Institutions of higher learning, on the other hand, received generous support from the Old Regime because they performed a valuable service for the state. First of all they trained lawyers and clergymen for the bureaucracy and the church, the bulwarks of established authority. Perhaps even more important, they provided young gentlemen with a body of knowledge which raised them above the common run of humanity. The man who had learned to read Greek and Latin wore

---

[9] From *Collected Poems 1909–1962* by T. S. Eliot, copyright, 1936, by Harcourt, Brace & World, Inc.; copyright, © 1963, 1964, by T. S. Eliot. Reprinted by permission of the publisher.

an invisible mark of distinction identifying him as a member of the leisured class. True, in many cases he forgot most of what he had studied soon after leaving the classroom, and sometimes he had been too busy drinking and wenching to have learned much in the first place. Yet usually he retained enough to cite from time to time some classical authority. And this accomplishment sufficed for that conspicuous consumption of learning which in many circles passed for culture.

The advent of industrialism forced a fundamental change in the basis of education. To begin with, for the first time in history the laboring populace was freed from unremitting drudgery and provided with enough leisure to make universal literacy an attainable goal. Secondly, the growing complexity of the processes of production and distribution created a demand for trained workers and made mastery of the three R's essential for even the menial occupations. Finally, the shift of the center of political power from the upper to the lower classes which resulted from the growth of democracy in government necessitated a new program of popular instruction. "We must educate our masters" became the slogan of every government far-sighted enough to realize that the era of the masses had arrived.

THE MODERNIZATION OF INSTRUCTION

An educational revolution occurred in the West in the latter part of the nineteenth century, as one country after another hastened to prepare its citizenry for new civic responsibilities. England in 1870 promulgated a law establishing a system of primary schooling open to all children, and ten years later classroom attendance became a legal obligation. France made elementary school instruction free and compulsory in 1882. Prussia nationalized her primary schools in 1872 and ended the payment of tuition in 1888. Basic education became obligatory in Switzerland in 1874, in Italy in 1877, in Holland in 1878, and in Belgium in 1879. Although enrollment in an elementary school was generally not required beyond the pupil's tenth year, illiteracy in Europe and America began to decline with remarkable rapidity. Within the lifetime of a single generation the essential tools of learning became available to the countless millions who from time immemorial had been condemned to an existence of total ignorance.

The content of education also changed. The classical curriculum, which originally served a practical purpose, had become a venerated idol. Its study was supposed to sharpen the intellect, purify morals, ennoble the spirit, and strengthen judgment. Moreover, it offered the advantage of differentiating between the gentleman and the boor, for no man who had to earn his livelihood by labor could afford to devote himself to it. Yet learning was too vital an enterprise to be permanently reduced to a social ornament. Among those demanding a thoroughgoing reform of instruction was Thomas H. Huxley, who brilliantly satirized the typical attitude of the Victorian English family toward the academic training which its sons received:

> At the cost of from one to two thousand pounds of our hard-earned money, we devote twelve of the most precious years of your lives to school. There you shall toil, or be supposed to toil; but there you shall not learn one single thing of all those you will most want to know directly you leave school and enter upon the practical business life. You will in all probability go into business, but you shall not know where, or how, any article of commerce is produced, or the difference between an export and an import, or the meaning of the word "capital." You will very likely settle in a colony, but you shall not know whether Tasmania is part of New South Wales, or *vice versa* . . . . Very probably you may become a manufacturer, but you shall not be provided with the means of understanding the working of one of your own steam engines, or the nature of the raw products you employ; and when you are asked to buy a patent, you shall not have the slightest means of judging whether the inventor is an impostor who is contravening the elementary principles of science or a man who will make you as rich as Croesus. You will very likely get into the House of Commons. You will have to take your share in making laws which may prove a blessing or a curse to millions of men. But you shall not hear one word respecting the political organization of your country; the meaning of the controversy between free traders and protectionists shall never have been mentioned to you; you shall not so much as know that there are such things as economical laws. The mental power which will be of most importance in your daily life will be the power of seeing things as they are without regard to authority; and of drawing accurate general conclusions from particular facts. But at school and at college you shall know of no source of truth but authority; nor exercise your reasoning faculty upon anything but deduction from that which is laid down by authority.[10]

Little by little academic practice adjusted to new economic and political conditions. The natural sciences, the social sciences, arts and letters, and modern languages began to appear among the course offerings of the secondary schools and universities. The reform of higher education was a slow process, for institutions of advanced learning continued to draw their student body largely from the well-to-do classes, and hence they retained an intellectually and socially aristocratic character. Yet they were eventually forced to modify their curriculum in response to the needs of a new industrial age. The domination of philosophy and the classics came to an end as the foundation of academic training gradually broadened. A Europe in which technology played an increasingly important role could not go on neglecting the study of physics, chemistry, and biology. The value of the social disciplines was less obvious, but with time educators came to recognize that the function of learning was not only to preserve but to transform the intellectual heritage of the past. In an era of growing democratization history, economics, political science, sociology, and anthropology could contribute to a clearer understanding of the momentous

---

10 Thomas H. Huxley, *Science and Education* (New York: D. Appleton and Co., 1898), pp. 95–96.

changes which society was undergoing. An alteration in the content of instruction was thus the inevitable result of an alteration in the structure of the community itself.

TRADITION AND PROGRESS IN CULTURE

Such changes in the nature of the educational process inevitably aroused the opposition of those accustomed to older forms of knowledge. As early as 1914 the conservative essayist Paul Elmer More in an article suggestively entitled "Natural Aristocracy" protested against what he considered the vulgarization of learning:

> Let us, in the name of a long-suffering God, put some bounds to the flood of talk about the wages of the bricklayer and the trainman, and talk a little more about the income of the artist and teacher and public censor who have to remain in opposition to the tide. Let us have less cant about the great educative value of the theatre for the people and less humbug about the virtues of the nauseous problem play, and more consideration of what is clean and nourishing food for the larger minds. Let us forget for a while our absorbing desire to fit the schools to train boys for the shop and the counting-room, and concern ourselves more effectively with the dwindling of those disciplinary studies which lift men out of the crowd. Let us, in fine, not number ourselves among the traitors to their class who *invidiae metu non audeant dicere* [do not dare to speak out for fear of ill will].[11]

But the knights in shining armor who rode forth with sharpened pencils to fight the good fight of culture against barbarism were Don Quixotes tilting at windmills. Whether they liked it or not, the genteel tradition of learning was declining along with the patrician environment which it had reflected. Its place was being taken by new concepts of pedagogy appropriate to a civic order committed to the goal of mass welfare. John Dewey, the champion of progressive education, spoke for those who refused to seek truth in authority:

> The foundation of democracy is faith in the capacities of human nature; faith in human intelligence and in the power of pooled and cooperative experience. It is not belief that these things are complete but that if given a show they will grow and be able to generate progressively the knowledge and wisdom needed to guide collective action. Every autocratic and authoritarian scheme of social action rests on a belief that the needed intelligence is confined to a superior few, who because of inherent natural gifts are endowed with the ability and the right to control the conduct of others; laying down principles and rules and directing the ways in which they are carried out. It would be foolish to deny that much can be said for this point of view. It is that which controlled human relations in social groups for much the greater part of human history. The democratic faith has emerged very, very recently in the history of mankind. Even where democracies now exist, men's minds and feelings are still permeated with ideals about leadership imposed from above, ideas that

---

11 From "Natural Aristocracy" by Paul Elmer More, from *The Unpopular Review*, April–June, 1914. Reprinted by permission of Holt, Rinehart and Winston, Inc.

develop in the long early history of mankind. After democratic political institutions were nominally established, beliefs and ways of looking at life and of acting that originated when men and women were externally controlled and subjected to arbitrary power persisted in the family, the church, business and the school, and experience shows that as long as they persist there, political democracy is not secure.[12]

The crisis in education created by the changing function of knowledge was only one aspect of a vast process of social reorganization arising out of industrialism. There was no doubt a good deal of cant in the professional pedagogical pontification about adjustment to life and training for citizenship in the classroom. Yet the alternative had to be more than a return to the good old days when the little red schoolhouse dispensed learning and discipline without fads or frills. Even in the halcyon days before the First World War a worried editor of the *Nation* was complaining about the declining level of intellectual achievement in the United States: "Boys come into college with no reading and with minds unused to the very practice of study; and they leave college, too often, in the same state of nature. There are even those, inside and outside of academic halls, who protest that our higher institutions of learning simply fail to educate at all. That is slander; but in sober earnest, you will find few experienced college professors, apart from those engaged in teaching purely utilitarian or practical subjects, who are not convinced that the general relaxation is greater now than it was twenty years ago." That must surely have been the lament of the good city fathers of Athens who put Socrates to death for corrupting the minds of the young; it must have been the view of the schoolmen of the medieval universities who solemnly proclaimed that the reading of those vulgarians Petrarch and Chaucer would distract students from the classics and prove the ruination of academic standards. In each age in which the form of learning changed under the influence of a new way of life there were those who made dire predictions about the decay of morality and the stultifying of intelligence. To them every dawn looked red.

The point is that much of the criticism directed against mass culture ignored the essential character of modern society. Not that the strictures about popular taste were without foundation. The yellow press, the dime novel, the horror film, the "soap opera," the "juke box," the calendar illustration, each in its own way purveyed sensationalism or sentimentality. But were such forms of entertainment any more vulgar than the bearbaiting and cockfighting which used to amuse the aristocracy? Was the violence portrayed in thousands of neighborhood motion-picture theaters any more barbaric than the morbid curiosity which once attracted fashionable ladies and gentlemen to the public execution of criminals? It took centuries to transform a boorish, illiterate feudal chieftain into a connoisseur of art

---

12 John Dewey, "Democracy and Educational Administration," *School and Society* (Chicago: University of Chicago Press, 1899), p. 67.

and a patron of literature. There was no reason to expect that the improvement of plebeian sensibilities would take less time.

The Greeks had once looked down on the Romans as intellectual parvenus; the Romans had considered the Germans country bumpkins; the nobleman had made fun of the bourgeois for being a *nouveau riche;* the bourgeois had derided the workingman trying to master good grammar and good breeding; and so it went. In the light of historical experience, however, no people and no class could claim a monopoly of culture. Every social order of the past had created its unique intellectual synthesis out of common philosophic, esthetic, scientific, and educational experiences. The modern world was still engaged in the search for some new, all-embracing system of thought which could express its fundamental convictions in universal terms. It was only to be expected that in such a moment of moral crisis cries would be raised against the abandonment of the familiar old deities. But the twentieth century could not escape its own time. The civic faith which it was seeking to create had to express a basic belief in scientific progress, material welfare, social justice, and political democracy.

Further Reading

*W. C. Dampier, *A History of Science and Its Relations with Philosophy and Religion* (London, 1946) and *F. S. Taylor, *A Short History of Science and Scientific Thought* (New York, 1949) are standard works. On physics see C. T. Chase, *The Evolution of Modern Physics* (New York, 1947); on chemistry, T. M. Lowry, *Historical Introduction to Chemistry* (London, 1936); and on geology, H. B. Woodward, *History of Geology* (New York, 1911). C. Singer, *A History of Biology* (New York, 1950) and R. H. Shryock, *The Development of Modern Medicine* (New York, 1947) are solid but less readable than such popularized works as *P. H. De Kruif, *Microbe Hunters* (New York, 1958) and H. Zinsser, *Rats, Lice, and History* (Boston, 1935). The theory of evolution is described by W. Irwin, *Apes, Angels, and Victorians* (New York, 1955); and *J. Barzun, *Darwin, Marx, Wagner* (Garden City, 1958). *B. Russell, *The A.B.C. of Relativity* (New York, 1925) and *L. Barnett, *The Universe and Dr. Einstein* (New York, 1952) consider the scientific image of nature.

*J. T. Merz, *A History of European Thought in the Nineteenth Century,* 4 vols. (New York, 1896–1914) has become almost a classic. *H. S. Hughes, *Consciousness and Society* (New York, 1961) is a brilliant study of the reorientation of European social thought in the opening decades of the twentieth century. H. E. Barnes, *The New History and the Social Studies* (New York, 1925) depicts the development of the social sciences. *P. A. Sorokin, *Contemporary Sociological Theories* (New York, 1928) is a sound guide to sociology; A. C. Haddon and A. H. Quigin, *History of Anthropology* (New York, 1910), to anthropology; C. Gide and C. Rist, *History of Economic Doctrines from the Physiocrats to the Present Day* (Boston, 1948), to economic theory;

G. H. Sabine, *A History of Political Theory* (New York, 1950), to political science; and *G. P. Gooch, *History and Historians in the Nineteenth Century* (Gloucester, Mass., 1949), to modern historiography. G. Murphy, *Historical Introduction to Modern Psychology* (New York, 1929) is a good survey, but for psychoanalysis see in addition *S. Freud, *An Outline of Psychoanalysis* (New York, 1940) and E. Jones, *The Life and Work of Sigmund Freud,* 3 vols. (New York, 1953–1957). H. S. Hughes, *Oswald Spengler* (New York, 1952); P. Geyl, *From Ranke to Toynbee* (Northampton, Mass., 1952); and *D. Riesman, *The Lonely Crowd* (Garden City, 1953) are studies in cultural pessimism.

*H. Höffding, *A History of Modern Philosophy,* 2 vols. (New York, 1955) is a well-known, substantial book. A. L. Lindsay, *Kant* (Gloucester, Mass., 1934) presents an appraisal of the founder of philosophic idealism, while *H. Marcuse, *Reason and Revolution: Hegel and the Rise of Social Theory* (New York, 1941) deals with its most controversial exponent. *C. Brinton, *Nietzsche* (Cambridge, Mass., 1941) is an urbane biography of the prophet of the superman. E. Friedell, *A Cultural History of the Modern Age,* 3 vols. (New York, 1930–1932) describes important modern intellectual movements. A. C. McGiffert, *The Rise of Modern Religious Ideals* (New York, 1915) is a thoughtful and balanced exposition. E. A. Burtt, *Religion in an Age of Science* (New York, 1929) and *C. Dawson, *Religion and Culture* (New York, 1958) analyze the role of religion in an industrial society.

G. Brandes, *Main Currents in Nineteenth Century Literature,* 6 vols. (New York, 1923) is a comprehensive work by an eminent literary critic. E. Faure, *History of Art,* 5 vols. (New York, 1921–1930) has won an international reputation. P. H. Lang, *Music in Western Civilization* (New York, 1941) presents an excellent account. There are several works dealing with the relationship between the content of learning and the structure of society, among them J. K. Folsom, *Culture and Social Progress* (New York, 1928) and R. B. Fosdick, *The Old Savage in the New Civilization* (Garden City, 1928). The following are especially concerned with the problem of intellectual training in a democracy: *B. Russell, *Education and the Modern World* (New York, 1932); and G. S. Counts, *The Social Foundations of Education* (New York, 1934). A description of changing pedagogic patterns in the leading states of Europe appears in F. W. Roman, *The New Education in Europe* (New York, 1930); and A. D. C. Peterson, *A Hundred Years of Education* (London, 1952).

CHAPTER 20

The Contemporary
World

*The Second World War had the effect of destroying a system of in-*ternational relations which had prevailed in the West for five hundred years. Ever since the fifteenth century, when the national monarchy became the dominant form of political organization, a balance of power among the major countries had been maintained by the art of diplomacy or by recourse to war. Whenever any state threatened to become strong enough to dominate the others, a coalition would be formed to restore the equilibrium. Charles V of the Holy Roman Empire, Louis XIV and Napoleon I of France, William II of Germany, each discovered that too much power could be as dangerous as too little. In a world in which diplomatic affairs were conducted in the spirit of Machiavelli's *Prince,* no ruler could allow his neighbor to acquire a preponderant influence. The weaker concerted to oppose the stronger, and in combination they succeeded in reestablishing the international equipoise. Sometimes the mere threat of force was enough to redress the balance; more commonly a war was required. In any case, the techniques of statesmanship reflected a diplomatic situation in which no one of the leading governments could achieve a position of hegemony.

1. The New International Order

THE RESULT OF THE SECOND WORLD WAR was to weaken the major states of Europe to the point where, with one exception, they could no longer be properly described as great powers. Not only were Germany and Italy forced to agree to unconditional surrender, but even such victorious countries as England and France were winners in name only. Enfeebled financially as well as ideologically, they ceased to play a leading role on the diplomatic stage. The traditional balance of power began to disintegrate because there were no longer several strong governments on the Continent. In its place there developed a dualism of power which reflected the fact that after 1945 there were only two great western states, the Soviet Union and the United States. Having emerged from the Second World War in a stronger political and economic position than before, they were able to dominate international relations. Not since the days of the Roman Empire had there been such a high concentration of power. But whereas Rome had been able to provide its citizens with the *Pax Romana,* a period of tranquillity extending for almost three hundred years, the postwar world of the mid-twentieth century was less fortunate. For the statesmen in Moscow and Washington were divided by fundamental differences in their philosophies of government.

THE COLLAPSE OF THE BALANCE OF POWER

As far as the Soviet Union was concerned, the defeat of the Axis meant that it could emerge from the isolation in which it had been kept by the capitalistic states during the first twenty years of its existence. It ceased to be a pariah among nations and even began to exert a strong influence on countries beyond its borders. First of all, there were the secondary states of eastern Europe which during the interwar period had maintained a diplomatic barrier against the Soviet Union. In the final stages of the Second World War they had been overrun by the Red Army, so that Stalin could impose his will on their governments by the threat of armed force. Second, the defeat of the Wehrmacht by the Russian forces endowed the Kremlin with new prestige and strengthened the communist parties in western Europe. Finally, the economic decline resulting from the war won new converts for radical doctrines which promised the masses of the world security in the classless society of the future. Not since the chaotic days after the First World War had the chances of a Marxist victory been better.

It was America which was primarily responsible for checking the expansionist designs of the Kremlin, because it alone possessed the necessary physical resources. In 1945 there was a strong desire among the people of the United States to demobilize their armies and regain that sense of cozy security which they had known through most of their history. Yet almost against their will they found themselves drawn into international complications which threatened to lead to a new war. Just as the Romans after the Carthaginian wars discovered that great political power brought with it heavy political responsibility, so the Americans after the Second World War found themselves compelled to assume duties which they did not seek and to which they were not accustomed.

Since the domination of Europe by the Soviet Union would have left the western hemisphere isolated in a communist sea, self-interest demanded that Washington become the leader of the forces aligned against Russia. It was too late to save the eastern borderlands of the Continent from the control of Moscow, but farther west economic and military assistance from the New World strengthened the opposition to Stalin. The result was the formation of two great alliances, one commanded by the Kremlin, the other directed from the White House.

THE REORGANIZATION OF THE CONTINENT

After hostilities came to an end in 1945, the reorganization of the Continent was carried out partly by an authoritarian communism, partly by a democratic capitalism. In the east Russia had a free hand. To begin with, she annexed several strategically located territories extending along her prewar frontiers. Finland was forced to cede Petsamo and the western shore of Lake Ladoga; Estonia, Latvia, Lithuania, and part of East Prussia were incorporated into the Soviet Union; Poland gave up her eastern provinces; Romania lost Bessarabia and northern Bucovina; and Czechoslovakia surrendered Carpathian Ruthenia.

Moreover, in the years following the collapse of the Axis Moscow succeeded in gaining political control over its weak neighbors. The technique employed to achieve this end involved first the formation of a coalition government representing the center and the left. Then would come a gradual suppression of the bourgeois parties which left the radicals firmly in the saddle. Ultimately the state was reduced to a satellite fawning on the Kremlin. One after another the countries of eastern Europe underwent the transformation from "popular front" to "people's democracy." By the beginning of 1948 Mátyás Rákosi in Hungary, Marshal Tito in Yugoslavia, Ana Pauker in Romania, Joseph Cyrankiewicz in Poland, Georgi Dimitrov in Bulgaria, Klement Gottwald in Czechoslovakia, and Enver Hoxha in Albania were recreating their states in the image of the Soviet Union. As for their foreign policies, a conference held in Warsaw in September 1947 established the Communist Information Bureau (Cominform) to coordinate the diplomatic activities of all communist governments under the ultimate direction of Stalin.

In the meantime the United States was encouraging the revival of democratic governments and capitalistic economies in western Europe. Unlike the Kremlin, Washington did not use the weapon of the coup d'état, relying rather on the effects

Petsamo

N O R W A Y

S W E D E N

F I N L A N D

25°

Porkkala
(Leased to USSR)

Oslo

Stockholm

Helsinki

L. Ladoga

U. S. S. R.

Estonia

DENMARK

Copenhagen

Baltic Sea

Latvia

Lithuania

ANNEXED
BY USSR

Moscow

55°

East
Prussia

Berlin

Occupied

by

Poland

POLAND

Warsaw

Eastern
Poland

CENTRAL and EASTERN
EUROPE in 1947

GERMANY

Prague

0   200   400

MILES

CZECHOSLOVAKIA

Vienna

Carpathian Ruthenia

Northern Bucovina

SWITZ.

AUSTRIA

Budapest

Bessarabia

HUNGARY

ROMANIA

Belgrade

Bucharest

YUGOSLAVIA

Black Sea

ITALY

Adriatic Sea

DOBRUDJA

Rome

Sofia

BULGARIA

ALBANIA

Istanbul

Ankara

GREECE

TURKEY

Athens

of civic and financial rehabilitation. Convinced that under normal social conditions the peoples of the Continent would continue to accept differences in class and property which were traditional in their culture, the United States made a determined effort to alleviate mass suffering in the Old World. The United Nations Relief and Rehabilitation Administration spent almost four billion dollars immediately after the war to provide the necessities of life to lands freed from the Axis. And its relief program was supplemented with direct loans advanced by the United States to needy governments throughout the world. The results were gratifying from the American point of view. While the industrial proletariat of Europe generally continued to accept socialism in one form or another, the middle class, in alliance with the peasantry, the bureaucracy, and the church, succeeded in maintaining political control in the western states. France, Belgium, Holland, Norway, and Denmark all returned to the parliamentary form of government under which they had lived before the war. Even Italy, after more than twenty years of fascist dictatorship, decided, not without some prodding by the occupying forces of the United States and Great Britain, to establish a representative democracy.

The opposing camps met head on in central Europe. At the end of the war their armies were in complete possession of enemy territory, and therefore their first serious disputes arose with regard to its administration. On the punitive measures to be taken against Germany there was general agreement. A policy of denazification was initiated throughout the country, culminating in the trial and execution of ten of Hitler's close associates. Demilitarization was also carried out with such thoroughness that not a trace was left of the powerful war machine

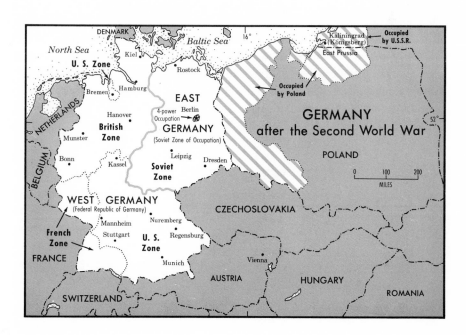

which had almost conquered the Continent. Even on the question of reparations which Stalin demanded there was little difference of opinion. As a result, a defeated nation, exhausted physically after six years of warfare, was crippled economically, by the confiscation of much of its remaining industrial equipment.

Yet while the victorious allies acted in harmony to effect the destruction of fascism, they could not reconcile their views concerning a political system to take its place. The Americans, the British, and the French, whose zones of occupation comprised more than two-thirds of the total area under military government, favored the creation of representative institutions similar to those of the Weimar Republic. The Russians, on the other hand, had no intention of allowing the establishment in the heart of Europe of a parliamentary capitalistic state opposed to the Soviet Union. The outcome was the gradual formation of two Germanys, one a middle-of-the-road democracy with close ties to the United States, the other a communist dictatorship dependent on the support of Moscow.

THE UNITED NATIONS

Winston Churchill was one of the first democratic statesmen to realize that the great wartime alliance could not overcome the differences among its members regarding the organization of the peace. Even before the surrender of the Axis he had begun to distrust the intentions of the Kremlin. One year later, on March 5, 1946, he delivered a speech at Westminster College in Fulton, Missouri, bluntly describing the problem facing the parliamentary governments of the West: "From Stettin in the Baltic to Trieste in the Adriatic, an iron curtain has descended across the Continent. Behind that line lie all the capitals of the ancient states of central and eastern Europe . . . all these famous cities and the populations around them lie in what I might call the Soviet sphere." To oppose Russian aggression he urged close collaboration between America and the United Kingdom: "If the population of the English-speaking Commonwealth be added to that of the United States, with all that such co-operation implies in the air, on the sea, and in science and industry, there will be no quivering, precarious balance of power to offer its temptation to ambition or adventure. On the contrary there would be an overwhelming assurance of security."

To many of his listeners, however, talk of power politics and military alliances was a will-o'-the-wisp. The game of armed diplomacy had been played throughout history without preventing conflict among the great powers. Was there any reason why it should prove more effective in the postwar world? Surely it would be better to rely instead on some new form of international organization for the maintenance of world security. True, the League of Nations had failed to avert a ruinous war. But a careful study of its mistakes might make possible the formation of a more perfect association of peace-loving peoples.

So great was the longing of the masses of the West for political stability that while the Second World War was still in progress the grand coalition against fascism announced on October 30, 1943: "The Governments of the United States of America, the United Kingdom, the Soviet Union and China . . . recognize the necessity of establishing at the earliest practicable date a general international organization, based on the principle of the sovereign equality of all peace-loving states, and open to membership by all such states, large and small, for the maintenance of international peace and security." To implement this declaration exploratory conversations were held at Dumbarton Oaks in Washington, D.C., from August to October 1944. Then early in February 1945 Roosevelt, Stalin, and Churchill met at Yalta in the Crimea to concert plans for the military defeat of the Axis, the reestablishment of international stability, and the guarantee of the peace by a new league of nations. About two months later delegates from fifty countries gathered in San Francisco to draft the constitutional charter of the proposed association of states. Finally, on October 24, 1945, the United Nations came officially into existence.

The charter of the United Nations provided for the establishment of two major deliberative bodies, the General Assembly and the Security Council. The former, in which each state was to have one vote, possessed advisory rather than mandatory power. The latter, on the other hand, was endowed with considerable

YALTA CONFERENCE. At the time of this historic meeting of Churchill, Roosevelt, and Stalin there was still hope that after the war the world would be free of political insecurity.

authority to deal with international conflicts. Composed of five permanent members, the United States, the Soviet Union, Great Britain, France and China, and of six other nations elected by the General Assembly for terms of two years, it had the right to "take such action by air, sea, or land forces as may be necessary to maintain or restore international peace and security." The great powers were thus in effect entrusted with the primary responsibility for enforcing law and order among the lesser governments. Furthermore, the Economic and Social Council was formed to encourage cooperation among countries "with respect to international economic, social, cultural, educational, health, and related matters." The Trusteeship Council was designed to supervise the administration of those colonies taken away from the defeated nations in the two world wars which were not yet ready for self-government. Finally, the International Court of Justice was founded to help settle diplomatic disputes referred to it by sovereign states. The fundamental purpose of all these organizations was stated in the first article of the charter of the United Nations: "To maintain international peace and security, and to that end: to take effective collective measures for the prevention and removal of threats to the peace, and for the suppression of acts of aggression or other breaches of the peace, and to bring about by peaceful means, and in conformity with the principles of justice and international law, adjustment or settlement of international disputes or situations which might lead to a breach of the peace."

Yet the realization of this purpose was possible only as long as the leading states of the world, especially the United States and Russia, were able to continue the policy of collaboration which they had adopted during the struggle against the Axis. In other words, the success of the United Nations after the Second World War, like that of the League of Nations after the First World War or of the Quadruple Alliance after the Napoleonic era, depended on the maintenance of the diplomatic harmony among the victors which had been originally established under wartime conditions. Together the great powers could impose their will on the weaker countries and thus prevent an international dispute from developing into an armed conflict. But once they themselves became divided, the United Nations lost much of its effectiveness as an instrument for the enforcement of peace. Any consistent plan of action then became difficult, because Article 27 of the charter provided that each of the permanent members of the Security Council had the right to veto any important decision which it considered incompatible with its interests.

This provision came to be bitterly criticized in the democratic countries for enabling the Soviet Union to obstruct the efficient operation of the United Nations. But as a matter of fact at both the Yalta Conference and the San Francisco Conference American statesmen were as ready as the Russians to accept the veto. Remembering what had happened twenty-five years before, when the Treaty of Versailles was rejected by a suspicious Senate, they decided to appease isolationist sentiment in the New World with an ironclad guarantee of the sovereignty of

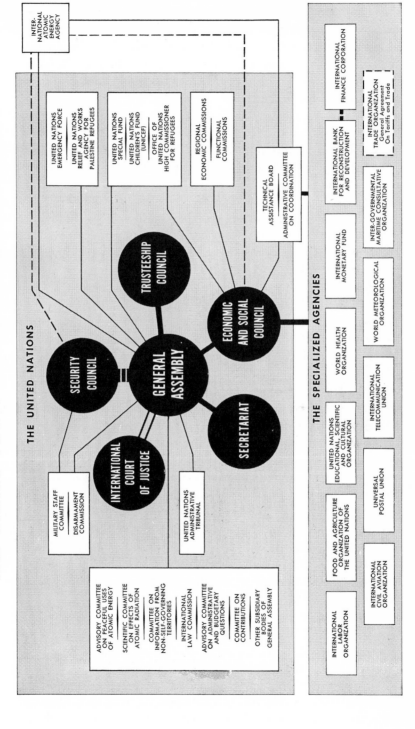

THE UNITED NATIONS AND RELATED AGENCIES

THE UNITED NATIONS

INTER-NATIONAL ATOMIC ENERGY AGENCY

UNITED NATIONS EMERGENCY FORCE

UNITED NATIONS RELIEF AND WORKS AGENCY FOR PALESTINE REFUGEES

UNITED NATIONS SPECIAL FUND

UNITED NATIONS CHILDREN'S FUND (UNICEF)

OFFICE OF UNITED NATIONS HIGH COMMISSIONER FOR REFUGEES

REGIONAL ECONOMIC COMMISSIONS

FUNCTIONAL COMMISSIONS

TECHNICAL ASSISTANCE BOARD

ADMINISTRATIVE COMMITTEE ON COORDINATION

TRUSTEESHIP COUNCIL

SECURITY COUNCIL

GENERAL ASSEMBLY

ECONOMIC AND SOCIAL COUNCIL

INTERNATIONAL COURT OF JUSTICE

SECRETARIAT

MILITARY STAFF COMMITTEE

DISARMAMENT COMMISSION

UNITED NATIONS ADMINISTRATIVE TRIBUNAL

ADVISORY COMMITTEE ON PEACEFUL USES OF ATOMIC ENERGY

SCIENTIFIC COMMITTEE ON EFFECTS OF ATOMIC RADIATION

COMMITTEE ON INFORMATION FROM NON-SELF-GOVERNING TERRITORIES

INTERNATIONAL LAW COMMISSION

ADVISORY COMMITTEE ON ADMINISTRATIVE AND BUDGETARY QUESTIONS

COMMITTEE ON CONTRIBUTIONS

OTHER SUBSIDIARY BODIES OF GENERAL ASSEMBLY

THE SPECIALIZED AGENCIES

INTERNATIONAL FINANCE CORPORATION

INTERNATIONAL BANK FOR RECONSTRUCTION AND DEVELOPMENT

INTERNATIONAL TRADE ORGANIZATION General Agreement On Tariffs and Trade

INTERNATIONAL MONETARY FUND

INTER-GOVERNMENTAL MARITIME CONSULTATIVE ORGANIZATION

WORLD HEALTH ORGANIZATION

WORLD METEOROLOGICAL ORGANIZATION

UNITED NATIONS EDUCATIONAL, SCIENTIFIC AND CULTURAL ORGANIZATION

INTERNATIONAL TELECOMMUNICATION UNION

FOOD AND AGRICULTURE ORGANIZATION OF THE UNITED NATIONS

UNIVERSAL POSTAL UNION

INTERNATIONAL LABOR ORGANIZATION

INTERNATIONAL CIVIL AVIATION ORGANIZATION

the United States. As it turned out, their precautions were unnecessary. In almost all significant questions Washington could count on the support of the majority of the other governments, while Moscow was forced to oppose hostile votes with vetoes. Yet if the situation had been reversed, if America had found herself consistently outvoted in the United Nations, she too would in all likelihood have made use of the special right conferred by the charter.

The disintegration of the wartime coalition meant that popular hopes for peace could not be realized. Instead a diplomatic struggle between the communist and the capitalist states retarded the recovery of the world. Some observers of the international scene were reminded of the atmosphere of crisis which preceded the outbreak of the Second World War. There were even those who openly prophesied for the United Nations the same fate which had befallen the League of Nations. Much of their criticism, however, was ill-founded. To be sure, the danger of a new armed conflict was real enough. But despite the fact the United Nations failed to live up to the expectations of many of its supporters, the achievements to its credit were sufficiently impressive to justify its existence.

For millions of hungry people throughout the world the United Nations Relief and Rehabilitation Administration meant the difference between health and sickness. The International Bank facilitated economic progress in devastated or backward countries. The International Labor Organization urged improvements in the standard of living of the working class. The United Nations Educational, Scientific, and Cultural Organization sought to overcome national exclusiveness by encouraging intercultural understanding. Most important of all, the Security Council and the General Assembly constituted a stock exchange of diplomatic policies where opposing governments could discuss the political problems facing them. True, the debates between Russia and America sometimes reached the heights of futility. But as long as their delegates continued to argue around the conference table, they were not likely to start dropping bombs. Suggestions that the Soviet Union be expelled from the United Nations were therefore rejected by the democratic leaders, who did not wish to transform an international organization designed to maintain peace into an out-and-out military alliance directed against the communist states. It was better to let the long argument on the shores of the East River in New York go on, while the West recovered from the effects of a ruinous military conflict. Besides, there was always the hope that some day an agreement could finally be reached.

2. The Recovery of the West

THE RIVALRY between the parliamentary and the communist states had an important effect on their internal development. In the case of the former, it meant an

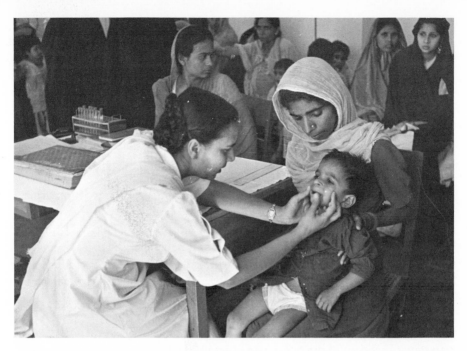

THE ACHIEVEMENTS OF THE UNITED NATIONS. The maternity center conducted by the World Health Organization in Pakistan (*above*) is an example of the important humanitarian work carried on under the auspices of the United Nations; while the photograph of Secretary General U Thant and Russian and American diplomats during the Cuban missile crisis of 1962 (*below*) reminds us that the United Nations has been successful in helping the diplomats of the world to solve some international crises at the conference table.

even greater political and economic dependence on the United States than would have been the case under conditions of diplomatic stability. For it was obvious during the early postwar years that Europe could not resist the Soviet Union with its own resources. Only the strength of the New World made possible the survival of democratic capitalism in the face of Russian hostility.

THE UNITED STATES

By 1945 the United States had become a colossus among nations. While achieving a steadily rising standard of living for its own population, it was at the same time feeding and defending half of the world from Berlin to Tokyo. Despite the gloomy predictions of economists who could still remember the great depression, the end of the war failed to halt the growth of its productive capacity. Military expenditures to meet the threat of Russian aggression, the demand from abroad for foodstuffs and manufactured goods, and finally the appetite of the consumer at home for houses, automobiles, and television sets, all in combination generated the greatest wave of prosperity since the formation of the republic. At first the Democrats under President Harry S Truman claimed credit for this material well-being, but good times proved to be non-partisan. Industry and agriculture went on producing in increasing abundance during the Republican administration of Dwight D. Eisenhower in the 1950's, as well as under his Democratic successors John F. Kennedy and Lyndon B. Johnson in the 1960's. Both parties, moreover, recognized the continuing need for welfare legislation by increasing public housing, raising the minimum-wage scale, subsidizing the farm population, financing flood control and soil conservation, and improving the status of the Negro. And both pursued a diplomatic policy of opposition to Moscow and Peking by providing financial and military assistance to all governments ready to combat communism.

WESTERN EUROPE

The United Kingdom was the chief beneficiary of the generosity of the New World. Britain had undergone a serious relative economic decline since the nineteenth century, when her factories dominated the markets of the world. The movement for independence among colonial peoples, the competition of other great industrial states, and two world conflicts had left her in a condition of national exhaustion. The extent of popular dissatisfaction was clearly revealed in the election of 1945, when the indomitable prime minister of the war years, Winston Churchill, was soundly defeated, and the Labor party under Clement R. Attlee came to power.

In keeping with its campaign promises, the new government extended the social-insurance system and introduced a plan for free medical care. In 1946 it put the overseas cable and wire services and the coal mines under public ownership, and in 1947 it nationalized the railroads, canals, and docks. But social reform alone was not the answer to financial insecurity. Loans of some five billion dollars from the United States and Canada alleviated the economic problem without solving it, so that rationing of food had to be retained without substantial relaxation until 1948. Restrictions on the purchase of clothing remained in force even longer. Finally, in 1949 the pound sterling was devalued from $4.03 to $2.80 in order to stimulate the languishing export trade. Such Spartan measures succeeded little by little in restoring fiscal stability, but they did nothing to enhance the popularity of the socialist government. In the election of 1951 the Conservative party won a majority, just as the program of national austerity was beginning to show results. Two years later the coronation of the youthful Elizabeth II was greeted by millions of her jubilant subjects as inaugurating a reign like that of her illustrious sixteenth-century namesake. Yet it was clear that the country remained exposed to financial and political dangers. The 1960's was a decade of steady progress, although the predominance which the United Kingdom had formerly enjoyed was only a memory. Now it had to adjust to the status of a second-class power.

While the difficulties which the English had to face were primarily economic, the French were afflicted by a crisis of national spirit. Their country had escaped severe physical damage during the war by a prompt capitulation to the enemy, and the population, which had hardly increased in more than seventy years, could still live in abundance on the most fertile lands of western Europe. But military defeat, colonial unrest, and the intensification of class resentment inflicted wounds which material well-being alone could not heal. In the postwar years the proletariat of France became more radical and the bourgeoisie less conciliatory than before. And there was still the conservative argument that ever since the French Revolution republicanism had divided and weakened the nation, so that only a return to some form of rule by a strong man could revive its sense of purpose.

Immediately after the liberation of Paris it looked as if a new spirit of civic unity had developed in France. On September 9, 1944, General Charles de Gaulle formed the Provisional Government of the French Republic, which initiated the work of economic reconstruction and political reorganization. By 1946 coal, gas, electricity, aviation, and banking had been nationalized, the armed forces had been modernized and enlarged, and an ambitious foreign policy befitting a major power had been initiated. But most Frenchmen were unwilling to sacrifice individualism for order. In the National Constituent Assembly elected on October 21, 1945, could be found the usual Gallic multiplicity of parties, and the new constitution adopted a year later was indistinguishable in most important respects from the old.

The Fourth Republic like the Third was plagued with ministerial instability and parliamentary confusion. In ten years some twenty cabinets came and went, each eventually overthrown because of its inability to reconcile the opposing forces on the political scene. On the left the Communist party was planning for a dictator-ship of the proletariat. On the right the Reunion of the French People was preach-ing the need for a concentration of government authority. In the middle moderate statesmen, among them Antoine Pinay, Joseph Laniel, Robert Schuman, Georges Bidault, Pierre Mendès-France, and Edgar Faure, continued to fight against revo-lutions in southeast Asia and North Africa and to struggle with inflated prices and labor strikes at home. Always in the midst of one crisis or another, the state went on muddling through in the familiar fashion of French republicanism, divided and confused. Finally, in June 1958 a hopeless impasse in parliament and the threat of a mutiny in the army led to de Gaulle's return to power. Some three months later a new constitution won overwhelming popular approval, and the Fourth Republic was officially replaced by the Fifth.

The new leader of the nation stabilized political conditions at home, liquidated what was left of the colonial empire overseas, and sought to revive French grandeur in international affairs. But while most of his countrymen accepted the regime with varying degrees of approval, there was growing apprehension about what system of government would succeed the aging president.

In Italy there was a peaceful transition from authoritarianism to democracy. Yet at first the outlook was bleak, for a lost war had aggravated all the chronic

CHARLES DE GAULLE. The president of the French Republic became a symbol of the revived and assertive Europe of the 1960's.

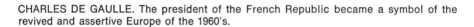

economic ills of the country. It went without saying that fascism was discredited, but what would replace it? After the fall of Mussolini communism emerged as a powerful political movement supported by exploited factory workers and even by some landless peasants. Resisting it were the middle-of-the-road parliamentary parties expressing the views of the bourgeois businessman, the white-collar professional, and the church-going farmer. Their triumph in the struggle with radicalism was partly at least a result of the policy pursued by the democratic victor states.

To alleviate privation, the United Nations Relief and Rehabilitation Administration in 1946 alone shipped $450 million worth of essential supplies to Italy. National pride, moreover, was flattered by the prompt return of political control over virtually the entire country to the government in Rome. Under the terms of the peace treaty of February 10, 1947, the Italians suffered only minor losses of territory in Europe. The surrender of their costly overseas possessions and the reduction of their army to three hundred thousand men were actually blessings in disguise. The presence of American and British troops, moreover, provided security against a radical coup. On June 2, 1946 elections to the Constituent Assembly gave 207 seats to the moderate Christian Democratic party and 41 seats to the Liberal party, while the Socialist party received 115 and the Communist party 104. At the same time a national referendum decided in favor of the establishment of a republic by a vote of 12,717,923 to 10,719,284. After the adoption of a democratic constitution on December 22, 1947, Italy was ruled by the statesmen of the center, of whom Alcide de Gasperi was the ablest. Poverty among the lower classes remained a serious problem. The left continued to receive the endorsement of about a third of all voters. Even fascist and monarchist organizations revived. Yet the new regime displayed greater determination in dealing with economic and social questions than any which had been in power since the achievement of national unification almost a hundred years before. Although the south remained a depressed region, the great boom of the 1960's produced a significant improvement in the standard of living. All in all, democracy in Italy was proving to be a viable and effective form of government.

Germany in the meantime provided proof that under conditions of modern warfare the distinction between winner and loser was often artificial. In 1945 a land of ruined cities and hungry people lay prostrate before the victorious powers. In the wake of defeat came despair, while the occupying forces demilitarized and denazified. To make matters worse, the country was forced to receive some ten million refugees and expellees from the east; her industrial output was reduced to half the volume of 1938; and she was deprived of territories normally providing about 25 per cent of her food supply by the assignment to Polish administration of the region beyond the Oder and the Neisse rivers. Never before had a leading state of the West suffered such a catastrophic collapse.

Yet before long the democratic powers decided that they could not go on indefinitely maintaining a slum in the heart of Europe. First of all, they would be endangering their own economic position. And second, in the developing struggle between capitalism and communism German factories and even German arms could play an important role. The introduction in 1948 of currency reform in the western zones of occupation was therefore designed to stimulate traditional Teutonic industriousness. One year later the territories under the control of America, England, and France formed the Federal Republic of Germany in accordance with a new democratic constitution. The first chancellor of the republic was Konrad Adenauer of the Christian Democratic party, a septuagenarian politician who governed his country like some stern but patient father controlling a houseful of unruly children.

The result of financial and civic reform was a surprisingly swift recovery. Ten years after unconditional surrender the industrial output of the western region of Germany far exceeded its level before the war. Moreover, the prerogatives of sovereignty, including even the right to maintain an army, had been restored. It was one of the ironies of the postwar scene that in 1950, while victorious England was still forced to retain a system of rationing, defeated Germany ended all restrictions on the purchase of goods. While the propertied classes were the chief beneficiaries of the "economic miracle" of the 1950's and 1960's, the position of labor improved as well. The undiminished strength of the Social Democratic party revealed, however, that the urban proletariat remained loyal to the doctrines of socialism.

The United States did not forget the small democracies. Belgium, Holland, Norway, Denmark, Greece, and Austria received funds to help revive their industry and agriculture which had been impaired by years of alien occupation. For that matter, the fascist countries were also enlisted in the struggle against radicalism. In 1953 the United States and Spain concluded an agreement by which the former obtained bases in the Iberian peninsula, while the latter received economic aid which strengthened the regime of General Franco. Similarly the authoritarian government of Premier Salazar in Portugal succeeded in maintaining cordial relations with the democratic powers by allowing them to use airfields in the Azores during the war and by cooperating with them against Russia afterwards. Throughout western Europe American support helped to restore and stabilize a state system which the Second World War had threatened to destroy.

RUSSIA

The role which the Kremlin played on the other side of the Iron Curtain was similar to the one which the White House performed on this side. Russia, like America, had come out of the war in a stronger diplomatic and military position than when she went in. In foreign affairs her main concern became the consolidation and expansion of the important political gains which she had made during the hostilities. And at home she had to deal above all with the problem of repairing the vast damage caused by the invasion of the Axis. Both tasks were begun under the direction of Stalin, who was now at the pinnacle of his power. His domestic opponents had been purged; his enemies abroad had been defeated. The Red dictator could exercise greater authority than the tsars had ever possessed. In the army his word was law. Even the removal of the savior of Moscow and captor of Berlin, Marshal Georgi K. Zhukov, from the command of the armed forces evoked not a word of protest. Among biologists he was accepted as the arbiter of scientific theories, championing Trofim D. Lysenko's teachings against those of Gregor Mendel, which the rest of the world accepted. He even assumed the role of music critic supreme, condemning the works of such eminent composers as Dmitri Shostakovich and Sergei Prokofiev for bourgeois tendencies. Like Ozymandias in Shelley's poem, he could boast: "Look on my works, ye Mighty, and despair!"

The legacy of his limitless power, however, was fear and hatred. After the death of the autocrat on March 5, 1953, the most damaging attack on his lifework came not from some conservative monarchist or middle-class liberal, but from one of his own protégés, Nikita S. Khrushchev:

> Stalin acted not through persuasion, explanation, and patient cooperation with people, but by imposing his concepts and demanding absolute submission to his opinions. Whoever opposed this concept or tried to prove his viewpoint and the correctness of his position was doomed to removal from the leading collective and to subsequent moral and physical annihilation. . . . Stalin originated the concept "enemy of the people." This term automatically rendered it unnecessary that the ideological errors of a man or men engaged in a controversy be proven; this term made possible the usage of the most cruel repression, violating all norms of revolutionary legality, against anyone who in any way disagreed with Stalin, against those who were only suspected of hostile intent, against those who had bad reputations. . . . In the main, and in actuality, the only proof of guilt used, against all norms of current legal science, was the "confession" of the accused himself; and as subsequent probing proved, "confessions" were acquired through physical pressures against the accused.[1]

But despite their criticisms, the successors of Stalin differed from him in temperament rather than objective. The apparatus of oppression was relaxed, yet the dictatorship of the party remained. The government maintained its control over the economy, and the secret police continued to function. Moreover, while the cult of one man was replaced by an experiment in collective leadership, within the walls of the Kremlin a struggle for political mastery went on. In 1953 Lavrenti P. Beria appeared to be the power behind the scenes; in 1954 it was Georgi M.

---

[1] *New York Times,* June 5, 1956. © 1956 by The New York Times Company. Reprinted by permission.

PARADE IN MOSCOW. This picture suggests the economic and military progress which the Soviet Union has made since the Second World War.

Malenkov; in 1955 Nikita S. Khrushchev; in 1964 Alexei I. Kosygin and Leonid I. Brezhnev. Although factions within the communist hierarchy vied for power, there was no evidence of popular opposition to the doctrines of Marxism. The man in the street remained convinced that the established order was in essence just. His faith was reinforced, moreover, by the economic and technological progress of his country, which in 1957 startled the capitalistic world by becoming the first to launch an artificial satellite revolving in an orbit around the earth, and which continued to achieve remarkable successes in space exploration during the following years. To a people which had never known political freedom or material well-being the promise of the future seemed to justify past sacrifices.

THE COMMUNIST SATELLITES

The vassal states of the Soviet Union meekly conformed to the wishes of the Kremlin. Soon after the war Poland, Romania, Hungary, Bulgaria, Yugoslavia, Albania, Czechoslovakia, and the German Democratic Republic, formed in the Russian zone of occupation, began to establish the dictatorship of the Communist party, to collectivize agriculture, to nationalize factories and banks, and to engage in a test of strength with the church. They organized security police systems and built corrective labor camps, launching periodic campaigns against ideological dissenters. Even dedicated left-wingers, among them Traicho Kostov in Bulgaria, Laszlo Rajk in Hungary, and Rudolf Slansky in Czechoslovakia, suffered imprisonment or death because of suspicions in Moscow that they were secretly planning to pursue an independent policy. Only Marshal Tito of Yugoslavia succeeded in defying Russia, and he was punished with expulsion from the communist camp in 1948.

With the death of Stalin, however, the grip of the Kremlin began to loosen. There was much talk about following several paths to the classless society in accordance with special national conditions. In 1955 Khrushchev and Tito compromised the differences between their governments on terms which represented a moral victory for the latter. One year later the communist leader of Poland, Wladyslaw Gomulka, succeeded in winning a measure of autonomy for his country. Yet although the Soviet Union was prepared to tolerate some differences within the Marxist system, it remained opposed to any attack on the system itself. Thus, when in the fall of 1956 a popular uprising in Hungary sought to overthrow the radical government, the Red Army marched against the Magyars and suppressed the rebellion by force of arms. Disregarding all the pronouncements about "national sovereignty, mutual advantage, and equality," Moscow made it clear that it had no intention of permitting the reestablishment of the barrier of hostile states which had stood in its way in the interwar period.

THE HUNGARIAN REVOLUTION. The two dead Russian soldiers were victims of a violent but unsuccessful uprising in Budapest in 1956 against Soviet domination.

After 1953 the Communist parties of the satellite nations, while still opposed to parliamentary democracy, relaxed some of their oppressive economic and civic restrictions. In the face of antiradical popular sentiments, moreover, they advanced a program of reform which was not without beneficent results. They ended the dominant position of the conservative landed aristocracy; they increased the output of factories and mines; they improved the quality of popular instruction; they curbed the rampant chauvinism of the educated classes. Their rule was dictatorial and brutal, but they succeeded in destroying the historic social system of the eastern borderlands of the Continent. During the 1960's, furthermore, they began to tolerate a measure of political criticism and dissent. The lasting result of their activities was that, even in the event of their fall from power, the task of restoring the old order would be like attempting to unscramble an omelet.

THE NEW ERA

While the outcome of the struggle between democratic capitalism and authoritarian communism remained in doubt, there was no question that Europe had suffered a political decline. It could still manufacture goods and grow crops; it could still produce works of art and achieve advances in science. Indeed, the progress of technology assured for its masses a higher standard of living than they had ever known before. But it could no longer command obedience in a world which was increasingly adopting the way of life of the Occident. The ordeal of total war and the strain of colonial conflict had exhausted the Continent. Like Hellas after the death of Alexander the Great, Europe might continue to enlighten the barbarian. Its capacity for the subjugation of alien peoples, however, was dwindling. Not only was the colored man rebelling against the rule of the European with increasing success, but the European himself was no longer the unchallenged master of his own house. Whether he liked it or not, he had to choose between two alternatives neither of which would have been conceivable before the First World War. Either he aligned with the United States, which lay beyond the frontiers of the Old World, or he was forced to become a client of Russia, a land only partly occidental. The existence of this dilemma was a measure of his decline. Economic progress remained an attainable goal, but political hegemony was a thing of the past. The heroic age of Europe had come to an end.

3. The Colonial World in Revolt

THE EAST was in the meantime experiencing the exhilaration of a great awakening. Its political revival, which had begun early in the twentieth century, was stimulated by military conflicts and social upheavals in Europe. Most of the Orient had escaped the devastation of war, and even in those regions which became battlefields economic backwardness actually facilitated recovery. It was easier to rebuild a Burmese village or a Bedouin encampment than Berlin, London, or Warsaw. Besides, from the point of view of native nationalism, physical suffering was a fair price for the relaxation of alien rule. After 1918 the English, the French, and the Dutch had been forced to make important political concessions to the colonial masses; after 1945 their resistance to anti-imperialistic demands began to collapse completely. For the Orient, therefore, the major developments of the postwar years were a logical extension of the administrative improvements and constitutional reforms initiated during the interwar period.

Some of the colonial powers, such as Great Britain and the United States, accepting gracefully what could not be changed, succeeded in maintaining cordial relations with their former possessions. Others, particularly France and Holland, attempted to hold their dependencies by force of arms, only to discover that they no longer had the military resources to suppress nationalism in the East. They were defeated, and what is more, the struggle cost them much of the goodwill they still retained among their emancipated subjects. For whether under the leadership of liberals, communists, or party bosses, the dark-skinned races were resolved to win the right to self-determination.

THE FAR EAST

In the Far East the most important political effect of the Second World War was the defeat of the country which for forty years had been paramount along the western shore of the Pacific. Japan, like Germany, paid the penalty of defeat by the loss of her position as a great nation. But, unlike Germany, she did not suffer the disaster of territorial partition. By surrendering under circumstances which in effect made the United States the major occupying power, she ensured a uniform reorganization of her civic and economic institutions. The man entrusted with the task of governing the defeated enemy was General Douglas MacArthur, who played the role of Yankee proconsul with an enthusiasm inspiring the observation: "The Japanese emperor has renounced his divinity. It has been taken up by General MacArthur." Under his direction Japan adopted a program of far-reaching reform. A new constitution promulgated on November 3, 1946 declared the people to be the source of sovereignty; it introduced government by a cabinet responsible to parliament; it defined the freedom of the citizen in a bill of rights; it conferred on women a status of legal equality with men; and it proclaimed that war was "forever renounced as a means of settling disputes with other nations." At the same time the leading exponents of the prewar policy of aggression were executed or imprisoned, and thousands of their followers were excluded from participation in politics. The armed forces were dissolved; the secret police was abolished; the system of popular education was liberalized; and the formation of labor unions was encouraged. Finally, measures were initiated to transform landless peasants into independent farmers and to break the power of the great industrial and financial combines known as the *Zaibatsu*. The effect was a revolution from above democratizing the social structure of a country still dominated by an aristocracy of birth and wealth.

To demonstrate her faith in the new parliamentary regime as well as to win an important ally against communism, the United States on September 8, 1951 signed a peace treaty with Japan, by which the latter regained her national sovereignty. Yet the loss of all of her possessions outside the home islands meant that a population approaching a hundred million had to find subsistence in an area no larger than that on which twenty-eight million had lived a century before when Commodore Matthew C. Perry first sailed into Edo Bay. A security pact concluded with Washington, moreover, permitted American troops to remain in her territories. To be sure, they were no longer to act as an army of occupation, but rather "to deter armed attack." Yet expressions of mutual regard could not disguise the fact that the Land of the Rising Sun was still within the American sphere of influence. What made this political decline bearable was a rapid economic revival which raised the Japanese standard of living to its highest point in history. Technological progress was making possible the material security which colonial expansion and military conquest had failed to achieve.

The collapse of Japan enabled China to claim at last the position of the leading power in the Far East. Yet her triumph also exposed her once again to domestic strife. As long as they faced the Nipponese armies, the middle-of-the-road Kuomintang under Chiang Kai-shek and the Communist party under Mao Tse-tung were forced to collaborate against their common enemy. But once Tokyo had surrendered, old animosities began to rise to the surface.

From 1945 to 1950 the nation went through a civil war in which the leftists gradually won the upper hand. First of all, they received substantial support from the Soviet Union. Second, their armed forces proved superior in leadership and discipline to their opponents. And finally, their program of radical economic reform made a strong appeal to millions of poverty-stricken workers and peasants. The government of the republic, on the other hand, frittered away whatever political and military advantages it had possessed when the struggle began. As for the United States, immediately after the surrender of the Japanese it attempted to mediate between the two opposing camps. Even after the efforts of General George C. Marshall to arrange a truce had failed because of intransigency on both sides, Washington went on giving the Nationalists financial assistance, which by 1948 amounted to more than two billion dollars. But money alone could not buy honesty and efficiency in Nanking. As the Red armies continued to make headway against the anticommunists, the White House decided to cut its losses. Convinced that nothing less than the intervention of American troops could save the Kuomintang, it finally assumed a hands-off attitude.

The American policy of neutrality toward the struggle in China hastened the defeat of the Nationalists. By 1950 Chiang Kai-shek had been driven to the island of Formosa (Taiwan), leaving the mainland completely in the hands of the leftists. The latter proceeded to introduce an ambitious program of socialization and industrialization under the dictatorial leadership of the Communist party. Furthermore, a pact of friendship with the Soviet Union established a formal alliance between the two Marxist states.

Meanwhile the Nationalists on Formosa, now that the horse had been stolen, were rushing to lock the stable. The troops they managed to save from the debacle were reorganized and retrained; bureaucratic corruption was suppressed; the economy of the island was strengthened; and the system of administration was democratized. There was even bold talk about the reconquest of the mainland from communism. Yet the fact was that an insular province with a population of some eleven million people and an army of perhaps six hundred thousand aging soldiers could hardly expect to undertake a military campaign against an enemy whose armed forces were among the largest in the world. Only in the event of a war between China and America, or of a successful revolution against the communist government on the mainland, could the Kuomintang hope to regain its lost authority. In the meantime the new regime in Peking was consolidating its political strength, fostering economic growth, and emerging as a great world power.

INDIA

In India the victory of nationalism was easier. For one thing, there was a world of difference between the parliamentarians in London and the militarists in Tokyo. And second, the religious hostility of Hindu and Moslem was not as uncompromising as the ideological opposition of communist and conservative. As soon as the war was over, Prime Minister Attlee entered into negotiations with the political leaders of the subcontinent to determine the conditions under which the liberation of their country should take place. But no agreement was reached. The Indian National Congress, loyal to the teachings of Mohandas K. Gandhi, advocated the establishment of a united democratic state in which the various cultural communities could live peacefully side by side. This plan appealed particularly to the adherents of Hinduism, who constituted a majority of the nation. The All-India Moslem League under Mohammed Ali Jinnah, however, insisted on nothing less than the creation of a separate state for the followers of Islam, to be known as Pakistan. Otherwise, it maintained, there could be no effective protection of the Mohammedan minority against the bigotry of the Hindus. On August 15, 1947 after all efforts to find a mutually acceptable compromise had failed, two new countries were formed in India.

The Union of India, with a population of more than four hundred million people and an area of some 1,300,000 square miles, was politically the more important. Governed in the spirit of western democracy, she followed a policy of agricultural and industrial reform at home and of neutrality between Russia and America in foreign affairs. The essential objectives of her diplomacy were defined in 1954 in the five principles or Panch Shila: respect for other countries' territorial integrity and sovereignty; non-aggression; non-interference in other nations' internal affairs; equality and mutual benefit; and peaceful coexistence. But the Republic of Pakistan, with about ninety-five million inhabitants in two widely separated regions

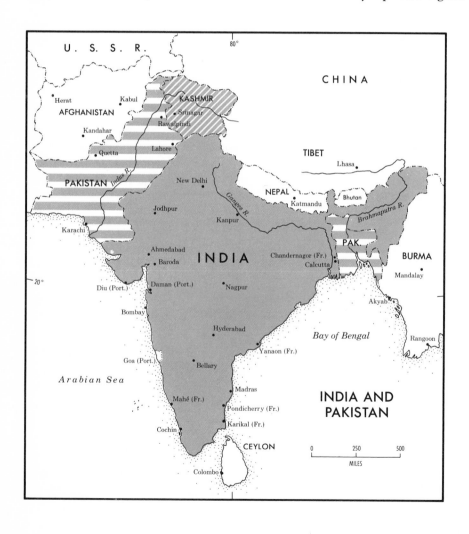

totaling 365,000 square miles, at first took her stand on the side of the capitalistic countries. Influenced in her philosophy of state by the teachings of the Koran, she was naturally opposed to the antireligious doctrines of Marxism. But hostility toward India, particularly over the control of Kashmir, forced her into closer relations with communist China. Both India and Pakistan suffered from overpopulation and underdevelopment, aggravated by the economic dislocation which political separation created. And yet despite their common history, despite their common needs and purposes, they remained divided by religious hostilities and territorial disputes. From the point of view of civic and material progress, the partition of the subcontinent was a surrender of national welfare to fear and prejudice.

SOUTHEAST ASIA

The neighboring states of southeast Asia also won their political independence after the Second World War. The British, once they recognized the inevitability of the decline of imperialism, adapted their colonial policies to changing conditions. Since they could not suppress native nationalism, they attempted to influence it by a program of conciliation. In 1946 Ceylon received the right to self-government in domestic affairs; in 1948 Burma was recognized as a free republic; and in 1957 Malaya won the status of a sovereign power. Similarly, the United States in 1946 redeemed the promise of the Tydings-McDuffie Act of 1934 with the establishment of the Republic of the Philippines, an act of generous statesmanship which was rewarded by a close political and economic collaboration between Manila and Washington.

The Dutch, however, were not disposed to part with their overseas possessions so easily. Immediately after the surrender of Japan they returned to the East Indies, only to find that the nationalists under Achmed Sukarno had proclaimed the independence of the islands. There followed four years of intermittent warfare, until on December 27, 1949 the government of Queen Juliana was forced to agree to the independence of the United States of Indonesia. The new country soon embarked on a policy of expansion which brought it into diplomatic conflict with the states of the West.

The French in Indochina opposed demands for the end of imperialistic rule with even greater determination than the Dutch. Yet the result was the same. After fighting against their colonial subjects for nine frustrating years they were finally forced by the defeat at Dien Bien Phu in 1954 to admit the futility of further hostilities. The most populous districts of the north were surrendered to the communists led by Ho Chi Minh, while the bulk of the southern part went to the moderates under Ngo Dinh Diem. But a left-wing insurrection in what was now called South Vietnam threatened to topple the government there and achieve the reunification of the country under a Marxist regime. Early in the 1960's, there-

A VIETNAMESE POLITICAL DEMONSTRATION. Buddhist monks and women in Saigon yank at a barbed wire barricade set up by the police in 1963, as they express their dissatisfaction with the government in power.

fore, the United States decided to intervene in southeast Asia to prevent the region from falling completely under the control of communist governments.

THE MIDDLE EAST

The conflicting objectives of European imperialism, Arab patriotism, and Jewish nationalism had created a diplomatic powder keg in the Middle East. Among Zionists the effect of the Second World War was to strengthen their determination to establish an independent nation in Palestine. The extermination by National Socialism of millions of their defenseless coreligionists served to emphasize the need for a sovereign authority capable of opposing anti-Semitism, while the plight of the hundreds of thousands of survivors of the holocaust who were in search of a place of refuge provided an additional argument for proclaiming a Jewish state in the Holy Land. The position of the Arabs was that the criminal atrocities of the Axis in eastern Europe were no justification for any change in the ethnic composition of western Asia. And the British, who had been entrusted with the administration of Palestine after the First World War, had only one desire, to withdraw as soon as possible from a country in which both sides looked upon them as intruders.

After a proposal of the United Nations to partition Palestine had been rejected by the Arabs, the United Kingdom surrendered her authority on May 14, 1948. That same day a Zionist provisional government under David Ben Gurion announced the formation of the state of Israel. The result was a war which continued for about a year between the new republic and its Arab enemies. The Jews held their own, and an uneasy armistice was finally concluded which left them in control of about half of the Holy Land. They adopted a system of government based on the principles of parliamentary democracy, and in the diplomatic struggle between the United States and the Soviet Union their sympathies were on the side of Washington. But serious dangers still threatened them. Economically they managed to make ends meet only through the contributions of their coreligionists in the New World, since the arid soil of Palestine could not support a swiftly growing population of two million inhabitants. Militarily, moreover, they had to face hostile neighbors who had lost one campaign, but who were determined to avenge their defeat the moment an opportunity arose.

For the Arabs the conflict with Israel was only one aspect of a greater struggle against the political influence of the West. In 1945 there had been formed the League of Arab States, an association of countries which included Egypt, Syria, Lebanon, Iraq, Transjordania, Saudi Arabia, and Yemen, with a combined popu-

THE INAUGURATION OF CHAIM WEIZMANN AS FIRST PRESIDENT OF ISRAEL. This picture shows an important episode in 1949 in the creation of a new state by an ancient people.

lation of approximately forty-five million people and an area extending from the Persian Gulf to the Libyan Desert. Under its direction the lands of the Middle East proceeded to free themselves from the remnants of colonial rule. Foreign troops were withdrawn from Syria and Lebanon in 1946; national independence was achieved in Libya in 1951; Morocco and Tunisia became sovereign states in 1956; and Algeria won her freedom in 1962.

The most colorful of the leaders in the struggle against imperialism was Gamal Abdel Nasser, an officer in the Egyptian army, who became the dominant figure in the government in Cairo after the deposition of King Farouk in 1952. The impoverished masses of his countrymen idolized him as their deliverer from foreign oppression, while jealous politicians regarded him as an ambitious climber exploiting the force of nationalism to further his own career. All agreed, however, that no other figure on the political scene in the Middle East possessed his flair for the dramatic. The supreme test of his skill as a statesman came in 1956, when as a result of the withdrawal of a promise of financial support by the democratic states he seized the Suez Canal Company. The reply to this move was a lightning military campaign by Israeli, British, and French troops against the Egyptian armed forces, which were easily defeated. The Nile lay defenseless before the invaders. And yet the dashing dictator actually managed to transform a military disaster into a diplomatic victory. Since neither the United States nor the Soviet Union wanted to antagonize patriotic sentiment within Islam, Nasser was saved from a total debacle by the intervention of the United Nations. The world organization deprived the victors of their conquests and left the vanquished to enjoy a major political triumph.

In the course of the hostilities the Kremlin had offered to help the Egyptians oppose the designs of "bourgeois imperialism." Thereafter the prestige of Russia rose throughout the Middle East. There were even important Arab leaders ready to enter into an alliance with Moscow, not because of any sympathy with Marxism, but in order to play off communism against capitalism. Such a course was tempting, although it was not without its dangers. In the diplomatic agreements which the Soviet Union had concluded with the countries of eastern Europe after the Second World War the Russians had usually gotten the best of the bargain. Furthermore, leftist expansionism had proved as oppressive as rightist imperialism. Lastly, in the event of an armed conflict for control of the Mediterranean, the first victims of war would be the masses of Islam.

AFRICA

The influence of native nationalism was felt as far as the Dark Continent. In the interwar period there had already been evidence of the discontent of the black man with white rule, and after 1945 the demand for self-determination for Africa became more insistent. Sometimes it found expression in barbaric secret societies like the Mau Mau in Kenya, which launched a campaign of terror against colonial domination under the slogan: "Take back the land which the white man has stolen from us!" Sometimes it took the form of open demonstrations of political disaffection, as when some fifty thousand persons in the Gold Coast participated in a nationalist riot in 1948. And sometimes it was used by colored leftists like Jomo Kenyatta to advance radical doctrines in the guise of protests against imperialism.

The response of the whites to the growing civic consciousness of the Negro varied. In the Union of South Africa it was an even stricter program of racial segregation introduced by the Boers of the Nationalist party. The Belgians and the Portuguese farther north attempted to oppose native nationalism with a policy of ethnic toleration and economic progress. For the French in West Africa and in Equatorial Africa, the ideal remained assimilation, that is, the acceptance by the educated and propertied blacks of the culture of the mother country in return for their admission to the rights of citizenship.

As for the possessions of Great Britain, they were governed on the assumption that the process of political development in colored colonies would not be essentially different from what it had been in white colonies. The authorities in London accordingly sought to prepare the way for a system of self-rule in which the Europeans would at least in the beginning be predominant, but in which the interests of the indigenous population would also be represented. In 1950, for example, the new constitutions promulgated for Nigeria and Sierra Leone envisaged a considerable measure of participation in civic affairs by Negroes. In 1953 came the establishment of the Central African Federation, composed of Northern Rhodesia, Southern Rhodesia, and Nyasaland, and governed by a parliament of thirty-five members among whom were six natives. And in 1957 the Gold Coast became the free and sovereign state of Ghana, the first land in black Africa to complete transition to national independence.

During the 1960's the movement for the liberation of the Dark Continent became irresistible, as one European state after another hastened to emancipate the colonies which could no longer be retained anyway. President de Gaulle of France, hoping to retain a measure of influence over African affairs by a policy of conciliation, granted freedom to the overseas territories, although the mother country continued to extend economic aid to them. The Belgians suddenly decided to withdraw from the Congo, plunging the inexperienced new nation into a period of chaos and revolution. Great Britain proceeded less abruptly, but she too surrendered voluntarily the great bulk of her African possessions. The result was the end at last of the colonial rule of the West which had been established some eighty years before. In 1955 there had been only five free states in Africa: Egypt, Ethiopia, Liberia, Libya, and the Union of South Africa. Five years later there were twenty-seven. And ten years later the entire continent was independent except for the Portuguese and Spanish colonies and a few British possessions still preparing for nationhood.

LIBERATION FROM IMPERIALISM

It was clear that the relationship between Occident and Orient was changing. The former was still preponderant in economic and military resources, but these were no longer sufficient to support its political domination. Occasionally through the use of persuasion, more commonly by the application of force, the dark-skinned races were freeing themselves from alien rule. The end of the era of imperialism, to be sure, was not always an unmixed blessing. In comparison with European standards, native methods of government were often less efficient and sometimes less honest. Moreover, in many cases colored politicians regarded the civic rights of their countrymen even more cavalierly than the foreign bureaucrats had done. Perhaps worst of all, economic ties which had been fostered under the auspices of the West were frequently severed by newly emancipated countries eager to assert their right of self-determination. Yet even after the first outburst of enthusiasm inspired by the proclamation of independence subsided, there was little nostalgia among the native masses for colonialism. In London, Paris, and The Hague disgruntled soldiers and administrators who had lost their jobs overseas went on predicting a dire future for their former colonies. Yet colored peoples preferred freedom to

DAG HAMMARSKJOLD AND THE CONGO QUESTION. This photograph taken in 1961 shows the Secretary General of the United Nations conferring with a Liberian diplomat regarding the problems of Africa.

security or efficiency or even honesty. They were determined to make their own way at all costs. And foreign criticism of their policy, no matter how justified, only intensified their determination. The truth was that imperialism was succumbing to the political resurgence of the colonial world.

4. The Cold War

THE MOST PRESSING PROBLEM confronting the postwar world was the danger of another great military conflict. Modern science had made any future armed struggle among the major states seem so comprehensive and devastating that a diplomacy of neutrality was becoming impossible. There could no longer be a distinction between combatants and noncombatants, only between winners and losers. For that matter, the unlimited capacity for destruction of new offensive weapons suggested that the difference between victory and defeat might prove meaningless, for each side was in a position to inflict enormous damage upon the other.

Never before the twentieth century had wars been waged for such objectives as "peace and justice in the life of the world" or "world order under law." Yet never before the twentieth century had peace treaties provided so little security for the world. The statecraft of reactionary aristocrats like Metternich and Castlereagh or of clever opportunists like Bismarck and Cavour had given the West a century of relative tranquillity. The idealism of democratic leaders like Woodrow Wilson and Franklin D. Roosevelt, on the other hand, produced only a brief truce after 1918 and an even briefer one after 1945. In his address of April 18, 1955, President Achmed Sukarno of Indonesia expressed the prevailing mood of a generation disillusioned by the constant frustration of its hopes: "Yes, we are living in a world of fear. The life of man today is corroded and made bitter by fear. Fear of the future, fear of the hydrogen bomb, fear of ideologies. Perhaps this fear is a greater danger than the danger itself, because it is fear which drives men to act foolishly, to act thoughtlessly, to act dangerously."

WARTIME DIPLOMACY

The origins of the diplomatic crisis which the postwar world faced lay in the war itself. The outbreak of hostilities in 1939 signified that the political structure of the West, weakened by the shock of the First World War, was in danger of total collapse. The question was what would replace it. Yet the victorious powers failed to deal with the organization of the peace until military operations were almost over. The democracies contented themselves with vague declarations like the Atlantic Charter of August 14, 1941, by which the United States and Great Britain promised to work together for a never-never land of brotherly love among nations. At the same time the Soviet Union was delivering pious pronouncements about the destruction of fascism and the friendship of peace-loving states. As Stalin put it: "It is not so difficult to keep unity in time of war since there is a joint aim to defeat the common enemy, which is clear to everyone. The difficult task will come after the war when diverse interests tend to divide the Allies."

From the point of view of military efficiency it was probably best to avoid discussion of controversial political issues until the Axis had been defeated. But at the same time the task of diplomatic negotiation became more difficult as the day of victory approached. The processes of war and peace could not be logically separated, since the outcome of one was bound to determine the conditions of the other. The decision to postpone serious consideration of the postwar settlement until the enemy was on the verge of surrender meant that by the time the statesmen finally met around the conference table there was little they could do except recognize an international situation which the generals had created by force of arms.

Early in February 1945 Roosevelt, Stalin, and Churchill met at Yalta in order to reach an agreement concerning the organization of the peace. In an atmosphere of cordiality, heightened by the good news from the front, they succeeded in reaching a friendly understanding on most of the questions with which they had to deal. It was not difficult to make preparations for the establishment of the United Nations and for the occupation of the Third Reich. The fate of eastern Europe was a more delicate problem, but there the Soviet Union held all the trump cards. In its retreat westward the Wehrmacht had abandoned this region to the Red Army, which made sure that ministries friendly toward communism were formed in the countries which it "liberated." The democracies therefore decided to accept a state of affairs which they were powerless to alter in return for a promise by Moscow of "the earliest possible establishment through free elections of governments responsive to the will of the people." Finally, Russia agreed to enter the war against Japan on the condition that the territories and rights in the Far East which she had lost by the Treaty of Portsmouth of 1905 would be restored.

Since many of his military experts were warning him that it might take eighteen months or more to defeat the Japanese armies, Roosevelt consented to pay Stalin's price. As it turned out, his acquiescence was unnecessary, for Tokyo decided to sue for peace before the Kremlin entered the conflict in Asia on August 8, 1945. Yet the criticism that the ailing president unleashed the demon of communism by making too many unnecessary concessions was by and large unjustified. Granted that he underestimated the political ambitions of the Kremlin and overestimated his own ability to charm Stalin into cooperation, even a statesman made of sterner stuff could not have halted the expansion of the Soviet Union.

The fact was that the total collapse of Germany and Japan created a power vacuum from which Moscow was bound to profit. Its neighbors in Europe were in effect occupied by the Red Army. Whether the democratic powers recognized the preponderance of Russia in the eastern borderlands or not, nothing short of a new major war could put an end to it. As for Asia, while it is true that Roosevelt invited the intervention of the Kremlin, Stalin would in any case hardly have consented to an extension of the influence of a capitalistic state over the entire western shore of the Pacific. With or without the approval of the United States he was sure to take advantage of the debacle of the Japanese by launching an invasion of China from bases in Siberia. Far from creating the problems which beset the postwar world, the Yalta Conference merely confirmed their existence. As James F. Byrnes, who had gone to the Crimea with the American delegation, pointed out: "It was not a question of what we would let the Russians do, but what we could get the Russians to do."

THE POSTWAR ALLIANCE SYSTEMS

Although the end of hostilities had been greeted in the victorious countries as the beginning of an era of international security, not many months passed before disillusionment set in. For there was obviously a vast difference of opinion among the wartime allies regarding the execution of the settlements reached at the Yalta Conference. To the democratic states they implied a guarantee of parliamentary capitalism in Europe. To the Kremlin, on the other hand, they meant an extension of the power of the Soviet Union commensurate with the magnitude of its victory over the Axis. No sooner had the enemy been defeated, therefore, than the grand coalition against fascism began to disintegrate.

First there was a dispute about the attempt of Moscow to maintain a foothold in Iran, which its troops had entered in the course of the war. Then appeared the new party line of the communist movement which once again became hostile toward bourgeois governments. Before long the regimes formed in eastern Europe under Russian auspices threw aside the mask of moderate reformism and revealed themselves as out-and-out satellites of Stalin. Finally the impressive victories of the armies of Mao Tse-tung in China increased the prestige of the Kremlin among the nations of Asia. By 1947 there could no longer be any doubt about the political intentions of Moscow. As one Russian diplomatic success followed another, the statesmen of the democracies turned to the United States as the only power still capable of opposing the expansion of the Soviet Union.

When he first became chief executive on April 12, 1945, President Harry S Truman was one of the millions of Americans who hoped for continuing collaboration among the victorious countries. The aggressive foreign policy pursued by Stalin, however, soon convinced him that only a strong stand by the parliamentary states could contain the radical dictator. When Russia began to menace Greece and Turkey, he decided that the moment had come to proclaim a new departure in the diplomacy of the United States. In a speech delivered on March 12, 1947 he made clear the readiness of his administration to accept the responsibility which communist expansion had thrust upon it. Urging Congress to extend financial aid to the two threatened nations, he told America that "the free peoples of the world look to us for support in maintaining their freedom."

Four months later the principles of the Truman Doctrine were applied in the Marshall Plan, a project advanced by General George C. Marshall who had recently been appointed Secretary of State. It provided long-term financial assistance by the United States to those countries of Europe which were ready to uphold representative institutions but which were hampered in their efforts by material hardship. By 1952 the authorities in Washington had approved the expenditure of some thirteen billion dollars for the economic recovery of the Old World. The results were by and large satisfactory. While the Soviet Union still constituted a threat to the security of the democracies, the advance of the Kremlin on the Continent came to a halt, and the danger of revolution in western and southern Europe receded.

The employment of economic weapons to combat Moscow was followed logically by the mobilization of military resources. On April 4, 1949 the foreign

DRAFTING THE NORTH ATLANTIC TREATY. Gathered around a conference table in Washington during the spring of 1949 are the representatives of eight governments opposed to the expansion of the Soviet Union.

ministers of the United States, Great Britain, France, Belgium, the Netherlands, Luxemburg, Italy, Portugal, Norway, Denmark, Iceland, and Canada signed the North Atlantic Treaty, which provided that an armed attack on any one of the parties was to be considered an attack against all. The American Secretary of State Dean Acheson described the strategy dictating the formation of this alliance: "We have also learned that if the free nations do not stand together, they will fall one by one. The stratagem of the aggressor is to keep his intended victims divided, or, better still, set them to quarreling among themselves. Then they can be picked off one by one without arousing unified resistance. We and the free nations of Europe are determined that history shall not repeat itself in that melancholy particular." In the Far East a similar diplomatic alignment directed against communism came into existence in 1954 with the conclusion of the Southeast Asia Treaty by the United States, Great Britain, France, Australia, New Zealand, the Philippines, and Thailand. Its effectiveness, however, was limited by the absence of such important Asian states as India, Indonesia, and Burma.

At the same time the leaders of the Soviet Union were busy marshaling their forces. In 1950 a pact of mutual assistance negotiated by Moscow and Peking strengthened the influence of the Kremlin in Asia. And in 1955 the Warsaw Treaty authorized the Kremlin to station its troops in the satellite countries of eastern

Europe and placed their armies under the command of Marshal Ivan Konev of Russia. Thus, ten years after the defeat of fascism, two armed camps divided by fundamental political and economic differences again confronted each other.

NEW INTERNATIONAL CONFLICTS

Even more ominous than the military alliances of the democratic and the communist states were the new international conflicts which followed the return of peace. In June, 1948 a diplomatic crisis arose when the Kremlin decided to score an inexpensive political success by forcing the democratic powers to evacuate their forces from Berlin. The former capital of the Third Reich, although deep within the region of Germany assigned to the Soviet Union, had been placed under the administration of all four occupying powers. By halting rail and road traffic between the city and the western zones, Moscow hoped to force the American, British, and French troops into a withdrawal from a starving metropolis. Only the transportation of essential supplies by air enabled the isolated western garrisons to hold out, until in May 1949 the Russians admitted defeat by lifting the blockade.

One year later hostilities broke out in Korea. After its surrender by the Japanese at the end of the Second World War the country had been partitioned by Russia

THE BERLIN WALL. Here is the barrier erected in 1961 by the government of East Germany to prevent the flow of population to the West, a frightening symbol of the effects of the Cold War.

and the United States along the thirty-eighth parallel for the purpose of temporary administration. As in the case of Germany, the division proved to be lasting. Even when foreign troops were finally withdrawn after an occupation of almost four years, they left behind them two rival governments. The radicals led by Kim Il Sung controlled the north; the conservatives under Syngman Rhee were established in the south. On June 25, 1950 the armies of North Korea opened an invasion designed to unite the nation under a leftist regime. The result was a full-scale armed conflict which lasted three years. The Republic of Korea was supported by the troops of the United States and its allies, while the forces of the communist Korean People's Democratic Republic were reinforced by hundreds of thousands of "volunteers" from China. When a truce was finally concluded on July 27, 1953 total casualties were in the neighborhood of three million men, while the military expenditures of the United States alone were $22 billion. As for the boundary between the two sides, it was just about where it had been before the shooting started, along the thirty-eighth parallel.

No sooner had the fighting in Korea come to an end than developments in Indochina threatened to lead to a major war. The struggle between the leftist nationalists under Ho Chi Minh and the colonial authorities reached a climax in 1954. The insurrectionists were clearly gaining the upper hand despite American dollars and French casualties. Their capture of the stronghold of Dien Bien Phu proved that they could not be defeated by the forces which the Fourth Republic had at its disposal. Only the armed intervention of the United States might crush the danger of Marxism in Indochina as it had almost done in Korea. President Eisenhower had to make a crucial decision. Having only recently brought to a conclusion one frustrating struggle in the Far East which had almost turned into a world war, he was in no mood to embark upon another. Besides, the involvement of American troops in the jungles of southeast Asia could tempt the Kremlin to seek gains in central Europe or along the Mediterranean. Washington therefore consented to an agreement which left most of the northern half of Indochina to the radicals, while the south was placed under the control of a moderate native regime. Once again a conflict between communism and democracy had ended in a stalemate. But in the early 1960's the United States intervened in South Vietnam to prevent the victory of left-wing guerrillas who were gaining the upper hand in a war against the established government. This fateful step revived the danger of a major conflict on the Asian mainland by threatening to bring Peking into the struggle.

For by now China had emerged as a third superpower alongside America and Russia. The end of the foreign and domestic conflicts which had torn China for more than a century meant that she could now develop her strength undisturbed. With a population well in excess of half a billion people, she was the largest nation in the world. The end of alien domination finally enabled her to exploit her vast natural resources in her own interest. The communist leadership proved harsh and autocratic, but also bold and energetic. Although the standard of living remained low in comparison with the Occident, China achieved an industrial expansion which could not be ignored. Her success in developing an atomic bomb, for example, was a measure of the technological progress she had made. Her foreign policy, moreover, grew increasingly ambitious. She sought to rally the colored masses of the world against the capitalistic states, even arguing that a major war would not be an excessive price to pay for the global victory of Marxism. When Russia refused to abandon the policy of peaceful coexistence with the West, the two great communist nations became divided by differences of opinion almost as great as those which stood between them and the anticommunist camp.

Yet most statesmen on both sides of the Iron Curtain wanted peace. Although they differed regarding the legitimate objectives of government, they also recognized that another world war would bring destruction to conqueror and conquered alike. Not only did the major countries therefore announce repeatedly that what they sought above all was international stability, but they conferred again and again concerning the best means to achieve it. The foreign ministers of the United States, the Soviet Union, the United Kingdom, and the French Republic met in London in 1945 to attempt to reach a friendly settlement. They met once more in Paris in 1946; then in Moscow in 1947. An even more important gathering took place in Geneva in 1955, when President Eisenhower, Russian Premier Nikolai A. Bulganin, British Prime Minister Anthony Eden, and French Premier Edgar Faure discussed the diplomatic situation. And in 1960 the democratic statesmen traveled to Paris for an ill-fated summit meeting with Khrushchev. All in all, the declarations of pacific intentions issued by each of the powers would have filled volumes.

Yet the world knew no peace, because the opposing alliance systems regarded each other with fear and hostility. They were almost convinced that "a house divided against itself cannot stand," that mankind could not remain indefinitely half authoritarian, half democratic. At times the United States insisted that its diplomacy aimed at nothing more than "containment," that is, a limitation of the gains of Marxism to the boundaries it had achieved by 1949. At other times, however, it spoke of "liberation," the suppression of communism in those regions in which it had become dominant after 1939. The Soviet Union was equally inconsistent in its statements of political objectives. There were occasions when it maintained that its purpose was peaceful coexistence with the capitalistic states in which the relative merits of the two rival economic systems could be tested by friendly competition. But then there were occasions when it returned to the more familiar theme that the proletarian fatherland must oppose by force the plutocratic democracies. As for Peking, its ultimate diplomatic goal was the leadership of the colonial peoples of the world against the anticommunist nations in the West.

The most significant element of hope in this situation was the reluctance of the leading powers to precipitate open hostilities. New military weapons like atomic bombs, jet airplanes, rocket projectiles, and intercontinental missiles threatened to inflict such enormous damage on the combatants of the future that neither communism nor democracy could feel sure of its ability to survive the ordeal of war. Therefore, despite belligerent notes and pronouncements, despite even acts of direct provocation, neither the White House nor the Kremlin nor even Peking was eager to start shooting. Indeed, when it actually came to an armed conflict, as in Korea in 1950 or in Egypt in 1956, they used their influence to prevent it from developing into a major struggle. Yet in 1914 the great powers had also sought to avoid a major struggle, only to discover that they were no longer in a position to control the crisis which was driving them all to self-destruction. Was there any assurance that they would be more successful now in preventing a world war? Tense and uneasy, the world continued to grope for a way out of an armed truce which was neither war nor peace.

5. *The Meaning of the Twentieth Century*

THE EXPERIENCES OF WAR, revolution, and depression have cast a pall of anxiety over the twentieth century. Ours is an age in which familiar institutions and attitudes are exposed to unfamiliar situations and demands. Such periods are not uncommon in the history of man, but they invariably produce a sense of bewilderment among those whom they force to abandon an accustomed way of life. Shortly after the First World War the British poet A. E. Housman expressed the anguish of a society shaken by a terrible physical ordeal:

> And how am I to face the odds
> Of man's bedevilment and God's?
> I, a stranger and afraid
> In a world I never made.[2]

He was echoing the sentiments of those who liked to think of themselves as the *lost generation*. Yet only a hundred years earlier another British poet, William Wordsworth, was bewailing the England of his day:

> She is a fen
> Of stagnant waters: altar, sword, and pen,
> Fireside, the heroic wealth of hall and bower,
> Have forfeited their ancient English dower
> Of inward happiness.

---

[2] From "The laws of God, the laws of man" from *The Collected Poems of A. E. Housman*. Copyright 1922 by Holt, Rinehart and Winston, Inc. Copyright 1950 by Barclays Bank Ltd. Reprinted by permission of Holt, Rinehart and Winston, Inc., The Society of Authors as the literary representative of the Estate of A. E. Housman, and Messrs. Jonathan Cape Ltd., publishers of A. E. Housman's *Collected Poems*.

Three hundred years before that a great political thinker, Niccolò Machiavelli, looked at his native country and lamented that "Italy should be reduced to her present condition, and that she should be more enslaved than the Hebrews, more oppressed than the Persians, and more scattered than the Athenians; without a head, without order, beaten, despoiled, lacerated, and overrun, and that she should have suffered ruin of every kind." And some two thousand years before that the world-weary preacher of the Old Testament was warning mankind: "I have seen all the works that are done under the sun; and behold, all is vanity and vexation of spirit."

The point is that the very nature of social change imposes upon every age new tasks and responsibilities which at times seem insupportable to those who must struggle with them. Only long afterwards does the scholar look into the past and tell us that the despairing Wordsworth lived in the midst of that great outburst of creative energy known as romanticism; that Machiavelli bemoaned the fate of his nation in the shadow of the magnificent artistic achievements of the Renaissance; that the unknown disillusioned author of Ecclesiastes was the heir of a rich cultural tradition which gave mankind the ideal of universal monotheism. Similarly it is safe to assume that what history will see in the twentieth century is not what the twentieth century sees in itself. For the price which today's existence demands in physical toil and mental strain is forgotten tomorrow, and only the vital accomplishment bequeathed by the present to the future remains. The problem is to recognize this accomplishment taking shape amid the hurly-burly of the marketplace where men labor for their daily bread. In order to solve it we must become detached observers of a world in which we are also active participants; we must rise above our own interests and commitments in the life which goes on around us. Clearly a task of such complexity is to be approached with a sense of intellectual humility.

In the light of historical experience, the twentieth century appears to be concerned with social justice as intensely as the nineteenth century was concerned with political freedom. In other words, our age is one in which men are determined to free themselves from the economic inequities and insecurities which in the past were accepted as the inevitable accompaniment of life in the community. Parliamentarianism, socialism, fascism, each in turn has had to take into account this vast popular yearning for security and has had to make an accommodation to it. Seen from this point of view, the cold war becomes a struggle to determine whether a higher degree of mass welfare will be achieved under democratic capitalism or authoritarian communism.

This struggle may end in the ultimate victory of one side or the other; or it may result in a stalemate gradually leading to a mutual adjustment, such as that which followed the religious conflicts of four hundred years ago. In any case, unless a new world war accompanied by enormous physical destruction should suddenly depress the level of material civilization, the demand for a stable and paternalistic social order is likely to grow. The ideals of civic freedom and private property may solve the problems of the future as they overcame the dangers of the past, but only by recognizing the need to adapt themselves to the changing conditions of human progress. The strength of democracy lies not in a rigid adherence to outworn formulas, but in its ability to meet a new challenge in the spirit of liberty and honesty.

Perhaps even more important than the quest for social justice is the longing for national justice. The current reaction of the oriental peoples against colonialism is nothing more than what the occidental states experienced in the past. It is motivated by the same principle of nationalism; it aims at the same arbitrariness and jingoism. Yet successful resistance to its demands is in the long run impossible. For among colored as among white men the desire for political freedom cannot be suppressed. A recognition of the decline of imperialism need not imply an uncritical acceptance of all the extravagant claims of native patriotism. Asia and Africa have their demagogues no less than Europe and America. All can meet, however, in the common determination to work for a better world order. What the East wants from the West, even more than territorial gain or economic advantage, is understanding and respect. If the Occident can learn to satisfy this thirst for dignity on the part of the Orient, it will succeed in coming to terms with those whom it formerly ruled. The two need each other more than they are prepared to admit, because the interdependence of the world which industrial progress has created makes their cooperation essential for the welfare of mankind. In view of the end of the era of colonial domination, the twentieth century faces the task of forging new ties of friendship among the races of the earth.

Finally, we are in the midst of a technological revolution which in its far-reaching social effects can be compared only to that great communal revolution of six thousand years ago when men first began to live in cities. The advance of science harnessed to the demand for material welfare is creating a new civilization fundamentally different from any which the world has seen in the past. For the first time mankind looks forward to the day when the bugaboos which have haunted its history will disappear. Famines, epidemics, natural disasters, economic shortages, all the frustrations which have afflicted human society in the past are diminishing. With them will perhaps diminish the resentments and dissatisfactions which have traditionally driven nations to war. Proper planning, moreover, can make possible an increase in the output of goods greater than the increase in the size of population, so that the time is in sight when the energies of the masses of humanity will no longer be completely absorbed by the process of mere physical survival. Leisure and the cultivation of the mind, which depends on leisure, will cease to be a monopoly of well-to-do classes deriving their power from political influence or economic advantage. Instead the rationalization of production may make possible the emergence of a popular culture accessible to all strata of society.

For the twentieth century, as for every century before it, there is a promise of progress capable of inspiring men to action and sacrifice. Its realization is no easy task, and it must not give rise to that shallow optimism which marred the thought of many well-intentioned intellectuals in the Age of Enlightenment. Yet neither is there need to despair of the fate of man who has historically displayed a remarkable talent for meeting the problems with which life confronts him. Before humanity lies the prospect of an exciting future. Its outline cannot be seen clearly, but it is surely suggested by the vision of one of the great thinkers of our age, the philosopher George Santayana:

> A man's feet must be planted in his country, but his eyes should survey the world. What a statesman might well aim at would be to give the special sentiments and gifts of his countrymen such a turn that, while continuing all vital traditions, they might find less and less of what is human alien to their genius. Differences in nationality, founded on race and habitat, must always subsist; but what has been superadded artificially by ignorance and bigotry may be gradually abolished in view of universal relations better understood. There is a certain plane on which all races, if they reach it at all, must live in common, the plane of morals and science.[3]

Further Reading

Good accounts of political developments since the end of the Second World War may be found in J. B. Harrison, *This Age of Global Strife* (Philadelphia, 1952) and *H. W. Gatzke, *The Present in Perspective* (Chicago, 1965). The collapse of the balance of power is described by G. L. Arnold, *The Pattern of World Conflict* (New York, 1955); and A. J. and V. M. Toynbee, *The Realignment of Europe* (New York, 1955). For the formation and organization of the United Nations there are the following works: S. Arne, *United Nations Primer* (New York, 1945); V. M. Dean, *The Four Cornerstones of Peace* (New York, 1946); and H. V. Evatt, *The United Nations* (Cambridge, Mass., 1948). W. N. Hogan, *The United Nations: Background, Organization, Functions, Activities* (New York, 1952) deals with various agencies of the United Nations.

On the recovery of the West see B. Ward, *The West at Bay* (New York, 1948); C. Brinton, *The Temper of Western Europe* (Cambridge, Mass., 1953); and T. H. White, *Fire in the Ashes: Europe in Mid-Century* (New York, 1953). Important studies of individual countries include the following: for England, L. D. Epstein, *Britain: Uneasy Ally* (Chicago, 1954) and D. G. Somervell and H. Harvey, *The British Empire and Commonwealth* (London, 1954); for France, G. Wright, *The Reshaping of French Democracy* (New York, 1948) and *A. Werth, *France, 1940–1955* (New York, 1956); for Italy, H. S. Hughes, *The United States and Italy* (Cambridge, Mass., 1953) and M. Grindrod, *The Rebuilding of Italy* (New York, 1955); and for Germany, H. C.

---

[3] George Santayana, *Reason in Society* (New York: Charles Scribner's Sons, 1905), p. 175.

Wallich, *Mainsprings of the German Revival* (New Haven, 1955) and E. Davidson, *The Death and Life of Germany* (New York, 1961). H. Seton-Watson, *From Lenin to Malenkov* (New York, 1954) is useful for the last years of the Stalin regime. Events since then are examined by E. Crankshaw, *Russia without Stalin* (New York, 1956) and D. J. Dallin, *The Changing World of Soviet Russia* (New Haven, 1956). A sound analysis of the industrial expansion of Russia is to be found in H. Schwartz, *Russia's Soviet Economy* (Englewood Cliffs, N.J., 1954). *H. Seton-Watson, *The East European Revolution* (London, 1956) considers the communist satellites.

H. V. Hodson, *Twentieth-Century Empire* (London, 1948) and *E. Staley, *The Future of Underdeveloped Countries* (London, 1954) look at the changing relationship of East and West. H. S. Quigley and J. E. Turner, *The New Japan* (Minneapolis, 1956) describes the problems facing Nipponese democracy, while *H. Feis, *The China Tangle* (Princeton, 1953) surveys the postwar development of China. *T. G. P. Spear, *India, Pakistan, and the West* (New York, 1952) deals with the achievement of independence in the Indian subcontinent. For southeast Asia see J. K. King, *Southeast Asia in Perspective* (New York, 1956). N. Izzeddin, *The Arab World* (Chicago, 1953) depicts the civic aspirations of Islam, and J. C. Hurewitz, *The Struggle for Palestine* (New York, 1950) treats the conflict in the Holy Land. C. W. Stillman, ed., *Africa in the Modern World* (Chicago, 1955) is a thoughtful introductory work.

W. L. Neumann, *Making the Peace, 1941–45* (Washington, 1949) describes the war aims of the victorious powers. *J. L. Snell, ed., *The Meaning of Yalta* (Baton Rouge, 1956) is the best account of the crucial international conference. W. Lippmann, *The Cold War* (New York, 1947) and K. Ingram, *History of the Cold War* (London, 1955) seek to analyze the struggle between democratic capitalism and authoritarian communism. The attempt of the United States to halt the advance of Russia through economic rehabilitation is examined by S. E. Harris, *The European Recovery Program* (Cambridge, Mass., 1948); and *G. F. Kennan, *Realities of American Foreign Policy* (Princeton, 1954). H. Hoskins, *The Atlantic Pact* (Washington, 1949) and D. Middleton, *The Defense of Western Europe* (New York, 1952) explain the function of the North Atlantic Treaty. On the cold war there are such works as N. A. Graebner, *The New Isolationism* (Cardiff, Wales, 1956); W. W. Kaufmann, ed., *Military Policy and National Security* (Princeton, 1956); and *H. L. Roberts, *Russia and America* (New York, 1956).

H. S. Hughes, *An Essay for Our Times* (New York, 1950) and *R. Aron, *The Century of Total War* (Boston, 1955) consider the contemporary world from a historical perspective. *C. Kluckhohn, *Mirror for Man* (New York, 1949) applies the teachings of anthropology to social problems, while *R. Niebuhr, *The Children of Light and the Children of Darkness* (New York, 1944) attempts to define the significance of theology for a democratic community. F. S. C. Northrop, *The Taming of the Nations* (New York, 1952) and A. H. Richmond, *The Colour Problem* (New York, 1955) plead for greater understanding among peoples and races. The effect of population growth on the standard of living is discussed by W. S. and E. S. Woytinsky, *World Population and Production* (New York, 1953); and K. Sax, *Standing Room Only: The Challenge of Overpopulation* (Boston, 1955). Julian Huxley, *Science and Social Needs* (New York, 1935) and W. Esslinger, *Politics and Science* (New York, 1955) assess the influence of scientific progress on civic development. *B. Ward, *Faith and Freedom* (New York, 1958) is an eloquent plea for courage in a time of trouble.

Index